LATIN
IS
FUN

Book II

Lively lessons for advancing students

John C. Traupman, Ph.D.
St. Joseph's University
Philadelphia

When ordering this book, please specify *either* **R 605 W** *or*
LATIN IS FUN, BOOK II

Dedicated to serving
AMSCO
our nation's youth

Amsco School Publications, Inc.
315 Hudson Street / New York, N.Y. 10013

Illustrations by Tom O'Sullivan and Ed Malsberg

ISBN 0-87720-565-5

Printed in the United States of America

1 2 3 4 5 6 7 8 9 10   01 00 99 98 97 96 95 94

Preface

Quintilian, the foremost Roman educator, said: "Be sure to make learning fun lest the youngsters get to hate the subject before they learn it." That is the principle on which this book is based. At the same time great care has been taken to use genuine Latin structure and idiom in devising the exercises, readings, and conversations so that students will be prepared to read Latin authors with comprehension upon completion of this course.

LATIN IS FUN, BOOK II continues the natural, personalized, enjoyable, and rewarding program of language acquisition begun in the first course. BOOK II provides all the elements for a full second course. It aims at oral proficiency, as well as proficiency in listening, writing, and reading, thus meeting the requirements of the national proficiency standards for this level of Latin.

LATIN IS FUN, BOOK II is designed to broaden students' level of achievement in basic skills, with emphasis on realistic, meaningful communication. Through the topical contexts, students will also expand their vocabulary, their control of structure, and their ability to communicate about their daily lives in task-oriented and social situations.

LATIN IS FUN, BOOK II consists of four parts. Each part contains five lessons, followed by a *Recognitiō* (review) unit, in which structures are recapitulated and practiced through various *activitātēs* (activities). These *activitātēs* include games and puzzles as well as conventional exercises.

Each lesson includes a step-by-step sequence of the following student-directed elements, which are designed to make the materials directly accessible as well as give students the feeling that they can have fun learning and practicing their Latin.

Culture

Each lesson begins with a *Modicum cultūrae* (essay dealing with a specific topic on Roman culture) designed to create the context for the chapter as a whole. This is particularly important for students who are being introduced to a culture that in many ways was quite different from their own. This is not a "cultural extra" but an integral part of the unified lesson. Together with the *Modicum cultūrae*, the cultural concepts in the rest of the lesson will be better understood. The vocabulary, structures, and readings are integrated with the cultural essay.

Vocabulary

Unlike traditional Latin textbooks that introduce each chapter with vocabularies in isolation, each lesson presents topically and thematically related vocabulary through sets of drawings that convey the meanings of new words and expressions in Latin without recourse to English. This device, sometimes individual vignettes, sometimes composite scenes, enables students to make direct and vivid association with the Latin terms and their meanings. The *activitātēs* that follow directly also use pictures to help students practice words and expressions.

To produce interesting, realistic readings and conversations from the very outset, the book provides additional vocabulary side by side with the readings.

Structure

LATIN IS FUN, BOOK II introduces new structural elements in small learning components — one at a time, followed directly by appropriate *activitātēs*. By following this simple, straightforward, guided presentation, students make their own discoveries and formulate their own conclusions and in the process gain a feeling of accomplishment. The aim is not simply to cover a certain amount of grammar; grammatical elements are introduced as they are required by the readings and conversations.

Conversation

To encourage students to use Latin for communication, each lesson includes a conversation and a dialog exercise. All conversations are illustrated in cartoon-strip fashion, containing a "punch line" to drive home a point and to add a touch of light humor. The conversations are repeated in dialog exercises, but with gaps that students are asked to fill in, based on the previous conversation. The conversations are meant not merely to be read once but to be repeated and practiced in order to achieve oral proficiency.

Reading

Each lesson contains a short narrative or playlet that features the new structures and vocabulary and reinforces previously acquired vocabulary. Each reading selection not only is a vehicle for the presentation of these elements but also deals with a topic of intrinsic interest related to real, everyday experiences of ancient Rome and our own age. Cognates and near-cognates are used extensively to show the relationship between the Latin language and culture and English.

Personal Information

One of the goals of the entire program is to enable students to personalize language by relating the situation in the lesson to their own lives. The "personal questions" at the end of each lesson give the students an opportunity for their own input.

The Latin Connection

Since one of the chief reasons why students study Latin is to enhance their command of English vocabulary, each lesson ends with an exercise in derivatives, based on the Latin words that occurred in the lesson. These exercises in English derivatives are more elaborate than those that were provided in LATIN IS FUN, BOOK I. To understand some of the English derivatives, the students will probably have to consult an English dictionary or get help from the teacher.

Pronunciation

The practice of indicating long and short vowels is based on the *Oxford Latin Dictionary*, Oxford University Press, 1968–82.

Teacher's Manual with Answers; Testing

A separate *Teacher's Manual with Answers* includes suggestions for teaching all elements in this book, additional oral practice, some bibliography information for further study, suggestions for activities and student projects, and a complete key for all exercises and puzzles.

The *Manual* also includes a Quiz for each lesson, a Unit Test for each part, and two Achievement Tests. These tests are designed to be simple in order to give ALL students a sense of accomplishment. The tests use various techniques through which mastery of structure and vocabulary as well as comprehension may be evaluated. Teachers may use these tests as they appear or modify them to fit particular needs. Keys are provided for all test materials.

Contents

Pars Prīma

I **Lūdī Olympicī** 2
Demonstratives

II **Thermae** 16
Volō/nōlō; Reflexive Verbs

III **Superstitiō** 29
Future Tense

IV **Spectācula Rōmāna** 47
Future Tense (continued); Ablative of Means

V **Animālia** 58
Comparative Degree

RECŌGNITIŌ I (Lectiōnēs I–V) 79

Pars Secunda

VI **Rōmulus et Remus** 92
Relative Pronouns; Interrogative Adjectives

VII **Medicīna et valētūdō** 110
Pluperfect Tense

VIII **Dominus et servus** 126
Present Participles

IX **Vehicula et viae** 140
Locative Case; **īdem, eadem, idem**

X **Amor et mātrimōnium** 155
Irregular Adjectives

RECŌGNITIŌ II (Lectiōnēs VI–X) 172

Pars Tertia

XI **Perseus** 186
Passive Voice: Present, Imperfect, Future

XII **Tempestās** 204
Perfect and Pluperfect Passive; Deponent Verbs

XIII   **Agricultūra**   222
        Fīō; Perfect Passive Participle
XIV   **Lūsūs**   237
        Defective Verbs; Infinitives
XV   **Māne et noctū**   251
        Indirect Statements
RECŌGNITIŌ III (Lectiōnēs XI–XV)   266

Pars Quārta

XVI   **Status fēminārum Rōmānārum**   280
        -urus Conjugation
XVII   **In officīnā tignāriā**   294
        Present Subjunctive
XVIII **Mons Vesuvius**   312
        Imperfect Subjunctive
XIX   **Jūstitia crīminālis**   325
        Pluperfect Subjunctive
XX   **Rēs pūblica**   340
        Ablative Absolute
RECŌGNITIŌ IV (Lectiōnēs XVI–XX)   357

Proficiency Test   369
Vocābula Latīna-Anglica   379
Vocābula Anglica-Latīna   395
Grammatical Index   407
Topical Index   408

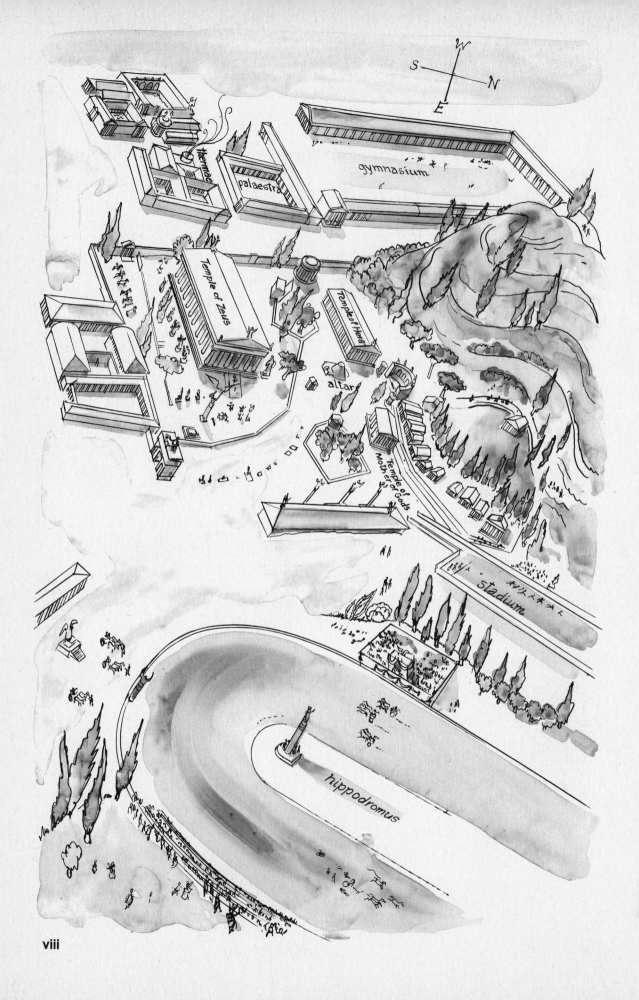

PARS

PRIMA

I _Lūdī Olympicī_

Demonstratives

1 Modicum cultūrae

The Olympic games, held every four years since 776 B.C., were an athletic event for Greeks only until the Romans conquered Greece in 146 B.C. and forced the Greeks to allow Romans to compete. The games continued to be held at the original site at Olympia in Greece, but it did not take long for "Olympic fever" to make itself felt among the Roman people. Even the Roman emperor Nero entered the chariot race. Although he fell out of his chariot during the race, he was allowed to win. After all, who would be bold enough to defeat the mad Emperor Nero in a race and lose his head for it?

The games, which lasted five days, included running, jumping, discus throwing, javelin throwing, boxing, wrestling, and chariot racing. These were the kinds of skills that were important for success in ancient warfare. There were two age groups: boys up to the age of 18 and men over the age of 18. Girls were not allowed to participate, and no females were allowed to attend the games except the priestess of the goddess Demeter.

The athletes trained in two buildings: a smaller, square building, called a **palaestra,** which means "wrestling place," although boxers also trained there, and the **gymnasium,** a much longer building that contained a track for the runners under a covered portico and space for discus and javelin throwers. Some sports that are popular in modern Olympic games, such as swimming, diving, basketball, and gymnastics, were not part of ancient Olympic games.

The Olympic grounds were divided into three parts. The first was the area where the athletes practiced. In it were the **palaestra,** the **gymnasium,** and the baths. The second and central area was the sacred precinct where the temple of Zeus (called Jupiter by the Romans), the temple of Hera (Juno), and the temple of the Mother of the Gods stood. The games were held in honor of Zeus, whose temple contained a 45-foot-high statue of Zeus made of ivory and gold. This statue was one of the seven wonders of the world. Near the temple was a huge sacrificial altar to Zeus composed of the ashes of sacrificial animals. It rose to a height of 32 feet. There were also buildings that housed the Olympic officials, and throughout the sacred precinct there were hundreds of statues to the gods and to successful Olympic heroes. The third area contained the race track (**hippodromus -ī** _m_), where the horse races took place, and the stadium, where all the other events took place. (_See illustration on page viii_)

A month before the games began, in July or August, a truce was declared throughout Greece, so that all those who wished to attend the games at Olympia could travel safely. Before the games, all the athletes took a solemn oath that they had trained hard for at least ten months and that they would not cheat in the competitions. At the end of the games, the winner of each event was crowned with wild olive branches cut from a tree near the temple of Zeus. When the hero returned to his hometown, he was given high honors as well as a substantial amount of money.

The ancient Olympic games lasted over a thousand years, until a Christian emperor put an end to them because they were in honor of a pagan god.

2 Vocābula

aurīga -ae m

curriculum -ī n

jaculum -ī n

discus -ī m

cursor -ōris m

jaculātor -ōris m

discobolus -ī m

caestus -ūs m

gymnasium -ī n

luctātor -ōris m

palaestra -ae f

pugil -is m

4 Lectio I

___ ACTIVITĀS _____

A. **Quid id est?** Write the correct Latin name below each picture. Give the genitive case and the gender of each:

1. _cursororis m_ 2. _Iaculum in_ 3. _caestus us m_

4. _Iaculateroris m_ 5. _discobolus in_ 6. _aurigae m n_

7. _discus in_ 8. _pugilis m_ 9. _palaestra e f_

10. _gymnasium in_ 11. _curriculum in_ 12. _luctatoris oris m_

As you read the story below about Ajax and Claudius at the Olympic games, keep your eye on the demonstrative adjectives **hīc, haec, hoc** (*this*) and **ille, illa, illud** (*that*). Demonstrative adjectives are used to point out someone or something. As you will see, they are declined much like the adjective **bonus, bona, bonum.** These demonstrative adjectives are printed in bold type.

Erat aestās. Erat prīmus diēs lūdōrum Olympicō-rum. Āthlētae ubīque sē exercēbant. Magna turba circumstābat et āthlētās spectābat.

Ajax, puer Graecus ex Spartā et amīcus suus, Claudius, ex Campāniā modō ad Olympiam pervēnērunt. Ajax semel anteā Olympiam vīsitāvit. Claudius autem numquam anteā Olympiam vīsitāvit.

"Estne grandis statua Jovis in hōc templō?" rogāvit Claudius. "Nōn est," respondit Ajax. "**Hōc** templum est templum Jūnōnis, sed **illud** est templum Jovis. **Illa** statua est ūna ex septem mīrāculīs mundī. Sed **illud** templum posteā vīsitāre possumus. Prīmō ad palaestram eāmus."

Duo amīcī palaestram intrāvērunt. "Ecce," inquit Ajax, "**hī** āthlētae sunt pugilēs et **illī** sunt luctātōrēs. **Hī** pugilēs caestūs gestant."

"Certantne pugilēs et luctātōrēs in **hāc** palaestrā?" rogāvit Claudius. "Minimē," respondit Ajax. "In **hōc** locō āthlētae sē exercent et palaestricus **illōs** attentē observat. Āthlētae in stadiō ultrā **illa** templa certant."

"Suntne āthlētae etiam in **illō** aedificiō proximō?" rogāvit Claudius.

"Sānē. **Illud** aedificium est gymnasium. In **illō** aedificiō cursōrēs sē exercent, discobolī discōs conjiciunt, jaculātōrēs jacula conjiciunt. Quamob-rem **illud** aedificium tam longum est."

"Licetne observāre **illōs** āthlētās?" rogāvit Claudius.

"Licet," respondit Ajax. "**Illī** āthlētae sunt amīcis-simī, sed **hīc** palaestricus est strictissimus. Vīsne vi-dēre aurīgās et equōs et curricula in hippodromō?"

---

ubīque *everywhere*
sē exercēre *to train, exercise*
turba -ae *f crowd*
circumstō -stāre -stetī -statum *to stand around*
Ajax, Ajācis *m boy's name*
Campānia -ae *f Campania (a district south of Rome)*
modō *just*
perveniō -venīre, -vēnī, -ventum *to arrive*
semel *once*   **anteā** *before*
grandis -is -e *large, huge*

mīrāculum -ī *n wonder*
prīmō *first*
eāmus *let's go*

palaestricus -ī *m coach*
attentē *closely*
ultrā *prep (+ acc) beyond, on the other side of*
certō -āre *to compete*
proximus -a -um *nearby, next*

conjiciō -jicĕre -jēcī -jectus *to hurl, throw*
quamobrem *that's why*
tam *so*

licet *it is allowed, we are allowed*

amīcus -a -um *friendly*
strictus -a -um *strict*
vīsne? *do you want?*
hippodromus -ī *m race track, hippodrome*

"Minimē, Ajax. Ego aurīgās et equōs et curricula in Circō Maximō saepe vīdī."

"Bene!" inquit Ajax. "Nunc eāmus ad gymnasium, deinde ad templum Jovis, ubi **illam** statuam grandem vidēre possumus. Pōmerīdiē certāmina in stadiō spectāre possumus."

eāmus *let's go*

pōmerīdiē *this afternoon*
certāmen -inis n *contest, competition*

___ ACTIVITĀS ___

B. Respondē ad quaestiōnēs:

1. Ubi est domus Ajācis?

2. Ubi est domus Claudiī?

3. Quotiens Ajax Olympiam anteā vīsitāvit?

4. Quotiens Claudius Olympiam anteā vīsitāvit?

5. Quid est ūnum ex septem mīrāculīs mundī?

6. Quis sē exercet in palaestrā?

7. Certantne āthlētae in palaestrā?

8. Ubi certant āthlētae?

9. Quis pugilēs et luctātōrēs attentē observat?

10. Quid conjiciunt discobolī?

You have just met some of the forms of **hīc, haec, hōc,** meaning *this*. They either modify nouns, and then they are called demonstrative adjectives, or they can stand alone, and then they are called demonstrative pronouns, meaning *this one* or simply *he, she,* or *it.* Let's look at the entire declension:

	MASCULINE	FEMININE	NEUTER
SINGULAR			
NOMINATIVE	hīc	haec	hōc
GENITIVE	hūjus	hūjus	hūjus
ACCUSATIVE	hunc	hanc	hōc
DATIVE	huic	huic	huic
ABLATIVE	hōc	hāc	hōc
PLURAL			
NOMINATIVE	hī	hae	haec
GENITIVE	hōrum	hārum	hōrum
ACCUSATIVE	hōs	hās	haec
DATIVE	hīs	hīs	hīs
ABLATIVE	hīs	hīs	hīs

In the singular, the genitive has the same form for masculine, feminine, and neuter. So also the dative case. Did you notice that all endings except two in the plural are the same as the plural endings of **bonus, bona, bonum**? Which

two endings are different? _____

Make sure that you understand the difference between the demonstrative ADJECTIVE and the demonstrative PRONOUN. Look at these two examples:

Hīc **pugil est rōbustus.**	*This boxer is strong.*
Hīc **est rōbustus.**	*This one (He) is strong.*

In the first example, **hīc** modifies **pugil** and so is a demonstrative adjective. In the second example, **hīc** stands alone and so is a demonstrative pronoun.

PITFALL: **Hīc** may be an adjective meaning *this*, a pronoun meaning *this one*, or an adverb meaning *here, in this place*. Another adverb, **hūc**, means *here, to this place*. Note the difference:

Venī hūc!	*Come here!*
Ajax est hīc.	*Ajax is here.*

In the first sentence, *here* implies motion; in the second sentence, *here* implies position.

— ACTIVITĀTĒS

C. Fill in the correct form of the demonstrative adjective:

1. _____ pugil

2. _____ pugilēs

3. _____ palaestra

4. in _____ palaestrā

5. per _____ palaestram

6. contrā _____ luctātōrem

7. contrā _____ luctātōrēs

8. cum _____ luctātōribus

9. _____ gymnasium

10. sine _____ discīs

D. Look over the sentences carefully and complete them with the correct forms of the demonstrative adjectives:

1. _____ gymnasium est magnum.

2. Āthlētae in _____ gymnasiō sē exercēbant.

3. Templum Jovis est proximum _____ gymnasiō.

4. Columnae _____ templī sunt altae.

5. _____ turba hūc venit ex omnibus partibus Graeciae.

6. In _____ palaestrā omnēs āthlētae sunt pugilēs.

7. Lūdī Olympicī _____ virō et _____ feminae nōn placent.

8. _____ palaestricus est jūstus.

9. _____ pugilēs sunt ferōcēs.

10. Quis timet _____ luctātōrēs?

11. _____ virī sunt pugilēs excellentēs.

12. Sine _____ caestibus pugil vincĕre nōn potest.

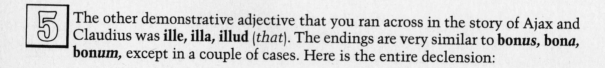

The other demonstrative adjective that you ran across in the story of Ajax and Claudius was **ille, illa, illud** (*that*). The endings are very similar to **bonus, bona, bonum,** except in a couple of cases. Here is the entire declension:

	MASCULINE	FEMININE	NEUTER
	SINGULAR		
NOMINATIVE	ille	illa	illud
GENITIVE	illīus	illīus	illīus
ACCUSATIVE	illum	illam	illud
DATIVE	illī	illī	illī
ABLATIVE	illō	illā	illō
	PLURAL		
NOMINATIVE	illī	illae	illa
GENITIVE	illōrum	illārum	illōrum
ACCUSATIVE	illōs	illās	illa
DATIVE	illīs	illīs	illīs
ABLATIVE	illīs	illīs	illīs

As you can see, the genitive and dative singular have the same form through-out. Although the forms are irregular, they are easily remembered. The plural is regular throughout. **Ille** sometimes means *that famous*.

— ACTIVITĀTĒS

E. Supply the correct form of **ille, illa, illud:**

1. Quid est _____ aedificium?

2. Jaculātor _____ discum longissimē conjēcit.

3. _____ discobulī hūc veniunt ex Graeciā.

4. Quis in _____ curriculō stat?

5. Vīsne spectāre _____ equōs?

6. Ajax _____ puerō discum novum dedit.

7. _____ templum est veterrimum.

8. _____ āthlētae sunt cursōrēs ex Campāniā.

9. Tectum _____ templī est aurātum (*gold-plated*).

10. Caestūs _____ pugilis sunt gravēs.

11. Rotae _____ curriculōrum sunt fractae.

12. _____ discobolus nōn procul ab Olympiā habitat.

F. In the following sentences, insert the correct form of **hīc, haec, hōc** in the first slot and the correct form of **ille, illa, illud** in the second slot:

1. _____ templum est novum, sed _____ est vetus.

2. _____ statua est grandis, sed _____ est parva.

3. _____ āthlētae sunt cursōrēs, sed _____ sunt jaculā-tōrēs.

4. In _____ gymnasiō sunt jaculātōrēs; in _____ sunt pugilēs.

5. Caesar _____ gladiātōrī pecūniam dedit, sed _____ gladiātōrī nihil dedit.

6. _____ aurīgae sunt victōrēs, sed nōn _____ .

7. _____ discobolus ūnum discum habet; _____ duōs habet.

8. _____ pugil cum _____ pugile certāre potest.

9. In _____ hippodromō sunt aurīgae, sed in _____ hippodromō sunt curriculī.

10. _____ jaculum mihi placet sed _____ jaculum nimis longum mihi est.

11. Discus _____ discobolī nōn longē volat, sed discus _____ discobolī longissimē volat.

12. In _____ gymnasiō āthlētae sē exercent sed nōn in _____ gymnasiō.

6
Another demonstrative meaning *that* is **iste, ista, istud,** which is declined exactly like **ille, illa, illud.** When it modifies a noun, it is a demonstrative adjective, and when it stands alone, it is a demonstrative pronoun. It is sometimes used with a feeling of contempt:

Quis timet istum gladium?   *Who is afraid of that sword of yours?*
Iste senātor pecūniam accēpit.   *That (disgraceful) senator accepted money.*

But sometimes **iste** simply means *that* without any feeling of contempt.

— ACTIVITĀTĒS ——————————————————————

G. Fill in the correct form of **iste, ista, istud:**

1. _____ pugil   5. cum _____ aurīgā

2. _____ jaculum   6. sine _____ jaculātōribus

3. in _____ gymnasiō   7. contrā _____ luctātōrem

4. _____ cursōrēs   8. ab _____ palaestrā

H. Complete the sentences by inserting the correct form of **hīc, haec, hōc** in the first slot of each sentence and the correct form of **iste, ista, istud** in the second slot:

1. _____ cursor est vēlox, sed _____ est tardus.

2. _____ pugilēs sunt Graecī, sed _____ sunt Rōmānī.

3. Ego saepe cum _____ luctātōre pugnō sed numquam cum _____ luctātōre.

4. Exspectā mē in _____ locō, nōn in _____ palaestrā.

5. _____ palaestricī sunt benignī sed _____ sunt strictī.

6. Praefersne _____ discum an _____ discum?

7. _____ āthlētae discōs conjiciunt, sed _____ conjiciunt jacula.

8. Palaestricus aquam _____ pugilī dedit sed nōn _____ pugilī.

9. Cūr _____ luctātōrem timēbās sed nōn _____ ?

10. Ego in _____ domō habitābam, nōn in _____ .

DIALOGUS

Vocābula

multō nimis *much too*
lentus *-a -um* *slow*
mē paenitet *I am sorry*
validus *-a -um* *strong*

licet *well*
exspectō *-āre* *to wait*
tum *then*
erō *I will be*

QUAESTIŌNĒS PERSŌNĀLĒS

1. Potesne currĕre vēlōciter?

_____

2. Potesne salīre longē?

_____

3. Vīsne certāre in lūdīs Olympicīs?

_____

4. Vīsne vidēre lūdōs Olympicōs?

_____

5. Praefersne pugilēs an luctātōrēs an cursōrēs?

_____

6. Praefersne vidēre lūdōs Olympicōs in Graeciā an in patriā tuā?

_____

7. Ubi erunt (*will be*) proximī lūdī Olympicī?

_____

8. Exercēsne tē cōtīdiē?

_____

COMPOSITIŌ

You have been an athlete in previous Olympic games in Greece. Your friends are eager to attend the next games. Explain to them what the various athletes do or where they carry on their activities.

_____

_____

_____

_____

_____

COLLOQUIUM

Complete this conversation with expressions based on the previous conversation or create your own expressions:

THE LATIN CONNECTION

1. Did you know that a **gymnasium** was not only a place where people exercised but also where philosophers gave lectures? That is why in some countries of Europe "gymnasium" is the word for high school.

2. What is a "cursor" on a computer screen? _____

    Why is it called that? _____

3. What is "cursive" script? _____

4. What is a pugilist? _____

5. The verb **conjiciō** consists of the prefix **con-** and the verb **jacĕre**. The principal parts of **conjiciō** (*to throw*) are:

    conjiciō   **conjicĕre**   **conjēcī**   **conjectus**

    That last principal part is a past participle meaning *thrown* or *having been thrown*. You will see in a later lesson just how it works. Right now notice that the verb *conjecture* derives from the last principal part. Write out the principal parts of the following verbs and give the English derivatives from the last principal part:

    EXAMPLE: **ējiciō ējicĕre ējēcī ējectus**   *to eject; ejection*

1. injiciō _____

2. interjiciō _____

3. objiciō _____

4. prōjiciō _____

5. rejiciō _____

6. subjiciō _____

II *Thermae*

Volō/nōlō; Reflexive Verbs

1 | Modicum cultūrae

Roman public baths were much more than simply shower stalls and bathtubs. They resembled our modern YMCAs. Remember that most people in Rome lived in apartments, which had no toilets or bathrooms. In place of toilets, people used chamber pots (**matell*a* -*ae*** *f*). Only the homes of the rich contained a toilet (**lātrīn*a* -*ae*** *f*) and a bath (**balneum -*ī*** *n* or **balne*a* -*ae*** *f*). Public baths (**balne*a* -*ōrum*** *npl*), therefore, became one of the most important centers of Roman life. Citizens of every class enjoyed their use.

In earlier periods of their history, Romans seldom used the bath and then only for cleanliness and health, not as a luxury. The Roman author Seneca tells us that in the old days Romans washed their legs and arms daily and bathed their whole body once a week. Of course, people enjoyed swimming in the Tiber river as much for fun as for cleanliness. The earliest public baths were simple, often dingy, and used by the lower classes. In addition to public baths, private owners ran commercial bathhouses, charging a small fee. Every town had at least one public bath, and many larger towns had several. By the year A.D. 300, Rome had 856 such baths.

Gradually the baths became more pleasant and elaborate. The term **therm*ae*** (**-*ārum*** *fpl*), which originally meant *hot springs*, was applied to those magnificent structures erected by various Roman emperors to win popularity. These huge establishments contained, in addition to bathing facilities, lounges where Romans could chat with their friends, libraries, reading rooms, lecture halls, as well as snack shops (**popīn*a* -*ae*** *f*), barbershops, and places to exercise (**palaestr*a* -*ae*** *f*).

Rome could boast of several lavish **therm*ae*.** The largest in the whole Roman Empire was built by the emperor Diocletian in the heart of Rome and was dedicated in A.D. 306. It took 40,000 men to build it; it could hold 30,000 bathers. The admission fee was a fraction of a cent. The **therm*ae*** were the poor people's country club in the heart of the city, where they could forget about their dingy apartments and enjoy exercising, swimming, a massage, reading books that they could not afford at home, and catch up on the latest gossip. There were separate hours for men and women. The hours for women were in the morning; the afternoons were reserved for men. The **therm*ae*** of Diocletian were supplied with water from an aqueduct that had been built four hundred years earlier and brought water from fifty-seven miles away in the Sabine Mountains. The water was stored in a huge reservoir outside the baths that was about the size of a football field. From this reservoir, water was distributed through larger and smaller lead pipes to all the pools, tubs, basins, and fountains.

The chief rooms of the **thermae** were the dressing rooms (**apodytērium -ī** *n*) (which were notorious for pickpockets), the hot bath (**caldārium -ī** *n*), the warm bath (**tepidārium -ī** *n*), and the cold bath (**frīgidārium -ī** *n*). There was also a massage room (**unctōrium -ī** *n*) and a sauna (**lacōnicum -ī** *n*), toilets (**lātrīna -ae** *f*), and storerooms for equipment (**cella -ae** *f*). In the Baths of Diocletian, there was even a full-size theater. There were several large swimming pools (**piscīna -ae** *f*).

The remains of the Baths of Diocletian can still be visited today. They now contain a large church and a smaller one, a museum, a planetarium, and a movie theater instead of bathing facilities.

The general plan of the Baths of Diocletian will give you an idea of what these **thermae** included. It is impossible today to identify all the smaller rooms.

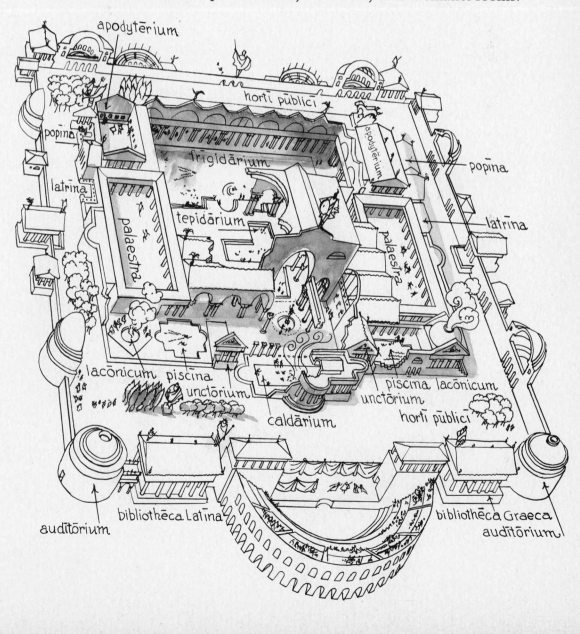

ACTIVITĀS

A. Here are some typical scenes in a Roman bath. Match the sentences with the pictures they describe:

Puer in piscīnam salit.
Puellae in palaestrā pilā lūdunt.
Puer vestēs in apodytēriō exuit.
Puellae ante fontem in tepidāriō stant.
Virī librōs in bibliothēcā legunt.
Philosophus in audītōriō docet.
Virī in lacōnicō sedent et sūdant.

Duo virī in palaestrā onera levant.
Trēs puellae in piscīnā in frīgidāriō natant.
Puerī ē piscīnā in caldāriō exeunt.
Multae fēminae thermās intrant.
Puer tomāclum et pānem in popīnā emit.

1. _____

2. _____

3. _____

4. _____

5. _____

6. _____

7. _____

8. _____

9. _____

10. _____

11. _____

12. _____

2 | Now read this conversation between Marcus, his older brother Lucius, and their cousin Rufus from the small town of Ardea in the district of Latium. Rufus is visiting Rome. Pay special attention to the forms of **volō** (*I want*) and **nōlō** (*I don't want*), which appear in bold type. The present tense of these verbs is irregular, but you should have no trouble spotting them and understanding them:

MARCUS: Vīsne, Rūfe, īre cum frātre meō et mēcum ad thermās novās?

RŪFUS: Ad thermās? Quae sunt "thermae"? Numquam dē thermīs audīvī.

quae? *what?*

LŪCIUS: Numquam dē thermīs audīvistī? Thermae sunt balneum grande ubi piscīnae et palaestrae et bibliothēcae et audītōrium sunt. Multī librī bonī sunt in bibliothēcā. In audītōriō philosophī docent.

grand*is* -*is* -*e* big, huge
audītōrium -*ī* n lecture hall
philosophus -*ī* m
  philosopher

RŪFUS: Omittē bibliothēcam et audītōrium. Neque librōs legĕre **volō** neque philosophōs audīre **volō**. Quid tū et frāter tuus facĕre **vultis?**

omittō -*ĕre* omīsī omissus
  to skip, forget about

MARCUS: In palaestrā pilā lūdĕre possumus aut trochōs volvĕre.

pil*a* -*ae* f ball (Note: The
  Romans said "play *with* a
  ball.")
troch*us* -*ī* m hoop
  volvō -*ĕre* -*ī* volūtus to
    roll
  parvul*us* -*ī* m little boy

RŪFUS: Trochum volvĕre **nōlō**. Nōn parvulus sum. Sed fortasse pilā lūdĕre possumus.

LŪCIUS: Et sī **vīs**, discum aut jaculum conjicĕre possumus. Omnēs amīcī nostrī pilā lūdĕre **volunt.**

RŪFUS: Bene! Post exercitātiōnem, in piscīnā in frīgidāriō natāre **volō**. Postquam sūdāvī, aquam frīgidam, nōn tepidam amō.

bene! *fine!*
  exercitātiō -*ōnis* f exercise
sūdō -*āre* to sweat
tepid*us* -*a* -*um* lukewarm,
  warm
quidnī? *why not?*

MARCUS: Quidnī? Ego quoque in piscīnā frīgidā natāre **volō**. Deinde, sī **vīs**, in piscīnam in tepidāriō salīre possumus. Frāter meus in piscīnā in frīgidāriō natāre **nōn vult.**

RŪFUS: Estne unctōrium in thermīs?

unctōrium -*ī* n massage room

MARCUS: Sānē. Est unctōrium cum optimīs unguentīs in tōtō orbe terrārum. Et post natātiōnem, unctiō est vērum oblectāmentum!

unguentum -*ī* n perfumed
  oil, perfume
natātiō -*ōnis* f swim
unctiō *ōnis* f massage
  oblectāment*um* -*ī* n
    delight

RŪFUS: Post unctiōnem, fortasse puellīs bellīs in tepidāriō occurrĕre possumus!

LŪCIUS: Mē paenitet, sed nōn licet puellīs in thermīs cum puerīs natāre. Sed in hortīs publicīs extrā thermās multae puellae bellae frequenter deambulant.

occurrō -*ĕre* -*ī* occursum
  (+ dat) to meet
licet it is allowed
hortī publicī -*ōrum* mpl park
deambulō -*āre* to stroll,
  walk around

RŪFUS: Eō cāsū, cūr nōn istās thermās omnīnō omittimus et statim . . .

eō cāsū in that case

MARCUS: Nōn, nōn, Rūfe. Prīmum ad thermās eāmus; posteā puellās petĕre possumus.

petō -*ĕre* -*īvī* -*ītus* to chase
  (after)

___ ACTIVITĀS _____

B. Respondē ad quaestiōnēs:

1. Quae sunt "thermae"?

   _____

2. Ubi in thermīs puerī pilā lūdunt?

   _____

3. Quid faciunt Rōmānī in bibliothēcā?

   _____

4. Ubi in thermīs philosophī docent?

   _____

5. Cūr Rūfus trochum volvĕre nōn vult?

   _____

6. Ubi in thermīs puerī natāre possunt?

   _____

7. Quid est vērum oblectāmentum post natātiōnem?

   _____

8. Ubi sunt hortī pūblicī?

   _____

3 | In the conversation between Rufus, Marcus, and Lucius, you came across the forms of the present tense of **volō.** Now let's look over the entire present tense of **volō** (*I want*) and **nōlō** (*I don't want*):

ego	**volō**	**nōlō**
tū	**vīs**	**nōn vīs**
is/ea/id	**vult**	**nōn vult**
nōs	**volumus**	**nōlumus**
vōs	**vultis**	**nōn vultis**
eī, eae/ea	**volunt**	**nōlunt**

The principal parts (first person present, present infinitive, first person perfect) of the two verbs are:

volō	**velle**	**voluī**
nōlō	**nōlle**	**nōluī**

The imperfect forms are **volēbam, volēbās,** etc., **nōlēbam, nōlēbās,** etc.

— ACTIVITĀTĒS —————————————————

C. Substitute the appropriate forms of **nōlle** in place of the forms of **velle**:

1. In hāc piscīna natāre [volō] ———————————————.

2. Illae puellae in flūmine natāre [volunt] ———————————.

3. Ad thermās īre [volumus] —————————————————.

4. Cūr tū Rōmam aestāte vīsitāre [vīs] ————————————?

5. Ubi tū et amīcus tuus natāre [vultis] —————————————?

6. Marcus in hanc piscīnam salīre [vult] ———————————.

7. Nōs nunc unctiōnem habēre [volumus] ——————————.

8. Cūr tū in hortīs pūblicīs deambulāre [vīs] ————————?

D. Supply the correct form of **velle** in the following sentences:

1. Rūfus puellīs occurrĕre ————————————————.

2. Post unctiōnem, fēminae in hortīs publicīs deambūlāre ————.

3. Ego et pater meus āthlētās in palaestrā spectāre —————————.

4. Lūcius in hōc lacōnicō sedēre et sūdāre —————————.

5. Sī tū et Marcus tomācla emĕre ——————————, eāmus ad illam popīnam.

6. Simul atque ego piscīnam videō, in eam salīre —————————.

7. Lūcius et ego Ardeam et alia oppida in Latīo vīsitāre ————.

8. Virī in palaestrā onera levāre ————————————————.

E. Read over the following sentences carefully and then supply the correct form of **nōlle:**

1. Quamquam bene natāre possum, hodiē natāre —————————.

2. Quia hodiē calidum est, hī puerī in caldāriō sedēre —————.

3. Virī Rōmānī ante merīdiem ad thermās īre —————————.

4. Antequam in piscīnam saliō, in lacōnicō sūdāre —————————.

5. Sī tū in audītōrium īre _____, philosophum audīre nōn potes.

6. Vōsne in bibliothēcā librōs legĕre _____?

7. Multī ē Campaniā thermās novās Rōmae vidēre _____.

8. Postquam ego thermās vīsitāvī, ista balnea intrāre _____.

F. As we saw earlier, the imperfect tense endings are regular. Substitute the correct form of **nōlle** for **velle:**

1. Ego herī ad thermās īre [volēbam] _____.

2. Quis in hāc piscīnā natāre [volēbat] _____?

3. Amīcī meī mē in tepidāriō exspectāre [volēbant] _____.

4. [Volēbāsne] _____ mēcum in hortīs pūblicīs deambulāre?

5. Senātōrēs cum populō in lacōnicō sedēre [volēbant] _____.

6. Puer cum āthlētīs pilā lūdĕre [volēbat] _____.

4 In Lesson I, you met the expression **Āthlētae sē exercent** *(The athletes are training).* The verb **sē exercent** is called REFLEXIVE because the action does not go from the subject to some object but reflects back to the subject. The sentence **Āthlēta sē lavat** may mean *the athlete is washing* or *the athlete is washing himself; himself* is the reflexive pronoun.

A reflexive verb uses regular simple accusative pronouns in the first and second persons, singular and plural; but it uses **sē** in the third person, singular and plural:

mē lavō	*I wash/am washing (myself)*
tē lavās	*you wash/are washing (yourself)*
sē **lavat**	*he/she washes/is washing (himself/herself)*
nōs lavāmus	*we wash/are washing (ourselves)*
vōs lavātis	*you wash/are washing (yourselves)*
sē **lavant**	*they wash/are washing (themselves)*

In Latin, the reflexive pronoun is often separated from the reflexive verb.

— ACTIVITĀS

G. Complete the sentences with the correct reflexive pronouns:

1. Puella _____ in speculō videt.

2. Vidēsne _____ in speculō?

3. Marcus _____ in speculō videt.

4. Āthlētae _____ ante certāmen exercēbant.

5. Ego et amīcī in hāc palaestrā _____ exercēbāmus.

6. Quamobrem tū et frāter tuus _____ nōn exercēbātis?

7. Quamquam multī in palaestrā erant, cum istīs _____ exercēre nōluī.

8. Amīcī meī _____ in caldāriō lavābant.

5 | Certain verbs, as you may recall, take the dative rather than the accusative case, such as **noceō -ēre -uī** (*to harm*); **confīdō -ĕre -ī** (*to trust*); **diffīdō -ĕre -ī** (*to distrust*). When these verbs are used reflexively, they require the dative of the reflexive pronoun. Again, the reflexive pronoun in the dative case is the same as the simple dative pronoun in the first and second persons singular and plural; in the third person singular and plural, the reflexive pronoun is **sibi**:

mihi noceō	*I hurt/am hurting myself*
tibi nocēs	*you hurt/are hurting yourself*
sibi **nocet**	*he/she/it hurts/is hurting himself/herself/itself*
nōbīs nocēmus	*we hurt/are hurting ourselves*
vōbīs nocētis	*you hurt/are hurting yourselves*
sibi **nocent**	*they hurt/are hurting themselves*

__ ACTIVITĀTĒS _____

H. Complete the following sentences with the correct reflexive pronouns:

1. Ille āthlēta _____ nocuit.

2. Quōmodo _____ nocuistī?

3. Hī āthlētae _____ diffīdunt.

4. Quandō ego et Claudius pilā lūdēbāmus, _____ nocuimus.

5. Hīc discobulus _____ nocuit.

6. Quia ego timidus sum, in perīculō numquam _____ confīdō.

I. Some of the following verbs take the accusative, while others take the dative case of the reflexive pronoun. Complete the sentences with the correct reflexive pronouns:

1. Claudius _____ in tepidāriō lavābat.

2. Quamobrem Claudius _____ nōn confīdit?

3. Claudī, sī _____ lavāre vīs, remanē in caldāriō.

4. Amīcī meī, sī _____ lavāre vultis, salīte in hanc piscīnam.

5. Quot āthlētae _____ in palaestrā nocuērunt?

6. Puerī, nōlīte nocēre _____ .

7. Rūfe, nōlī nocēre _____ .

8. Propter timōrem _____ saepe diffīdimus.

QUAESTIŌNĒS PERSŌNĀLĒS

1. Habetne familia tua piscīnam?

2. Praefersne natāre in flūmine an in piscīnā?

3. Praefersne natāre in frīgidāriō an tepidāriō an caldāriō?

4. Natāvistī umquam in oceanō?

5. Potesne natāre bene an male?

6. Lūdisne pilā cum amīcīs tuīs?

DIALOGUS

Vocābula

tantus -a -um *such big*
nē . . . quidem *not even*
balneolum -ī *n little bath*
dēsīderō -āre *to miss*
Miserum Rūfum! *Poor Rufus!*
quotiens? *how often?*

licet tibi *are you allowed*
semel aut bis *once or twice*
addūcō -ĕre adduxī adductus *to take to*
stagnum -ī *n pond*

COMPOSITIŌ

Assume that you live in ancient Rome. Your cousin in Ardea has never seen the baths. Write your cousin four statements that will describe what the **thermae** are like.

1. _____

2. _____

3. _____

4. _____

THE LATIN CONNECTION

A. Perhaps you have heard the expression: "She was the *belle* of the ball." From

which Latin word is *belle* derived? _____

B. People might say of a smart girl: "She is a *fount* of knowledge." From which Latin

word is *fount* derived? _____

C. Can you give another English word for each of the following words and then give the Latin word from which it is derived?

1. tepid   _____   _____

2. unguent   _____   _____

3. licit   _____   _____

4. grand   _____   _____

5. legible   _____   _____

6. omit   _____   _____

7. disc   _____   _____

8. cell   _____   _____

9. latrine   _____   _____

10. puerile   _____   _____

COLLOQUIUM

Complete the dialog with ideas taken from the previous conversation or create answers of your own:

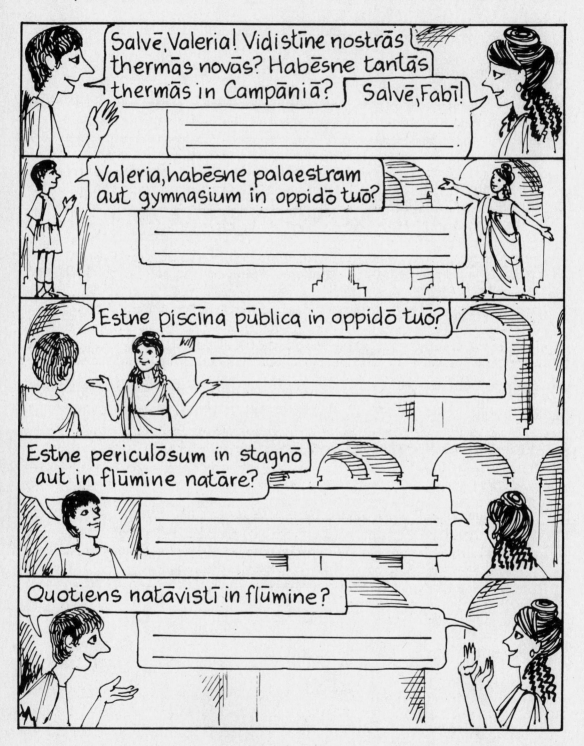

III Superstitiō

Future Tense

1 Modicum cultūrae

If you were to drop in suddenly on the ancient Romans, you would be amazed at the strange methods they used to try to look into the future. Priests, called **haruspicēs** (*haruspex -icis* m), tried to interpret the will of the gods by examining the internal organs of sacrificial animals. The slightest abnormal condition of the liver, for instance, could indicate doom. **Haruspicēs** also marked off a section of the sky, called a **templum,** and divided it into sections with an augural staff (**lituus -ī** m). Depending on the section in which lightning was seen, they made various predictions. Another group of priests called augurs (**augur -uris** m) also marked off the sky into sections and made predictions according to the directions of birds flying through the **templum.** The augurs even made predictions by watching chickens eat. If the chickens refused to eat, disaster was predicted. The augurs also interpreted the sounds and moves that chickens made as they ate.

The Romans often retold the story of a navy commander named Appius Claudius the Handsome. Just before a naval battle off Sicily, he had the augur observe the chickens that he carried aboard the ship in a coop. When he was told that the chickens would not eat (bad omen!), he flung them into the sea, saying "If they won't eat, then they will drink." When he lost the naval battle, everyone blamed him for not believing in the omens that the chickens gave.

The Romans saw an omen in any event that was the least bit unusual. Dreams, natural phenomena like thunder, hail, and floods, and the birth of deformed animals were all considered omens. Even the founding of Rome by Romulus and his brother Remus was based on augury.

Astrologers were very influential in Rome. Even the emperor Augustus and the emperors that came after him regularly consulted astrologers. How many items can you name that are regarded today as signs of good luck or bad luck? How do people today try to find out what the future holds?

2 Vocābula

Ariēs -etis m

Taurus -ī m

Geminī -ōrum mpl

29

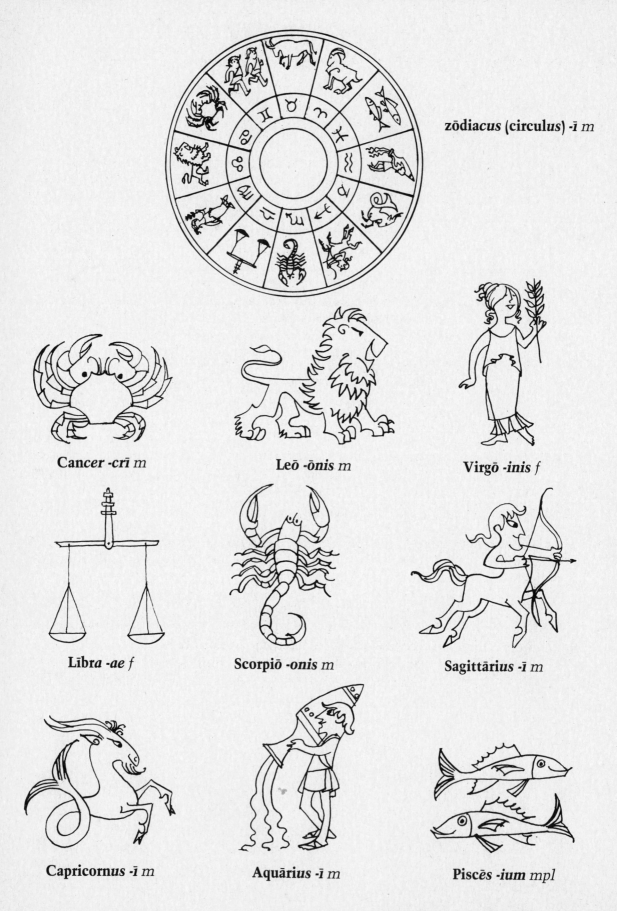

zōdiacus (circulus) -ī m

Cancer -crī m

Leō -ōnis m

Virgō -inis f

Lībra -ae f

Scorpiō -onis m

Sagittārius -ī m

Capricornus -ī m

Aquārius -ī m

Piscēs -ium mpl

augur -uris *m*   **astrologus -ī** *m*   **harūspex -icis** *m*

③ Hōroscopium

Learn to read the horoscope. Pay attention to the verbs in bold type. These verbs are in the future tense:

Sī tū inter vīcēsimum prīmum diem Martiī et vīcēsimum diem Aprīlis nātus(-a) es, tuum signum zōdiacī est Ariēs. Elementum tuum est ignis. Tū es persōna līberālis, benigna, fidēlis, sed interdum audax et violenta. Amīcōs tuōs semper **juvābis** et inimīcōs tuōs nōn **timēbis.**

ignis -is *m fire*
līberālis -is -e *generous*

juvō -āre -ī -tus *to help*
inimīcus -ī *m enemy*

Sī tū inter vīcēsimum prīmum diem Aprīlis et vīcēsimum prīmum diēm Māiī nātus(-a) es, tuum signum zōdiacī est Taurus. Elementum tuum est terra. Tū es persōna patiens et fortis et valida, sed interdum arrogans, tarda, īrācunda, superstitiōsa. Post multa perīcula, magnum successum **habēbis.** Aliī tibi **invidēbunt** propter successum tuum.

terra -ae *f earth*
fortis -is -e *brave*
īrācundus -a -um *quick-tempered*

invideō -ēre -vīsī (+ *dat*) *to envy*

Sī inter vīcēsimum secundum diem Māiī et vīcēsimum prīmum diem Jūniī nātus(-a) es, signum tuum zōdiacī est Geminī. Tuum elementum est aër. Tū es persōna sincēra et astūta et justa sed etiam mūtābilis et avāra et inquiēta. Dīligenter **labōrābis,** sed mentem tuam saepe **mūtābis.**

aër aëris *m air*

mūtābilis -is -e *fickle*
  avārus -a -um *greedy*
  inquiētus -a -um *restless*
mens mentis *f mind*
mūto -āre *to change*

Sī tū inter vīcēsimum secundum diem Jūniī et vīcēsimum diem Jūliī nātus(-a) es, tuum signum zōdiacī est Cancer. Elementum tuum est aqua. Tū es persōna cum sensū commūnī. Memoriam excellentem et cor bonum habēs. Animālia parva amās. Tū es persōna prūdens et intellegens sed interdum nimis cauta et timida. Quia tū persōna cauta es, vītam longam **habēbis.**

nimis *too*
  cautus -a -um *cautious*

Sī tū inter vīcēsimum tertium diem Jūliī et vīcēsimum tertium diem Augustī nātus(-a) es, signum tuum zōdiacī est Leō. Elementum tuum est ignis. Es persōna audax et ambitiōsa et fortis sed interdum superba et arrogans et nimis audax. Corpus validum habēs. Rapidē currĕre potes. Nihil tē **terrēbit.** Aliquandō domum magnam et pecūniam multam **habēbis.**

superbus -a -um *proud*
validus -a -um *strong*
nihil *nothing*

Sī tū inter vīcēsimum quārtum diem Augustī et vīcēsimum tertium diem Septembris nātus(-a) es, signum tuum zōdiacī est Virgō. Elementum tuum est terra. Es persōna studiōsa et astūta et industria, sed interdum fastīdiōsa et tristis et nimis cauta. Vestēs pulchrās amās. Antequam aliquid facis, singula dīligenter consīderās. Quia līberālis ergā omnēs es, multōs amīcōs semper **habēbis.**

fastīdiōsus -a -um *picky*

singula -ōrum *npl details*
consīderō -āre *to consider*
  ergā (+ *acc*) *toward*

Sī tū inter vīcēsimum quārtem diem Septembris et vīcēsimum tertium diem Octōbris nātus(-a) es, signum tuum zōdiacī est Lībra. Elementum tuum est aër.

Es persōna polīta et ēlegans et obēdiens, sed etiam fastīdiōsa et irrītābilis et interdum difficilis. Vēr et autumnus tibi placent, sed aestās tibi praecipuē placet. Quia tū persōna justa es, aliquandō advocātus aut jūdex **eris.**

polīt*us* **-a -um** *polite, refined*

vēr vēris *n spring*
aestās -ātis *f summer*
  praecipuē *especially*
jūdex -icis *m judge*

Sī tū inter vīcēsimum quārtum diem Octōbris et vīcēsimum secundum diem Novembris nātus(-a) es, signum tuum zōdiacī est Scorpiō. Elementum tuum est aqua. Tū es persōna neque dīves neque pauper, neque nimis audax neque nimis timida. Multōs labōrēs in vītā **habēbis,** sed eōs facile **superābis.**

neque . . . neque *neither . . . nor*
labōrēs -um *mpl troubles*
superō -āre *to overcome*

Sī tū inter vīcēsimum tertium diem Novembris et vīcēsimum diem Decembris nātus(-a) es, signum tuum zōdiacī est Sagittārius. Elementum tuum est ignis. Quia tū persōna ambitiōsa es, labōrem numquam **timēbis.** Semper dīligenter **laborābis.** Multam pecūniam **merēbis.** Sed persōna obstināta et impatiens et cerebrōsa es. Forsitan aliquandō mīles aut āthlēta aut senātor **eris.** Multās terrās **vīsitābis** in Eurōpā et Asiā et Āfricā. Nōmen tuum **erit** clārum.

labor -ōris *m work*
mereō -ēre -uī *to earn*
cerebrōsus -a -um *hot-headed*
forsitan *perhaps*
clārus -a -um *famous*

Sī tū inter vīcēsimum prīmum diem Decembris et vīcēsimum diem Jānuāriī nātus(-a) es, signum tuum zōdiacī est Capricornus. Elementum tuum est terra. Tū es persōna cauta et sēria et dīligens, sed interdum obstināta et mūtābilis et frīgida ergā aliēnōs. Quia tū persōna sēria et dīligens es, forsitan aliquandō **eris** magister (magistra) aut medicus(-a). Parentēs viam ad successum tibi **mōnstrābunt.**

sērius -a -um *serious*
frīgidus -a -um *cool*
  aliēnus -ī *m stranger, foreigner*

Sī tū inter vīcēsimum prīmum diem Jānuāriī et duodēvīcēsimum diem Februāriī nātus(-a) es, signum tuum zōdiacī est Aquārius. Elementum tuum est aër. Tū es persōna honesta et līberālis et studiōsa. Sed interdum tū es rebellis et difficilis. Apud condiscipulōs semper populāris **eris.** Aliquandō theātrum tē **vocābit** et tū **eris** actor clārus (actrix clāra). Vītam fortūnātam **habēbis.**

apud (+ acc) *among*
condiscipulus -ī m *classmate*

Sī tū inter undēvīcēsimum diem Februāriī et vīcēsimum diem Martiī nātus(-a) es, signum tuum est aqua. Es persōna tenera et amābilis et artifex sed etiam timida et mūtābilis et interdum tristis. Sed tū es fidēlis amīcīs tuīs. Tū habēs mentem sānam in corpore sānō. Ergo tū **eris** bonus negōtiator aut āthlēta. Multa praemia **merēbis.**

tener -era -erum *tender*
artifex -ficis *artistic*

sānus -a -um *sound*
negotiātor -ōris m *business person*
praemium -ī n *award*

__ ACTIVITĀTĒS _____

A. Now that you have learned something about the significance of the signs of the zodiac, see whether you can identify them on sight and write their Latin names below their pictures. And while you're at it, how about writing the genitive ending and the gender as well!

1. _____   2. _____   3. _____

4. _____   5. _____   6. _____

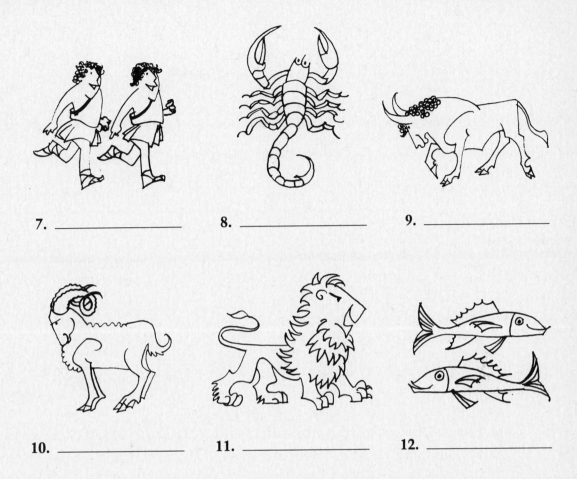

7. _____   8. _____   9. _____

10. _____   11. _____   12. _____

B. Read over the following descriptions carefully. Then identify the sign of the zodiac:

1. Ego sum animal magnum et ferox. Dentēs lon-
gōs et acūtōs habeō. Juba longa mihi est. Cum
ego rugiō, omnia animālia in silvīs timent, quia
ego sum rex bestiārum.

   acūtus -a -um *sharp*
   juba -ae f *mane*
   cum *when*
   rugiō -īre -iī *to roar*

   Ego sum _____.

2. Ego sum animal grande. In fundō habitō. Her-
bam multam consūmō, sed ego lac agricolīs nōn
dō, sed vaccae lac agricolīs dant. Duo cornua
habeō, et cum vexillum rubrum videō, ego
oppugnō.

   cornu -ūs n *horn*
   vexillum -ī n *flag*
   oppugnō -āre *to charge*

   Ego sum _____.

3. Nōs sumus frātrēs. Eōdem diē nātī sumus.
Eāsdem vestēs saepe gestāmus. Vultūs nostrī si-
millimī sunt. Diem nātālem eundem celebrā-
mus.

   īdem eadem idem *the same*
   gestō -āre *to wear*
   vultus -ūs m *looks, expression*

Nōs sumus _____.

4. Nōs duo neque manūs neque crūra habēmus. Dīcĕre nōn possumus, quia vox nōbīs nōn est. Caudam habēmus. Cum in aquā sumus, respīrāre possumus sed extrā aquam respīrāre nōn possumus. Pinnās habēmus. Flūmina et stāgna nōbīs placent.

dīcō -*ĕre* dīxī *to speak*
  vox vōcis *f voice*
caud*a* -*ae* f *tail*
  respīrō -*āre* *to breathe*
  extrā (+ *acc*) *outside of*
pinn*a* -*ae* f *fin*

Nōs sumus _____.

5. Animal parvum sed periculōsum sum. In dēsertīs habitō. In harēnā calidā rēpĕre amō. Tria crūra in dextrā parte corporis meī habeō et tria in sinistrā parte. Etiam duo bracchia mihi sunt. In caudā meā habeō acūleum venēnātum. Ictus meus magnum dolōrem facit.

dēsert*a* -*ōrum* npl *desert*
harēn*a* -*ae* f *sand*
  rēpō -*ĕre* rēpsī *to crawl*
dexter -*tra* -*trum* *right*
  pars partis f *side*
sinister -*tra* -*trum* *left*
  bracchium -*ī* n *claw*
acūle*us* -*ī* m *sting*
  venēnāt*us* -*a* -*um*
    poisonous
ict*us* -*ūs* m *bite, sting*
  faciō -*ĕre* fēcī *to cause*

Ego sum _____.

Until now, all the verbs have been in either the present or the past tense. How do you describe actions and events that will happen in the future? The horoscope told you some things that will happen to you in the future. Let's look at some examples:

Virgō benigna multās amīcās habēbit.
A kind girl will have many friends.
Quid Rōmānī dē astrologīs cōgitābunt?
What will the Romans think about astrologers?
Quid crās in forō gestābimus?
What will we wear in the forum tomorrow?

If you compare the imperfect forms of the verbs of the first and second conjugations with the forms of the future, you will see how simple it is to form the future tense. The imperfect tense is formed as follows:

I	portā	-bam
		-bās
		-bat
II	tenē	-bāmus
		-bātis
		-bant

To form the future tense, use the same stem and add the future personal endings:

$$
\left.\begin{array}{l}
\text{-bō} \\
\text{-bis} \\
\text{-bit} \\
\text{-bimus} \\
\text{-bitis} \\
\text{-bunt}
\end{array}\right\}
$$

I   portā
II tenē

What is the typical vowel in the imperfect endings? _____ .

What is the typical vowel in the future endings? _____ .

__ ACTIVITĀTĒS _____

C. Write out the future tense of the following verbs:

	portāre	tenēre	dare
ego	_____	_____	_____
tū	_____	_____	_____
is, ea, id	_____	_____	_____
nōs	_____	_____	_____
vōs	_____	_____	_____
eī, eae, ea	_____	_____	_____

D. Read over the following sentences carefully to see what they say. Then convert the verb from the imperfect to the future tense:

1. Astrologī caelum frequenter observābant. _____

2. Augustus astrologōs consultābat. _____

3. Cūr tū mentem tuam sine causā mūtābās? _____

4. Ego consīderābam scorpiōnēs esse perīculōsōs. _____

5. Tiberius virginem Germānam amābat. _____

6. Vidēbāsne multōs cancrōs in orā maritimā? _____

7. Agricola vaccās et taurōs in fundō habēbat. _____

8. Augurēs lituum in manū sinistrā tenēbant. _____

9. Vidēbātisne capricornum cum ūnō cornū? _____

10. Aquāriī aquam leōnibus in amphitheātrō dābant. _____.

E. Complete the sentences with the correct future-tense forms of the verbs:

1. (observāre) Astrologī astra et planētās _____.

2. (vīsitāre) Cūr Augustus astrologum _____?

3. (celebrāre) Quis diem nātālem crās _____?

4. (dēmonstrāre) Astrologusne Sagittārium _____?

5. (consultāre) Omnēs Rōmānī astrologōs _____.

6. (manēre) Ego et pater in urbe _____.

7. (merēre) Quantam pecūniam astrologus _____?

8. (placēre) Nōnne hōroscopium tuum tibi _____?

9. (vidēre) Augurēs avēs nōn _____.

10. (habēre) Tū et frāter sānam mentem et corpus sānum _____.

5 The endings of the future tense of **īre** (*to go*) are regular, that is, they are the same as for verbs like **portāre** and **tenēre**. The entire stem is simply **ī-**. The stem of **abīre** (*to go away*) is **abī-**; the stem of **exīre** (*to go out*) is **exī-**; the stem of **adīre** (*to go to, approach*) is **adī-**.

___ ACTIVITĀTĒS _____

F. Write out the future tense of **īre** (*to go*) and **abīre** (*to go away, leave*):

	īre	abīre
ego	_____	_____
tū	_____	_____
is, ea, id	_____	_____
nōs	_____	_____
vōs	_____	_____
eī, eae, ea	_____	_____

G. Change the verbs from the imperfect to the future tense:

1. Post cēnam omnēs amīcī meī abībant. _____

2. Quis ē domō astrologī exībat? _____

3. Augurēs aram ante templum adībant. _____

4. Quandō tū ē pistrīnā cum pāne exībās? _____

5. Ego et avia mea ad bibliothēcam redībāmus. _____

H. Change the verbs from the present to the future tense:

1. Multī mīlitēs in bellō pereunt. _____

2. Āthlēta ad stadium cōtīdiē it. _____

3. Augurēs et haruspicēs templum ineunt. _____

4. Astrologus aliēnōs numquam adit. _____

5. Ego et Titus astrologum adīmus. _____

6 Do you want to know what will happen to you in the future? Do you want to get some hints on how astrology works? In ancient Rome, astrologers were often called **mathēmaticī,** probably because the astrologers had to do a lot of computing. Suppose you were strolling through the Roman forum and stopped to listen to an astrologer trying to drum up business. Listen!

Ego sum mathēmaticus aut astrologus, quia ego astra in caelō cōtīdiē observō et mōtiōnēs astrōrum dīligenter dēnotō. Itaque futūra praedīcĕre possum, quoniam astra in caelō omnia in terrā afficiunt, perinde āc lūna aestūs ōceanī afficit. Lūna plēna multōs hominēs afficit. Nōs omnēs sub ūnō ex duodecim signīs zōdiacī nātī(-ae) sumus. Ergō diēs nātālis noster est maximī mōmentī.

mōtiō -ōnis f movement
dēnotō -āre to mark down
    futūra -ōrum npl future
    praedīcō -ĕre -dīxī to predict
afficiō -ĕre -fēcī to influence
    perinde āc just as
aestus -ūs m tide
    plēnus -a -um full
momentum -ī n importance

Nōlīte dēcernĕre dē rēbus magnīs nisi prius hōroscopium vestrum consultātis. Crēde mihi, astrologia est scientia vēra, nōn superstitiō! Sī mē consultābitis, ego vōs juvābō. Nīmīrum, pensitābitis multam pecūniam prō meō consiliō.

dēcernō -ĕre -crēvī to decide
    magnus -a -um important
    nisi prius unless first
scientia -ae f science
nīmīrum of course
    pensitō -āre to pay
consilium -ī n advice

— ACTIVITĀS _____

I. Now that you have heard the man's "sales pitch," see if you can answer the following questions:

1. What is the first thing he does as an astrologer?

   _____

2. What does he record?

   _____

3. What do the stars influence?

   _____

4. What does the moon influence?

   _____

5. What does the full moon influence?

   _____

6. Which day in our lives determines our future?

   _____

7. What should we do before we decide on anything important?

   _____

8. According to him, what is astrology?

   _____

9. What will he do if you consult him?

   _____

10. What does he say in the end that may make you think twice about his absolute sincerity?

   _____

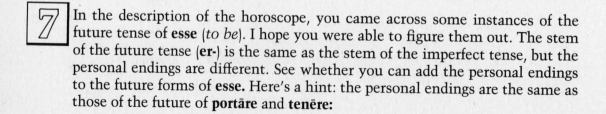

7 In the description of the horoscope, you came across some instances of the future tense of **esse** (*to be*). I hope you were able to figure them out. The stem of the future tense (**er-**) is the same as the stem of the imperfect tense, but the personal endings are different. See whether you can add the personal endings to the future forms of **esse**. Here's a hint: the personal endings are the same as those of the future of **portāre** and **tenēre:**

	IMPERFECT	FUTURE
ego	eram	er _____
tū	erās	er _____
is, ea, id	erat	er _____
nōs	erāmus	er _____
vōs	erātis	er _____
eī, eae, ea	erant	er _____

8 Do you remember how you formed the present tense of **posse** (*to be able*)? Do you recall that **posse** is a combination of the root **pot-** (which means *able*) and **esse** (*to be*)? Do you remember when the **t** was changed to **s** in the present tense? To form the future, add the future forms of **esse** to the root **pot-**:

ego	_____
tū	_____
is, ea, id	_____
nōs	_____
vōs	_____
eī, eae, ea	_____

___ ACTIVITĀTĒS _____

J. Change the verb in the following sentences from the imperfect to the future:

1. Bona fortūna tibi erat. _____

2. Cūr tam līberālis erās? _____

3. Condiscipulī meī erant studiōsī. _____

4. Nōs erāmus āthlētae clārī. _____

5. Astrologus ante templum hodiē erat. _____

K. Complete with the correct forms of the future tense of **posse**:

1. Astrologī nōn semper futūra praedīcĕre _____.

2. Nōs astra noctū vidēre _____ .

3. Ego hōroscopium tuum legĕre nōn _____ .

4. Tū et soror tua astrologum consultāre _____ .

5. Augurēs Rōmānī futūra per avēs praedīcĕre _____ .

6. Lūna aestūs ōceanī afficĕre _____ .

7. Omnēs discipulī signa zōdiacī circulī discĕre _____ .

8. Num ego fēlix esse _____ sine hōroscopiō?

9. Augurēs Rōmānī gallīnās crās observāre _____ .

10. Ego multam pecūniam astrologō pensitāre nōn _____ .

_____QUAESTIŌNĒS PERSŌNĀLĒS_____

1. Quandō est tuus diēs nātālis?

_____

2. Quid est tuum signum Zōdiacī circulī?

_____

3. Quandō est diēs nātālis mātris tuae?

_____

4. Quid est ejus signum?

_____

5. Quandō est diēs nātālis patris tuī?

_____

6. Quid est ejus signum?

_____

7. Potestne hōroscopium praedīcĕre futūra tua?

_____

DIALOGUS

Vocābula

quod *which*
fēlix -īcis *lucky*
debeō -ēre -uī *to owe*

dēnārius -ī *m dollar*
infēlix -īcis *unlucky*

COLLOQUIUM

Pretend that you are the astrologer in this dialog. Complete it by answering the questions:

Astrologe, quōmodō futūra mea praedīcěre poteris?	_____ _____ (Say that you will observe the stars and the signs of the zodiac.)
Quot signa sunt in zōdiacō circulō?	_____ _____ (Answer the question and then ask what his sign is.)
Signum meum est Sagittārius. Estne signum meum fēlix an infēlix?	_____ _____ (Respond affirmatively and give your opinion of the sign.)
Num multōs labōrēs in vītā habēbō? Vītam bonam et secūram habēbō?	_____ _____ (Give your opinion and then ask for 200 dollars.)

RĒS PERSŌNĀLĒS

Imagine that you have consulted a Roman astrologer. He says that any of the following can be yours in the future, but you have to choose only three, putting the most important first, and the least important last. Use numbers 1 to 3 to indicate your choice:

_____ longa vīta		_____ multī amīcī
_____ multa pecūnia		_____ familia amābilis
_____ fēlix vīta		_____ successus in vītā
_____ lībertās		_____ corpus sānum

COMPOSITIŌ

Ask three of your friends what their signs are. Then get some ideas from the horoscope of this lesson and tell each of them what is "in their stars." For each friend, list the first name, the sign, and then the horoscope reading:

First name: _____ Sign: _____

Horoscope: _____

_____

First name: _____ Sign: _____

Horoscope: _____

_____

First name: _____ Sign: _____

Horoscope: _____

_____

THE LATIN CONNECTION

A. One of the signs of the zodiac is Lībra, which means either "a pair of scales" to weigh things or "a pound." What English abbreviation meaning "pound" comes

from **lībra?** _____

B. Can you give the Latin words from which these English words derive?

1. superstition _____

2. cautious _____

3. astronaut _____

4. circle _____

5. mutant _____

6. ignite _____

7. fortitude _____

8. success _____

9. mental _____

10. corporal _____

11. memorial _____

12. superb _____

13. judicial _____

14. alien _____

15. vocal _____

16. reptile _____

17. predict _____

18. momentous _____

IV Spectācula Rōmāna

Future Tense (continued); Ablative of Means

1 Modicum cultūrae

The Romans did not have a word for "sports." No Roman author ever wrote a book on sports. In fact, there were no "weekends" on the Roman calendar on which great sporting events might be held. The Romans, unlike people of modern countries, did not have organized teams representing cities, towns, and schools. Instead, wealthy citizens and public officials, and later on the emperors, provided games and entertainment to celebrate a military victory, a religious festival, an election campaign, or even a public funeral.

Boxing and wrestling matches, as well as circus acts (jugglers, tight-rope walkers, acrobats), were staged in the Roman forum or the Circus Maximus until amphitheaters were built. By far the most popular events were the gladiatorial shows and wild-animal hunts (**vēnātiō -ōnis** *f*). Admission was free since the producer of the shows wished to win popularity.

The gladiators were usually slaves, prisoners of war, or condemned criminals. Occasionally free-born citizens became gladiators for the excitement of the sport. They lived and trained in the gladiatorial school (**lūdus -ī** *m*) under the watchful eyes of their trainers (**lanista -ae** *m*). Some gladiators won many victories, gained their freedom and popularity, and even became rich. But most of them lived and died miserably.

To add variety to the show, gladiators were grouped into various classes according to the type of armor they wore or their method of fighting. For example, a net man (**rētiārius -ī** *m*) was armed only with a trident and a fishing net, which he tried to throw over his opponent. A Thracian (**Thrax -ācis** *m*) was armed with a helmet, shin guards, a small round shield, and a curved dagger. Others fought on horseback and looked very much like medieval knights. Most gladiators had their entire right arm wrapped up to the shoulder in leather straps. One class of gladiators fought without holes in their visors, so that they had to fight blindfolded for the amusement of the spectators. Some (**bestiārius -ī** *m*) fought wild animals with a spear; others, mostly criminals, were simply thrown unarmed to the wild beasts, which had been brought to Rome from Asia and especially from North Africa.

On the day of the show (**spectāculum -ī** *n*), at the blare of trumpets, the gladiators paraded around the arena to the cheers of the crowds and saluted the producer of the games. Then the gladiators paired off to fight. Often there were several pairs fighting at one time. The gladiators fought to the accompaniment of music. The contests continued till noon.

During the lunch break, jugglers, magicians, clowns, and animal trainers would entertain the crowd. The afternoon performance might be a battle with wild animals. When the Colosseum was dedicated by the emperor Titus in A.D. 80, some 5,000 animals were slaughtered during the hundred-day holiday.

Another favorite spectator sport was the chariot race in the Circus Maximus. And the emperor Augustus built an artificial lake near the Tiber, where mock naval battles would be fought. The ships were smaller than sea-going vessels, but the battles were dangerous and even deadly.

2 The equipment that the gladiators wore may be new to you. Look it over carefully and try to remember the name of each item:

___ ACTIVITĀS ___

A. See whether you can identify the equipment that these gladiators are wearing:

In Lesson III, you learned how to form the future tense of verbs of the first and second conjugations and of **sum** and **possum.** Now it's time to learn the future tense of the remaining verb families. Read the following story of the rebellion of the gladiators, led by Spartacus in 73 B.C. Pay special attention to the verbs in bold type. These are verbs of the **-ĕre, -īre** and **-iō** families in the future tense:

In urbe Capuā erat amphitheātrum magnum. Nōn procul ab amphitheātrō erat lūdus gladiātōrius, ubi multī gladiātōrēs ex omnibus partibus orbis sē exercēbant. Servī erant. Lanistae eōrum erant crūdēlissimī et saepe mīserōs gladiātōrēs ferulīs verberāvērunt.

nōn procul ab (+ abl) *not far from*
lūdus -ī m *school*
orbis -is m *world*
servus ī m *slave*
ferula -ae f *whip*
verberō -āre *to beat*

Quōdam diē, ūnus ē gladiātōribus, nōmine Spartacus, amīcōs suōs convocāvit et dīxit: "Amīcī meī, quōusque ad dēlectāmentum populī Rōmānī pugnābimus? Quōusque ad glōriam dominōrum nostrōrum vītās nostrās **āmittēmus?** Quōs timēmus? Lanistās nostrōs? Sed gladiōs, sīcās, scūta, parmās habēmus. Ītalia patria vestra nōn est. Vōs ex Asiā et Graeciā et Germāniā et Galliā et longinquā Britanniā ad Ītaliam vēnistis. Nunc est tempus redīre ad patriās vestrās.

quōdam diē *one day*
convocō -āre *to call together*
quōusque *how long*
  ad (+ acc) *for*
  dēlectāmentum -ī n *entertainment*
dominus -ī m *owner, master*
āmittō -ĕre āmīsī āmissus *to lose*
quōs *whom*
longinquus -a -um *distant*

Nōndum inter nōs **contendēmus.** Nōndum contrā bestiās in arēnā **contendēmus.** Nōn prō dominīs

nōndum *no longer*
  inter nōs *with each other*

nostrīs sed prō lībertāte nostrā **contendēmus.** Contrā legiōnēs Rōmānās bellum **gerēmus.** Sī vōs fortiter **contendētis, vincētis.** Numquam mīlitēs Rōmānī nōs vīvōs **capient.** Ad montem Vesuvium **fugiēmus.** Servī undique ad nōs **fugient** et ūnā cum nōbīs contrā Rōmānōs **contendent.** Victōria nōbīs **erit!** Superābimus!"

Ūnus ē gladiātōribus clāmāvit: "Sī tū, Spartace, nōs **dūcēs** et **dēfendēs,** certē **vincēmus.** Nullus Rōmānus nōs **vincet.**

Spartacus respondit: "Crēdite mihi, ego vōs **dūcam** et **dēfendam.** Nōbīs **erit** victōria, nōbīs **erit** lībertās.

Spartacus et gladiātōrēs duōs annōs contrā Rōmānōs fortiter pugnāvērunt sed dēnique Rōmānī Spartacum necāvērunt.

contendō *-ĕre -dī -tum to fight*
bellum gerĕre *to fight a war*
vincō *-ĕre* **vīcī victus** *to win*
vīvus *-a -um alive*
  capiō *-ĕre* **cēpī captus** *to take, capture*
  fugiō **fugĕre fūgī** *to flee*
undique *from everywhere*
  ūnā cum *(+ abl) together with*
superō *-āre to overcome*
nullus *-a -um no*

necō *-āre to kill*

4 If you look over the story you have just read very carefully and pay particular attention to the words in bold type, you will find the personal endings of the future tense for all persons singular and plural. Can you now write those personal endings?

SINGULAR   PLURAL

_____   _____

_____   _____

_____   _____

Let's compare the forms of the future tense with the forms of the present tense of **dūcĕre:**

	PRESENT	FUTURE
eġo	dūc*ō*	dūc*am*
tū	dūc*is*	dūc*ēs*
is, ea, id	dūc*it*	dūc*et*
nōs	dūc*imus*	dūc*ēmus*
vōs	dūc*itis*	dūc*ētis*
eī, eae, ea	dūc*unt*	dūc*ent*

You can see for yourself how easy it is to confuse the present tense with the future tense. What is the typical vowel in the personal endings of the present tense? _____ What is the typical vowel in the personal endings of the future

tense? _____ In which two forms is there a shift of accent in the future tense?

_____

Now you can easily form the future of **-īre** verbs, like **audīre,** and of **-iō** verbs, like **accipĕre.** Notice that the **i** belongs to the stem:

	audiō	**accipiō**
ego	audi _____	accipi _____
tū	audi_____	accipi _____
is, ea, id	audi_____	accipi _____
nōs	audi _____	accipi _____
vōs	audi _____	accipi _____
eī, eae, ea	audi _____	accipi _____

_ ACTIVITĀTĒS _____

B. How good are you at predictions? Can you predict the future forms of verbs? Underline each verb in the following list that will form the future with **-ābō:**

1. praedīcĕre
2. pugnāre
3. habēre

4. superāre
5. exercēre
6. convocāre

C. This time it'll be a little tougher to decide which verbs will form the future with **-ēbō,** since their infinitives end in **-ēre:**

1. placēre
2. merēre
3. dīcĕre
4. tenēre

5. timēre
6. crēdĕre
7. legĕre
8. movēre

D. You'll need all the help you can get from augury to predict correctly this time, because all the following verbs have exactly the same infinitive but some belong to the **-ĕre** family of verbs and form the first person future with the ending **-am,** like **defend***am;* others form the future with the ending **-iam,** like **fug***iam* (*I will flee*). The trick is to remember whether the first person singular of the present tense ends in **-ō,** like **defendō,** or in **-iō,** like **perficiō.** Underline the verbs that will form the future with **-iam:**

1. accipĕre
2. dūcĕre
3. currĕre

4. capĕre
5. afficĕre
6. dēfendĕre

 Before going on to exercises with the future tense, let us first see how the Romans used the ABLATIVE OF MEANS OR INSTRUMENT:

Gladiātor *gladiō* **contendet.**   *The gladiator will fight WITH A SWORD.*

Gladiātor *cum Rōmānīs* **contendet.**   *The gladiator will fight WITH (against) THE ROMANS.*

In the first example, **gladiō** is the means or instrument; therefore, no preposition is used. The form of **gladiō** is called the ablative of means or the instrumental ablative. In the second example, **Rōmānīs** are persons and so the preposition **cum** is used. Let's test the difference in some sentences.

___ ACTIVITĀTĒS _____

E. Read over the following sentences and decide whether the preposition **cum** is needed with the noun in the ablative or not. Underline the correct expression. Notice that all of the verbs are in the future tense:

1. Astrologus futūra (stellīs/cum stellīs) praedīcet.
2. Gladiātor crūra sua (cum ocreīs/ocreīs) prōteget.
3. Bestiāriī (bestiīs/cum bestiīs) contendent.
4. Mīlitēs patriam suam (vītīs suīs/cum vītīs suīs) dēfendent.
5. Rētiārius (cum tridente/tridente) crās pugnābit.
6. Bestiārius panthērās (sīcā/cum sīcā) occīdet.

F. Read over the following sentences carefully. Then put the verb into the future tense. The nouns in the ablative of means or instrumental ablative are in bold type to draw your attention to them:

1. Ego et Syrus **gladiīs** contendimus. _____

2. Quōmodo sine **scūtō** contendis? _____

3. Gladiātōrēs glōriae causā contendunt. _____

4. Ego aut **scūtō** aut **parmā** contendō. _____

5. Quis palmam (*palm*) victōriae accipit? _____

6. Gladiātōrēs nunc galeās induunt. _____

7. Bestiārius tigrēs et ursōs **hastā** occīdit. _____

8. Cūr tū et frāter tuus **cum aliēnō** contenditis? _____

G. For each of the following sentences, two verbs are given. But be careful! Only one verb fits the sense. Put that correct verb into the future tense to complete the sentence:

1. (accipĕre/fugĕre) Rētiārius palmam victōriae _____ .

2. (prōtegĕre/occīdĕre) Galea caput gladiātōris _____ .

3. (contendĕre/capĕre) Nōs mox in arēnā _____ .

4. (accipĕre/dēfendĕre) Mīlitēs urbem fortiter _____ .

5. (prōtegĕre/contendĕre) Cūr tū sine parmā _____ .

6. (fugĕre/capĕre) Servus ā lūdō gladiātōriō _____ .

H. Be on your toes for this next activity. The verbs are from all conjugations. Change them to the future tense. Be sure to use the correct future ending:

1. Gladiātōrēs lanistās semper timent. _____

2. Post proelium rētiāriī ocreās exuunt. _____

3. Ego et avus meus stadium intrāmus. _____

4. Lanista gladiātōrem ferulā verberat. _____

5. Multī spectātōrēs in stadium veniunt. _____

6. Quid in lūdō gladiātōriō invenīs? _____

7. Potestne Thrax rētiārium vincĕre? _____

8. Caesar palmam victōrī dat. _____

9. Quot gladiātōrēs in arēnā pugnant? _____

10. Nōs omnēs ob glōriam contendimus. _____

I. A **lanista** is asking a young trainee some questions. He is too nervous to answer. Can you answer for him in complete sentences?

1. Gestābisne scūtum an parmam?

   _____

2. Contendēsne cum Thrāce an cum rētiāriō?

   _____

3. Nōnne galeam gestābis?

   _____

4. Pugnābisne sīcā an gladiō?

   _____

5. Num bestiae tē terrēbunt?

   _____

6. Contendēsne prō pecūniā an lībertāte?

   _____

7. Necābisne adversārium tuum sī vincēs?

   _____

8. Accipiēsne palmam victōriae sī vincēs?

   _____

———————— QUAESTIŌNĒS PERSŌNĀLĒS ————————

1. Praefersne pugnam inter gladiātōrēs an inter bestiās et bestiāriōs?

   _____

2. Praefersne animālia prōtegĕre an occīdĕre?

   _____

3. Praefersne vidēre bestiās in amphitheātrō an in vīvāriō *(zoo)*?

   _____

4. Considerāsne pugnās gladiātōriās esse bonās an malās?

   _____

5. Quot animālia domestica habēs domī tuae?

   _____

DIALOGUS

Listen to this conversation between Davus, a young trainee, and Thrax, a big, seasoned gladiator:

Vocābula

mī amīce *my friend*	**vīsne?** *do you want?*
vincō -ĕre vīcī victus *to defeat*	**taberna vīnāria -ae** f *wine shop*
quam *how*	**serus -a -um** *late*
audeō -ēre *to dare*	**uxor -ōris** f *wife*
abhinc *ago*	**irātus -a -um** *angry*

COLLOQUIUM

Complete the dialog on the model of the conversation, but substitute your own words wherever you can:

—————————— COMPOSITIŌ ——————————

Your friend from abroad has come to visit you in Rome and to see his/her first gladiatorial show in the amphitheater. Tell your friend a few things about the gladiators and the weapons with which they will fight.

_____

_____

_____

_____

_____

(THE LATIN CONNECTION)

You have come across the word **occīdĕre** (_to kill_) several times. It is a combination of the prefix **-ob** and **caedĕre.** When a prefix is added to **caedere,** it becomes **-cīdere.** The **b** of the prefix **ob-** changes to the first letter of **-cīdere,** and so we get **occīdĕre.** From this verb, we get the noun **cīdium,** which means _killing_. There are many combinations. For instance, **homicīdium,** meaning "the killing of a human being," gives us our word _homicide_. Give the meaning of the following Latin words and the English words derived from them:

EXAMPLE:	MEANING	DERIVATIVE
homicīdium	_killing of a man_	_homicide_
1. frātrīcidium	_____	_____
2. fungicīdium	_____	_____
3. genocīdium	_____	_____
4. germicīdium	_____	_____
5. herbicīdium	_____	_____
6. infanticīdium	_____	_____
7. insecticīdium	_____	_____
8. mātricīdium	_____	_____
9. patricīdium	_____	_____
10. pesticīdium	_____	_____

V Animālia

Comparative Degree

1 Modicum cultūrae

Most of the animals familiar to us were known to the Romans. As the Roman Empire spread, the Romans imported exotic animals from all over the world. As we learned in Lesson IV, great numbers of them were slaughtered in the amphitheater for the entertainment of the people. The Romans called these performances "hunts" (**vēnātiōnēs**), but they were hardly that, since the animals did not have a fair chance in the arena. These "hunts" were popular for some 400 years.

Animals were important in religion. Augurs and soothsayers used animals to predict the future. And you may remember that certain animals were associated with the gods. For instance, the eagle (**aquila -ae** *f*) was sacred to Jupiter, and the peacock (**pāvō -ōnis** *m*) was sacred to Juno. When these animals made their appearance, the Romans believed that they brought some message from the gods. Many animals were sacrificed to the gods to gain their goodwill.

Animals were also important in war. Donkeys and mules were used as beasts of burden to haul heavy loads. Horses played an important role in the cavalry. Elephants were, so to speak, the "tanks" of ancient warfare. Hannibal used elephants to carry supplies from Spain across the Alps into Italy in the Second Punic War.

Animals were, of course, also used as pets. For instance, goats were often hitched to little chariots or wagons to pull the children around.

2 Vocābula

sciūrus -ī m

apis -is f

mūlus -ī m

mannus -ī m

pāpiliō -ōnis m

arānea -ae f

cervus -ī m

caper, caprī m

panthēra -ae f
leopardus -ī m

castor -is m

crocodīlus -ī m

formīca -ae f

serpens -entis m

— ACTIVITĀTĒS

A. Here are some cages (**cavea -ae** *f*) in a zoo (**vīvārium -ī** *n*). The names of the animals are missing. Some of them you just met; others you learned before. Write their names below the cages. If there is one animal, use the singular form; if there are two, use the plural form:

1. _____   2. _____   3. _____

4. _____   5. _____   6. _____

7. _____   8. _____   9. _____

B. Look over this list of animals and list them according to their usual habitat. As you pick each animal for a category, cross it off the list:

apis	castor	mūlus	sciūrus
aquila	cervus	panthēra	sīmia
ariēs	crocodīlus	pāpiliō	taurus
cancer	elephantus	serpens	tigris
caper	mannus		

ON THE FARM	IN THE AIR	IN THE FIELDS/ WOODS	IN THE JUNGLE
_____	_____	_____	_____
_____	_____	_____	_____
_____	_____	_____	_____
_____	_____	_____	_____
_____	_____	_____	_____

③ First you learned Latin adjectives in the simple form, called the positive degree (**clārus** *-a -um*). Then you learned the adjective in the highest degree, called the superlative degree. Do you remember the endings of the superlative degree of

clārus? _____. If you wrote **clārissimus**, give yourself a pat on the back.

Do you remember the superlative endings of an adjective that ends in **-er**, like

pulcher, pulchra, pulchrum? _____.
If you do, you have a superlative memory. And what are the superlative end-

ings of an adjective that ends in **-ilis, -ilis, -ile**, like **facilis?** _____.

Now we will see not only the positive and superlative but also the COMPAR-ATIVE DEGREE (in English, *faster, easier, more beautiful*). In Latin, the ad-verb meaning *more* is **magis.** The Latin comparative ending **-ior** sounds a little like the English comparative ending *-ier*:

(arbor) **alta**   **altior**   **altissima**

(serpens) **longus**   **longior**   **longissimus**

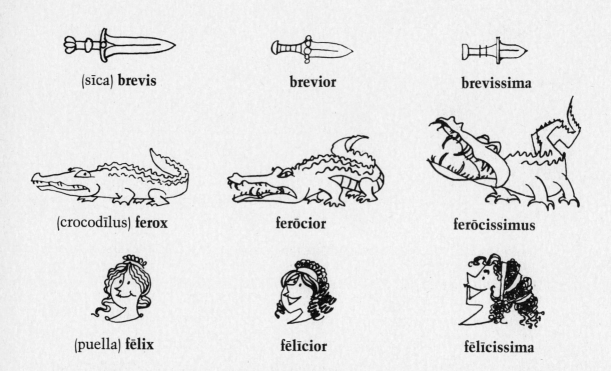

(sīca) **brevis**   **brevior**   **brevissima**

(crocodīlus) **ferox**   **ferōcior**   **ferōcissimus**

(puella) **fēlix**   **fēlīcior**   **fēlīcissima**

How observant are you? Did you notice that the comparative ending of the adjective is the same for the masculine and feminine? What is that ending?

_____. The neuter ending of the comparative is different, however, as we will see later on. Right now, just look at the last two examples, **ferox** and **fēlix.** They are single-ending adjectives of the third declension. The full stem of such adjectives is to be seen in the genitive case: **ferox, ferōcis; fēlix, fēlīcis.**

What is the full stem of **ferox?** _____ What is the full stem of **fēlix?**

_____. Notice that the full stem is used in the comparative and superlative degrees.

__ ACTIVITĀTĒS _____

C. Try a few comparisons of your own. Write the sentences below the pictures, noting the gender of each noun:

EXAMPLE:

Hīc serpens est longus.   Ille serpens est longior.   Iste serpens est longissimus.

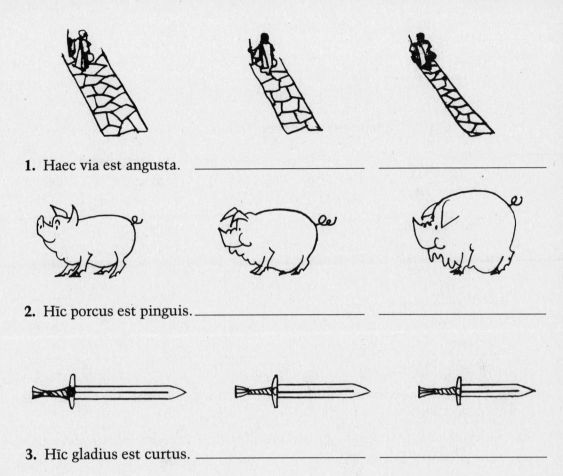

1. Haec via est angusta. _____ _____

2. Hīc porcus est pinguis. _____ _____

3. Hīc gladius est curtus. _____ _____

D. Give the masculine/feminine comparative form and the superlative form of the following adjectives:

POSITIVE	COMPARATIVE	SUPERLATIVE
1. **tardus** *-a -um* (*slow*)	_____	_____
2. **audax, audācis** (*bold*)	_____	_____
3. **ēlegans** *-antis* (*elegant*)	_____	_____
4. **similis** *-is -e* (*similar*)	_____	_____
5. **vēlox** *-ōcis* (*fast*)	_____	_____
6. **facilis** *-is -e* (*easy*)	_____	_____
7. **mītis** *-is -e* (*tame, mild*)	_____	_____

4 Let's consider the mystery of the disappearing **e** in some adjectives. How does it affect the comparative degree? Look over the following adjectives:

> **miser misera miserum** (*poor, miserable*)
> **pulcher pulchra pulchrum** (*beautiful*)
> **tener teneris tenere** (*tender, soft*)
> **ācer ācris ācre** (*sharp, keen*)

List the adjectives that drop the **e** in the feminine and neuter form:

_____ _____. The same adjectives drop the **e** in the comparative form. What is the comparative form of **miser?**

_____ ; of **pulcher?** _____ ; of **tener?** _____ ;

of **ācer?** _____

— ACTIVITĀS —

E. Complete the sentences by identifying the pictures and providing the proper form of the adjective in the comparative degree:

EXAMPLE:

Apis est pulchra.   Pāpiliō est pulchrior.

1. _____ est dīligens. _____ est _____.

2. _____ est ācer. _____ est _____.

3. _____ est ferox. _____ est _____.

4. _____ est teneris. _____ est _____.

5. _____ est vēlox. _____ est _____.

6. _____ est obstinātus. _____ est _____.

7. _____ est fortis. _____ est _____.

8. _____ est timida. _____ est _____.

So far we have seen the comparative adjective only in the masculine/feminine forms. The neuter form ends in **-ius.** That neuter form is also the form of the comparative adverb. The sentence sense will tell you whether, for example, **velōcius** is the neuter comparative adjective or the comparative adverb. The following sentences demonstrate this difference:

> **Aquila est animal *velōcius* quam pāpiliō.**
>
> *An eagle is a faster animal than a butterfly.*

> **Aquila volat *velōcius* quam pāpiliō.**
>
> *An eagle flies faster than a butterfly.*

In the first sentence, **velōcius** is an adjective modifying the noun **animal.** In the second sentence, **velōcius** is an adverb modifying the verb **volat.**

> PITFALL: Don't confuse an adjective in the positive degree like **sērius** (*serious*) or **medius** (*central*) with a comparative neuter adjective like **velōcius** (*faster*).

___ ACTIVITĀS _____

F. In the following sentences, pay particular attention to the gender of the noun that the comparative adjective modifies. Then write the comparative adjective in the space provided:

1. Domus est aedificium altum. Templum est aedificium _____.

2. Parma est gravis. Scūtum est _____.

3. Hasta est ācris. Gladius est _____.

4. Arānea est insectum dīligens. Apis est animal _____.

5. Rētiārius est fortis. Bestiārius est _____.

6. Mannus est timidus. Cervus est _____.

7. Medicīna est amāra. Acētum est _____.

8. Castor est bellus. Sciūrus est _____.

9. Leopardus est ferox. Crocodīlus est _____.

10. Astrologus est astūtus. Augur est _____.

So far we have been dealing with comparative adjectives only in the nominative case. Of course, they are declined just like any adjective of the third declension. To refresh your memory, the declension of **gravis** (*heavy*) is given in full in the table below and even some of the comparative forms. Complete the table. But be careful. Remember that a neuter adjective, just like a neuter noun, has the same form in the accusative as in the nominative case:

	POSITIVE		COMPARATIVE	
	MASC./FEM.	NEUTER	MASC./FEM.	NEUTER
			SINGULAR	
NOM.	gravis	grave	gravior	gravius
GEN.	gravis	gravis	graviōris	graviōris
ACC.	gravem	grave	_____	_____
DAT.	gravī	gravī	_____	_____
ABL.	gravī	gravī	_____	_____
			PLURAL	
NOM.	gravēs	gravia	_____	graviōra
GEN.	gravium	gravium	_____	_____
ACC.	gravēs	gravia	_____	_____
DAT.	gravibus	gravibus	_____	_____
ABL.	gravibus	gravibus	_____	_____

__ ACTIVITĀS _____

G. Each of the following sentences has an adjective in the positive degree. Write the corresponding comparative degree in the space provided:

1. Gladiātor tunicam longam gestāvit. _____

2. Lanista cum illīs servīs miserīs vēnit. _____

3. Castor caudam curtam habēbat. _____

4. Numquam crocodīlōs ferōcēs vīdī. _____

5. Astrologus hōroscopium fēlix mihi praedixit. _____

6. Ego in urbe pulchrā diū habitāvī. _____

7. Puella illum mannum mītem amat. _____

8. Sciūrī in arbore altā sedēbant. _____

9. Ego leōnēs ferōcēs in vīvāriō vīdī. _____

10. Aliēnus ē terrā longinquā venit. _____

---

7 In English, we generally compare two or more things, using the adverb *than*. In Latin, the word is **quam**:

Crocodīlus est perīculōsior *quam* serpens.　　　*A crocodile is more dangerous than a snake.*

But the Romans often skipped **quam** and put the noun in the ablative case after the comparative:

Crocodīlus est perīculōsior *serpente*.　　　*A crocodile is more dangerous than a snake.*

We can also compare two things and state that they are equal:

Leō est *tam* ferox *quam* panthēra.　　　*A lion is as ferocious as a panther.*

___ ACTIVITĀS _____

H. Rewrite the following sentences using **quam** and the nominative in place of the ablative:

1. Porcus est pinguior ove.

_____

2. Cervus est mītior leōne.

_____

3. Leopardī sunt vēlōciōrēs elephantīs.

_____

4. Mūlī sunt tardiōrēs equīs.

_____

5. Formīcae sunt industriōrēs apibus.

___

8 There are certain adjectives in English that have irregular forms in the comparative and superlative degrees: *good, better, best; bad, worse, worst*. There are also Latin adjectives (and adverbs) that have irregular comparatives and superlatives. Here are some of the most important ones:

	M/F	NEUTER	
bonus *-a -um* *good*	**melior** *better*	**melius**	**optimus** *-a -um* *best*
malus *-a -um* *bad*	**pējor** *worse*	**pējus**	**pessimus** *-a -um* *worst*
magnus *-a -um* *big*	**mājor** *bigger*	**mājus**	**maximus** *-a -um* *biggest*
parvus *-a -um* *small*	**minor** *smaller*	**minus**	**minimus** *-a -um* *smallest*
superus *-a -um* *high, on high*	**superior** *higher*	**superius**	**suprēmus** *-a -um* **summus** *-a -um* *highest*

> PITFALL: Don't confuse **summus** (*highest*) with the verb **sumus** (*we are*).
> Note that the first has a double **m**, the second has a single **m**.

___ ACTIVITĀTĒS ___

I. Rewrite the following sentences, substituting the ablative of comparison for **quam** and the nominative:

1. Mūs est minor quam castor.

___

2. Equus est mājor quam mannus.

___

3. Hiems est pējor quam autumnus.

___

4. Aestās est melior quam hiems.

___

5. Arbor est superior quam domus.

_____

6. Elephantī sunt mājōrēs quam leopardī.

_____

7. Līlium est melius quam viola.

_____

8. Scūtum est mājus quam parma.

_____

J. Compare the animals using the clues given. First state the comparison using **quam** and the nominative; then repeat, using the ablative:

EXAMPLE: parvus

Fēlēs est minor quam porcus.
Fēlēs est minor porcō.

1. vēlox

_____

_____

2. intellegens

_____

_____

3. ferox

_____

_____

4. bonus

_____

_____

5. perīculōsus

_____

_____

⑨ Let's read a story of a girl whom a goddess changed into a spider (**arānea** *ae f*) because of her pride:

In Lȳdia erat puella, nōmine Arachnē. Vestēs pulcherrimās texēbat. In vestibus pictūrās admīrābilēs pinxit. Puellae ex omnibus partibus Lȳdiae vēnērunt et opus admīrābile spectāvērunt. Omnēs puellae invidēbant Arachnae. "Minerva certē tē hanc artem docuit," dīcēbant puellae. Arachnē autem magnā cum īrā respondit: "Nūgās! Minerva nōn est, nōn erat et nōn erit mea magistra. Ego eam ad certāmen prōvocābō! Facile eam vincam, quamquam dea est!"

Lȳdia *-ae f* ancient kingdom (now a part of Turkey)
texō *-ĕre -uī -tum* to weave
  admīrābilis *-is -e* wonderful
pingō *-ĕre pinxī pictus* to embroider
opus *-ĕris n* work
certē *surely*
  ars artis *f* skill
īra *-ae f* anger
  nūgae *-ārum fpl* nonsense
certāmen *-ĭnis n* contest
prōvocō *-āre* to challenge
  quamquam *although*

Minerva verba superba audīvit et dixit: "Arachnē est puella superba et audax. Ad ejus casam ībō et eam monēbō." Jam stetit Minerva ante casae jānuam, nōn ut dea sed ut anus. "O, Arachnē," ait Minerva, "certā cum aliīs puellīs sed nōlī prōvocāre deās! Minerva erit īrāta."

superbus -a -um *proud*

moneō -ēre -uī -itus *to warn*
ut *as*
    anus -ūs *f old lady*
īrātus -a -um *angry*

"Misera anus," respondit Arachnē, "nūgās dīcis. Deās nōn timeō. Nulla puella et nulla dea texĕre et pingĕre potest melius quam ego. Sī dea ipsa veniet, eam ad certāmen prōvocābō."

ipsa *herself*

Tum Minerva formam anūs exuit et suam formam vēram induit. Omnēs puellae deam adōrāvērunt. Arachnē sōla nōn erat territa, et iterum deam ad certāmen prōvocāvit. Sine morā Minerva et Arachnē certāmen incipiunt. Minerva in purpureō veste beneficia deōrum deārumque ergā hominēs pingit. Contrā, Arachnē maleficia Jovis pingit. Nē Minerva quidem pulchrum opus carpĕre potuit. Minerva autem magnā cum īrā dixit: "Tū certē splendidē texĕre et pingĕre potes. Sed Jovem et omnēs deōs arrogantiā tuā offendistī. Itaque tē in arāneam mūtābō. Nōn jam pulchrās vestēs texēs; ex hōc tēlas texēs." Subitō Arachnē minor atque minor fīēbat. Prō crūribus et manibus, nunc octō crūra habēbat. Arachnē nunc arānea fīēbat.

adōrō -āre *to adore, worship*
solus -a -um *alone*
    territus -a -um *scared*
    iterum *again*
mora -ae *f delay*
incipiō -ĕre incēpī inceptus
    to begin
    purpureus -a -um *crimson*
beneficium ī *n kindness,*
    good deed
contrā *on the other hand*
    maleficium -ī *n evil deed*
nē . . . quidem *not even*
    carpō -ĕre -sī -tus *to find*
    fault with
offendō -ĕre -ī offēnsus *to*
    offend
nōn jam *no longer*
    tēla -ae *f web*
    ex hoc *from now on*
    subitō *suddenly*
fīēbat *(she) became*
    prō *(+ abl) instead of*

___ ACTIVITĀS _____

K. Respondē ad quaestiōnēs:

1. Ubi habitābat Arachnē?

_____

2. Quid Arachnē texēbat?

_____

3. Quid in vestibus pinxit?

_____

4. Quis Arachnae invidēbat?

_____

5. Quem Arachnē ad certāmen prōvocāvit?

_____

6. Quam formam Minerva assumpsit?

_____

7. Ubi Minerva vēram formam iterum induit, quid aliae puellae fēcērunt?

_____

8. Quis sōla nōn erat territa?

_____

9. Quid Minerva in veste pinxit?

_____

10. Quid pinxit Arachnē in veste?

_____

_____ COMPOSITIŌ _____

You are a caretaker in a children's day-care center that has all kinds of stuffed animals with which the children play. List some of the questions that the children ask about the animals. For example, they want to know: "Is a fox faster than a rabbit?" "Can a peacock fly?" "Is a bear bigger than a pig?"

1. _____

2. _____

3. _____

4. _____

5. _____

DIALOGUS

Vocābula

quaesō *please*	**orbis** (*-is* m) **terrārum** *world*
quod *which?*	**nimium** *too*
nesciō *I don't know*	**interrogātum -ī** n *question*
incertus -a -um *unsure*	**pōnō -ĕre posuī positus** *to put, ask*

RĒS PERSŌNĀLĒS

Supply the Latin names of the animals that apply in your case. Notice that the first four answers must be in the accusative case:

1. Ego amō mannōs magis quam _____.

2. Timeō arāneās magis quam _____.

3. Amō sciūrōs magis quam _____.

4. Amō columbās magis quam _____.

5. Pāpiliōnēs mihi placent magis quam _____.

Think of all the students that you know. Compare sets of two, using one of the adjectives in the list below or any other taken from the general vocabulary at the end of the book. Of course, you can simply use their first names in English:

> EXAMPLES: līberālis   Thomas est tam līberālis quam Jennifer.
> *Thomas is as generous as Jennifer.*
>
> Thomas est līberālior quam Jennifer.
> *Thomas is more generous than Jennifer.*

altus (*tall*)   crūdus (*crude*)   sērius (*serious*)
amābilis (*lovable*)   curtus (*short*)   sincērus (*sincere*)
bellus (*cute*)   fēlix (*lucky, happy*)   studiōsus (*studious*)
benignus (*kind*)   fidēlis (*loyal*)   superbus (*proud*)
cārus (*dear*)   honestus (*honest*)   timidus (*shy*)
clēmens (*gentle*)   insānus (*crazy*)   vēlox (*fast*)

1. _____

2. _____

3. _____

4. _____

5. _____

COLLOQUIUM

Your little brother is very curious. Supply your own answers to his questions:

Vocābula

mel, mellis *n honey*
colligō -*ĕre* collēgī collectus *to gather*
nux, nucis *f* nut
macula -*ae f spot*

niger nigra nigrum *black*
pellis -*is f hide, skin*
tantus -*a* -*um so much*
sciō scīre scīvī scītus *to know*

THE LATIN CONNECTION

Answer the questions and then put in parentheses the Latin word from which the italicized English word is derived:

EXAMPLE: What is a *maladjusted* child?
A badly adjusted child. (**malus -a -um**)

1. What is a *serpentine* road?

_____

2. What is the *velocity* of a bullet?

_____

3. What kind of person is an *optimist*?

_____

4. What kind of person is a *pessimist*?

_____

5. What is a *minor* mistake?

_____

6. What is a *major* blunder?

_____

7. What is a *supreme* sacrifice?

_____

8. What is the *summit* of a mountain?

_____

9. When a person obeys his *superior*, whom is he obeying?

_____

10. What are *textiles*?

_____

11. What kind of person is a *malefactor*?

_____

12. What are royal *vestments*?

_____

13. What kinds of insects are *arachnids*?

_____

14. What kinds of winged animals have an *apiary* as their home?

_____

15. What quality does a girl of *pulchritude* possess?

_____

16. What do you do when you *abbreviate* a word?

_____

17. *Gladioli* are common flowers. What shape do their leaves have?

_____

18. When a situation *ameliorates*, in what way is it changing?

_____

Recōgnitiō I
(Lectiōnēs I–V)

Lectiō I

a. Demonstrative adjective/pronoun meaning *this* (*one*), *these*:

SINGULAR

NOMINATIVE	hīc	haec	hōc
GENITIVE	hūjus	hūjus	hūjus
ACCUSATIVE	hunc	hanc	hōc
DATIVE	huic	huic	huic
ABLATIVE	hōc	hāc	hōc

PLURAL

NOMINATIVE	hī	hae	haec
GENITIVE	hōrum	hārum	hōrum
ACCUSATIVE	hōs	hās	haec
DATIVE	hīs	hīs	hīs
ABLATIVE	hīs	hīs	hīs

b. Demonstrative adjective/pronoun meaning *that* (*one*), *those*:

SINGULAR

NOMINATIVE	ille	illa	illud
GENITIVE	illīus	illīus	illīus
ACCUSATIVE	illum	illam	illud
DATIVE	illī	illī	illī
ABLATIVE	illō	illā	illō

PLURAL

NOMINATIVE	illī	illae	illa
GENITIVE	illōrum	illārum	illōrum
ACCUSATIVE	illōs	illās	illa
DATIVE	illīs	illīs	illīs
ABLATIVE	illīs	illīs	illīs

c. The demonstrative **iste, ista, istud,** meaning *that* (*one*) has the same endings as **ille, illa, illud.** It is sometimes used with a feeling of contempt.

Lectiō II

a. The conjugation of **volō** (*I want, wish*) and **nōlō** (*I do not want, I do not wish*)

ego	**volō**	**nōlō**
tū	**vīs**	**nōn vīs**
is/ea/id	**vult**	**nōn vult**
nōs	**volumus**	**nōlumus**
vōs	**vultis**	**nōn vultis**
eī/eae/ea	**volunt**	**nōlunt**

b. The principal parts of these two verbs are:

volō	**velle**	**voluī**
nōlō	**nōlle**	**nōluī**

c. The reflexive verb uses the regular simple pronoun in the first and second persons singular and plural and **sē** in the third person, singular and plural:

mē lavō	*I wash/am washing (myself)*
tē lavās	*you wash/are washing (yourself)*
sē lavat	*he/she washes/is washing (himself/herself)*
nōs lavāmus	*we wash/are washing (ourselves)*
vōs lavātis	*you wash/are washing (yourselves)*
sē lavant	*they wash/are washing (themselves)*

Lectiō III

a. To form the future tense of the first two families of verbs (**-āre** and **-ēre**), add the future personal endings to the stem:

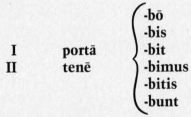

I	**portā**
II	**tenē**

- **-bō**
- **-bis**
- **-bit**
- **-bimus**
- **-bitis**
- **-bunt**

The formation of the future tense of the remaining verb families follows a different pattern.

b. The future endings of the verb **īre** (*to go*) are regular; that is, the endings are the same as for verbs like **portāre** and **tenēre**. The entire stem is **ī-**: **ībō** (*I will go*), **ībis** (*you will go*), and so on.

c. The future tense of **sum** consists of the stem **er-** plus the personal endings:

ego	**erō**	*I will be*
tū	**eris**	*you will be*
is/ea/id	**erit**	*he/she/it will be*
nōs	**erimus**	*we will be*
vōs	**eritis**	*you will be*
eī/eae/ea	**erunt**	*they will be*

Lectiō IV

a. To form the future of verbs of the **-ĕre** family, take the present stem and add the personal endings, which are different from the personal endings of the first two verb families:

ego	**dūc*am***	*I will lead*
tū	**dūc*ēs***	*you will lead*
is/ea/id	**dūc*et***	*he/she/it will lead*
nōs	**dūc*ēmus***	*we will lead*
vōs	**dūc*ētis***	*you will lead*
eī/eae/ea	**dūc*ent***	*they will lead*

b. To form the future of the **-īre** family of verbs like **audīre** and of the **-iō** family of verbs like **accipĕre,** remember that the **i** belongs to the stem. The future of **audiō** is **audi*am*** (*I will hear*), **audi*ēs*** (*you will hear*), and so on. The future of **accipiō** is **accipi*am*** (*I will receive*), **accipi*ēs*** (*you will receive*), and so on.

c. The ablative of means (also called the instrumental ablative) does not take a preposition in Latin. It is equivalent to the English preposition *with* or *by*.

Rōmulus Remum *gladiō* necāvit.   *Romulus killed Remus with a sword.*

Lectiō V

a. To form the comparative degree of adjectives, add **-ior** to the stem for the masculine and feminine genders and **-ius** for the neuter gender. Remember that the full stem of single-ending adjectives of the third declension (**ferox, fēlix**) is in the genitive case (**ferōcis, fēlīcis**), where the stems are **ferōc-** and **fēlīc-**. The complete declension of the comparative degree of an adjective like **fēlix** follows:

	MASC./FEM.	NEUTER
	SINGULAR	
NOMINATIVE	**fēlīcior**	**fēlīcius**
GENITIVE	**fēlīciōris**	**fēlīciōris**
ACCUSATIVE	**fēlīciōrem**	**fēlīcius**
DATIVE	**fēlīciōrī**	**fēlīciōrī**
ABLATIVE	**fēlīciōre**	**fēlīciōre**
	PLURAL	
NOMINATIVE	**fēlīciōrēs**	**fēlīciōra**
GENITIVE	**fēlīciōrum**	**fēlīciōrum**
ACCUSATIVE	**fēlīciōrēs**	**fēlīciōra**
DATIVE	**fēlīciōribus**	**fēlīciōribus**
ABLATIVE	**fēlīciōribus**	**fēlīciōribus**

b. Adjectives that drop the **e** in the feminine and neuter of the positive degree (**pulcher, pulchra, pulchrum**) and also drop the **e** in the comparative degree: **pulchrior, pulchrius.**

c. The comparative degree of the adverb has exactly the same form as the neuter of the adjective. Thus, **fēlīcius** is the comparative degree of the adverb meaning *more happily.*

d. The comparative degree of certain adjectives is irregular and must be memorized. Here are some of the most important ones:

	MASC./FEM.	NEUTER	
bonus *-a -um* good	**melior** *better*	**melius**	**optimus** *-a -um* *best*
malus *-a -um* bad	**pējor** *worse*	**pējus**	**pessimus** *-a -um* *worst*
magnus *-a -um* big	**mājor** *bigger*	**mājus**	**maximus** *-a -um* *biggest*
parvus *-a -um* small	**minor** *smaller*	**minus**	**minimus** *-a -um* *smallest*
superus *-a -um* high, on high	**superior** *higher*	**superius**	**suprēmus** *-a -um* **summus** *-a -um* *highest*

e. In Latin, when two items are compared, the Romans used either **quam** (*than*) or they omitted **quam** and put the following noun in the ablative case. It is called the ablative of comparison:

Crocodīlus est perīculōsior *quam* **serpens.** **Crocodīlus est perīculōsior serpente.**	*A crocodile is more dangerous than a snake.*

f. We can also compare two things and state that they are equal:

Leō est *tam* **ferox** *quam* **panthēra.**	*A lion is as ferocious as a panther.*

___ ACTIVITĀTĒS _____

A. Quis est augur? Read the following sentences and then decide which one of the five men they describe. Put an X in the correct circle:

Togam gestat.   Numquam rīdet.
Comam in capite habet.   Vēlum suprā caput gestat.
Barbam nōn habet.   Lituum manū dextrā tenet.

○   ○   ○   ○   ○

B. Here are six pictures. Complete the description below each picture by using the correct form of **velle:**

1. Infans dormīre _____ .

2. Āthlēta sē lavāre _____ .

3. Ego et Claudia pilā lūdĕre _____ .

4. Vōs in piscīnā natāre _____ .

5. Tū jaculum conjicĕre _____ .

6. Pugilēs pugnāre _____ .

C. First, write the Latin word next to the English word. Then circle the Latin word in the puzzle below. The words may read from right to left, from left to right, up or down, or diagonally:

1. statue _____

2. Olympia _____

3. boxing glove _____

4. helmet _____

5. beaver _____

6. here _____

7. goat _____

8. air _____

9. dagger _____

10. three _____

11. net _____

12. lion _____

13. snack shop _____

14. storeroom _____

15. shin guard _____

16. in front of _____

17. racing chariot _____

18. exercise place _____

19. games _____

20. earth _____

21. slave _____

22. gymnasium _____

M	U	I	S	A	N	M	Y	G	T
A	U	O	C	A	S	T	O	R	R
R	C	L	E	O	V	R	E	T	E
T	E	Y	U	S	U	V	R	E	S
S	L	M	I	C	A	P	E	R	U
E	L	P	D	S	I	C	A	R	T
A	A	I	U	O	C	R	E	A	S
L	G	A	L	E	A	E	R	S	E
A	N	T	E	S	T	A	T	U	A
P	O	P	I	N	A	V	H	I	C

D. Cruciverbilūsus:

HORIZONTĀLE

1. wrestling place
5. site of Olympic games
10. snack shop
11. that one (*masc.*)
13. summer
15. his own
16. air
18. himself
21. then, at that time

23. net
24. play, school
26. I love
27. trip
28. temple
31. this (*fem. abl.*)
33. to
34. she
35. fire
36. me

37. from, by
39. man
40. his, her, its
42. crowd
43. he is
44. I do not want
45. weight
47. ring
49. you love (*pl.*)
50. part

PERPENDICULĀRE

1. boxers
2. in front of
3. often
4. king
6. wolf
7. pony
8. spiders
9. to compete
10. foot
12. light

14. so many
17. also, even
19. why
20. to change
22. apples
24. lion
25. but
26. friend
27. so

29. person
30. ball
32. certain
38. good (*neuter*)
39. it flies
41. already
42. your
46. or
48. as, when

E. You consulted a Roman astrologer for your horoscope, but he forgot to share a few predictions with you. Use the secret numbers to break the code and find out what the stars have in store for you. The numbers tell you which letter to put above the lines:

C O D E					
A_1	B_2	C_3	D_4	E_5	F_6
G_7	H_8	I_9	J_{10}	L_{11}	M_{12}
N_{13}	O_{14}	P_{15}	Q_{16}	R_{17}	S_{18}
T_{19}	U_{20}	V_{21}	X_{22}	Y_{23}	Z_{24}

1.
— — — — — —   — — — — — —   — —
12 20 11 19 1 18   19 5 17 17 1 18   9 13

— — — — — —   — —   — —
5 20 17 14 15 1   5 19   9 13

— — — —   — — — — — — — — —.
1 18 9 1   21 9 18 9 19 1 2 9 18

2.
— — — — — — —   — — —   — —
6 1 12 9 11 9 1   19 20 1   19 5

— — — — — —   — — — — — —.
18 5 12 15 5 17   1 12 1 2 9 19

3.
— —   — — — — —   — — — — — — — —
19 20   14 12 13 9 1   15 5 17 9 3 20 11 1

— — — — —   — — — — — — — — —.
21 9 19 1 5   18 20 15 5 17 1 2 9 18

4.
— —   — — — — —   — — — — — —
19 20   21 9 19 1 1   11 14 13 7 1 12

— —   — — — — — — —
5 19   6 5 11 9 3 5 12

— — — — — — —.
8 1 2 5 2 9 18

5.
— — — — — — — — —   — — — —
1 11 9 16 20 1 13 4 14   5 17 9 18

— — — — — — —   — — — — — — — — — —
15 5 17 18 14 13 1   3 11 1 17 9 18 18 1 12 1

— — — — — —   — — — —.
3 11 1 18 18 9   19 20 1 5

F. How many of these items do you remember? Fill in the Latin words, then read down the boxed column of letters to find out where all of these items can be seen:

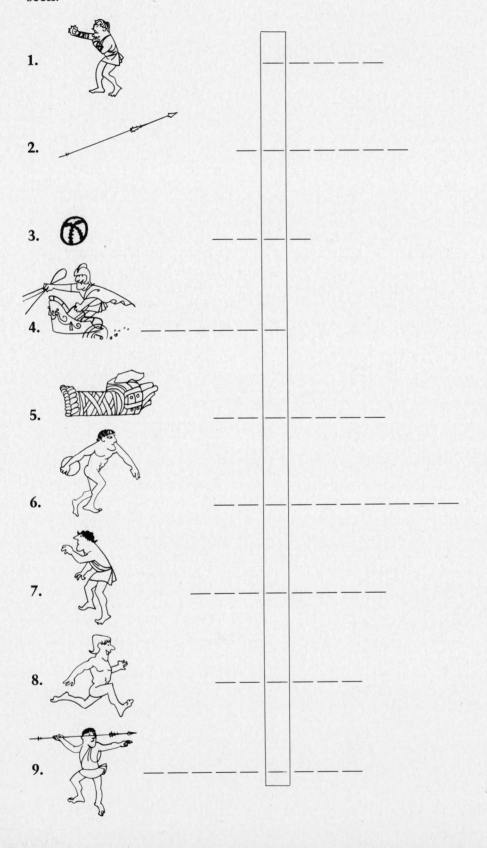

1. _ _ _ _ _ _ _

2. _ _ _ _ _ _ _

3. _ _ _ _

4. _ _ _ _ _ _

5. _ _ _ _ _ _

6. _ _ _ _ _ _ _

7. _ _ _ _ _ _

8. _ _ _ _ _

9. _ _ _ _ _

G. You go to the zoo and find that the zoo keeper got the letters of the labels of animals all mixed up. Unscramble the names to identify the animals correctly. Then unscramble the letters in the circles to find out what they all share in common:

S I P A   ⬜ ⬜ ⬜ ⬜

R E P A C   ⬜ ⬜ ⬜ ⬜ ⬜

U M S U L   ⬜ ⬜ ⬜ ⬜ ⬜

N E P T H A R A   ⬜ ⬜ ⬜ ⬜ ⬜ ⬜ ⬜

C L O R D O C I U S   ⬜ ⬜ ⬜ ⬜ ⬜ ⬜ ⬜ ⬜ ⬜ ⬜

The secret word is: ⬜ ⬜ ⬜ ⬜ ⬜ ⬜ ⬜ ⬜ .

H. Picture story. You should have no trouble reading about this trip to Olympia. Whenever you come to a picture, read it as if it were a Latin word. Try to put the proper endings to the words you supply:

Marcus est [picture] Rōmānus, tredecim annōs nātus.

Marcus et [picture] Olympiam vīsitāre volunt.

Ab [picture] ad [picture] mense Augustō nāvigābunt.

Pater [picture] et [picture] spectāre vult. In Olympiā

nempe [picture] nōn certant. Marcus autem [picture]

et 🖼 spectāre praefert, quia Marcus ipse

◎ conjicĕre amat. Marcus etiam / in Campō Martiō

interdum conjiciēbat. Sī tempus restābit, Marcus et

pater ad hippodromum ībunt, ubi 🖼 et 🖼

pulchra et 🖼 vēlōcēs vidēbunt. Postquam certāmina

vīdērunt, ad 🖼 Jovis ībunt, ubi est 🖼 aurea Jovis.

Nōn procul ab 🖼 est 🖼 nōmine Alphēus, ubi

Marcus et pater 🖼 poterunt. Post quīnque diēs ad

🖼 iterum redībunt. Quam magnificum tempus habēbunt!

Vocābula

nempe *as you know*
autem *now*
ipse *himself*
restō -āre restitī *to remain, be left over*

hippodromus -ī *m racetrack,*
hippodrome
iterum *again*

PARS
SECUNDA

VI Rōmulus et Remus

Relative Pronouns; Interrogative Adjectives

 ### Modicum cultūrae

Some of the most interesting stories that Roman children loved to hear were those about the earliest days of the city of Rome, which, according to tradition, was founded on April 21, 753 B.C. Rome is said to have been built on seven hills, but it all started on the Palatine Hill, which the Romans called a mount (**mons, montis** *m*). It would have been hard even for the Romans of the time of the emperor Augustus 700 years later to imagine what the area around the Palatine, Capitoline, and Aventine hills looked like before it became crowded with buildings and paved roads.

The little valley at the foot of the Palatine and Capitoline hills was just a meadow, which was swampy a good deal of the year. Later it was to become the marketplace where peasants set up booths (**taberna** *-ae f*) to sell their produce and wares. Later it became the Roman Forum, full of public buildings, such as temples, courthouses (**basilica** *-ae f*), and senate building (**cūria** *-ae f*).

A second valley, between the Palatine and Aventine, became the race track called the Circus Maximus, where chariot races and all kinds of events were held. The cattle market (**forum boārium**) was located in the area between the Palatine and the Capitoline, close to the Tiber river. Nearby, a simple wooden bridge spanned the Tiber river.

The Palatine Hill was the home for a group of peasants and shepherds, who lived in primitive huts. Someday it would become the most fashionable district of Rome, where the rich would build their mansions and the emperors would someday build their magnificent palaces, whose ruins are still to be seen there.

The Aventine Hill, which later became the residential quarter for the poorer people, was covered with grass and clusters of trees.

The Capitoline Hill had two peaks. On one of them, the great temple to Jupiter would be built. The other peak was the fortified citadel (**arx, arcis** *f*), where the people could take refuge in times of attack. Here would be located the **augu-rāculum,** the official spot where the augur took the auspices for the city. The depression between the two peaks was covered with a dense cluster of trees.

Beyond the Capitoline Hill, in a wide loop of the Tiber river, was a big open field called the **Campus Martius** (*Field of Mars*), which was used for military training and athletic exercise.

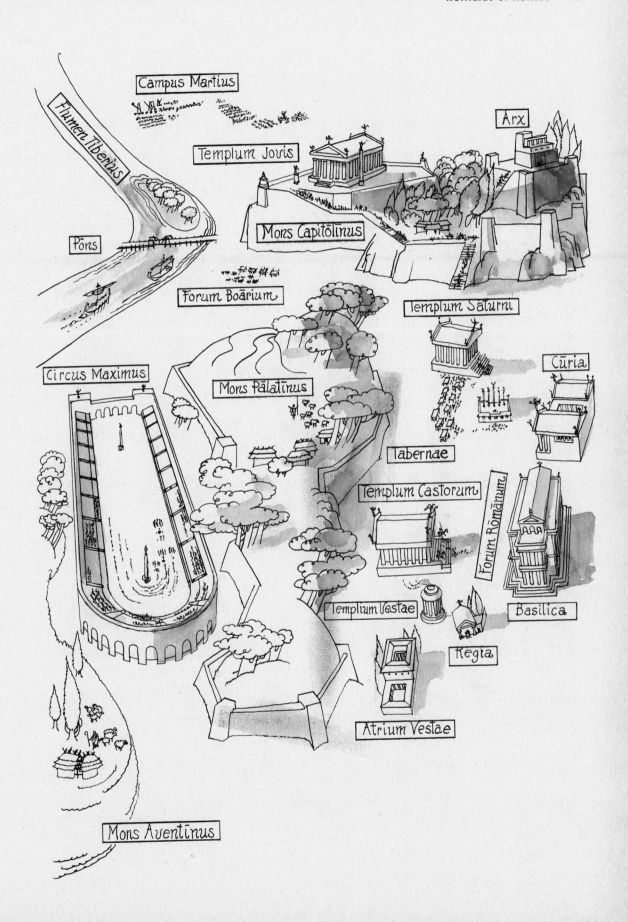

ACTIVITĀS

A. How many features of early Rome can you identify?

Before we go to the story of how Rome was founded, let's look at RELATIVE PRONOUNS. A relative pronoun introduces a relative clause. The relative pronoun relates back to a previous noun (the antecedent):

Gladiātor *quī fortiter pugnat* saepe victor est.	*The gladiator who fights bravely is often the victor.*

Quī is the relative pronoun; **gladiātor** is the antecedent. In Latin, you can tell where the relative clause begins and ends. It begins with the relative pronoun and ends with the verb. In English we sometimes skip the relative pronoun: *Jason is the player (whom/that) I admire most.* In that sentence, the relative pronoun (*whom* or *that*) can be omitted. In Latin, the relative pronoun is never skipped. Although the Romans never omitted the relative pronoun, they sometimes skipped the antecedent:

Quī multam pecūniam habet, multōs amīcōs habet.	*(A person) who has a lot of money has a lot of friends.*

In Latin, the relative pronoun may be masculine (**quī** = *who/that*), feminine (**quae** = *who/that*) or neuter (**quod** = *which/that*). Remember that in Latin "things" can be masculine, feminine, or neuter: **digitus** *m*; **coma** *f*; **bracchium** *n*. Now look at the following sentence very carefully:

Gladiātor, quī in arēnā pugnāvit, rētiārium occīdit.

What is the relative pronoun in this sentence? _____.

What is the antecedent? _____ What is the gender? _____

___ ACTIVITĀTĒS _____

B. Note carefully the gender of each of the following nouns and then write the appropriate relative pronoun in the space provided:

1. gladius	_____	**6.** pater	_____
2. lanista	_____	**7.** māter	_____
3. hasta	_____	**8.** insectum	_____
4. scūtum	_____	**9.** apis	_____
5. sīca	_____	**10.** castor	_____

C. Complete the following sentences with the appropriate relative pronoun. Then put each relative clause in brackets:

1. Bestiāriī nōn timent leōnem _____ in arēnā est.

2. Apis est insectum _____ mel colligit.

3. Castor est animal _____ prope fluvium habitat.

4. Sciūrus _____ in arbore sedet nūcem edit.

5. Pāpiliō _____ in agrō nostrō est multōs colōrēs habet.

6. Ego numquam vīdī cervum _____ tam vēlōciter currĕre potest.

7. Amīcus meus in urbe habitat _____ prope flūmen sita est.

8. Gladiātor parmam gestāvit _____ gravissima erat.

9. Mihi nōn placet senātor _____ superbus est.

10. Arānea est insectum _____ tēlās texĕre potest.

3 The plural forms of relative pronouns are **quī, quae, quae.** Notice that the first two plurals are the same as the singular. Only the neuter is different. Of course, the antecedent as well as the verb will tell you whether the pronoun is singular or plural.

___ ACTIVITĀS _____

D. Complete the sentences with the correct forms of the plural relative pronouns. Then put brackets around the relative clauses:

1. Bestiāriī _____ animālia timent in arēnā pugnāre nōn dēbent.

2. Formīcae sunt insecta _____ in cavernīs sub terrā habitant.

3. Vīdistī umquam mannōs et equōs _____ in prātō sunt?

4. Sciūrī sunt animālia _____ arborēs facile ascendĕre possunt.

5. Pāpiliōnēs _____ veterrimī sunt volāre nōn possunt.

6. Pāpiliōnēs habent ālās _____ flāvae et rubrae et caeruleae sunt.

7. Ego mūlōs habeō _____ gravia onera portāre possunt.

8. Panthērae _____ in vīvāriō habitant nōn laetae sunt.

9. Bestiāriī multa animālia occīdērunt _____ ex Africā vēnērunt.

10. Gladiātōrēs _____ ē lūdō Capuae fūgērunt contrā Rōmānōs pugnāvērunt.

4 Earlier you learned the interrogative pronouns and have often seen them in sentences. What is the interrogative pronoun meaning *who*? _____.

What is the interrogative pronoun meaning *what*? _____. You were not aware of it, but, as you just learned the relative pronouns **quī, quae, quod,** you also learned the INTERROGATIVE ADJECTIVES:

Quī vēnātor leōnem occīdit?	*Which hunter killed the lion?*
Quae soror est maxima nātū?	*Which sister is the oldest?*
Quod animal tēlās texit?	*Which animal spins cobwebs?*

The plural interrogative adjectives (**quī, quae, quae**) are used in the same way.

— ACTIVITĀS

E. Some of the following sentences call for the singular, some call for the plural interrogative adjectives. Write the correct form in the space provided:

1. _____ senātor est jūdex?

2. _____ homō amīcum nōn adjuvat?

3. _____ animal per tōtam hiemem dormit?

4. _____ animālia in aquā habitant?

5. _____ fēmina novam vestem nōn amat?

6. _____ fundus equōs et vaccās nōn habet?

7. _____ augur futūra praedīcĕre nōn potest?

8. _____ urbs prope Tiberim Flūmen jacet?

9. _____ montēs prope forum sunt?

10. _____ pistor pānem tuum facit?

5 Having had a bit of practice with the relative pronouns in the nominative case, let's see what they look like in the accusative case:

	SINGULAR	PLURAL
NOM.	**quī** (*who*), **quae** (*who*), **quod** (*which*)	**quī** (*who*), **quae** (*who*), **quae** (*which*)
ACC.	**quem** (*whom*), **quam** (*whom*), **quod** (*which*)	**quōs** (*whom*), **quās** (*whom*), **quae** (*which*)

As usual, the neuter accusative form is the same as the nominative. Did you also notice that some of the accusative endings are the same as the noun endings that you already know? Which three forms in the accusative case (singular or plural) have the same endings as the corresponding nouns?

_____   _____   _____

___ ACTIVITĀTĒS ___

F. Nominative or accusative? Read the sentences carefully and then underline the correct form of the relative pronoun:

1. Quis cēpit sciūrum (quī/quem) in hortō nostrō fuit?
2. Mannus (quī/quem) in prātō est vēlōciter currĕre potest.
3. Leopardus (quī/quem) vēnātōrēs in monte cēpērunt ferōcissimus est.
4. Medicus fēminam sānāvit (quae/quam) dolōrem dentis habuit.
5. Pars corporis (per quae/per quam) audīmus est auris.
6. Augur (quī/quem) senātōrēs consultāvērunt est astūtus.
7. Nōs omnēs hominem amāmus (quī/quem) benignus est.
8. Urbs (per quae/per quam) Tiberis Flūmen fluit est Rōma.
9. Via (quae/quam) per Forum Rōmānum currit est Via Sacra.
10. Vir (quī/quem) ante Jovis templum in Monte Capitōlīnō vīdī est augur.

G. Singular or plural? Complete the sentences with the correct relative pronoun in the accusative case. Then put brackets around the relative clause:

1. Astrologus _____ Augustus consultāvit ex Graeciā vēnit.

2. Stellae _____ in caelō vīdimus sunt clārae et pulchrae.

3. Gladiātōrēs _____ Spartacus in arēnā occīdit geminī erant.

4. Scūtum _____ Spartacus gestāvit oblongum erat.

5. Vīdistīne tabernās _____ Rōmānī in forō aedificāvērunt?

6. Montēs inter _____ Circus Maximus jacet sunt Palātīnus et Aventīnus.

7. Templum _____ augurēs vīsitant in arce stat.

8. Pons _____ Rōmānī fabricāvērunt trans Tiberim in Etrūriam dūcit.

9. Numqam vīdī novam basilicam _____ Rōmānī aedificāvērunt.

10. Aedificium _____ senātōrēs cōtīdīe intrant est cūria.

Let's read one of those stories about early Rome that Roman children loved to hear. As you read it, pay particular attention to the relative pronouns. Some of the relative pronouns are in the ablative case. Even though they haven't been explained as yet, see whether they cause you any real problem. If they do, you are free to complain to your teacher about them!

Rōmulus et Remus geminī erant. Eōrum māter erat Rhea Silvia, et eōrum pater erat Mars, quī deus bellī erat. Eōrum avus erat Numitor, quī rex Albae Longae erat. Ejus frāter, Amūlius, autem Numitōrem ē regnō expulit et ipse regnum occupāvit.

Alba Longa -ae *f hill town SE of Rome*
regnum -ī *n kingdom*
expellō -ĕre expulī expulsus *to expel*
ipse *himself*

Amūlius, quia fīliōs Rheae Silviae timuit, eam Virginem Vestālem fēcit; geminōs autem in arcā inclūsit et in flūmen Tiberim injēcit. Sed arca quae geminōs continēbat, ad rīpam fluitāvit. Jupiter enim, quī omnia videt, geminōs servāre voluit. Lupa, quae forte dē Monte Aventīnō dēscendit, infantēs invēnit et eōs lacte suō nūtrīvit. Lupa eōs sīcut catulōs suōs prōtēxit.

Virgō Vestālis *Vestal Virgin*
arcā -ae *f chest*
inclūdō -ĕre inclūsī inclūsus *to lock up, enclose*
injiciō -ĕre injēcī injectus *to throw into*
contineō -ēre -uī contentus *to contain*
rīpa -ae *f bank*
fluitō -āre *to float*
lupa -ae *f she-wolf*
forte *by chance*
nūtriō -īre -ī(v)ī -ītus *to nourish, to nurse*
sīcut *just as*
catulus -ī *m cub*
pastor -ōris *m shepherd*

Post paucōs diēs Faustulus, quī pastor erat et in Monte Palātīnō habitābat, ad illum locum vēnit in quō infantēs dormiēbant. Faustulus, quī vir benignus erat, infantēs ad casam suam in Montem Palātīnum tulit. Faustulus infantēs Rōmulum et Remum nōmināvit. Faustulus et uxor ejus, Laurentia, geminōs libenter ēducāvērunt. Puerī vītam fēlīcem sine cūrīs dūcēbant. Modō in Monte Aventīnō, modō in Monte Capitōlīnō lūdēbant; et modō in valle, quae inter montēs jacet, lūdēbant. Saepe lupam vīdērunt quae infantēs nūtriēbat. Lupa autem semper amīca eīs fuit.

ferō ferre tulī lātus *to bring, take*
nōminō -āre *to name*
libenter *gladly*
ēducō -āre *to raise*
cūra -ae *f care, worry*
modō ... modō *sometimes ... sometimes*
vallēs -is *f valley*
amīcus -a -um *friendly*

Post multōs annōs, geminī urbem novam condĕre volēbant in illō locō in quō Faustulus et Laurentia eōs ēducāvērunt. Sed prius necesse erat ōmen prosperum petĕre. Itaque Rōmulus in Monte Palātīnō inaugurāvit. Remus autem in Monte Aventīnō inaugurāvit. Ōmen prīmum Remō ēvēnit, nam sex vulturēs per ejus templum in caelō volāvērunt. Remus exultāvit et clāmāvit: "Ego hīc in Monte Aventīnō novam urbem condam. Et populus faciet mē prīmum rēgem."

condō -dĕre -didī -ditus *to found*
prius *adv first*
prosperus -a -um *favorable*
inaugurō -āre *to look for an omen*
ōmen -inis *n omen*
eveniō -īre ēvēnī ēventum *to occur*
nam *conj for*
exultō -āre *to jump for joy*

Tunc maximē Rōmulus, quī in Monte Palātīnō sedēbat, duodecim vulturēs in suō templō observāvit. "Ecce," inquit Rōmulus, "duplicem numerum vulturum observāvī; itaque ego urbem novam condam, et urbs nōmen meum accipiet. Ego prīmus rex urbis erō. Circum Montem Palātīnum ego dūcam mūrum, quī urbem novam prōteget.

tunc maximē just then

ecce look
  duplex, duplicis *double*

mūrum -dūcĕre *to build a wall*

Sīc contrōversia amāra inter frātrēs geminōs exārsit, deinde īra, dēnique caedēs; nam Rōmulus frātrem gladiō necāvit et urbem ā sē nōmināvit. Rōmulus multōs annōs Rōmae regnāvit et post ejus mortem in caelum ascendit et fīēbat deus. Nōmen ejus in caelō est Quirīnus.

amārus -a -um *bitter*
  exārdēscō -ĕre exārsī *to flare up*
caedēs -is *f murder*
ā sē *after himself*
rēgnō -āre (+ *dat*) *to rule over*
caelum -ī *n heaven*
  fīēbat *he became*

___ ACTIVITĀS _____

H. Answer in complete Latin sentences the following questions about the story that you have just read:

1. Quī erant parentēs geminōrum?

_____

2. Quis erat Rōmulī et Remī avus?

_____

3. Quis erat Numitōris frāter malus?

_____

4. Cūr Amūlius geminōs occīdĕre voluit?

_____

5. Quī deus geminōs servāre voluit?

_____

6. Quis geminōs lacte suō nūtrīvit?

_____

7. Quis Rōmulum et Remum ēducāvit?

_____

8. In quō monte Remus inaugurāvit?

_____

9. In quō monte Rōmulus inaugurāvit?

_____

10. Quis erat prīmus rex Rōmae?

_____

<table>
<tr><td>7</td><td>Let us now look at the ablative case of the relative pronouns. What is the ablative ending of a masculine noun of the second declension, like amīcus?</td></tr>
</table>

_____ Of a feminine noun of the first declension, like **stella?** _____ Of

a neuter noun of the second declension, like **scūtum?** _____ Those are also the endings of the ablative singular of relative pronouns. In the plural, the ablative forms of the masculine, feminine, and neuter are all the same: **quibus.** Here, then, are the forms of the relative pronouns thus far:

	MASCULINE		FEMININE		NEUTER	
			SINGULAR			
NOM.	**quī**	(*who*)	**quae**	(*who*)	**quod**	(*which*)
ACC.	**quem**	(*whom*)	**quam**	(*whom*)	**quod**	(*which*)
ABL.	**quō**	(*whom*)	**quā**	(*whom*)	**quō**	(*which*)
			PLURAL			
NOM.	**quī**	(*who*)	**quae**	(*who*)	**quae**	(*which*)
ACC.	**quōs**	(*whom*)	**quās**	(*whom*)	**quae**	(*which*)
ABL.	**quibus**	(*whom*)	**quibus**	(*whom*)	**quibus**	(*which*)

The ablative case is often, but not always, preceded by a preposition. Remember that the ablative of means does not use a preposition:

Collis *in quō* Rōmulus vulturēs observāvit erat Palātīnus.

The hill on which Romulus observed the vultures was the Palatine.

Diēs *quō* Rōmulus Rōmam condidit est festus diēs.

The day on which Romulus founded Rome is a holiday.

Tēlum *quō* Rōmulus Remum necāvit erat gladius.

The weapon with which Romulus killed Remus was a sword.

Pars corporis *quā* vidēmus est oculus.

The part of the body with which we see is the eye.

How well do you observe? Did you notice that **quō** in the second sentence used no preposition because it is the ablative of time and that **quō** in the third sentence did not have a preposition because it is the ablative of means or instru-

ment? What is the gender of **quō** in the first sentence? _____;

of **quō** in the second sentence? _____; of **quō** in the third sentence? _____; of **quā** in the fourth sentence? _____.

What is the antecedent of **quā** in the fourth sentence? _____.

___ ACTIVITĀTĒS _____

I. Complete the sentences with the correct forms of the relative pronouns in the ablative case:

1. Oppidum, in _____ Numitor regnāvit (*ruled*), erat Alba Longa.

2. Parentēs ex _____ Rōmulus et Remus nātī sunt erant Mars et Rhea Silvia.

3. Arca in _____ Amūlius geminōs inclūsit ad flūminis rīpam fluitāvit.

4. Flūmen in _____ arca fluitāvit erat Tiberis.

5. Mons in _____ Faustulus habitāvit erat Palātīnus.

6. Collis dē _____ lupa dēscendit erat Aventīnus.

7. Locus in _____ lupa geminōs nūtrīvit nōn procul ā Palātīnō aberat.

8. Casa, in _____ Faustulus et Laurentia puerōs ēducāvērunt, in Monte Palātīnō erat.

9. Vallēs in _____ geminī lūdēbant nunc est Forum Rōmānum.

10. Casae in _____ pastōrēs habitābant erant parvae et simplicēs.

J. The antecedent to which the pronoun relates does not always come immediately before the relative pronoun. Look carefully at the following sentences to be sure that you know what the antecedent is. Draw an arrow from the relative pronoun to the antecedent and then supply the proper form of the relative pronoun:

EXAMPLE: **Partēs** corporis **quibus** vidēmus sunt oculī nostrī.
The parts of the body with which we see are our eyes.

1. Gladiātor bracchium suum mihi exhibuit in _____ vulnus grave fuit.

2. Scīsne signum zōdiacī circulī sub _____ ego sum nāta?

3. Apēs aculeum habent _____ icĕre (*to sting*) possunt.

4. Trēs puerī in Albā Longā erant cum _____ ego lūdēbam.

5. Pastōrēs arcam in flūmine vīdērunt in _____ geminī dormiēbant.

6. Romulus frātrem suum occīdit cum _____ contrōversiam habēbat.

7. Arachnē erat puella superba et arrogans cum _____ Minerva certāvit.

8. Claudia digitum manūs sinistrae mihi exhibuit in _____ ānulum aureum gestābat.

⑧ Read how Romulus doubled the population of his new city in record time:

Roma, quae iam oppidum magnum et validum erat, perpaucōs cīvēs adhūc habuit. Itaque Rōmulus fugitīvōs undique in oppidum novum invītāvit et asȳlum eīs dedit in Monte Capitōlīnō. Multī agricolae pastōrēsque ex agrīs ad novum oppidum convēnērunt. Casās in Monte Capitōlīnō aedificāvērunt. Etiam ovīlia prō ovibus suīs aedificāvērunt in valle quae inter Capitōlīnum et Palātīnum jacēbat. Rōmulus eōs omnēs fēcit cīvēs Rōmānōs.

iam *by now*
perpaucī -ae -a *very few*
   cīvis -is m *citizen*
   adhūc *till now*
undique *from all around*
ex agrīs *from the countryside*
ovīle -is n *sheepfold*

Sed nōndum uxōrēs habēbant. Ergo Rōmulus Sabīnōs quī in oppidīs vīcīniīs habitābant ad lūdōs invītāvit. "Venīte," inquit Rōmulus, "ad nostrum oppidum novum. Splendidōs lūdōs edam. Hospitālitātem Rōmānam vōbīs adhibēbō. Et adferte uxōrēs fīliāsque vestrās."

nōndum *not yet*
Sabīnī -ōrum mpl *hill tribe near Rome*
   vīcīnus -a um *neighboring*
ēdō -ēdĕre ēdidī ēditus *to provide, put on*
adhibeō -ēre -uī -itus *to show*
   adferō -ferre -tulī -lātus *to bring along*
benignē *warmly*
   excipiō -ĕre excēpī exceptus *to welcome*

Magna multitūdō Sabīnōrum ad lūdōs vēnit. Rōmānī eōs benignē excēpērunt. In valle quae inter Palātīnum et Aventīnum jacet consīdēbant, in quā Circus Maximus nunc est. Rōmānī et Sabīnī lūdōs attentē aspiciēbant cum subitō Rōmulus signum dedit. Juvenēs Rōmānī ex sēdibus exsiluērunt; virginēs Sabīnās rapuērunt; eās ad casās suās portāvērunt et eās in mātrimōnium duxērunt.

consīdō -ĕre consēdī consessum *to sit down*
aspiciō -ĕre aspexī aspectus *to watch*
   cum subitō *when suddenly*
juvenis -is m *young man*
   sēdēs -is f *seat*
   exsiliō -īre -uī *to jump up*
   virgō -inis f *girl*
rapiō -ĕre -uī -tus *to seize, kidnap*
in mātrimōnium dūcĕre *to marry*

Tristēs parentēs virginum timōre in oppida sua refūgērunt. Sed post aliquot annōs, Sabīnī Rōmānīs bellum indixērunt. Sabīnī cum Rōmānīs diū et ācriter pugnāvērunt in valle in quā nunc Forum Rōmānum est. Subitō fēminae Sabīnae inter infestās

timōre *out of fear*
refugiō -ĕre -ī *to flee back*
indīcō -ĕre indixī indictus (+ dat) to declare (war) on
diū et acriter *long and hard*
infestus -a -um *hostile*

aciēs cucurrērunt. Hinc marītōs hinc patrēs suōs ōrāvērunt: "Marītī, nōlīte necāre patrēs nostrōs!" Et "Patrēs, nōlīte pugnāre cum vestrīs generīs!"

Repentīnum silentium fuit. Deinde dūcēs utrimque prōdiērunt. Nōn modō pācem fēcērunt, sed etiam ūnam cīvitātem ex duābus creāvērunt.

aciēs -ēī *f battle line*
hinc . . . hinc *on one side . . . on the other side*
marītus -ī *m husband*
ōrō -āre *to beg*
gener -ī *m son-in-law*
repentīnus -a -um *sudden*
silentium -i *n silence*
utrimque *from both sides*
prōdeō -īre -iī *to step forward*
nōn modō . . . sed etiam *not only . . . but also*
pax pācis *f peace*
cīvitās -ātis *f state*
creō -āre *to create*

__ ACTIVITĀS __

K. Respondē ad quaestiōnēs:

1. Quid Rōmulus fugitīvīs dedit?

2. Ubi Rōmulus asȳlum dedit?

3. Quid in valle inter Capitolīnum et Palātīnum aedificāvērunt?

4. Cūr Rōmulus Sabīnōs ad lūdōs invītāvit?

5. Ubi Rōmānī et Sabīnī lūdōs aspexērunt?

6. Quis signum juvenibus Rōmānīs dedit?

7. Quis virginēs Sabīnās rapuit?

8. Quō (*where*) Rōmānī virginēs portāvērunt?

9. Quis bellum Rōmānīs indīxit?

10. Quis inter infestās aciēs cucurrit?

DIALOGUS

Here's a conversation that may have taken place between Faustulus and Laurentia when the twins were found:

Vocābula

mūnusculum -ī n *gift*
conjiciō -ĕre conjēcī conjectus *to guess*
sit *(it) is*

fīliolus -ī m *baby boy*
aliquis *somebody*
cicōnia -ae f *stork*

COLLOQUIUM

Complete the dialog on the model of the conversation. Try to make little changes of your own:

QUAESTIŌNĒS PERSŌNĀLĒS

1. In quā urbe habitās?

_____

2. Estne urbs magna an parva?

_____

3. Estne flūmen prope urbem tuam?

_____

4. Quot scholae in urbe tuā sunt?

_____

5. Quot hominēs in tuā urbe habitant?

_____

6. Praefers habitāre in urbe vetere an novā?

_____

7. Quae urbs est optima in tōtō orbe terrārum?

_____

COMPOSITIŌ

Some of the most interesting stories deal with Rome when it was just a small town of farmers and shepherds. Retell in your own words something about Romulus and Remus.

_____

_____

_____

_____

_____

THE LATIN CONNECTION

A. Which English word is derived from **hospitālitās?** _____

What is the genitive form of this feminine noun? _____

All Latin words ending in **-itās** are feminine and are abstract nouns. (Abstract nouns, like *virtue, goodness,* cannot be seen with the eyes or felt with the hands, but can be seen in the mind.) All these Latin nouns ending in **-itās** give us an English noun ending in *-ity.*

B. Give the English derivative of the following Latin nouns:

1. **ūnitās -ātis** *f* (from **ūnus**) _____

2. **sānitās -ātis** *f* (from **sānus**) _____

3. **mortālitās -ātis** *f* (from **mortālis**) _____

4. **nōbilitās -ātis** *f* (from **nōbilis**) _____

5. **sēcūritās -ātis** *f* (from **sēcūrus**) _____

C. As indicated above, each of these abstract Latin nouns in turn is derived from a Latin adjective. Can you supply the meaning of each?

1. ūnus _____   4. nōbilis _____

2. sānus _____   5. sēcūrus _____

3. mortālis _____

D. There are other words that come from **ūnus:** unanimous (being of one mind), unison (being of one sound), universal (all turned to one). Can you give the definition of the following English words?

1. unicorn _____

2. uniform _____

3. unify _____

4. union _____

5. uniparental _____

6. unique   _____

7. unit   _____

8. united   _____

E. What does ē **plūribus ūnum** mean? _____

F. Can you think of three other English words that end in *-ity* and give the Latin source?

1. _____   _____

2. _____   _____

3. _____   _____

G. What are the English derivatives of the following Latin words? Some Latin words have more than one English derivative. List as many of each as you can:

1. arca   _____

2. nūtrīre   _____

3. ēducāre   _____

4. inaugurāre _____

5. exultāre   _____

6. nōmināre   _____

VII Medicīna et valētūdō

Pluperfect Tense

1 Modicum cultūrae

It may come as a surprise to learn that there were no doctors in Rome for the first five hundred years of its existence. Those who fell ill were either cured with some herbs or died. The ancients were always experimenting with herbs for their healing value. Knowledge of this herbal medicine, mixed with a bit of witchcraft and magic, was handed down from father to son. Not only were there no doctors, there were also no public hospitals. Anyone could practice medicine. There were no medical schools and no governmental or professional organizations to regulate the sale of medicines and drugs. Quacks with a smattering of medical knowledge often found great popularity in Rome.

The Romans' knowledge of the human body was primitive by our standards. It was widely believed that the liver was the seat of love, the heart the seat of intelligence, the bile the seat of hatred, the lungs the seat of pride, the spleen the seat of laughter, and the brain the seat of anger. The Romans did not know that blood circulated through the body. That fact was not discovered until the eighteenth century.

When doctors finally arrived in Rome from Greece and the Near East, they had little prestige. Many of them were slaves or men of the lower classes. The first doctor to take up permanent residence in Rome came from Greece in 219 B.C. Many doctors quickly accumulated huge fortunes, but their wealth did not usually bring them respect and dignity, and the Romans never completely lost their prejudice against doctors. The learned Roman scholar Marcus Terentius Varro, who was in charge of the library of Emperor Augustus, ranked doctors next to dyers and blacksmiths.

Wealthy families with large numbers of slaves often had a doctor permanently in the household. Some had male and female medical slaves, as well as an infirmary. Not until the fourth century did the state provide scientific training for those who would become public doctors, whose duty was to heal all who consulted them, the poor free of charge. But doctors did not have to take examinations or get a degree. Private doctors continued to practice as they pleased.

And yet the Roman ideal was "**mens sāna in corpore sānō** (*a sound mind in a sound body*)." The Roman doctors and the Roman people felt that most ills could be overcome by proper diet and exercise. Some ills had to be treated with medicinal herbs. The Romans laid stress on good health (**valētūdō** *-inis f*). Their usual expression for good-bye was "**Valē!**," literally, "Be in good health!" The old expression "farewell" comes closer to the Latin sense than "good-bye."

Before you look at the new vocabulary in Section 2, see if you remember these body parts from your first course in Latin:

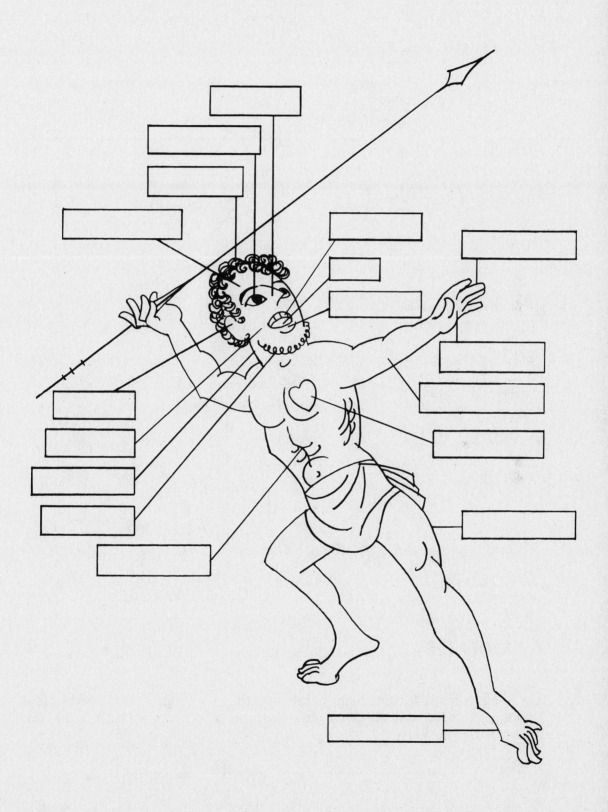

2 Vocābula

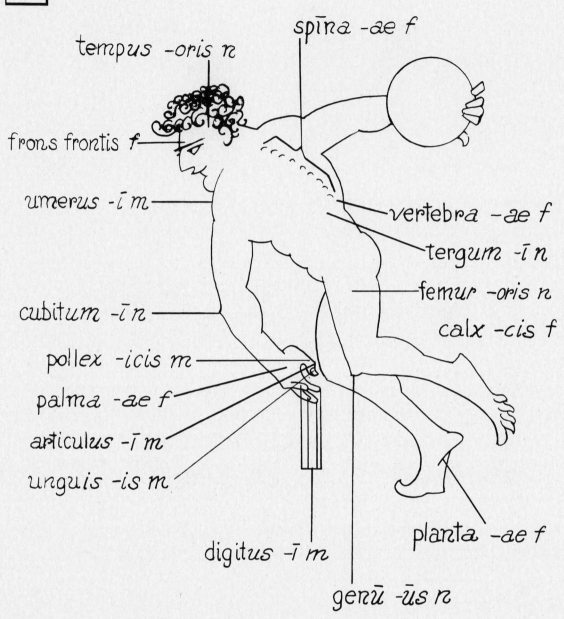

tempus -oris n

spīna -ae f

frons frontis f

umerus -ī m

vertebra -ae f

tergum -ī n

femur -oris n

calx -cis f

cubitum -ī n

pollex -icis m

palma -ae f

articulus -ī m

unguis -is m

digitus -ī m

planta -ae f

genū -ūs n

____ ACTIVITĀTĒS ____

A. The Romans found it convenient to measure things with parts of the body. Here are the parts of the body that were often used in measurements. Can you give the Latin word for each?

1. finger _____   3. cubit _____

2. hand _____   4. foot _____

B. How good are you at finding body parts? In the following sentences you'll have to know the genitive case:

> EXAMPLE: Digitus est pars **manūs.**

1. Palma est pars _____.

2. Frons est pars _____.

3. Vertebra est pars _____.

4. Femur est pars _____.

5. Pollex est pars _____.

6. Calx est pars _____.

7. Cubitum est pars _____.

8. Spīna est pars _____.

9. Genū est pars _____.

10. Unguis est pars _____.

11. Planta est pars _____.

12. Tempus est pars _____.

C. Now that you're getting good at anatomy, see whether you can complete the following sentences:

1. Spīna est in _____.

2. Digitī sunt in _____.

3. Femur est in _____.

4. Frons est in _____.

5. Pollex est in _____.

6. Labra sunt in _____.

7. Cubitum est in _____.

8. Oculī sunt in _____.

9. Calx est in _____.

10. Vertebrae sunt in _____ .

11. Palma est in _____ .

12. Tempora sunt in _____ .

13. Aurēs sunt in _____ .

14. Coma est in _____ .

15. Dentēs sunt in _____ .

D. You are a Roman doctor and you are explaining the parts of the body to your medical students. Write the names of the parts of the body in the chart:

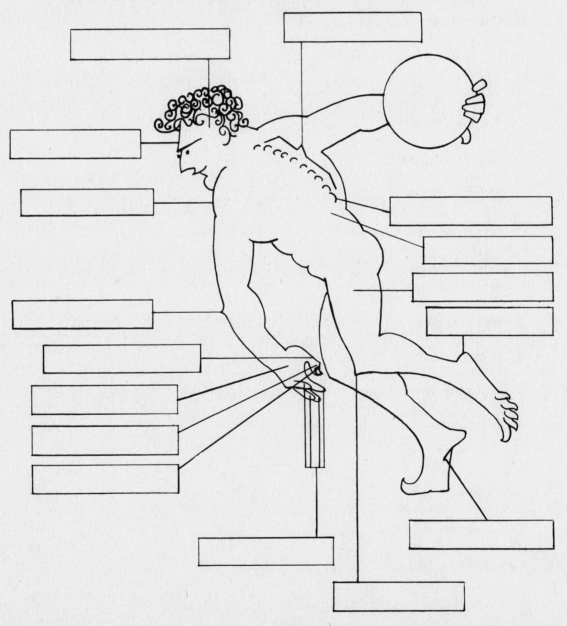

> ③ You have often watched an interview with athletes after a game on television. Let's visit the "locker room" (**cella -ae** *f*) of a Roman gladiator:

SCAENA: In cellā sub amphitheātrō. Vulnerātus gladiātor in lectō jacet post pugnam in arēnā. Nōmen gladiātōris est Thrax. Medicus Graecus intrat.

> **vulnerātus -a -um** *wounded*

MEDICUS: Quid est tibi, Thrax?

THRAX: In novissimā pugnā ego multa vulnera accēpī. Tōtum corpus meum dolet. Bracchia dolent; crūra dolent; tergum dolet. Crēde mihi, medice, fatīgātus sum.

MEDICUS: Exue tunicam tuam et exhibē mihi tua vulnera.

THRAX: Multa vulnera in corpore meō sunt. Est ūnum vulnus in fronte meā, alium in tempore dextrō, quattuor vulnera in pectore. Ecce, tōtum corpus meum est cruentum!

MEDICUS: Ita, Thrax. Et habēs alia vulnera: ūnum in femore, ūnum in umerō. Et ūnum in genū sinistrō videō.

THRAX: Nōn vulnera sōlum habeō sed etiam tumōrēs.

MEDICUS: Tumōrēs in bracchiīs et umerīs videō. Tōtum quidem bracchium sinistrum tumidum est.

THRAX: Poterisne mea vulnera sānāre? Habēsne remedia prō vulneribus et tumōribus meīs?

MEDICUS: Sānē. Vulnera et tumōrēs sānāre possum. Herbās et medicīnās et fasciās prō istīs vulneribus habeō. Vulnera in pectore tuō gravissima sunt. Sīc victō saepe contingit.

THRAX: Medice, nōn sum victus; ego victor in certāmine eram. Vulnera et tumōrēs adversāriī meī vidēre dēbēs. Iste habet multō plūra vulnera quam ego. Habet vulnera ubīque, etiam in tergō!

> **Quid est tibi?** *What's wrong with you?*
> **novissimus -a -um** *latest*
> **vulnus -eris** *n wound*
> **tōtus -a -um** *whole*
> **fatīgātus -a -um** *exhausted*
> **exhibeō -ēre -uī -itus** *to show*
>
> **pectus -oris** *n chest, breast*
> **cruentus -a -um** *bloody*
>
> **tumor -ōris** *m swelling, lump*
>
> **quidem** *in fact*
> **tumidus -a -um** *swollen, puffed up*
> **sānō -āre** *to heal*
>
> **herba -ae** *f herb*
> **fascia -ae** *f bandage*
> **gravis -is -e** *serious*
> **sīc contingit** (+ *dat*) *that's what happens*
> **victus -ī** *m loser*
> **adversārius -ī** *m opponent*
> **iste** *that guy*
> **multō plūra** *many more*
> **ubīque** *everywhere*

___ ACTIVITĀTĒS ___

E. Respondē ad hās quaestiōnēs:

1. Ubi est gladiātor?

2. Quandō gladiātor vulnera accēpit?

_____

3. Quot vulnera gladiātor in capite habet?

_____

4. Quot vulnera gladiātor in crūribus habet?

_____

5. Ubi sunt tumōrēs?

_____

6. Quae pars corporis est omnīnō (_entirely_) tumida?

_____

7. Ubi sunt vulnera gravissima?

_____

8. Quae remedia habet medicus?

_____

9. Estne gladiātor victus an victor?

_____

10. Quis habet vulnera in tergō?

_____

F. You are a Roman doctor. Make a diagnosis of the following patients who come to your office by matching the statements with the pictures:

Dolōrem tergī habet.
Pollex est fractus.
Sunt vulnera in femore et genū.
Planta et calx sunt inflammātae.
Trēs vertebrae spīnae sunt
  inflammātae.

Est vulnus in tempore dextrō.
Palma sinistrae manūs est tumida.
Oculī sunt inflammātī.
Tumōrem in fronte habet.
Cubitum est tumidum.

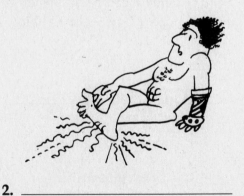

1. _____   **2.** _____

3. _____

4. _____

5. _____

6. _____

7. _____

8. _____

9. _____

10. _____

4 Thus far you have learned the present, imperfect, future and perfect tenses of verbs. There is one more tense that occurs from time to time: the PAST PERFECT, also called the PLUPERFECT. It is very easy to form. Take the perfect stem of any verb (that is, the third principal part of a verb minus the personal ending) and add the past tense of **sum:**

pugnāv + eram	*I had fought*	**pugnāv + erāmus**	*we had fought*
pugnāv + erās	*you had fought*	**pugnāv + erātis**	*you had fought*
pugnāv + erat	*he/she/it had fought*	**pugnāv + erant**	*they had fought*

The pluperfect tense refers to an action in the past that happened before another past action:

Medicus sānāvit gladiātōrem quem rētiārius *vulnerāverat.*
The doctor healed the gladiator whom the net man had wounded.

In this sentence, which action occurred earlier, the healing or the wounding?

_____ If you said the wounding, you are right. The verb **vulnerāverat** is in the pluperfect tense. You might say that it's the tense of the "double past."

__ ACTIVITĀTĒS _____

G. Change the verbs in the following sentences from the perfect tense to the pluperfect:

1. Cursor crūs frēgit. _____

2. Rētiāriī tridentēs in umerīs portāvērunt. _____

3. Medicus vulnus in pectore sānāvit. _____

4. Avia dolōrem articulōrum (*arthritis*) habuit. _____

5. Nōs dolōrēs capitis habuimus. _____

6. Bestiāriī vulnera in pectore accēpērunt. _____

7. Nōnne magnōs clāmōrēs in arēnā audīvistis? _____

8. Puella avem in palmā manūs suae tenuit. _____

9. Geminī in Monte Palātīnō diū habitāvērunt. _____

10. Lupa geminōs nūtrīvit. _____

H. Complete the sentences with the correct pluperfect form of the verb in parentheses:

1. (injicĕre) Arca, quam Amūlius in flūmen _____, ad rīpam fluitāvit.

2. (esse) Amūlius Numitōrem expulit ex urbe, in quā multōs annōs _____ rex.

3. (invenīre) Lupa nūtrīvit geminōs, quōs prope flūmen _____ .

4. (portāre) Laurentia infantēs ēducāvit, quōs Faustulus domum _____ .

5. (observāre) Mons in quō Remus vulturēs _____, erat Aventīnus.

6. (lūdĕre) Rōmulus urbem condidit in colle in quō ut puer _____ .

7. (servāre) Geminī nōn timuērunt lupam quae eōs _____ .

8. (capĕre) Juvenēs quī virginēs Sabīnās _____ erant Rōmānī.

9. (dare) Nōn sumpsī medicīnam quam medicus mihi _____ .

10. (accipĕre) Medicus sānāvit vulnus quod Thrax in certāmine _____ .

11. (cūrāre) Medicus quī familiam meam _____ in Graeciam transiit.

12. (venīre) Ille gladiātor quī ex Thrāciā _____, fortiter in arēnā certāvit.

_____ **COMPOSITIŌ** _____

You are a doctor in a hospital. As you make your rounds, ask three of your patients what's wrong with them. Be sure to record your questions and their answers, as doctors always do. Or perhaps you want to examine only one patient more thoroughly and ask that patient various questions.

1. _____

_____

2. _____

_____

3. _____

_____

DIALOGUS

Vocābula

pallidus *-a -um* pale
febris *-is* f fever
continuus *-a -um* continuous

gravēdō *-inis* f a cold
probātiō *-ōnis* f test

_____QUAESTIŌNĒS PERSŌNĀLĒS_____

1. Habēsne mentem sānam in corpore sānō?

_____

2. Quot tempora habēs?

_____

3. Quot umerōs habēs?

_____

4. Quot digitōs pedis habēs?

_____

5. Quot pollicēs habēs?

_____

6. Quō tempore annī habēs gravēdinēs?

_____

7. Quandō febrem continuam habēs, vīsitāsne medicum?

_____

8. Praefersne dolōrem capitis dolōrī stomachī?

_____

9. Nōnne scholam ob valētūdinem malam omīsistī?

_____

10. Quotiens (how often) omīsistī scholam annō novissimō ob valētūdinem malam?

_____

COLLOQUIUM

Supply your own answers in Latin in the following conversation:

Salvē. Quid agis hodiē?

_____
_____

(Say that you are sick.)

Quid est tibi? Cūr tam tristis es? Habēsne dolōrem capitis?

_____
_____

(Respond negatively. Say that your stomach hurts.)

Ego medicīnam adferre possum aut medicum vocāre possum.

_____
_____

(Say that you don't need a doctor.)

Quōmōdo tē adjuvāre possum?

_____
_____

(Supply your own answer.)

THE LATIN CONNECTION

A. Answer these questions about expressions derived from Latin:

1. Where would you find the *pectoral* muscle?

   _____

2. Where would you find a *temporal* bone?

   _____

3. When you *genuflect*, what part of the body do you bend?

   _____

4. With which part of the body do you indicate single *digits*?

   _____

5. What are *audio-visual* aids?

   _____

6. What is an *oral* examination?

   _____

7. Where would you find a *femoral* artery?

   _____

8. What kind of work is *manual* labor?

   _____

9. What is a *cordial* greeting?

   _____

10. With which part of the body would you produce a *nasal* sound?

    _____

11. Which part of your body do you put on the *pedal*?

    _____

12. What kind of punishment is *corporal* punishment?

    _____

13. What is another word for *vertebral* column?

    _____

14. When two people *confront* each other, with which part of their bodies do they face each other?

    _____

15. In which part of the body would you find the *humeral* bone?

_____

B. There are a lot of English words ending in *-al*. The *-al* that is tacked on to a word is called a suffix and means "of or pertaining to." We add the suffix in Latin to the *stem* of a noun. Remember that the complete stem of a Latin noun is found by dropping off the ending of the genitive:

nātiō, nātiōnis *f* (*nation*)

The stem is **nātiōn-**, to which we add the suffix *-al*, and we get *national* (of or pertaining to a nation).

In the following list of words, drop off the ending from the stem and add *-al*:

NOM.	GEN.	ENGLISH ADJECTIVE	ENGLISH MEANING
1. spīna	spīnae	spinal	of the spine
2. corpus	corporis		
3. mens	mentis		
4. vertebra	vertebrae		
5. dens	dentis		
6. pectus	pectoris		
7. frons	frontis		
8. digitus	digitī		
9. nāsus	nāsī		
10. auris	auris		
11. faciēs	faciēī		
12. caput	capitis		

C. You can add the suffix *-al* to nouns other than the parts of the body. In Latin, all adjectives formed in this way have three endings: **globus -ī** *m* (*globe*) gives us the adjectives **globālis -is -e.** The word *oval* comes from the Latin word "**ōvālis -is -e**," which comes from the noun **ōvum -ī** *n* (*egg*). Hence, oval means "egg-shaped."

From now on, when you come across such Latin adjectives, you'll understand them immediately, and it will no longer be necessary to give their meanings in the margin.

Here are some words that you have seen before. Give the Latin adjective with its endings and then the English adjective derived from it:

1. mūrus	mūrī	**mūrālis -is -e**	mural
2. bestia	bestiae		
3. parens	parentis		
4. fīlius	fīliī		
5. locus	locī		
6. pastor	pastōris		
7. astrum	astrī		
8. verbum	verbī		
9. fīnis	fīnis		
10. medicus	medicī		
11. initium	initiī		
12. rūs	rūris		
13. cultūra	cultūrae		
14. rex	rēgis		
15. vox	vōcis		

VIII Dominus et servus

Present Participles

1 Modicum cultūrae

Slavery was practiced not only among the Romans but also throughout the ancient world. There seemed to be an endless supply of slaves: prisoners of war; people who had fallen into debt under cruel laws that favored the money lenders; people, especially children, kidnapped by pirates; children of slave women; those guilty of crimes that resulted in the loss of liberty.

Slaves were trained in a wide range of trades and professions to increase the wealth of their masters. Cooks, blacksmiths, dyers, waiters, porters, carpenters, potters, tanners, farmers, gladiators, secretaries, accountants, architects, doctors, and dancers streamed to Rome from every quarter of the globe. As many as 10,000 slaves were sold in a single day on the small Greek island of Delos. Caesar and Pompey are said to have captured over a million people as slaves in Gaul and Asia.

Slave dealers (**mangō -ōnis** m) brought their slaves to the market in the Forum and elsewhere in the city and put them on a revolving platform (**catasta -ae** f) for display. Each slave had a sign (**titulus -ī** m) hung from the neck with all the information that the purchaser needed: age, nationality, abilities, and personal qualities. Slaves with intelligence and learning brought the highest prices. Not to own at least one slave was a sign of embarrassing poverty.

Slaves belonging to a household in the city (**familia urbāna**) generally had it easier than slaves belonging to an estate in the country (**familia rūstica**). Slaves who worked at the flour mill or in the mines or manned the oars of Roman galleys led the hardest life. Worst off were the members of chain gangs (**compeditī -ōrum** mpl) that worked on prison farms (**ergastulum -ī** n). They worked and even slept in chains.

According to Roman law, slaves were the absolute property of their masters, who could do with them whatever they wished. Many masters were kind and considerate, but others were mean and abusive. A slave could not own property, could not marry legally, and was denied legal protection against the master's mistreatment. Runaway slaves, when caught, were branded on the forehead with a red-hot iron. For the most serious offenses, a slave could be crucified or exposed to the wild beasts in the arena or burned alive. At the same time, unfair masters were always cautious about their safety, since it was not unusual for resentful and frustrated slaves to murder their masters. Rome witnessed some very serious slave rebellions. You will recall the rebellion led by Spartacus that defeated several Roman legions and came close to overthrowing the government.

Can you imagine what it was like for those thousands of boys and girls who were sold into slavery by the Roman conqueror and were transported out of their own country? For the rest of their lives, they were cut off from their families, friends, familiar surroundings, their native religion, as well as their native language. They knew only one law: obey or be punished.

Usually, slaves working on small family farms or in the city became, over the years, almost members of the family, sharing in the family religion. They were allowed to put aside their meager savings (**peculium -ī n**), which they could spend on pleasures or use to buy their freedom. Many faithful slaves were given freedom in the last will and testament of the master.

2 | Vocābula

__ ACTIVITĀS __

A. Match the sentences with the pictures they describe:

Servī ad molam labōrant.
Servus frūmentum in corbe fert.
Servus manicās gestat.
Mangō servōs ad catastam dūcit.
Servus aquam ex amphorā fundit.
Serva valvās armāriī claudit.
Servus pānēs in furnum inserit.
Serva aquam in situlā portat.

Serva in grabātō sedet.
Domina duās servās in catastā observat.
Trēs servī in catastā stant.
Serva vestēs in armārium ponit.
Servus farīnam subigit.
Serva candēlābrum incendit.

1. _____

2. _____

3. _____

4. _____

5. _____

6. _____

7. _____

8. _____

9. _____

10. _____

11. _____

12. _____

13. _____

14. _____

In English there are adjectives ending in -*ing* that come from verbs (the *smiling* boy). They are called "verbal" adjectives because they come from verbs. Another name for them is PARTICIPLE.

In Latin the present participles from the **-āre** family of verbs end in **-ans** (genitive: **-antis**) and are declined like **ēlegans**:

Servus aquam *portans* est validus.   *The slave carrying water is strong.*
Ego servum aquam *portantem* nōvī.   *I know the slave carrying water.*

Notice that in the first example **servus** is in the nominative case and so is the participle **portans,** which modifies **servus.** In the second example, **servum** is the direct object and, therefore, in the accusative case; and **portantem** must also be in the accusative case. Participles, like adjectives, agree with the noun they modify in number, gender, and case.

And here is something very important: In English the participle may come right before or after the noun that it modifies; in Latin the participle sandwiches its modifiers between itself and the noun:

> **Servus *aquam in amphorā portans* dominum strictum habet.**
> *The slave carrying water in a jar has a strict master.*

You can see that in Latin you know exactly where the participial phrase ends and the rest of the sentence continues because of the position of the participle at the end of the phrase.

The participles of the other verb families end in **-ens** (genitive: **-entis**):

dens *dolens*   *an aching tooth*
āthlētae in stadiō *currentēs*   *athletes running in the stadium*
cum servīs *effugientibus*   *with fleeing slaves*

The declension of these participles is just like that of **excellens** or **intellegens,** which you already know.

 Now read a letter written by a little slave boy to his mother and father, who were sold to a different master. Pay attention to the participles in heavy type. The letter begins with the typical greeting that the Romans always used:

Bassus parentibus suīs salūtem dat.   **salūtem dare** (+ *dat*) *to send greetings*

Mangō, vir crūdēlissimus, mē in manicīs in Forum Rōmānum duxit. Nōn sōlus eram. Multī aliī servulī mēcum erant. Virī Rōmānī circumstābant, **spectantēs** et **rīdentēs.** Nōs servulī autem erāmus perter-

sōlus *-a -um alone*
servulus *-ī m young slave*
circumstō *-stāre -stitī to stand around*

ritī. Titulum circum cervīcēs gestābāmus. In titulō erant nōmen, aetās, patria et artēs nostrae. Ab sōle **oriente** ad sōlem **occidentem** in forō stabāmus. Neque cibus neque aqua nobīs erat. Mangō nōs in catastā stāre coēgit. Virī Rōmānī, **circumstantēs,** nōs lustrāvērunt, **dīcentēs:** "Hīc servulus est nimis imbēcillus; ille servulus est nimis parvus; iste servus nullōs mūsculōs habet. Sed illī servulī sunt āthlēticī."

perterritus -a -um scared stiff
aetās -ātis f age
   ars artis f skill
oriens orientis rising
   occidens occidentis setting
cogō -ĕre coēgī coāctus to force
lustrō -āre to look (someone) over
imbēcillus -a -um weak
nullus -a -um no

Dēnique pistor ex oppidō Ōstiā **veniens,** mē et duodecim servulōs ēmit, **dīcens,** "Festīnāte, festīnāte, puerī! Ōstia est longinqua abhinc." Dominus noster nōn crūdēlis est sed sevērus. Numquam lūdĕre possumus. Labōrāmus ab sōle **oriente** ad sōlem **occidentem.**

dēnique finally
   Ōstia -ae f seaport of Rome
festīnō -āre to hurry up
longinquus -a -um far
   abhinc from here

Quattuor mensēs jam in pistrīnā labōrāmus. Duo servī validī frūmentum in amphorīs portant et id in molam infundunt. Duo servī molam versant et hōc modō frūmentum molunt.

jam labōrāmus we have been working
validus -a um strong
   frūmentum -ī n grain
   amphora -ae f (big) jar
mola -ae f mill
   infundō -fundĕre -fūdī -fūsus to pour into
   versō -āre to turn
molō -ĕre -uī -itus to grind
excipiō -ĕre excēpī exceptus to catch
subigō -ĕre subēgī subactus to knead
   modus ī m way
   pānēs loaves of bread
inserō -ĕre -uī -tus to put into, insert
coquō -ĕre coxī coctus to bake
admodum very
jaceō -ĕre -uī to lie
   lacrimō -āre to cry
vehementer terribly
   dēsīderō -āre to miss
agō agĕre ēgī actus to lead (a life)
   valēte good-bye

Ego farīnam ex molā in corbe excipiō et ad mensam adferrō. Trēs servulī ad mensam **stantēs** farīnam subigunt; hōc modō pānem ex farīnā faciunt. Dēnique ūnus servulus pānēs in furnum inserit et pānēs coquit.

Interdiū ego sum admodum occupātus; sed noctū, in grabātō **jacens,** saepe lacrimō. Ego vōs et avum aviamque, amīcos, patriam vehementer dēsīderō. Quam miser sum! Quam miseram vītam agō! Valēte.

Bassus

— ACTIVITĀS

B. Repondē ad quaestiōnēs:

1. Quis Bassum et aliōs servulōs in Forum Rōmānum duxit?

   _____

2. Quid Bassus circum manūs habuit?

   _____

3. Quid faciēbant virī Rōmānī circumstantēs?

   _____

4. Quid servulī circum cervīcēs gestābant?

   _____

5. Quid mangō in titulō inscripsit?

   _____

6. Quamdiū (*how long*) servulī in forō stābant?

   _____

7. Ubi mangō servulōs stāre coēgit?

   _____

8. Quis dēnique Bassum et servulōs ēmit?

   _____

9. Quid facit Bassus in pistrīnā?

   _____

10. Quem dēsīderat Bassus?

    _____

 Now that you have seen some present participles in action, let's look at the full declension of the participle:

	MASC./FEM.	NEUTER
SINGULAR		
NOMINATIVE	dīcens	dīcens
GENITIVE	dīcentis	dīcentis
ACCUSATIVE	dīcentem	dīcens
DATIVE	dīcentī	dīcentī
ABLATIVE	dīcente	dīcente

	MASC./FEM.	NEUTER
	PLURAL	
NOMINATIVE	dīcentēs	dīcentia
GENITIVE	dīcentium	dīcentium
ACCUSATIVE	dīcentēs	dīcentia
DATIVE	dīcentibus	dīcentibus
ABLATIVE	dīcentibus	dīcentibus

___ ACTIVITĀTĒS _____

C. Supply the correct nominative form of the participle and then give the English meaning:

1. (labōrāre) servulī _____

2. (occidĕre) sōl _____

3. (lacrimāre) puer _____

4. (dolēre) tergum _____

5. (ēsurīre) animal _____

D. Supply the correct form of the participle for the indicated verb and then give the English meaning:

1. (amāre) cum _____ patre   _____

2. (vīvĕre) sine _____ parentibus   _____

3. (dormīre) ab _____ servō   _____

4. (currĕre) in _____ equō   _____

5. (dolēre) prō _____ dente   _____

6. (effugĕre) ad _____ servum   _____

7. (pugnāre) inter _____ pugilēs   _____

8. (rīdēre) ob _____ virōs   _____

E. Read over the following sentences carefully. Then underline the correct form of the present participle:

1. Servus, molam (versans/versantem), est validus.

2. Pistor, in pistrīnā (stans/stantem), pānēs venditābat.

3. Duo servī, farīnam ex molā (excipiens/excipientēs) sunt frātrēs.

4. Servī timent dominum domō (veniens/venientem).

5. Ego prōtegam omnēs servōs (fugiens/fugientēs).

6. Mangōnēs, servōs in catastrā (venditans/venditantēs), sunt monstra.

7. Servulī, pānem in pistrīnā (coquentī/coquentēs), sunt pistōrēs bonī.

8. Servae, farīnam in mensā (subigens/subigentēs), ex Asiā veniunt.

9. Ego et frāter meus lupum, dē Monte Aventīnō (dēveniēns/dēvenientem), vīdimus.

10. Potestne medicus meum tergum (dolens/dolentem) cūrāre?

F. Read over the following sentences. Then supply the correct form of the participle of the indicated verb:

1. (portāre) Servus amphoram _____ pistrīnam intrāvit.

2. (stāre) Claudē, valvās armāriī in atriō _____!

3. (vocāre) Audīsne dominam, servōs ad sē _____?

4. (versāre) Servī, molam _____, admodum fatigātī erant.

5. (labōrāre) Quis invidet servulō ad molam _____?

6. (sedēre) Ego cibum dedī miserīs virīs ante templum _____.

7. (jacēre) Dominus verberāvit servulum in grabātō _____.

8. (infundĕre) Serva, aquam in amphoram _____, est bellissima.

9. (labōrāre) Compeditī, in ergastulō _____, miserrimī sunt.

10. (coquĕre) Servī, pānem _____, pecūlium mox habēbunt.

DIALOGUS

Vocābula

consīdō -ĕre consēdī consessum *to sit down*
adsum *here I am*
admodum mē paenitet *I am very sorry*
iterum *again*

tumeō -ēre -uī *to swell;* **tumens** *swollen*
mehercule! *by heaven!*
quidnam? *just what?*

COLLOQUIUM

Complete the dialog with expressions based on the conversation and the chapter as a whole:

COMPOSITIŌ

You are applying for a job in a Roman bakery. Tell the owner the various tasks that you can do in the bakery. Try to impress him with your skills. You might add some personal characteristics to help you land the job.

_____

_____

_____

_____

_____

_____

RĒS PERSŌNĀLĒS

A. As a slave in Rome, you could not be a senator, lawyer, or soldier. But you could be almost anything else if you had the ambition. If you were standing on the **catasta** in the Roman forum and were asked to give your preference, name five things that you would be willing to be or do. Can you give the reason for your choice in Latin? You may give your reason in English:

EXAMPLE: **Praeferō (volō) esse agricola, quia rūs amō.**

1. _____

2. _____

3. _____

4. _____

5. _____

B. Name three professions or jobs that you would not like. Begin with **Nōlō** . . . :

1. _____

2. _____

3. _____

THE LATIN CONNECTION

In Latin, the participle can act as an adjective: **amans pater** (*loving father*). The participle can also stand by itself and act as a noun: **amans** (*lover*), **amans patriae** *lover of country, patriot.*

An English word derived from a Latin participle may also be either an adjective or a noun. For example, the Latin participle **currens, currentis** gives us the following derivatives:

> *current* affairs (adjective)
> electrical *current* (noun)
> the *current* of a river (noun)

Write the nominative and the genitive of the participle of the following verbs. Then cross off the ending of the genitive and write the English derivative in the space provided. Remember that **-iō** verbs like **faciō** keep the **i** in the participle: **faciens, facientis**. Follow the pattern of the first verb in the list:

VERB	PARTICIPLE	ENGLISH DERIVATIVE
1. serpō -ĕre (*to crawl*)	**serpens, serpentis**	serpent
2. agō -ĕre (*to act, do*)		
3. recipiō -ĕre (*to receive*)		
4. studeō -ēre (*to study*)		
5. accidō -ĕre (*to happen*)		
6. repugnō -āre (*to fight back*)		
7. confīdō -ĕre (*to trust*)		
8. adjaceō -ēre (*to lie next to*)		
9. antecēdō -ĕre (*to go before*)		
10. praesideō -ēre (*to sit before, preside*)		
11. consultō -āre (*to consult*)		
12. dēficiō -ĕre (*to run low*)		
13. efficiō -ĕre (*to bring about*)		
14. fluō -ĕre (*to flow*)		

15. pertineō -ēre
    (*to belong to*)
16. contineō -ēre
    (*to hold together*)
17. conveniō -īre
    (*to come together,*
    agree)
18. dēterreō -ēre
    (*to frighten away,*
    prevent)
19. appareō -ēre
    (*to appear*)
20. ardeō -ēre
    (*to burn, glow*)
21. inhabitō -āre
    (*to inhabit*)
22. exspectō -āre
    (*to expect*)
23. observō -āre
    (*to observe*)
24. respondeō -ēre
    (*to answer*)
25. lateō -ēre
    (*to hide*)
26. sileō -ēre
    (*to be silent*)

Here is an aid to good spelling: English words derived from participles of the first conjugation end in -*ant* (*observant*); English words derived from any of the other conjugations end in -*ent* (*deterrent*). As is true for every rule, there are some exceptions, but the general principle should help your spelling.

IX *Vehicula et viae*

Locative Case;
īdem, eadem, idem

1 Modicum cultūrae

The most common means of transportation for ordinary people of the ancient world was the donkey, which was used for hauling loads as well as for personal travel. You might say that the donkey was the poor man's pickup truck. In the cities, the wealthy were carried in a litter (**lectīca -ae** *f*) or in a sedan chair (**sella gestātōria -ae** *f*). In the former, people traveled reclining on a couch; in the latter, seated. For comfort, they used soft cushions. For privacy, they used curtains (**vēlum -ī** *n*). The carriers were a team of strong, brightly dressed slaves of equal height. The number of slaves varied from two to eight, depending on the size of the litter. In many cities, Rome included, vehicles were forbidden during daylight hours in order to protect pedestrians in the narrow streets and to cut down on noise. Women of the highest rank and Vestal Virgins were allowed to travel in the city in a four-wheeled carriage (**pīlentum -ī** *n*) on special occasions, such as processions and public games.

For travel beyond the city, there was the chariot (**currus -ūs** *m*), in which the driver stood. Initially used for war, the chariot was adapted for civilian use. The two-wheeled cart (**carrus -ī** *m*) was used in transporting heavy loads. Heavier ones, often with solid wheels instead of wheels with spokes (**rota -ae** *f*), were drawn by oxen or horses. The smaller carts were pushed or pulled by men.

The most common word for wagon was **plaustrum -ī** *n*. Some had two wheels made of solid drums (**tympanum -ī** *n*) and were drawn by oxen or mules. Other wagons had four wheels.

For travel over longer distances, the four-wheeled carriage (**raeda -ae** *f*) was most common. It was used for carrying people and baggage and could carry as many as eight passengers. There was even the double-decker model, with people riding on the upper deck open to the sky, and the lower deck, which was enclosed with curtains. As you might expect, the wealthy had luxury models, while the common people had economy versions. Since most people living in a big city like Rome owned no vehicle, they could rent carriages (**raeda meritōria -ae** *f*) outside the city gates, just as people today who don't own a car or truck can rent one. The carriages were equipped with brakes (**sufflāmen -inis** *n*) and even with a trip-o-meter, a mileage gauge that indicated how many miles the passengers had traveled. A light, two-wheeled carriage without a top (**cisium -ī** *n*), designed for two persons, was used by those who wanted to travel fast and without baggage. Its design originated in Gaul, in what is now France.

Another two-wheeled traveling chariot (**essedum -ī** *n*) followed the lines of the war chariots of the Britons and Gauls. The smaller ones were driven by the traveler himself, and the larger ones by a driver. Although there are many references to the **essedum,** we do not know its exact shape.

The shape of the two-wheeled buggy called **carpentum** (**-ī** *n*) is known to us from Roman coins. It carried two or three passengers besides the driver. It was enclosed and had an arched cover overhead. For grand occasions it was richly adorned.

Ancient vehicles did not have rubber tires or springs to cushion the ride. The iron rims around the wheels made traveling a bone-jarring experience. The best streets and roads were paved with flat volcanic stones, which were carefully fitted together. Any spaces left between them were filled with smaller stones. But weathering and wear and tear over the years made the roads very bumpy by modern standards. It took the Romans over four hundred years to get around to building the first all-season highway (**via strāta,** literally, *paved road*). It was built in 312 B.C. under the direction of a crusty old Roman named Appius Claudius Caecus (the Blind) and was named Via Appia after him. Originally it ran south from Rome to Capua, a distance of 132 miles. Eventually it was extended to Brandisium on the Adriatic coast of southern Italy, a total distance of 360 miles. It took the Romans some sixty years to get around to setting up some milestones along the way to indicate distances and about two hundred years to set up mile markers every mile along the main highways.

The ancient Romans had not yet developed the system of hotels and motels along their highways. Whenever possible, travelers stayed at the homes of friends and relatives along the way. Most travelers had to put up with dismal inns (**caupōna -ae** *f*), which were generally as unsanitary and noisy as they were unsafe against thieves and robbers. Chances were the travelers had to share a bed with lice and bedbugs and put up with unappetizing food. Some travelers slept in their carriages (**carrūca dormītōria -ae** *f*) to avoid the gloomy, dirty inns. Bigger towns had more comfortable accommodations. Officials and soldiers were billeted in private houses by local officials.

2 Vocābula

carrus -ī m

cisium -ī n

raeda -ae f

currus -ūs m

rota -ae f

sella gestātōria -ae f

lectica -ae f

carpentum -ī n

mūlus -ī m

tympanum -ī n
plaustrum -ī m

bōs, bovis m

radius -ī m

― ACTIVITĀS

A. Match the sentences with the pictures they describe:

Senātor in hāc sellā gestātōriā sedet.
Duo bovēs hōc plaustrum trahunt.
Quattuor servī hanc lectīcam
  gestant.
Marītus et uxor in hōc cisiō sedent.
Vir hunc currum agit.
Duo mūlī hōc carpentum trahunt.

Ūnus radius rotae est fractus.
Haec raeda rotās quattuor habet.
Hōc plaustrum onus magnum fert.
Haec rota radiōs octō habet.
Vir in hāc lectīcā librum legit.
Hōc plaustrum nōn rotās sed
  tympana habet.

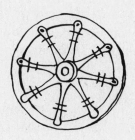

1. _____

2. _____

3. _____

4. _____

5. _____

6. _____

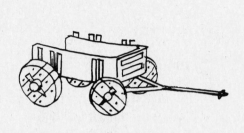

7. _____

8. _____

9. _____

10. _____

11. _____

12. _____

3 | The prepositions **ab** and **ad** are not used with the names of towns. There is a special case, called the LOCATIVE CASE, to indicate "in" or "at" a town. (Most Latin names of towns in Italy are feminine or neuter singular. Less common are feminine and masculine plural names.) Here are typical examples of names of towns along the Via Appia:

NOMINATIVE	ACCUSATIVE		ABLATIVE		LOCATIVE	
Rōma -ae f	**Rōmam**	*to Rome*	**Rōmā**	*from Rome*	**Rōmae**	*in/at Rome*
Lānuvium -ī n	**Lānuvium**	*to Lanuvium*	**Lānuviō**	*from Lanuvium*	**Lānuviī**	*in/at Lanuvium*
Formiae -ārum fpl	**Formiās**	*to Formiae*	**Formiīs**	*from Formiae*	**Formiīs**	*in/at Formiae*
Fundī -ōrum mpl	**Fundōs**	*to Fundi*	**Fundīs**	*from Fundi*	**Fundīs**	*in/at Fundi*

What is the locative ending of a feminine singular name? _____ Of a neuter

singular name? _____ Of a masculine or feminine plural name? _____ What is

the locative case of **rūs** (*country*) and **domus** (*home*)? _____ , _____

B. Here are the names of several towns on the Appian Way between Rome (in Latium) and Capua (in Campania). They are listed in the order in which you would see them traveling south. Give the form and English meaning of the locative case of each:

NOMINATIVE	LOCATIVE	MEANING
1. Bovill*ae* -*ārum* *fpl*	_____	
2. Alb*a* Long*a* -*ae* *f*	_____	
3. Arīci*a* -*ae* *f*	_____	
4. Lānuvi*um* -*ī* *n*	_____	
5. For*um* Appiī -*ī* *n*	_____	
6. Fērōni*a* -*ae* *f*	_____	
7. Terracīn*a* -*ae* *f*	_____	
8. Fundī -*ōrum* *mpl*	_____	
9. Itrī -*ōrum* *mpl*	_____	
10. Formi*ae* -*ārum* *fpl*	_____	
11. Minturn*ae* -*ārum* *fpl*	_____	
12. Capu*a* -*ae* *f*	_____	

4 Now let's read about a trip that Marcus, Cornelia, and their parents took along the Appian Way to Capua. Notice particularly the accusative cases of name places (*to* a place), ablative cases of name places (*from* a place), and locative cases. They appear in bold type:

Marcus et soror sua, Cornēlia, et parentēs iter per Viam Appiam facĕre constituērunt; nam **Capuam** in Campāniam īre volēbant. Marcus et Cornēlia erant excitātī, quia numquam anteā iter per Campāniam fēcerant. "Capua," inquit pater, "est noster

iter facĕre *to take a trip, travel*
constituō -ĕre -ī -tum *to decide (to)*
nam *conj for*

locus destinātus. Capua centum trīgintā mīlia passuum **Rōmā** abest. Crās māne prīmā hōrā **Rōmā** discēdēmus, nam iter erit longissimum."

Postrīdiē frāter et soror prīma lūce ex cubiculīs in viam festīnāvērunt, ubi servī raedam jam onerābant. Post jentāculum, Cornēlia et Marcus in raedam ascendērunt; deinde parentēs in raedam ascendērunt. Denique raedārius in raedam ascendit et equōs incitāvit. Raeda per urbis viās festīnāvit, et mox per Portam Capēnam* in Viam Appiam pervēnit.

Via Appia erat plēna vehiculōrum omnis generis. Marcus et Cornēlia tot vehicula numquam anteā vīderant: currūs, carrōs, lectīcās, plaustra, carpenta. Sed vehiculum velōcissimum erat cisium, in quō puer sē amīcae suae jactābat. Illud cisium omnia alia vehicula facile praeterībat. Vehicula tardissima erant plaustra et carrī, quōs bovēs trahēbant. Ā sinistrā et ā dextrā, Marcus et Cornēlia multās villās pulchrās vīdērunt. Vīdērunt etiam multōs servōs in agrīs et in olīvētīs labōrantēs. Circā hōram diēī tertiam, Montem Albānum subiērunt, ubi Alba Longa est. "Rōmulus et Remus," inquit māter, "**Albae Longae** ōlim nātī sunt." "Id sciō. Et Rhea Silvia erat māter eōrum," respondit Cornēlia.

Deinde **Arīciam** et **Lānuvium** pervēnērunt. Familia prandium **Lānuviī** sumpsit. "Festīnāte," clāmāvit pater, "sī **Terracīnam** sub nocte pervenīre volumus."

Post prandium, in raedam ascendērunt, et raedārius equōs incitāvit. Circā decimam diēī hōram **Fōrum Appiī** pervēnērunt, ubi erat statua Appiī Claudiī Caecī, quī Viam Appiam mūnīverat. "Ecce statuam!" exclāmāvit māter; Marcus autem et Cornēlia dormiēbant, nam fessī erant.

Post aliquot hōrās **Terracīnam** pervēnērunt. Hōc

***Porta Capēna** gate in the Roman wall where the Via Appia began.

---

locus destinātus -ī m destination
centum trīgintā mīlia passuum 130 miles (literally: 130 thousands of paces)
absum abesse āfuī to be distant
crās māne tomorrow morning
discēdō -ĕre discessī to depart
postrīdiē (on) the next day
lux lūcis f light; **prīmā lūce** at dawn
onerō -āre to load
ascendō -ĕre -ī to climb
raedārius -ī m driver, coachman
incitō -āre to urge on
perveniō -īre pervēnī (in or ad + acc) to arrive at, reach
genus -eris n kind, type
sē jactāre (+ dat) to show off to
praetereō -īre -īvī or **-iī** to pass
trahō -ĕre trāxī tractus to pull
olīvētum -ī n olive grove
subeō -īre -īvī or **-iī** to go up, climb
ōlim once upon a time

sub nocte before nightfall

mūniō -īre -īvī -ītus to build

fessus -a -um tired

oppidum in ōrā maritimā situm est. Raedārius rotam sufflāmināvit et raeda prō caupōnā constitit. Dum raedārius equōs pascit et eīs aquam dat, Marcus et Cornēlia cum parentibus caupōnam intrāvērunt. Caupōna erat plēna viātōrum. Aliī ad mensās cēnābant, aliī vīnum pōtābant et cantābant; aliī ante focum sedēbant et āleā lūdēbant.

Caupō Marcum et Cornēliam et parentēs ad mensam vocāvit et cibum eīs adposuit: assum, lactūcam, cāseum, pānem, fructum, et vīnum. Post cēnam familia dē itinere diū disputāvit. "Crās in marī natāre volam," dixit Cornēlia. "Ōra maritima nōn procul abest."

"Ego quoque," respondit Marcus. "Forsitan crās," dixit pater, "paulisper natāre poteritis. Sed deinde iter **Capuam** continuābimus. Crēdite mihi, iter inter Terracīnam et Capuam longa et dūra erit. Nunc dormīre temptāte, sī potestis."

Postrīdiē post natātiōnem in marī, familia **Terracīnā** discessērunt et sub nocte **Capuam** pervēnērunt.

rotam **sufflāmināre** to put on the brake
caupōna -ae f inn
consistō -ĕre constitī to stop
dum while
pascō -ĕre pāvī pastus to feed
viātor -ōris m traveler
cēnō -āre to eat supper
focus ī m fireplace
āleā lūdĕre to play dice; to gamble
caupō -ōnis m innkeeper
adpōnō -ĕre adposuī adpositus to serve
assum -ī n roast
disputō -āre dē (+ abl) to discuss
mare -is n (Mediterranean) sea
ōra maritima -ae f seashore
paulisper for a little while
dūrus -a -um rough, hard
temptō -āre to try
natātiō -ōnis f swim

ACTIVITĀS

C. Respondē ad hās quaestiōnēs:

1. Ubi Marcus et Cornēlia habitābant?

2. Ad quam urbem familia iter facĕre constituērunt?

3. Cūr Marcus et Cornēlia erant excitātī?

4. Quot mīlia passuum Capua Rōmā abest?

5. Quod nōmen est portae in mūrō Rōmānō?

6. Quae animālia plaustra et carrōs trahēbant?

_____

7. In quō oppidō familia prandium sumpsit? (Use locative)

_____

8. In quō oppidō statua Appiī Claudiī Caecī stābat? (Use locative)

_____

9. In quō oppidō familia cēnāvit? (Use locative)

_____

10. Quid Cornēlia et Marcus Terracīnae facĕre volēbant?

_____

5 In the account of the trip to Capua, distances were expressed in miles. A Roman mile was reckoned in paces, or a big step (**passus -ūs** m). One thousand paces (**mille passūs**) made one mile. Notice that the adjective **mille**, modifying the plural noun **passūs**, is indeclinable. From 2000 on, however, the word for thousand(s) (**mīlia -ium** npl) becomes a neuter plural noun, and **passus** is put into the genitive plural:

> **duo mīlia** _passuum_ _two miles_ (literally: two thousands of paces)
> **centum mīlia** _passuum_ _ten miles_ (literally: ten thousands of paces)

___ ACTIVITĀTĒS _____

D. Change the miles in parentheses to Roman miles:

1. (12 miles) Bovillae _____ Rōmā absunt.

2. (4 miles) Alba Longa _____ Bovillīs abest.

3. (45 miles) Terracīna _____ Rōmā abest.

4. (55 miles) Terracīna _____ Capuā abest.

5. (20 miles) Terracīna _____ Formiīs abest.

E. Complete the following sentences, putting the name of the town in parentheses in the proper case (accusative, ablative, or locative). Remember, no prepositions!

1. (at Lānuvium) Avus meus _____ habitat.

2. (from Lānuvium) Avus meus _____ ad Campāniam migrāvit (*moved*).

3. (from Arīcia) Marcus prīmā lūce _____ discessit.

4. (in Terracīna) Cornēlia prandium _____ sumpsit.

5. (to Fundī) Familia mea iter _____ fēcit.

6. (in Alba Longa) Caupōnae _____ vīnum malum habent.

7. (at Forum Appiī) Appius Claudius Caecus numquam _____ habitāvit.

8. (to Capua) Via Appia ab urbe Rōmā _____ dūcit.

9. (at Arīcia) Diāna templum clārissimum _____ habet.

10. (from Rome) Quandō Marcus _____ discessit, ad Campāniam īvit.

6 You are familiar with the simple pronouns **is, ea, id** (*he, she, it*). If we add the suffix **-dem,** they mean *the same:*

Eīdem servī hanc lectīcam herī gestābant.
The same slaves carried this litter yesterday.

Eōdem diē Marcus ab Latiō ad Campāniam discessit.
On the same day, Marcus departed from Latium for Campania.

Here is the entire declension:

	SINGULAR			PLURAL		
NOM.	īdem	eadem	idem	eīdem	eaedem	eadem
GEN.	ejusdem	ejusdem	ejusdem	eōrundem	eārundem	eōrundem
ACC.	eundem	eandem	idem	eōsdem	eāsdem	eadem
DAT.	eīdem	eīdem	eīdem	eīsdem	eīsdem	eīsdem
ABL.	eōdem	eādem	eōdem	eīsdem	eīsdem	eīsdem

Which letter was omitted in the masculine nominative singular? _____

Which letter dropped out of the neuter nominative singular? _____ There is one more point: Apparently the Romans didn't like the sound of **m** before **d** (**eumdem, eamdem**), and so they changed **m** to **n** (**eundem, eandem**). Now look over the plural forms. In what case do we see **m** changed to **n?** _____ .

__ ACTIVITĀS __

F. Complete the sentences with the correct form of **īdem, eadem, idem:**

1. Illae trēs tabernae sunt in _____ oppidō.

2. _____ raedārius raedam per Portam Capēnam herī ēgit (*drove*).

3. Marcus semper cum _____ amīcīs lūdit.

4. _____ mūlī raedam nostram trāxērunt.

5. Omnēs viātōrēs per _____ viam ad caupōnam pervēnērunt.

6. Senātōreś in _____ sellīs gestātōriīs iter Ardeam fēcērunt.

7. _____ rota iterum est fracta.

8. _____ pīlentum per urbis viās festīnāvit.

9. Mīlitēs mūrōs _____ oppidōrum oppugnābat.

10. Hīc caupō _____ cibum cōtīdiē adpōnit.

11. Ego _____ tabernam praetereō cum ad scholam eō.

12. Habitāsne in _____ insulā Rōmae?

____ COMPOSITIŌ ____

You are a used-vehicle vendor in a lot near the Appian Way. A customer drops in. Describe a couple of vehicles to the customer and explain how they can be used. Say how much each costs. Don't be reluctant to exaggerate, as used-car salespeople might.

_____

_____

_____

_____

_____

DIALOGUS

Buying from a used-wagon dealer? **Caveat emptor!** (*Let the buyer beware!*)

Vocābula

habitus -ūs m *condition*
cārus -a -um *expensive*
anicula -ae f *little old lady*
dīvitēs *the rich*

possideō -ēre possēdī possessus *to own*
tantummodo *only*
constat (+ *abl*) *it costs*
pedibus īre *to go on foot*

COLLOQUIUM

Complete the dialog with expressions taken from the conversation or expressions of your own:

Salvē, mī amīce. Vīsne _____ _____? Multa vehicula excellentia habeō. Omnia vehicula mea sunt _____.

Salvē. Vehiculum bonum emĕre volō, sed _____ _____ nōn habeō.

Hīc est _____ excellens et nōn cārum est.

Plaustrum? Ego agricola nōn sum, et neque _____ habeō.

Hīc est lectīca pulchra. Paene _____ _____. Anicula eam possēdit.

Mē paenitet, sed ego neque _____ _____ neque _____ sum.

Hīc est cisium splendidum. Erit vehiculum velōcissimum in Viā Appiā. _____ _____ _____ tē amābunt. Tantummodo mille dēnāriīs constat.

Mille dēnāriīs? Nesciō cūr, sed subitō _____ praeferō.

_____ *QUAESTIŌNĒS PERSŌNĀLĒS*_____

1. Fēcistīne umquam iter longum?

_____

2. Quae urbs erat locus destinātus itineris tuī longissimī?

_____

3. Quibuscum iter longissimum fēcistī?

_____

4. Praefersne itinera longa an brevia?

_____

5. Praefersne itinera in montēs an ad ōram maritimam?

_____

6. Quot vehicula familiae tuae sunt?

_____

7. Quandō sperās vehiculum tibi emĕre?

_____

8. Praefersne vehiculum magnum et cārum an vehiculum parvum et vēlox?

_____

(THE LATIN CONNECTION)

A. The English word *mile* comes from the Latin word **mille.** But **mille** means "one thousand." How do you explain it?

_____

B. One can say, "He went *via* the expressway to save time." What does *via* mean in that situation?

_____

C. From which Latin word is *itinerary* derived?_____

D. The verb **trahō trahĕre traxī tractus** means *to pull* or *to draw*. It can be combined with several prefixes. Read over the following sentences and then decide which compound form fits each sentence best:

abstract	extract	retract
contract	distract	subtract
detract	protract	attract

1. A dentist sometimes will _____ an aching tooth.

2. If you are not careful, you can _____ a disease.

3. The airplane will _____ its landing gear after takeoff.

4. Will you _____ the discount from the list price?

5. By his long-winded speech, the chairman _____ the meeting.

6. Your mother probably has used vanilla _____ when cooking.

7. This unfortunate action will _____ from his good name.

8. A drop of honey will _____ more flies than a barrel of vinegar.

9. Don't let outside noises _____ you.

X Amor et mātrimōnium

Irregular Adjectives

1 Modicum cultūrae

Almost all of Latin literature was written by male adults of the upper classes. This fact is, of course, unfortunate, since it would be interesting to read what young people thought and felt about the world around them. Even today, most books for children and young people are written by adults. Moreover, for the most part, what we know of romance of Roman teenagers and grown-ups comes from the pens of adults. Much of the romantic literature is in the form of myths. Later in this lesson, we will get an idea of such romantic myths from the love story about a young man named Pyramus and a young girl named Thisbe. It is a story told by the poet Ovid, who also wrote what was at that time a daring book called *The Art of Love* and a series of love letters supposedly written by women of mythology to their lovers.

You will be surprised to learn that boys and girls became engaged at a very early age. Cicero, the greatest Roman lawyer, public speaker, and politician, arranged for his daughter's engagement when she was ten years old and for her marriage when she was thirteen. This arrangement probably was typical of what usually happened; and it shows, as is still the case in some countries in modern times, that these matters were controlled entirely by the parents. It was a family arrangement designed to ensure that property stayed in the right hands. If, however, there was a strong dislike between the boy and the girl, the engagement could be broken off. At the time of the engagement, there would be a party or banquet.

In the early days of Rome, until 445 B.C., marriage between members of the wealthy patrician class and the poor plebian class was forbidden by law. Marriages between Roman citizens and foreigners were legal, but the children of such marriages were not Roman citizens unless the father was a Roman citizen. If a Roman girl married a non-Roman, the children were not considered Romans unless Rome had a special treaty conferring the right of intermarriage on the husband's town.

When the day of the wedding (**nuptiae -ārum** *fpl*) arrived, the girl dedicated her dolls (**pūpa -ae** *f*) to the household gods (**Lares -ium** *pl*) to symbolize that the carefree days of her childhood were over. The bride wore an orangey, flame-colored veil and a long white dress that reached to the ground. Her hair was divided by a spear-shaped comb into six strands, and for the first time she wore ribbons in her hair. On her head, she wore a crown of flowers (**corōna -ae** *f* **flōrida**).

The Latin verb for getting married was not the same for the boy and the girl. For the girl, the verb was **nūbō -ĕre nupsī, nupta** (+ *dat*). **Nūbĕre** means *to wear a veil*. The expression for the boy was **in mātrimōnium dūcĕre** or **uxōrem dūcĕre** (*to lead into matrimony* or *to lead a bride home*), since this "taking home the bride" was one of the official acts of a marriage.

The bride waited at her father's house for the bridegroom to come to lead her to his home. Before he took his bride home, the auspices were taken. May was a particularly ill-omened month. The most propitious time for marriage was the second half of June. If the omens were good, the bridal pair declared their consent by joining right hands at the direction of the matron of honor (**prōnuba -ae** *f*), who acted as a kind of representative of the goddess Juno, the patroness of marriage. The words spoken were "**Ubi Gaius, ego Gaia**" (*Where Gaius is, there I, Gaia, will be*). This formula remained unchanged, no matter what the names of the bridal couple.

A wedding reception was then held at the home of the bride, ending with a banquet (**cēna nuptiālis** *f*). Toward evening, the bridegroom conducted his bride to his home, accompanied by a procession (**dēductiō -ōnis** *f*) of relatives and friends. At the head of the procession were three boys, one of whom carried the lighted wedding torch with which the bride would light the fireplace in the home of the groom. The other two boys led the bride by the hand. The rest of the procession, including flute players, followed behind, singing wedding songs. On arriving at the home of the groom, the bride anointed the doorposts with fat and olive oil and wrapped strands of wool around the doorposts. She was then carried across the threshold to make sure that she wouldn't stumble as she entered since that would have been regarded as a very bad omen.

Once inside the home, the bride lighted the fire in the hearth with the torch. When the torch was put out, she threw it to the guests for good luck, just as a bride today throws her bouquet to those in her bridal group. The bridegroom then gave her fire and water as a sign of their future life together. The bride then gave her husband a dowry from her father. Thus ended the wedding ceremonies.

Vocābula

serta -ae f

nupta -ae f
corōna -ae f
vēlum -ī m

aedēs -is f

osculum -ī n

ānulus -ī m

nuptiae -ārum fpl

taeda -ae f nuptiālis

tibia -ae f

tībīcen -inis m

dēductiō -ōnis f
pompa -ae f nuptiālis

___ ACTIVITĀS _____

A. Match the sentences with the pictures they describe:

Puer taedam nuptiālem tenet.
Puer ānulum puellae dat.
Nupta sē ad nuptiās parat.
Tībīcen tībiā cantat.
Puer amōrem puellae monstrat.

Nupta corōnam flōridam gestat.
Marītus jānuam domūs sertīs decorat.
Nupta pūpam Laribus dedicat.
Duo puerī nuptam dūcunt.
Puer osculum puellae dat.

1. _____

2. _____

3. _____

4. _____

5. _____

6. _____

7. _____

8. _____

9. _____

10. _____

3 Now read the tragic love story of Pyramus and Thisbe, about which the Roman poet Ovid wrote:

Pȳramus et Thisbē domōs adjacentēs tenēbant. Alter erat juvenis pulcherrimus in urbe; altera erat virgō bellissima et tenera et amābilis. Tempore amor inter juvenem et virginem magis et magis crēvit. Pȳramus vērō Thisbēn in mātrimōnium dūcěre volēbat et Thisbē Pȳramō nūběre volēbat. Patrēs autem mātrimōnium prohibuērunt. Sed quod parentēs prohibēre nōn poterant, erat amor mūtuus inter amantēs, nam amor vincit omnia.

Rīma in pariete inter domōs erat. Nēmō autem anteā rīmam illam notāvit. Amantēs ipsī rīmam invēnērunt, nam amor viam semper inveniet. Postquam parentēs dormītum ībant, Pȳramus et Thisbē amōrem mūtuum per rīmam exprimēbant. Utrimque ōscula dabant et verba blanda inter sē

teneō -ēre -uī -tus to occupy, live in
  alter . . . altera the one . . . the other
juvenis -is m young man
  virgō -inis f young girl
tempore in time
  amor, amōris m love
magis et magis more and more
  crescō -ěre crēvī to grow
vērō in fact
prohibeō -ēre -uī -itus to prohibit, prevent
quod what
mūtuus -a -um mutual
  amans, amantis mf lover
rīma -ae f crack
  pariēs -etis m (inner) wall
notō -āre to notice
  ipse, ipsa, ipsum self (myself, yourself, etc.)

fēcērunt. Quō magis parentēs Pȳramum et Thisbēn sēgregāre temptābant, eō magis amor inter eōs crēvit.

Quōdam diē duo amantēs consilium sēcrētum iniērunt: fūrtim ē domō posterā nocte rēpēre et convenīre extrā urbem sub quādam mōrō. Illa mōrus erat proxima gelidō fontī.

Thisbē prīma ad mōrum pervēnit et sub arbore consēdit. Ecce leō ore cruentō ā recente caede ad fontem vēnit. Thisbē procul lūnae lūce leōnem vīdit et in spēluncam fūgit. Ut fūgit, vēlāmen dēmīsit. Leō vēlāmen ore cruentō laniāvit. Postquam aquam ex fonte pōtāvit, leō in silvam rediit.

Paulō post, Pȳramus ad mōrum pervēnit. Vestīgia leōnis et vēlāmen cruentum vīdit. "Ūna nox," ait, "duōs amantēs perdet. Tū, mea Thisbē, fuistī dignissima longā vītā. Ego ipse sum causa mortis tuae. Ego jussī tē noctū venīre in tam perīculōsum locum. Sine tē vīvēre nōlō." Vēlāmen Thisbēs ad mōrum tulit; oscula lacrimāsque vēlāminī dedit. Deinde pectus sīcā perfōdit.

Thisbē ē spēluncā vēnit et corpus cruentum Pȳramī vīdit. Thisbē caput pallidum ejus sustulit et multa oscula dedit. "Pȳrame!" clāmāvit, "cūr hōc fēcistī? Pȳrame, tua cārissima Thisbē tē nōminat. Audī vōcem meam!" Ut autem vēlāmen cruentum suum vīdit, tandem causam vēram mortis intellēgit.

Ad nōmen Thisbēs, Pȳramus oculōs, ā morte jam gravātōs, aperuit, sed nihil dīcēre poterat. "Manus tua et amor noster mortem tuam effēcērunt," clāmāvit Thisbē. "O parentēs miserrimī, quī nōs vīventēs sēgregāvistis, nunc ultima hōra vītae nōs junget."

Haec verba dīcens, pectus sīcā perfōdit et ē vītā discessit.

---

dormītum īre *to go to sleep*
exprimō -ĕre expressī, expressus *to express*
utrimque *on both sides (of the wall)*
  verba facĕre *to speak words*
  blandus -a -um *endearing*
quō magis . . . eō magis *the more . . . the more*
sēgregō -āre *to keep apart*
consilium inīre *to form a plan*
fūrtim repĕre *to sneak*
  posterus -a -um *the following*
convenīre *to meet*
  mōrus -ī f *mulberry tree*
gelidus -a -um *cold*
  fons, fontis m *spring*
caedēs -is f *kill*
lux, lūcis f *light*
spēlunca -ae f *cave*
  vēlāmen -inis n *wrap*
  dēmittō -ĕre dēmīsī dēmissus *to drop*
laniō -āre *to tear up*
paulō post *a little later*
  vestīgium -ī n *footprint*
perdō -dĕre -didī -ditus *to destroy*
dignus -a -um (+ abl) *deserving of*
jubeō -ēre jussī jussus *to tell, order*
ferō ferre tulī lātus *to bring*
sīca -ae f *dagger*
  perfodiō -ĕre perfōdī perfossus *to stab*
pallidus -a -um *pale*
  tollō -ĕre sustulī sublātus *to raise*
cārus -a -um *dear*
  nōminō -āre *to call by name*
ut *when, as*
tandem *finally*
gravātus -a -um *heavy*
efficiō -ĕre effēcī effectus *to bring about*
jungō -ĕre junxī junctus *to join*

discēdō -ĕre discessī *to depart*

___ ACTIVITĀS _____

B. Respondē Latīnē:

1. Quis erat virgō bellissima in urbe?

   _____

2. Quis erat juvenis pulcherrimus in urbe?

   _____

3. Quis mātrimōnium inter amantēs prohibuit?

   _____

4. Quid amantēs in pariete invēnērunt?

   _____

5. Quid Pȳramus et Thisbē faciēbant postquam parentēs dormītum ībant?

   _____

6. Secundum consilium, ubi convenīre constituērunt?

   _____

7. Quae fera ex silvā ad fontem vēnit?

   _____

8. Quō Thisbē fūgit?

   _____

9. Quid Thisbē casū (*accidentally*) dēmīsit?

   _____

10. Secundum Pȳramum, quae erat causa mortis Thisbēs?

    _____

4 If the suffix **-dam** is added to the forms of the relative pronouns (**quī, quae, quod**), the combinations mean "a certain":

Thisbē sub *quādam* arbore consēdit.   *Thisbe sat down under a certain tree.*

We had seen in the declension of **īdem, eadem, idem** that the Romans did not like the sound of **m** before **d** (**eumdem** was changed to **eundem**). What would, therefore, be the preferred form of **quemdam?** _____;

of **quamdam?** _____; of **quōrumdam?** _____;

of **quārumdam?** _____.

___ ACTIVITĀS _____

C. Underline the correct form of **quīdam, quaedam, quoddam:**

1. in (quōdam/quādam) urbe

2. ob (quōsdam/quāsdam) causās

3. in (quibusdam/quisdam) locīs

4. (quīdam/quaedam) juvenēs

5. ad (quendam/quoddam) oppidum

6. vēlum (quārumden/quārundem) nuptārum

 In the story of Pyramus and Thisbe, the intensifying pronoun **ipse, ipsa, ipsum** was used. It is declined like **bonus -a -um** except in the nominative masculine and genitive and dative singular:

	SINGULAR			PLURAL		
NOM.	ipse	ipsa	ipsum	ipsī	ipsae	ipsa
GEN.	ipsīus	ipsīus	ipsīus	ipsōrum	ipsārum	ipsōrum
ACC.	ipsum	ipsam	ipsum	ipsōs	ipsās	ipsa
DAT.	ipsī	ipsī	ipsī	ipsīs	ipsīs	ipsīs
ABL.	ipsō	ipsā	ipsō	ipsīs	ipsīs	ipsīs

When a form of **ipse** comes *after* the word it modifies, it means *self.* The forms of **ipse** mean *myself, yourself, himself, itself,* or *ourselves, yourselves, themselves:*

    ego ipse   *I myself*   **amantēs ipsī**   *the lovers themselves*

In English, *myself* may be reflexive or intensive, depending on the sentence as a whole, but in Latin there is one form for the reflexive and another form for the intensive. Look at these two examples:

INTENSIVE: **Virgō *ipsa* tabulātum lāvit.**   *The girl washed the floor herself.*
REFLEXIVE: **Virgō *sē* lāvit.**   *The girl washed herself.*

If the *self* word in English is intensive, you can substitute the word *personally.* An intensive simply adds emphasis:

    Pater *ipse* in nuptiīs interfuit.   *The father himself* (or *personally*)
                                     attended the wedding.

When **ipse** comes before the word it modifies, it is still intensive, but then it means *very* or *selfsame*:

Marītus vēnit *ipsō* diē quō nupta sua eum exspectāvit.   *The bridegroom came on the very day on which his bride expected him.*

__ ACTIVITĀS __

D. Complete with the correct form of **ipse, ipsa, ipsum:**

1. Marītus _____ nuptam domum dēduxit.

2. Parentēs _____ erant causa mortis amantium.

3. Thisbē dixit: "Ego _____ nunc ē vītā discēdam."

4. Pȳramus dixit: "Ego _____ nunc ē vītā discēdam."

5. Nupta _____ gratiās mihi ob donum ēgit.

[6] There are several Latin adjectives that have the same genitive and dative endings as **ipse**: **-īus** in the genitive and **-ī** in the dative. (You may remember that the demonstrative pronouns **ille** and **iste** have the same genitive and dative singular endings.) The most common of these adjectives are:

alius *-a -ud*	*another*
alter, altera, alterum	*the other*
ūllus *-a -um*	*any*
nūllus *-a -um*	*no*
ūnus *-a -um*	*one, alone*
tōtus *-a -um*	*whole*
sōlus *-a -um*	*only, alone*

__ ACTIVITĀS __

E. Complete the following sentences with the correct form of the adjective in parentheses. The nouns they modify are in bold type. (Remember that verbs like **confīdĕre** *to trust*, **crēdĕre** *to believe*, **placēre** *to please*, and **servīre** *to serve* take the dative case.):

1. (tōtus) Nupta per _____ **nuptiās** subrīdēbat (*smiled*).

2. (ūllus) Habēsne _____ **dōnum** nuptiāle prō nuptā?

3. (sōlus) _____ **amīcī** meī ad nuptiās meās nōn vēnērunt.

4. (tōtus) Populus _____ **oppidī** pompae aderant.

5. (nūllus) _____ **puellae** in nuptae domō erant.

6. (alter) Ego huic medicō sed nōn _____ **medicō** confīdō.

7. (ūnus) Ego tantummodo _____ **dominō** servīre possum.

8. (nūllus) Ego ipse _____ **astrologō** crēdō.

9. (ūnus) Hae nūptiae _____ **patrī** sed nōn alterī placent.

10. (alius) Ego dōnum nōn huic sed _____ **nuptae** dedī.

7 There's still a little more to be learned about **alius, alia, aliud** and **alter, altera, alterum.** First of all, did you notice that the neuter of **alius** is not **alium**, as you might expect, but **aliud** (just as the neuter form of **ille** is **illud**)? Furthermore, the genitive singular of **alius, alia, aliud** is **alterīus** for all three genders. Thirdly, **alius** and **alter** can be used in pairs with the following meanings:

alius ... alius	*one ... another*
aliī ... aliī	*some ... others*
alter ... alter	*the one ... the other*
alterī ... alterī	*some ... the others*

Alius Capuam amat, *alius* **Rōmam praefert.**

One likes Capua, another prefers Rome.

Aliī **bene cantāre possunt,** *aliī* **bene saltāre possunt.**

Some can sing well, others can dance well.

_ ACTIVITĀS _____

F. Complete the sentences by supplying the correct forms of **alius** and **alter**. When pairs are called for, the word is listed twice in parentheses. The word to be modified is in bold type:

1. (alius) **Nihil** _____ ā tē volō.

2. (alter ... alter) Marītus in _____ **parte** urbis habitat, nupta in _____ **parte.**

3. (alter ... alter) Pater _____ **fīliō** cisium dedit, _____ **fīliō** raedam.

4. (alter ... alter) Vīta _____ **marītī** fēlix est, sed vīta _____ **marītī** infēlix est.

5. (alius . . . alius) _____ **servī** in culīnā labōrant, _____ **servī** in olivētīs.

⑧ Let's look in on a Roman wedding:

Herī nuptiīs apud amīcam meam Tulliam, adfuī. Parentēs Tulliae laetissimī erant, quia Tullia Caeciliō, fīliō senātōris, nūbēbat. Pater ipse jānuam et postēs sertīs laureīs decorāverat. Amīcī ex omnibus partibus urbis ad nuptiās vēnērunt: aliī ā Monte Palatīnō, aliī ā Monte Aventīnō, et aliī ā Campō Martiō.

apud (+ *acc*) *at the house of*
ad**sum** **-esse -fuī** (+ *dat*) *to be present at*
laet**us** **-a -um** *happy*
post**is** **-is** *m doorpost*
laure**us** **-a -um** *of laurel*
decor**ō** **-āre** *to decorate*

Nupta erat bellissima. Vēlum flammeum et vestem albam et longam gestābat. Ānulum aureum nuptiālem in digitō sinistrae manūs habēbat, quem Caecilius eī dederat. Suprā caput corōnam flōridam gestābat.

vēl**um** **-ī** *n veil*
flamme**us** **-a -um** *flame-colored*
vest**is** **-is** *f gown*
suprā (+ *acc*) *on, on top of*
flōrid**us** **-a -um** *of flowers*

Tullia prīmō ante aedem in ātriō stetit, et pūpam suam Laribus dēdicāvit. Deinde Caecilius et nupta manūs dextrās conjunxērunt. Nupta cōram prōnubā dīxit: "Ubi Gaius, ego Gaia." Ad haec verba, omnēs in ātriō applaudēbant et clāmābant "Talassiō! Talassiō!" Deinde omnēs cēnam nuptiālem sumpsērunt. Post cēnam, pompa nuptiālis ā Tulliae domō ad Caeciliī domum prōcessit. Trēs puerī nuptam in pompā duxērunt. Alius taedam nuptiālem portāvit; alius nuptam manū dextrā dūxit et alius nuptam manū sinistrā dūxit. Tībīcinēs tībiīs cantābant et omnēs in pompā carmina cantābant. Interdum "Talassiō!" clāmābant.

aed**es** **-is** *f shrine*

conjung**ō** **-jungĕre -junxī -junctus** *to join*
cōram (+ *abl*) *in the presence of*
Talassiō! *traditional wedding cry*

prōcēd**ō -ĕre prōcessī prōcessum** *to proceed*

carm**en** **-inis** *n song*

Quandō pompa ad Caeciliī domum pervēnit, Caecilius ante jānuam constitit et nuptam trans līmen in ātrium portāvit. Omnēs amīcī et cognātī in ātriō convēnērunt, ubi Caecilius et Tullia ante aedem lībum nuptiāle ēdērunt. Deinde marītus ignem et aquam nuptae dedit. Nupta ignem in focō taedā nuptiālī accendit. Deinde omnēs amīcī et cognātī domum rediērunt. Caecilius et Tullia fēlīciter in perpetuum exinde vixērunt.

consist**ō -ĕre constitī** *to take up position*
līm**en** **-inis** *n threshold*
cognāt**us** **-ī** *m relative*
līb**um** **-ī** *n cake*
foc**us** **-ī** *m fireplace, hearth*
accend**ō -ĕre accendī accensus** *to light*

in perpetuum exinde *ever after*

— ACTIVITĀS

G. Respondē ad hās quaestiōnēs:

1. Quamobrem parentēs Tulliae laetissimī erant?

   _____

2. Quis jānuam et postēs sertīs laureīs decorāvit?

   _____

3. Quid nupta suprā caput gestābat?

   _____

4. Quō colōre erat vēlum?

   _____

5. Quid nupta in digitō habuit?

   _____

6. Quot puerī nuptam in pompā duxērunt?

   _____

7. Quid puer prīmus manū tenēbat?

   _____

8. Quī tībiīs cantābant?

   _____

9. Quid omnēs in pompā interdum clāmābant?

   _____

10. Quid marītus nuptae in ātriō suō dedit?

    _____

DIALOGUS

Vocābula

ratiō -ōnis f reason
rārō rarely
Quid aliud? What else?
prorsum absolutely
adōrō -āre to adore
Ita est That's right

purgō -āre to clean
obsōnō -āre to do the shopping
Itane? Is that so?
igitur then
omnīnō nōn not . . . at all
facerem would I do

COLLOQUIUM

Pretend you are Claudius. Complete the dialog with expressions based on the previous conversation and on the chapter as a whole:

Claudī, mī amīce, ubi est uxor tua? Estne domī an in forō?

Marce,
_____
_____
(Say that your wife is rarely at home.)

Cūr tam tristis es hodiē? Nōnne uxor tua domum cōtīdiē purgat?

_____
_____
(Say that she never cleans the house.)

Vultne uxor tua semper vestēs novās emēre, sicut omnēs uxōrēs?

_____
_____
(Say that clothes cost a lot of money.)

Misere Claudī! Coquitne uxor tua cibōs bonōs tibi. Estne uxor tua coqua bona?

_____
_____
(Say that she never cooks.)

Itane? Cūr igitur istam fēminam in mātrimōnium duxistī?

_____
_____
(Say that he doesn't understand. You love your wife.)

QUAESTIŌNĒS PERSŌNĀLĒS

1. Amāsne nuptiīs adesse?

_____

2. Habēbisne nuptiās magnās an parvās et prīvātās?

_____

3. Praefersne marītum dīvitem an pulchrum an amābilem (nuptam dīvitem an pulchram an amābilem)?

_____

4. Praefersne vēlum album an flammeum?

_____

5. Quō annō aetātis tuae nūbēs (uxōrem dūcēs)?

_____

6. Dēbetne pater an fīlia marītum sēligěre (*select*)?

_____

7. Labōrābisne forīs (*outside the home*) post mātrimōnium tuum?

_____

8. Quot līberōs spērās habēre in familiā futūrā tuā?

_____

—————————————— *COMPOSITIŌ* ——————————————

Someday you will get married. Describe the person and the qualities of your ideal partner in life.

_____

_____

_____

_____

_____

_____

_____

(THE LATIN CONNECTION)

A. The word *pupil* of the eye is derived from **pūpilla,** which means *little doll*. Can you explain the connection?

_____

B. What is the Latin meaning of the state of *Florida*?

_____

C. What is a *per capita* tax?

_____

D. What are *cognate* words? Can you give some examples?

_____

_____

E. What is a pilot's *solo* flight?

_____

F. What is the Latin source of the following words and what do they mean?

EXAMPLE: marital   **marītus**   of or pertaining to a husband or marriage

1. revive _____ _____

2. vestige _____ _____

3. secretive _____ _____

4. juvenile _____ _____

5. adjacent _____ _____

6. osculate _____ _____

7. prenuptial _____ _____

8. segregate _____ _____

9. posterity _____ _____

10. amateur _____ _____

11. vivid _____ _____

12. furtive _____ _____

13. nullify _____ _____

Recōgnitiō II
(Lectiōnēs VI–X)

Lectiō VI

a. Relative pronoun meaning *who, which, that*. The genitive and dative were not used but are given here for completeness:

	MASCULINE	FEMININE	NEUTER
SINGULAR			
NOMINATIVE	**quī**	**quae**	**quod**
GENITIVE	**cūjus**	**cūjus**	**cūjus**
ACCUSATIVE	**quem**	**quam**	**quod**
DATIVE	**cui**	**cui**	**cui**
ABLATIVE	**quō**	**quā**	**quō**
PLURAL			
NOMINATIVE	**quī**	**quae**	**quae**
GENITIVE	**quōrum**	**quārum**	**quōrum**
ACCUSATIVE	**quōs**	**quās**	**quae**
DATIVE	**quibus**	**quibus**	**quibus**
ABLATIVE	**quibus**	**quibus**	**quibus**

b. The relative pronoun agrees with its antecedent in number and gender, but its case is determined by its use in the relative clause.

c. The relative pronoun, in contrast to English, is never omitted.

Lectiō VII

The pluperfect or past perfect tense refers to an action in the past that happened before another past action. The pluperfect is a combination of the stem of the perfect tense (third principal part) and the imperfect tense of **sum**:

pugnāveram	*I had fought*	**pugnāverāmus**	*we had fought*
pugnāverās	*you had fought*	**pugnāverātis**	*you had fought*
pugnāverat	*he/she/it had fought*	**pugnāverant**	*they had fought*

Lectiō VIII

a. Present participles of the **-āre** family of verbs are formed by adding **-ans** to the present stem: **port** + **-ans** (*carrying*). The complete declension is as follows:

	SINGULAR		PLURAL	
	M/F	N	M/F	N
NOM.	portans	portans	portantēs	portantia
GEN.	portantis	portantis	portantium	portantium
ACC.	portantem	portans	portantēs	portantia
DAT.	portantī	portantī	portantibus	portantibus
ABL.	portante(-ī)	portante(-ī)	portantibus	portantibus

b. Present participles of the **-ēre** and **-ĕre** family of verbs are formed by adding **-ens** to the present stem: **mov + ens** (*moving*); **dīc + ens** (*saying*). The complete declension is as follows:

	SINGULAR		PLURAL	
	M/F	N	M/F	N
NOM.	movens	movens	moventēs	moventia
GEN.	moventis	moventis	moventium	moventium
ACC.	moventem	movens	moventēs	moventia
DAT.	moventī	moventī	moventibus	moventibus
ABL.	movente(-ī)	movente(-ī)	moventibus	moventibus

c. Present participles of the **-iō** and **-īre** family of verbs are also formed by adding **-ens** to the present stem, which ends in **i**: **accipi + ens** (*receiving*) and **audi + ens** (*hearing*). The complete declension is as follows:

	SINGULAR		PLURAL	
	M/F	N	M/F	N
NOM.	accipiens	accipiens	accipientēs	accipientia
GEN.	accipientis	accipientis	accipientium	accipientium
ACC.	accipientem	accipiens	accipientēs	accipientia
DAT.	accipientī	accipientī	accipientibus	accipientibus
ABL.	accipiente(-ī)	accipiente(-ī)	accipientibus	accipientibus

Lectiō IX

a. The prepositions **ab** and **ad** are not used with the names of towns and small islands. Thus **Romā** means *from Rome* and **Romam** means *to Rome*. Most Latin names of towns are feminine or neuter singular. Less common are feminine and masculine plural names.

b. There is a special case called the LOCATIVE CASE to indicate *in* or *at* a town or *in* or *on* a small island. The locative ending of a feminine singular name is **-ae.** The locative ending of a neuter singular name is **-ī.** The ending of masculine or feminine plural names of the second and first declensions is **-īs.** Examples of such names and the special words **rūs** (*country*) and **domus** (*home*) are as follows:

NOMINATIVE/GENITIVE	ACCUSATIVE	ABLATIVE	LOCATIVE
Rōma *-ae* f	**Rōmam** *to Rome*	**Rōmā** *from Rome*	**Rōmae** *in/at Rome*
Lānuvium *-ī* n	**Lānuvium** *to Lanuvium*	**Lānuviō** *from Lanuvium*	**Lānuviī** *in/at Lānuvium*
Formiae *-ārum* fpl	**Formiās** *to Formiae*	**Formiīs** *from Formiae*	**Formiīs** *in/at Formiae*
Fundī *-ōrum* mpl	**Fundōs** *to Fundi*	**Fundīs** *from Fundi*	**Fundīs** *in/at Fundi*
domus *-ūs* f	**domum** *home*	**domō** *from home*	**domī** *at home*
rūs, rūris n	**rūs** *to the country*	**rūre** *from the country*	**rūrī** *in the country*

c. If the suffix **-dem** is added to the simple pronouns **is, ea, id** (*he, she, it*), they mean *the same*. The complete declension is:

	SINGULAR			PLURAL		
NOM.	īdem	eadem	idem	eīdem	eaedem	eadem
GEN.	ejusdem	ejusdem	ejusdem	eōrundem	eārundem	eōrundem
ACC.	eundem	eandem	idem	eōsdem	eāsdem	eadem
DAT.	eīdem	eīdem	eīdem	eīsdem	eīsdem	eīsdem
ABL.	eōdem	eādem	eōdem	eīsdem	eīsdem	eīsdem

Lectiō X

a. If the suffix **-dam** is added to the forms of the relative pronoun (**quī, quae, quod**), the combinations mean *a certain*:

quīdam **vir**	*a certain man*
quaedam **urbs**	*a certain city*
quoddam **tempus**	*a certain time*

b. A group of adjectives has irregular genitive and dative endings: **-īus** in the genitive and **-ī** in the dative. The following adjectives fall into this group:

alius *-a -ud*	*another*	**ūnus** *-a -um*	*one, alone*
alter, altera, alterum	*the other*	**tōtus** *-a -um*	*whole, entire*
ullus *-a -um*	*any*	**sōlus** *-a -um*	*only, alone*
nullus *-a -um*	*no*	**ipse** *-a -um*	*self*

c. The intensifying pronoun/adjective **ipse, ipsa, ipsum** adds emphasis and must be distinguished from the reflexive pronoun:

INTENSIVE: **Servus *ipse* pecūniam cēlāvit.**
The servant himself hid the money.

REFLEXIVE: **Servus** *sē* **cēlāvit.**
The servant hid himself.

The complete declension of **ipse, ipsa, ipsum** serves as a model for all the pronoun/ adjectives of this group:

	SINGULAR			PLURAL		
NOM.	ipse	ipsa	ipsum	ipsī	ipsae	ipsa
GEN.	ips*īus*	ips*īus*	ips*īus*	ipsōrum	ipsārum	ipsōrum
ACC.	ipsum	ipsam	ipsum	ipsōs	ipsās	ipsa
DAT.	ipsī	ipsī	ipsī	ipsīs	ipsīs	ipsīs
ABL.	ipsō	ipsā	ipsō	ipsīs	ipsīs	ipsīs

—— ACTIVITĀS ——

A. Look at the picture. The name of the object is scrambled. Unscramble the letters and write out the Latin name:

1. _____

2. _____

3. _____

4. _____

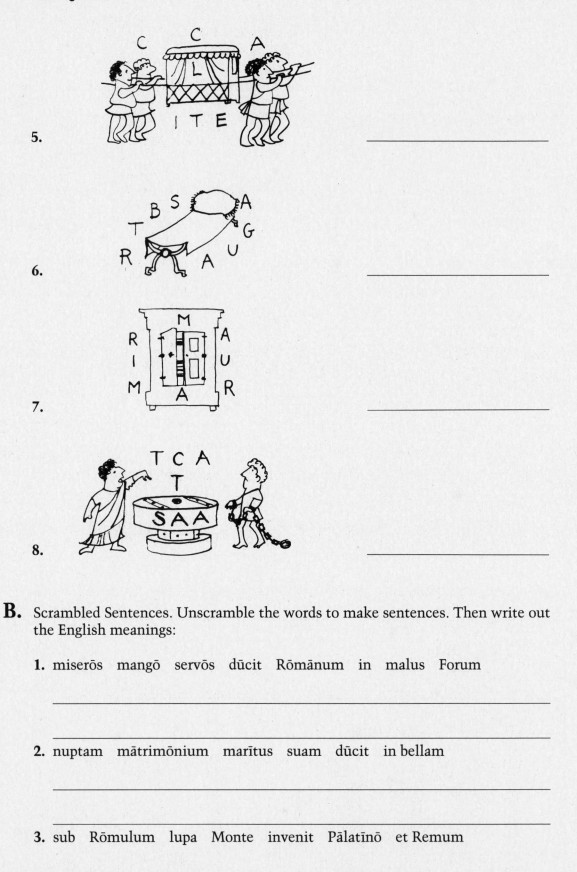

5. _____

6. _____

7. _____

8. _____

B. Scrambled Sentences. Unscramble the words to make sentences. Then write out the English meanings:

1. miserōs mangō servōs dūcit Rōmānum in malus Forum

_____

_____

2. nuptam mātrimōnium marītus suam dūcit in bellam

_____

_____

3. sub Rōmulum lupa Monte invenit Pālatīnō et Remum

_____

_____

4. grave gladiātor suum monstrāvit medicō vulnus

_____

_____

5. īvit Appiam in familia raedā tōta Viam novā per

_____

_____

6. senātōrem sex in portābunt gestātōriā servī sellā

_____

_____

C. Each group of words below belongs to the same _grammatical_ category (for example, all verbs, all ablatives, all nouns) except for one of the words in each group. Find the _grammatical_ misfit in each group and cross it out. Write the grammatical category of each group (adverbs, conjunctions, ablative nouns, etc.) in the space provided:

  1. insecta, scūta, terra, animālia, cubita   _____

  2. bene, deinde, ipse, saepe, rapidē   _____

  3. quī, quod, quae, quibus, quia   _____

  4. pistor, miser, mons, homō, augur   _____

  5. ille, haec, istud, hōc, autem   _____

  6. dīcit, movēbit, dūcet, accipiet, ambulābit   _____

  7. velle, nōlle, ferre, fonte, īre   _____

  8. condō, conjiciō, subitō, nōminō, veniō   _____

  9. puellam, dīcam, nuptam, arēnam, amphoram   _____

10. propter, quamquam, antequam, sī, dōnec   _____

11. cum, prope, inter, propter, sed   _____

12. fortiter, acriter, iter, celeriter, fidēliter   _____

13. bonum, parvum, tergum, tumidum, frīgidum   _____

14. aut, et, sed, -que, est   _____

15. nunc, mox, hōra, herī, hodiē   _____

D. Word Search. Hidden in the puzzle are the names of 22 things and places that a Roman would see or use when traveling down the Appian Way. First write the Latin words in the blank below. Then find and circle the words in the puzzle from left to right, right to left, up or down, or diagonally:

1. carriage _____

2. cart _____

3. chariot _____

4. coachman _____

5. horse _____

6. inn _____

7. innkeeper _____

8. litter _____

9. mule _____

10. ox _____

11. road _____

12. sea _____

13. spoke _____

14. town on Appian Way _____

15. town on Appian Way _____

16. town on Appian Way _____

17. traveler _____

18. trip _____

19. two-wheeled carriage _____

20. wagon _____

21. wheel _____

22. women's carriage _____

```
M  A  C  I  T  C  E  L  C  K  R
U  S  A  S  A  S  A  S  A  S  A
I  B  O  U  U  S  U  A  R  P  E
S  B  P  L  U  R  F  R  P  L  D
I  A  U  I  R  E  U  I  E  A  A
C  M  D  U  C  Q  N  C  N  U  R
V  A  C  S  A  U  D  I  T  S  I
R  I  U  L  U  U  I  A  U  T  U
R  A  A  P  P  S  X  X  M  R  S
V  O  E  T  O  C  A  R  R  U  S
H  I  T  D  O  N  E  R  A  M  U
S  S  A  A  A  R  A  I  T  E  R
```

E. From the list in the right column, choose the word that belongs to the same category of each numbered group and write its matching letter in the space provided:

1. nupta	pompa	marītus	prōnuba	_____	a. Rōmulus
					b. frons
2. raeda	cisium	carpentum	lectīca	_____	c. taeda
					d. grabātus
3. unguis	calx	umerus	spīna	_____	e. pānis
					f. plaustrum
4. Arīcia	Bovillae	Formiae	Terracīna	_____	g. bōs
					h. genu
5. mangō	catasta	manicae	titulus	_____	i. servus
					j. Fundī
6. tempus	planta	femur	articulus	_____	
7. mola	frūmentum	farīna	furnus	_____	
8. Laurentia	Palātīnus	Faustulus	lupa	_____	
9. armārium	mensa	candēlābrum	sella	_____	
10. mulus	mannus	equus	asinus	_____	

F. Cruciverbilūsus:

HORIZONTALE

1. marriage
7. from, by
9. you (*acc. sing.*)
10. for (*conj.*)
11. often
12. he was going
13. elbows
14. father
17. or

18. alone
19. and
20. senate building
22. thigh
24. spear
26. you are
28. heavy (*neuter*)
29. daggers (*acc.*)

30. they (*fem. pl.*)
31. shepherds
33. happy
36. it will be
37. mule
38. round shield
41. beaver
42. roads

PERPENDICULARE

1. slave dealers
2. temples
3. insect
4. wedding
5. as, when
6. my (*masc.*)
7. animals
8. mother
14. gates

15. your (*fem. sing.*)
16. you are
20. revolving auction block
21. spider
23. city
25. three
26. they (*masc.*)
27. oblong shield

28. sword
29. her own (*fem. sing.*)
32. Rome
33. wolf (*f.*)
34. himself
35. because
39. back, again (*prefix*)
40. I give

G. The Latin Connection. Some of the following English words you may never have seen before, but if you know their Latin origin, you should have a pretty good idea of their meaning. For each of the English words, give a Latin word from which it is derived. Sometimes the English word is derived from two Latin words. If you can, give both Latin words:

1. pacify _____
2. unify _____
3. solitaire _____
4. unanimous _____
5. unison _____
6. unicycle _____
7. unilingual _____
8. education _____
9. nutrition _____
10. nominal _____
11. valediction _____
12. digital _____
13. cubit _____
14. genuflect _____
15. total _____
16. sole _____
17. cell _____
18. dolorous _____
19. sinister _____
20. partial _____

21. pastoral _____
22. vocal _____
23. title _____
24. dominate _____
25. molar _____
26. valve _____
27. circumstantial _____
28. lacrimose _____
29. servile _____
30. cook _____
31. repugnant _____
32. convention _____
33. deterrent _____
34. timorous _____
35. rotation _____
36. radiate _____
37. amorous _____
38. Montana _____
39. unique _____
40. nuptials _____

H. Here are nine definitions. Fill in the missing word. Be sure that the noun is in the correct case. Then write the complete definition under the proper picture:

Quī _____ coquit est pistor.

Quī _____ agitat (*drives*) est raedārius.

Quī _____ agitat est aurīga.

Quī _____ pascit est pastor.

Quī _____ cūrat est medicus.

Quī _____ adpōnit est caupō.

Quī _____ venditat est mangō.

Quī _____ in mātrimōnium dūcit est marītus.

Quī _____ cantat est tībīcen.

1. _____

2. _____

3. _____

4. _____

5. _____

6. _____

7. _____

8. _____

9. _____

I. Antonyms. One way of showing your command of Latin vocabulary is to provide opposites. For each of the Latin words listed below, give the Latin opposite:

1. ad _____
2. aestās _____
3. inimīcus _____
4. anteā _____
5. malus _____
6. sine _____
7. nox _____
8. accipĕre _____
9. ex _____
10. mītis _____
11. grandis _____
12. lentus _____
13. longus _____
14. pax _____
15. magnus _____

16. vetus _____
17. calidus _____
18. ille _____
19. minimus _____
20. optimus _____
21. postquam _____
22. salvē! _____
23. marītus _____
24. vir _____
25. audax _____
26. difficilis _____
27. sinister _____
28. laetus _____
29. vērus _____
30. claudĕre _____

J. Synonyms. Another way of showing your command of Latin vocabulary is to produce synonyms, words that have the same meaning. For each of the following Latin words, provide a Latin synonym:

1. lentus _____
2. vēlox _____
3. validus _____
4. fortasse _____
5. propter _____

6. frequenter _____
7. atque _____
8. laetus _____
9. grandis _____
10. pariēs _____

PARS

TERTIA

XI *Perseus*

Passive Voice: Present, Imperfect, Future

1 Modicum cultūrae

Roman children were just as fascinated as modern children by stories about heroes who are bigger than life and can perform fantastic feats that no ordinary person can perform. Our modern Superman is just the latest in a long line of such heroes that go back to Greek and Roman times and even beyond. In fact, it was the lively imagination of the Greeks that was responsible for most of the stories of heroes that the Romans later adopted.

Hercules could qualify as Superman, even though he never flew through the air. He was sent on twelve missions impossible in which he regularly risked his life for the good of others. His only weapon was a big club. On one mission, he had to kill a lion; on another, he had to tame man-eating horses. But his toughest mission was to go down to the realm of the dead to bring back alive the three-headed hound of the Underworld, Cerberus. The great number of statues of Hercules that have been discovered all over the Mediterranean world is proof of his immense popularity. Even the Roman emperor Commodus had statues made of himself in the guise of Hercules.

But another hero, Perseus, comes closer to our idea of Superman. Mercury, the winged messenger of the gods, gave Perseus winged sandals so that he could soar through the air. Pluto, the god of the dead, gave him a magical winged helmet that made him invisible whenever he chose, and, as we will see, he acquired the means of turning people and animals to stone. Mercury gave him a curved magical sword, with which he always succeeds in killing his foes. Most heroes, Perseus included, were the sons of gods and often human mothers. Jupiter was the father of Perseus, and a Greek princess, Danaë, was his mother. Perseus was famous for two great feats: cutting off the head of Medusa and rescuing the princess Andromeda from a sea monster as she was chained to a cliff overlooking the sea.

The ancients found it hard to imagine that such supermen as Hercules and Perseus could simply die like ordinary mortals, and so they invented the story that these heroes were taken up to heaven to become constellations. You will need a good deal of imagination, however, to identify them in the sky, since only a few stars make up each constellation.

2 Vocābula

Perseus -ī m

parma -ae f

galea -ae f

solea -ae f

Gorgonēs -um f pl

Medūsa -ae f

Perseus -ī m

Cētus -ī m

Andromeda -ae f

Rēx Cēpheus -ī m

Rēgīna Cassiopēa -ae f

— ACTIVITĀS

A. Match the descriptions with the pictures:

Perseus in speculum spectat.
Solea ālās habet.
Perseus per aërem volat.
Galea ālās habet.

Perseus galeam induit.
Cētus est monstrum marīnum.
Gladius est curvus.
Perseus soleās induit.

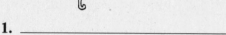

1. _____ .

2. _____ .

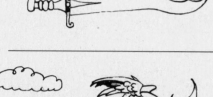

3. _____ .

4. _____ .

5. _____ .

6. _____ .

7. _____ .

8. _____ .

3. So far all the verbs have been in the active voice. When is a verb in the active voice? When the subject is the person or thing that does the action. But if the subject *receives* the action of the verb, we say that the verb is PASSIVE or in the passive voice. Look at the following pictures and you will see the difference between the active and passive voice. Note the changes in the Latin verb:

1. **Manūs meās** *lavō*.

Ego ā mātre meā *lavor*.

2. **Āthlētam** *salūtāmus*.

Ab āthlētā *salūtāmur*.

3. **Vulpēs cunīculum** *petit*.

Vulpēs ā leopardō *petitur*.

4. **Puerī canem** *petunt*.

Puerī ā cane *petuntur*.

Look at the first sentence. Which letter was added to **lavō** to form the passive?

_____ Now look at the second sentence, in which the verb is plural. To which

letter was the **s** in the ending changed to form the passive? _____ In the third
sentence the active verb in the third person singular is **petit** (*chases*). Which

letters were added to form the passive voice? _____ In the fourth sentence the
active verb in the third person plural is **petunt** (*they are chasing*). Which letters

were added to form the passive voice? _____

The verbs in the first two sentences belong to the **-āre** family of verbs; the verbs
of the last two sentences belong to the **-ĕre** family of verbs. In fact, the method
of changing the verbs from the present active to the present passive is always
the same, no matter to which family the verb belongs:

-ō	changes to **-or**	**-mus**	changes to **-mur**
-t	changes to **-tur**	**-nt**	changes to **-ntur**

Now look over the sentences above that have passive verbs. What preposition

occurs in them? _____ Which case does this preposition always take?

_____ This preposition tells "by whom" the action was
done. This case is called the ablative of personal agency. It is also often used
with animals: **ā cane** (*by a dog*).

4 Here's a story of the superman Perseus in action. Note in particular the passive
verbs in bold type:

Perseus erat fīlius Jovis; ejus māter erat Danaē.
Māter et fīlius in insulā Serīphō habitābant, in quā
Polydectēs erat rex. Danaē ā Polydectē **adamābātur,**
sed Danaē rēgem nōn amābat. Rex vērō eam in
mātrimōnium dūcĕre cupiēbat. Hōc consilium
autem neque mātrī neque fīliō placuit. Quamquam
māter ā rēge **adamābātur,** fīlius ā rēge **timēbātur.**

Danaē *-ēs f Greek female
name (acc:* **Danaēn**)
Polydectēs *-ae m Greek
male name (acc:*
Polydectēn)
adamō *-āre to love deeply*
vērō *in fact*
cupiō *-ĕre -īvī* (*or* *-iī*) *to wish*
cōnsilium *-ī n idea, plan*

Rex autem Perseum dīmittĕre cupiēbat. Itaque rex
constituit mittĕre eum in iter longinquum et perīculōsum. Rex Perseum ad sē vocāvit et dixit: "Abī
hinc ad terram longinquam, in quā Medūsa habitat.
Necā Medūsam et caput ejus ad mē reportā."

dīmittō *-ĕre* **dīmīsī** *to get rid
of*
longinquus *-a -um far-away,
distant*
abī hinc! *go (from here)!*
reportō *-āre to bring back*

Medūsa autem, sīcut suae duae sorōrēs, erant monstra horribilia, et Gorgōnēs **vocābantur.** Serpentēs in locō comae habēbant. Quīcumque faciem Medūsae aspiciēbat, statim in saxum **mūtābātur.**

Antequam Perseus discessit, Plūtō, deus inferōrum, galeam magicam eī dedit. Per hanc galeam magicam Perseus **reddēbātur** invīsibilis. Mercurius eī soleās ālātās dedit, quibus per aërem volāre poterat. Apollo magicum gladium curvum eī dedit, quō Medūsam necāre poterat. Minerva parmam speculārem eī dedit et dixit: "Nōlī aspicĕre Medūsam nisi per hanc speculārem parmam. In memoriā tenē: quīcumque faciem Medūsae aspiciet, in saxum **mūtābitur.**"

Perseus deinde soleās ālātās pedibus nexit et in aërem ascendit. Diū per caelum volāvit, dōnec ad eum locum pervēnit, in quō Medūsa cum cēterīs Gorgōnibus dormiēbat.

Perseus, in parmam speculārem inspiciens, Medūsae caput gladiō curvō magicō dētruncāvit. Cēterae Gorgōnēs statim ē somnō **excitābantur** et Perseum oppugnābant.

Perseus autem galeam magicam citō induit et in caelum ascendit, et caput Medūsae ad aulam Polydectae reportāvit. Rex malus id avidē aspexit et statim in saxum **mūtābātur.** Māter ejus, ex aulā currens, Perseum magnō cum gaudiō excēpit. "Mī fīlī," inquit māter lacrimans, "ego a rēge malō diū terrēbar. Nunc ā tē **servor.** Dēnique fēlīciter vīvĕre poterimus."

sīcut *like*
Gorgō -ōnis *f Gorgon*
in locō (+ *gen*) *in place of, instead of*
quīcumque quaecumque *whoever;* **quodcumque** *whatever*
aspiciō -ĕre aspexī aspectus *to look at*
discēdō -ĕre discessī *to leave, depart*
inferī -ōrum *mpl the dead, the underworld*
reddō -ĕre -idī *to render, make*
ālātus -a -um *winged*
speculāris -is -e *mirrorlike, shiny*
nisi *except*
in memoriā tenēre *to remember, keep in mind*

nectō -ĕre nexī *to tie*
dōnec *until*
cēterī -ae -a *the remaining, the rest of*

inspiciō -ĕre inspexī *to look into*
dētruncō -āre *to cut off*
somnus -ī *m sleep*
excitō -āre *to awaken*
oppugnō -āre *to attack*

aula -ae *f palace*
avidē *eagerly*

gaudium -ī *n joy*
excipiō -ĕre excēpī *to welcome*
dēnique *at last*

___ ACTIVITĀS ___

B. Respondē ad quaestiōnēs:

1. Quis erat pater Perseī?

2. Quod nōmen erat mātrī?

3. Ubi habitābant māter et fīlius?

_____

4. Quot sorōrēs habuit Medūsa?

_____

5. Quid est Gorgō?

_____

6. Quid Gorgōnēs in locō comae habēbant?

_____

7. Quid Perseum invīsibilem reddidit?

_____

8. Quī deus soleās ālātās Perseō dedit?

_____

9. Quid Apollo Perseō dedit?

_____

10. Quis dedit Perseō parmam speculārem?

_____

 Let's look at the active and passive forms of a verb of the **-āre** family in the present, imperfect, and future tenses. To keep things simple, we won't bother with the second person because the first and third persons of the verb occur much more frequently and should be learned first:

		ACTIVE		PASSIVE
PRESENT:	**vocō**	_I am calling, I call_	**vocor**	_I am called_
	vocat	_he/she/it is calling_	**vocātur**	_he/she/it is called_
	vocāmus	_we are calling_	**vocāmur**	_we are called_
	vocant	_they are calling_	**vocantur**	_they are called_
IMPERFECT:	**vocābam**	_I was calling, I called_	**vocābar**	_I was called_
	vocābat	_he/she/it was calling_	**vocābātur**	_he/she/it was called_
	vocābāmus	_we were calling_	**vocābāmur**	_we were called_
	vocābant	_they were calling_	**vocābantur**	_they were called_
FUTURE:	**vocābō**	_I will call_	**vocābor**	_I will be called_
	vocābit	_he/she/it will call_	**vocābitur**	_he/she/it will be called_
	vocābimus	_we will call_	**vocābimur**	_we will be called_
	vocābunt	_they will call_	**vocābuntur**	_they will be called_

ACTIVITĀTĒS

C. Here are the active forms of **mittĕre** (*to send*). Supply the corresponding passive forms. Remember that, as with the verb **vocāre, -o** changes to **-or, -mus** changes to **-mur, -t** changes to **-tur, -nt** changes to **-ntur:**

	ACTIVE	PASSIVE
PRESENT:	mittō	_____
	mittit	_____
	mittimus	_____
	mittunt	_____
IMPERFECT:	mittēbam	_____
	mittēbat	_____
	mittēbāmus	_____
	mittēbant	_____
FUTURE:	mittam	_____
	mittet	_____
	mittēmus	_____
	mittent	_____

6 You had seen earlier that, when the sentence has a passive verb, you can expect to find that the person (or animal) by whom the action is done is in the ablative case with the preposition **ā** or **ab:**

Medūsa *ā Perseō* necābitur.   *Medusa will be killed by Perseus.*

But if the action is done by means of something, no preposition is used:

Medūsa *gladiō curvō* necābitur.   *Medusa will be killed with a curved sword.*

— ACTIVITĀTĒS —

D. In the following sentences, distinguish between the ablative of personal agency, which requires the preposition **ā** or **ab,** and the ablative of means or instrument. Underline the correct phrase in parentheses:

1. Perseus (galeā magicā / ā galeā magicā) invīsibilis redditur.
2. Danaē (rēge malō / ā rēge malō) adamābātur.
3. Multī (ā Medūsae capite / Medūsae capite) in saxum mūtābantur.
4. Galea magica (Perseō / ā Perseō) gestātur.
5. Ego (ā Gorgōnibus / Gorgōnibus) facile terreor.
6. Perseus (ā rēge Polydectē / rēge Polydectē) magnopere timēbātur.
7. Medūsa et sorōrēs (multīs / ā multīs) Gorgōnēs vocantur.
8. Nōs omnēs (parentibus nostrīs / ā parentibus nostrīs) amāmur.

E. Convert the following sentences from the passive to the active. The object of the preposition will become the subject of the active sentence:

> EXAMPLE: Galea magica ā **Perseō** gestābātur.
> **Perseus** galeam magicam gestābat.

1. Perseus ā rēge in terram longinquam mittēbātur.

_____

2. Medūsa ā Perseō dētruncābātur.

_____

3. Medūsa propter superbiam suam ā Minervā in puellam dēformem (*ugly*) mūtābātur.

_____

4. Perseus et Danaē ab Acrisiō in insulam Serīphum mittēbantur.

_____

5. Caput Medūsae ā Perseō ad aulam Polydectae reportābātur.

_____

6. "Cūr tantum ā rēge Polydectē timeor?" rogāvit Perseus.

_____

7. Raeda nostra ā raedāriō optimō agitātur.

_____

8. Cibus bonus nōbīs ab illō caupōne adpōnitur.

_____

F. Convert the following sentences from the active to the passive. The direct object of the active sentence becomes the subject of the passive sentence, and the subject of the active sentence becomes the object of the preposition ā or **ab** or the instrumental ablative:

> EXAMPLE: Spectātōrēs **gladiātōrem** victōrem laudant.
> **Gladiātor** victor ā spectātōribus laudātur.

1. Perseus mātrem maximē amat.

_____

2. Perseus Medūsam dormientem necābit.

_____

3. Gorgōnēs Perseum oppugnābant.

_____

4. Māter nōs ē somnō māne excitābit.

_____

5. Serpentēs suprā Medūsae caput Perseum nōn terrent.

_____

6. Quis Perseum in terram longinquam mittet?

_____

7. Perseus speculum ante sē tenēbat.

_____

8. Fābulae dē Perseō mē semper dēlectant.

_____

G. Here's a description of several things going on right now. Say that the same things used to happen in the past by changing the sentences to the imperfect tense:

1. Aqua ab Aquāriō portātur.

_____

2. Aegrī ā medicō cūrantur.

_____

3. Vulnera rētiāriī ā medicō sānantur.

_____

4. Oculī meī fūmō inflammantur.

_____

5. Ego et Claudius ab avō et aviā ēducāmur.

_____

6. Haec medicīna ab aegrīs nōn sumitur.

_____

7. Ego ā magistrīs meīs semper attentē (*closely*) observor.

_____

8. Futūra ab auguribus Rōmānīs praedīcuntur.

_____

H. You are reminiscing with a friend about your childhood. Complete the following sentences with the correct passive imperfect form of the verb in parentheses:

1. (amāre) Ego ā parentibus semper _____ .

2. (dēfendĕre) Ego ā frātre majōre nātū interdum _____ .

3. (verberāre) Ego et frātrēs meī ā parentibus numquam _____ .

4. (addūcĕre) Ego et soror mea ad thermās ā mātre _____ .

5. (docēre) Ego ā magistrīs optimīs Latīnē _____ .

6. (vīsitāre) Multa oppida inter Rōmam et Capuam ā familiā meā _____ .

7. (narrāre) Multae fābulae dē Perseō ā patre mihi _____ .

8. (lavāre) Quandō infans eram, ego ā mātre cōtīdiē _____ .

I. Here are some things that happened in the past. You can become a great astrologer predicting that they will happen in the future by simply converting the verb of each statement from the imperfect to the future. But be careful. The future tense of the last four verbs is formed differently from the first four:

1. Duodecim vulturēs ā Rōmulō observābantur. _____

2. Urbs nova ā Rōmulō aedificābātur. _____

3. Urbs Rōma ā multīs aliēnīs vīsitābātur. _____

4. Ego prīmā lūce ē somnō excitābar. _____

5. Multa verba ā senātōribus in cūriā dīcēbantur. _____

6. Vox actōris per theātrum audiēbātur. _____

7. Medūsa et sorōrēs ā Perseō vincēbantur. _____

8. Ego et frāter meus ab aviā magnō cum gaudiō excipiēbāmur. _____

7 Now see how simple it is to learn the passive infinitive form. All you have to do is change the final **-e** to **-i:**

ACTIVE		PASSIVE	
portāre	to carry	**portārī**	to be carried
movēre	to move	**movērī**	to be moved
dūcĕre	to lead	**dūcī**	to be led
accipĕre	to receive	**accipī**	to be received
audīre	to hear	**audīrī**	to be heard

Did you notice that the passive infinitive of the **-ĕre** family of verbs and of the **-iō** family of verbs omits two letters? Which two letters were omitted in **dūcī**

and **accipī?** _____

__ ACTIVITĀTĒS _____

J. Form the active and passive infinitives of the following verbs:

1. amō   _____   _____

2. adjuvō   _____   _____

3. terreō   _____   _____

4. respondeō   _____   _____

5. scrībō   _____   _____

6. gerō   _____   _____

7. aspiciō   _____   _____

8. incipiō   _____   _____

9. mūniō   _____   _____

10. fīniō   _____   _____

K. Read over the following sentences. The sense will suggest which infinitive in parentheses is appropriate in each sentence. Underline the correct infinitive. Note that **videor** may mean *I am seen* but much more frequently means *I seem*:

1. Danaē ā rēge Polydectē (amāre/amārī) vidēbātur.
2. Caput Medūsae hominēs in saxum (mūtāre/mūtārī) poterat.
3. Gorgōnēs serpentēs in locō comae (habēre/habērī) dīcuntur.
4. Rex Polydectēs Perseum (dīmittĕre/dīmittī) cupīvit.
5. Gorgōnēs ā Perseō ē somnō (excitāre/excitārī) vidēbantur.
6. Perseus ā Gorgōnibus (oppugnāre/oppugnārī) dīcēbātur.
7. Perseus Medūsam (aspicĕre/aspicī) nōn poterat nisi per speculum.
8. Via Appia ab Appiō Claudiō Caecō (mūnīre/mūnīrī) dīcitur.

 Now let's read more about the adventures of Perseus. Passive verbs are in bold type:

Perseus, postquam Medūsam obtruncāvit et mātrem suam servāvit, per aërem volans, ad Aethiopiam vēnit ubi Cēpheus erat rex. Hīc rex fīliam bellissimam habēbat, quae Andromeda **vocābātur.** Rēgīna, quae Cassiopēa **vocābātur,** ōlim dē pulchritūdine fīliae suae sē jactāverat. Quōdam diē, dum rēgīna Cassiopēa et fīlia sua in orā maritimā stābant, māter dixit: "In aquā, mea fīlia, multae nymphae pulchrae habitant, sed tū es multō pulchrior quam omnēs istae nymphae."

Aethiopia *-ae f Ethiopia*

ōlim *once*
  pulchritūdō *-inis f beauty*
sē jactāre dē *(+ abl) to boast about*
  dum *while*

Subitō Neptūnus, hīs verbīs irātus, ex aquā surrexit et magnā vōce clāmāvit: "Ob hanc superbiam, sacrificium postulō. Necte fīliam tuam scopulō prope mare. Cētum, monstrum marīnum, mittam. Hōc mōnstrum fīliam tuam dēvorābit. Fīlia ā tē nōn **servābitur.** Neque ā patre suō **servābitur.**"

surgō *-ĕre* **surrexī** *to rise*
magnus *-a -um loud*
postulō *-āre to demand*
  scopulus *-ī m cliff*
marīnus *-a -um (of the) sea*
dēvorō *-āre to devour*

Itaque Andromeda ā servīs rēgis scopulō prope mare **nectēbātur,** dum Cēpheus et Cassiopēa et populus inopēs circumstābant. Cētus jam orae maritimae appropinquābat, cum subitō Perseus, per aërem volans, puellam trementem conspicuit. Omnēs in orā maritimā oculōs in puerum volantem convertērunt. Tamquam fulmen, Perseus dē caelō dēscendit et cētum gladiō magicō oppugnāvit. Ter Perseus corpus monstrī gladiō suō perfōdit. Ter cētus magnā vōce fremuit. Omnēs circumstantēs tremuērunt. Sed Per-

inopēs *helplessly*
appropinquō *-āre (+ dat) to approach*
tremō *-ĕre -uī to tremble*
  conspiciō *-ĕre* **conspexī** *to spot*
oculōs convertĕre in *(+ acc) to turn (the eyes on)*
tamquam *like*
  fulmen *-inis n lightning*
ter *three times*
fremō *-ĕre -uī to roar*

seus sōlus ā monstrō nōn **terrēbātur.** Iterum atque iterum Perseus cētum gladiō suō perfōdit. Dēnique Perseus monstrum necāvit et Andromedam līberāvit. Rex Perseō dixit: "Quia tū sōlus fīliam bellissimam servāvit, ego eam tibi in mātrimōnium dabō." Omnēs deinde ad aulam īvērunt, ubi Perseus Andromedam in mātrimōnium duxit.

iterum *again*

līberō *-āre to free*

Post multōs annōs, rex Cēpheus et rēgīna Cassiopēa et Andromeda et Perseus et cētus in constellātiōnēs **convertēbantur.** Etiam nunc eōs in caelō vidēre possumus.

L. Respondē ad quaestiōnēs:

1. Quōmodo Perseus ad Aethiopiam vēnit?

2. Quis erat rex Aethiopiae?

3. Quis erat rēgīna Aethiopiae?

4. Dē quō Cassiopēa sē jactāverat?

5. Quem deum Cassiopēa hīs verbīs offendit?

6. Quid Neptūnus ob Cassiopēae superbiam postulāvit?

7. Quid mīsit Neptūnus ex marī?

8. Ubi Andromeda nectēbātur?

9. Quis Andromedam Perseō in mātrimōnium dedit?

10. Ubi Cēpheum et Cassiopēam et Andromedam et Perseum et cētum vidēre possumus?

DIALOGUS

Vocābula

avē *hello*
quamobrem *why*
fīō *I become*
plānē *clearly, plainly*
forte *by chance*
sī forte vidēbō *if I happen to see*

certē *without fail*
blatta *-ae* f *cockroach*
nequīrēs *you couldn't*
continuō *continuously*
continuō inspicĕre *to keep looking into*
dīrectē *directly*

RĒS PERSŌNĀLĒS

A. List four things in Latin that happened to you in the past, using the passive voice:

EXAMPLE: Ego ab amīcīs adjuvābar. *I was helped by my friends.*

1. _____

2. _____

3. _____

4. _____

B. Name three persons who are your heroes and give the reasons why:

1. _____

2. _____

3. _____

COMPOSITIŌ

You have read about the adventures of Perseus and saw what kind of Superman (**Supervir -virī** *m*) he was and what he could do. Describe the physical appearance of modern Superman and explain what he is able to do:

_____

_____

_____

_____

_____

_____

COLLOQUIUM

Complete this dialog with expressions based on the previous conversation, substituting your own expressions wherever you can:

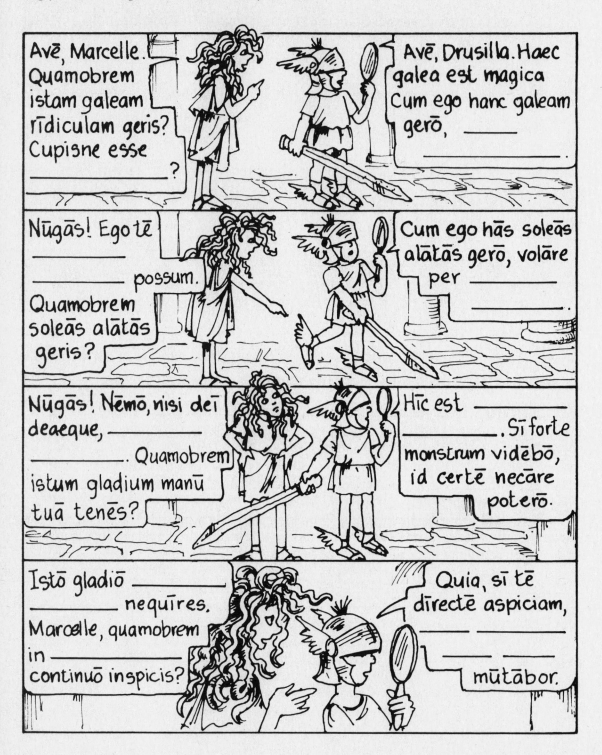

THE LATIN CONNECTION

A. What does the expression **et cetera** mean? _____

B. What is the common abbreviation for **et cetera?** _____

C. **Somnus** means *sleep*. What does a person suffer from who suffers from insomnia?

_____

D. The Latin suffix **-ficāre** means *to make, to cause* and is used in such combinations as **aedificāre** (*to make a building*), **sacrificāre** (*to make sacred*). The suffix **-ficāre** shows up in English as the suffix *-fy*, as in *sanctify* (to make holy), from **sanctus** (*holy*) and **-ficāre** (*to make*). Divide the following verbs into their parts and then give the meanings:

EXAMPLE: sanctify   **sanctus** *(holy)*   *to make holy*

1. deify _____ _____

2. diversify _____ _____

3. falsify _____ _____

4. fortify _____ _____

5. justify _____ _____

6. magnify _____ _____

7. nullify _____ _____

8. pacify _____ _____

9. personify _____ _____

10. simplify _____ _____

11. unify _____ _____

12. verify _____ _____

Your teacher will ask you to use each verb in a sentence to make sure that you know how to use it correctly.

XII _Tempestās_

Perfect and Pluperfect Passive; Deponent Verbs

1 Modicum cultūrae

Nowadays we rely on weather forecasts on television and radio and in the newspapers to plan our activities. The Romans, however, had to observe nature closely to obtain clues about the weather (**tempestās -ātis** _f_). Since farming and sailing were two important occupations and since success in both depended on knowledge of the weather, the Romans eagerly built up a body of weather lore, which they passed on from generation to generation. The rising and setting of various stars and constellations indicated to the sailors the beginning and end of the sailing season and the approach of storms at sea. They indicated to the farmers when to plow, sow, and harvest crops. The average Roman farmer and sailor probably knew more about astronomy than the average person knows today.

As you might expect, they attributed changes in the weather to the gods. Thus, Jupiter was the god of thunder, lightning, and rain. Iris was the goddess of the rainbow, and Aeolus was the god of the winds. In fact, the Romans did not look upon the stars as inanimate objects; they populated the skies with mythological persons and animals. In the last chapter you read how Perseus, Andromeda, Cepheus, Cassiopea, and even Cetus and Medusa's head wound up as constellations. You have learned before that the planets were identified with Roman gods. (How many of them do you remember?) And you saw in Lesson III that the twelve signs of the zodiac have Latin names. In fact, all eighty-eight constellations in the Northern Hemisphere have Latin names.

Did you know that, some 1500 years before Columbus, the Greeks and Romans knew that the earth was round and revolved around its own axis in twenty-four hours? One astronomer even figured out the circumference of the earth and divided the earth into the torrid, temperate, and frigid zones.

2 Vocābula

ventus -ī m

fulmen -inis n

nix, nivis f

grandō -inis m

imber -bris m

pluvius arcus -ūs m

glaciēs -ēī f

pila nivea -ae f

stīria -ae f

ACTIVITĀTĒS

A. Match the descriptions with the pictures:

Stīriae dē tectō dēpendent.
Pluvius arcus multōs colōrēs
   habet.
Ventus vehementer flat.
Puer in glaciē cadit.
Puerī virum ex nive faciunt.

Grandō in puerī caput cadit.
Puellae pilās niveās conjiciunt.
Fulmen inter nūbēs coruscat
   (*flashes*).
Imber dē caelō cadit.

1. _____

2. _____

3. _____

4. _____

5. _____

6. _____

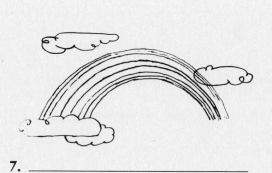

7. _____

8. _____

9. _____

B. There are certain impersonal verbs that we use in describing the weather. See whether you can figure out the meanings of the Latin verbs by looking at the pictures they describe:

1. Pluit.

2. Ningit.

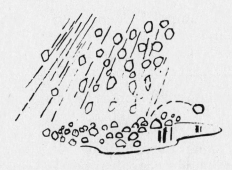

3. Grandinat.

4. Fulminat.

Now that you are familiar with the passive voice of verbs in the present, imperfect, and future tenses, let's learn the passive forms of the other two tenses: the perfect and the pluperfect.

Before we do that, we must look at the principal parts of verbs. Until now you have dealt with the first three principal parts of verbs:

> **portō**   *I carry, am carrying*
> **portāre**   *to carry*
> **portāvī**   *I carried, have carried*

There is a fourth principal part, called the PAST PASSIVE PARTICIPLE: **portātus -a -um**, which means *carried* or *having been carried*.

— ACTIVITĀS

C. Write out all four principal parts of the following verbs. They all go like **portō:**

EXAMPLE: portō   portāre   portāvī   portātus

1. amō   _____   _____   _____

2. optō   _____   _____   _____

3. vocō   _____   _____   _____

4. salūtō   _____   _____   _____

Very good! The formation of the principal parts of the **-āre** family of verbs is regular. But the principal parts of other verbs are not quite so regular. From now on, you will learn the principal parts of all verbs.

Now we can form the perfect passive tense. It consists of the perfect participle plus the present tense forms of **sum:**

portātus sum	*I was carried*	**portātī sumus**	*we were carried*
portātus es	*you were carried*	**portātī estis**	*you were carried*
portātus est	*he was carried*	**portātī sunt**	*they were carried*

> PITFALL: Don't confuse the auxiliary verb **sum** with **sum** as the main verb of a sentence:
>
> **Ego bonus *sum*.**   *I am good.*   (**Sum** is the main verb.)
> **Ego vocātus *sum*.**   *I was summoned.*   (**Sum** is the auxiliary verb.)

The pluperfect passive tense consists of the past participle plus the imperfect tense of **sum:**

portātus eram	*I had been carried*	**portātī erāmus**	*we had been carried*
portātus erās	*you had been carried*	**portātī erātis**	*you had been carried*
portātus erat	*he had been carried*	**portātī erant**	*they had been carried*

Actually, the participle has three endings just like the adjective **bonus -a -um**: **portā*tus* -a -um**. The subject of the sentence will determine which ending is to be used in the participle:

Andromeda ā Perseō līberāt*a* est.	*Andromeda was freed by Perseus.*
Monstrum marīn*um* ā Perseō necātum erat.	*A sea monster had been killed by Perseus.*
Hae trēs sorōrēs Gorgōnēs vocāt*ae* sunt.	*These three sisters were called Gorgons.*
Eīdem virī in lectīcā portātī erant.	*The same men had been carried in the litter.*

___ ACTIVITĀS _____

D. Change the following verbs from the perfect passive to the pluperfect passive:

1. Speculum ā Perseō manū sinistrā portātum est. _____.

2. Medūsa ā Perseō truncāta est. _____.

3. Ubi vulnerātī estis? _____.

4. Ego et soror in lectīcā portātī sumus. _____.

5. Ego ā patrē vocātus sum. _____.

6. Quamobrem tū ab omnibus amāta es? _____.

 As you read this story of a treasure hunt, you will come across several verbs in the perfect passive tense in bold type:

Erat diēs serēnus ultimā parte autumnī. Tempestās erat clāra. Sōl lūcēbat. Ego et amīcus Flaccus in ōrā maritimā ambulābāmus, cum Flaccus dixit: "Vidēsne illam insulam? Abhinc multōs annōs, thēsaurus vastus ā pīrātīs ibi **occultātus est** in cavernā sub scopulō. Vīsne ad insulam nāvigāre et thēsaurum quaerēre? Sī illum thēsaurum inveniē-mus, dīvitissimī erimus."

serēnus *-a -um calm, clear*
ultimus *-a -um last*
lūceō *-ēre* luxī *to shine*
abhinc *ago*
thēsaurus *-ī m treasure*
occultō *-āre to hide*
sub (+ *abl*) *at the foot of*

quaerō *-ere* quaesīvī quaesītus *to look for*

"Ita," ego respondī. Nāviculam Flaccī avidē conscendimus et vēla dedimus. Sed mox tempestās **mūtāta est.** Sōl nōn jam lūcēbat. Caelum nōn jam clārum sed nūbilum erat. Deinde imber cadĕre incēpit. Nōn sōlum pluit sed tonuit et fulmināvit. Ventī frīgidī ex septentriōnibus flābant. Propter imbrem et nebulam, neque ora neque insula conspicī poterat. Tonitrus ā nōbīs **audītus est** et fulmen **vīsum est.** Nāvicula fluctibus altīs **pulsāta est.**

"Dī superī," exclāmāvit Flaccus, "servāte nōs ā naufragiō."

Tunc maximē nāvis magna forte praeternāvigābat. Nāvicula nostra ā nāvis magistrō **conspecta est.** Ego et Flaccus dēnique **servātī sumus.**

"Cūr nāvigātis," interrogāvit nāvis magister, "cum pluit et tonat et fulminat? Haec tempestās est perīculōsa etiam nautīs."

"Nāvis magister," ego respondī, "quandō vēla dedimus, tempestās erat clāra. Neque pluēbat eō tempore neque tonābat neque fulminābat. Tantum posteā tempestās **mutāta est.**"

"Quō nāvigābātis?" interrogāvit nāvis magister.

"Ad insulam nōn procul abhinc, in quā ōlim thēsaurus vastus ā pīrātīs **occultātus erat.** Spēs nōbīs erat illum thēsaurum invenīre."

"Ille thēsaurus," rīdēbat nāvis magister, "jamprīdem **inventus est.** Ego ipse thesaurum in cavernā sub scopulō invēnī, et nunc ego divitissimus sum!"

conscendō -ĕre ī *to climb aboard*
vēla dare *to set sail*
mūtāta est *changed*
nūbilus -a -um *cloudy, overcast*
   cadō -ĕre cecidī casum *to fall*
incipiō -ĕre incēpī inceptus *to begin*
   tonō -āre -uī *to thunder*
   fulminō -āre *to lighten*
flō -āre *to blow*
nebula -ae *f fog, mist*
tonitrus -ūs *m thunder*
pulsō -āre *to batter, pound*
dī superī *gods above*
naufragium -ī *n shipwreck*
tunc maximē *just then*
   praeternāvigō -āre *to sail by*
(nāvis) magister -trī *m captain*

etiam *even*

tantum *only*

quō *where (to)*

nōn procul abhinc *not far from here*
spēs -ēī *f hope*

jamprīdem *long ago*

ACTIVITĀS

E. Respondē ad quaestiōnēs:

1. Ubi Flaccus et amīcus ambulābant?

2. Quid erat eōrum locus destinātus?

3. Quōmodo ad locum destinātum pervenīre (*reach*) cupiēbant?

_____

4. Quid in insulā occultātum erat?

_____

5. Ā quō occultātum erat?

_____

6. Quō tempore annī puerī nāvigāvērunt?

_____

7. Quālis (*what kind of*) tempestās erat quandō puerī vēla dedērunt?

_____

8. Cūr posteā neque ora neque insula conspicī poterat?

_____

9. Quid nāviculam pulsāvit?

_____

10. Ā quō puerī dēnique servātī sunt?

_____

If you take a Latin verb that is transitive (that is, it takes a direct object) and make it passive, it then can have an intransitive sense. For example, **lavāre** means *to wash* someone or something. If the Romans wanted to use it in an intransitive sense, they made the verb passive. You'll get the idea if you look at these pairs of sentences:

TRANSITIVE: **Manūs meās lavō.**   *I am washing my hands.*
INTRANSITIVE: **Nōn cotīdiē lavor.**   *I don't wash every day.*

TRANSITIVE: **Nāvis magister mentem mūtāvit.** *The captain changed his mind.*
INTRANSITIVE: **Tempestās repentē mutāta est.** *The weather suddenly changed.*

ACTIVITĀS

F. Do you think that you can tell the difference between a true passive verb and a passive verb that serves in an intransitive sense? Here's your chance. Mark the verbs in the following sentences as TRUE PASSIVE or INTRANSITIVE:

1. Infans ā mātre lavātur.   _____ _____

2. Āthlēta in tepidāriō lavātur. _____ _____

3. Sella ā servō mōta est.   _____ _____

4. Canis numquam mōtus est. _____ _____

5. Nix in imbrem mūtāta est. _____ _____

6. Omnia in nātūrā mūtantur. _____ _____

---

7 There are certain Latin verbs that are called DEPONENT VERBS, but it makes more sense to call them "fake passive verbs" because, although they have *passive* forms, they have *active* meanings. For example, **admīror** does NOT mean *I am admired* but *I admire*. Here are the principal parts of some very useful "fake passives":

admīror	**admīrārī**	**admīrātus sum**	*to admire*
conor	**conārī**	**conātus sum**	*to try*
videor	**vidērī**	**vīsus sum**	*to seem*
medeor (+ *dat*)	**medērī**	———	*to heal*
loquor	**loquī**	**locūtus sum**	*to speak*
nascor	**nascī**	**nātus sum**	*to be born*
sequor	**sequī**	**secūtus sum**	*to follow*
ūtor (+ *abl*)	**ūtī**	**ūsus sum**	*to use*
morior	**morī**	**mortuus sum**	*to die*
orior	**orīrī**	**ortus sum**	*to rise*

Notice that these verbs come from all families of verbs. As usual, those of the **-ĕre** family (**loquor, nascor, sequor, ūtor**) drop the letter **e** and **r** in the infinitive. **Morior** (*to die*) belongs to the **-iō** family of verbs and therefore also drops the **e** and **r** in the infinitive.

___ ACTIVITĀTĒS _____

G. To get used to the idea of seeing passive forms of verbs but understanding them in an active sense, give the English meanings of the following sentences:

1. Omnēs Perseum admīrantur. _____

2. Infans loquī conātur. _____

3. Hiems autumnum sequitur. _____

4. Rōmānī Latīnē locūtī sunt. _____

5. Senātor jūstus esse vidētur. _____

6. Sōl in oriente oritur. _____

7. Nōn cupiō morī. _____

8. Quot infantēs cōtīdiē nascuntur? _____

9. Pecūniā meā bene ūtor. _____

10. Medicī aegrīs medentur. _____

11. Quis tē secūtus est? _____

12. Quī Rōmae nascuntur, sunt Rōmānī. _____

H. Read over the following sentences carefully. Then convert the verb from the present to the pluperfect tense:

1. Omnēs Rōmānī Rōmulum admīrantur. _____

2. Omnēs līberī nivem cadentem admīrārī videntur. _____

3. Ego tē adjuvāre cōnor. _____

4. Gladiātōrēs gladiīs et ocreīs et scūtīs ūtuntur. _____

5. Sōl māne prīmā horā oritur. _____

6. Flōrēs hieme moriuntur. _____

7. Omnēs dē nive et glaciē loquuntur. _____

8. Frāterculus meus mē ubīque sequitur. _____

I. You are in a contrary mood today. Answer the following questions in the negative:

1. Dē tempestāte locūtus(-a) es?

_____

2. Amīcum tuum ad scholam herī secūtus(-a) es?

_____

3. Hodiēne magistram tuam admīrātus(-a) es?

_____

4. Cōnātus(-a) es cum amīcīs tuīs Latīnē loquī?

_____

5. Admīrātus(-a) es pluvium arcum post imbrem?

_____

J. Change the subject and the verb from the singular to the plural:

1. Vēnātor bestiās sequitur.

_____

2. Discipulus magistrō placēre conātur.

_____

3. Ego fulmina in caelō vidēre videor.

_____

4. Augur dē avibus loquitur.

_____

5. Augur lituō ūtitur.

_____

6. Nox diem sequitur.

_____

K. A friend of yours who does not know a bit of Latin has to write a report on constellations but doesn't know what the names of the constellations mean. Can you help your friend by giving the English meaning of the Latin names?

1. Aquila	_____	10. Sagitta	_____
2. Cētus	_____	11. Sculptor	_____
3. Columba	_____	12. Canis Major	_____
4. Lupus	_____	13. Canis Minor	_____
5. Mensa	_____	14. Musca	_____
6. Plaustrum	_____	15. Caput Medūsae	_____
7. Serpens	_____	16. Ursa Major	_____
8. Pāvō	_____	17. Ursa Minor	_____
9. Pictor	_____	18. Via Lactea	_____

L. Rewrite the following sentences with the verb in the perfect tense:

1. Pluvius arcus imbrem saepe sequitur.

_____

2. Glaciēs in viā esse vidēbātur.

_____

3. Nix in montibus altissima esse vidētur.

_____

4. Multī militēs in proeliō moriēbantur.

_____

5. Hieme omnēs dē grandine et glaciē et nive loquuntur.

_____

6. Hī ventī ex septentriōnibus oriuntur.

_____

7. Puerī mē pilīs niveīs icĕre (*hit*) conantur.

_____

8. Thēsaurus in cavernā sub scopulō occultārī vidēbātur.

_____
_____

_____ **COMPOSITIŌ** _____

All of us are influenced by the weather. It often restricts our activities. But it also provides us with many occasions for fun. Explain in Latin how the weather influences what you do:

_____
_____
_____
_____
_____
_____
_____
_____

DIALOGUS

Vocābula

foris *outside, outdoors*
nimis *too*
fiunt *get, become*
dēpendeō *-ēre -ī to hang down*

dētrahō *-ĕre dētraxī dētractus to pull off*
gustō *-āre to taste, eat*
exspectō *-āre to wait for*
libenter *gladly*

QUAESTIŌNĒS PERSŌNĀLĒS

1. Praefersne hiemem aestātī? Cūr?

   _____

2. Praefersne imbrem nivī? Cūr?

   _____

3. Lūdisne domī an forīs cum pluit?

   _____

4. Observāsne fulmen cum fulminat?

   _____

5. Consīderāsne fulmen in caelō esse pulchrum?

   _____

6. Manēsne domī an forīs cum tonat et fulminat?

   _____

7. Quid magis timēs, fulmen an tonitrum?

   _____

8. Exspectāsne pluvium arcum post imbrem?

   _____

9. Fēcistīne umquam virum ex nive?

   _____

10. Placetne tibi in nive lūděre?

    _____

11. Gustāvistīne umquam stīriam?

    _____

12. Īcistīne (_hit_) umquam quemquam (_anyone_) pilā niveā? Quem?

    _____

COLLOQUIUM

You are the second person in this dialog. Complete it on the model of the previous conversation:

Cupisne mēcum forīs lūdĕre?	_____ _____ (Say that it's cold outside today.)
Timēsne nivem et grandinem et glaciem?	_____ _____ (Say that you are not afraid of anything.)
Timēsne pilās niveās mēcum conjicĕre?	_____ _____ (Say that you don't throw snowballs at girls.)
Timēsne ventōs frīgĭdos ex septentriōnibus flantēs?	_____ _____ (Say that you prefer warm winds from the south.)
Cūr igitur mēcum forīs lūdĕre nōn vīs?	_____ _____ (Give your own response.)

THE LATIN CONNECTION

A. The fourth principal part of Latin verbs is often the source of not only other Latin words but also English words. If you drop the **-us** of the past passive participle and add **-or,** you get the doer of the action of the verb. If you drop the **-us** and add **-iō,** you get a noun that describes that action:

respirō -āre -āvī respirātus (*to breathe*):   **respirātor -ōris** m *breather, respirator*
respirātiō -ōnis f *breathing, respiration*

Now find the Latin and English derivatives in the same way for these verbs:

1. **celebrō -āre -āvī celebrātus** (*to celebrate*):   _____

   _____

2. **consultō -āre -āvī consultātus** (*to consult*):   _____

   _____

3. **decorō -āre -āvī decorātus** (*to decorate*):   _____

   _____

4. **līberō -āre -āvī līberātus** (*to free*):   _____

   _____

5. **exhibeō -ēre -uī exhibitus** (*to exhibit*):   _____

   _____

6. **moveō -ēre -ī mōtus** (*to move*):   _____

   _____

7. **prohibeō -ēre -uī prohibitus** (*to prohibit*):   _____

   _____

8. **agō -ĕre ēgī actus** (*to do*):   _____

   _____

9. **colligō -ĕre collēgī collectus** (*to gather*): _____

_____

10. **prōtegō -ĕre prōtexī prōtectus** (*to protect*): _____

_____

11. **trahō -ĕre traxī tractus** (*to pull*): _____

_____

12. **faciō -ĕre fēcī factus** (*to do*): _____

_____

13. **inspiciō -ĕre inspexī inspectus** (*to look into*): _____

_____

14. **audiō -īre -īvī audītus** (*to hear*): _____

_____

15. **inveniō -īre invēnī inventus** (*to find*): _____

_____

NOTE: Not every verb gives us two words derived from the past participle. For example, the past participle of **doceō** is **doctus.** From **doctus** we derive **doctor -ōris** m (*teacher*). (Physicians took over this word in the 19th century.) But **doctiō -ōnis** *f*, which would mean *teaching*, does not exist. Instead, the Romans used the word **doctrīna -ae** *f* for *teaching*. Sometimes a simple verb, such as **dūcō,** does not give us two derivatives in exactly the same way, but it gives us our word *duct*. Its compound **prōdūcō -dūcĕre -duxī -ductum** gives us again two words: *producer* and *production*.

B. 1. English took over the Latin word *thēsaurus*. What does it mean in English?

_____

2. When you hear "The preacher *fulminated* from the pulpit," what image do you get?

_____

3. What is an *incipient* headache?

_____

C. Give the Latin source for the following English derivatives. If the source is a verb, supply the infinitive:

1. tempest, tempestuous   _____

2. glacier, glacial   _____

3. translucent   _____

4. ultimate   _____

5. amble, ambulator   _____

6. inflate, deflate   _____

7. pulsate, pulsation, pulsator   _____

8. occult   _____

9. sequel, sequential, consequence   _____

10. mortuary, mortician, mortify   _____

11. orient, oriental, orientate, orientation   _____

12. utility, utilize   _____

XIII *Agricultūra*

Fīō; Perfect Passive Participle

1 Modicum cultūrae

It is hard for us today, living in an industrial age, to imagine what Roman life was like when practically everyone's father was a farmer. The colonial days in the United States came closest to what Roman life was like, especially during the first five or six hundred years of Roman history. In the early days of Rome, farming was regarded as the only respectable occupation in which a Roman citizen could engage. Manual labor on the farm was held in high esteem. Even senators and high government officials had their farms and country estates. Cato the Censor, who was widely respected in his own day and equally regarded by later generations as an ideal role model, worked in his fields side by side with his slaves. He has even left us a book on how to be a successful farmer. Business and commerce, even the practice of medicine, were considered below the dignity of a true Roman. In those early centuries, the Romans prided themselves on the simple life. People had what they needed to live on by diligently working their small plots of land. Luxuries were few. There was little reason for one family to be jealous of the wealth of another because they all had about the same standard of living. To make sure that there would be no vast gap between the rich and the poor, the Roman government passed a law limiting the amount of land that a man could own. Of course, the law was not very successful.

Naturally, it could not always stay that way. Gradually, raising herds of sheep and cattle became widespread because it was more profitable than raising wheat, barley, and vegetables on a small plot. As the centuries rolled by, large farms, worked by gangs of slaves under the supervision of foremen, caused the small farms to disappear.

In many districts of Italy, it became more and more profitable to cultivate the vine and olive and fruit trees, since cheap grain could be imported from Sicily and North Africa as tribute to be paid to Rome by the provincials, as the people who lived in the lands that had been conquered by the Roman armies were called. This grain from the provinces was used to feed the growing population of the city, to which the unsuccessful little farmers had moved. Since this grain was sold at very low prices, and sometimes below market price or even given away free by scheming politicians, the poor small farmer had no chance to make a profit or even survive. He fell into debt and in the end had to sell his farm to the large land owners. Even when Italy itself became more industrial in the early Empire (in the first and second century A.D.), most of the provinces were almost exclusively agricultural. Especially in Rome, people looked back on their world of small farms and hearty farmers as the most glorious time in their history.

222

2 Here are some of the typical activities carried on on a farm. And, of course, the farmers need the proper tools to perform their chores. Can you identify the activities and the tools?

segetēs metĕre

furca -ae f

arāre

falx -cis f

serĕre

arātrum -ī n

sārīre

irrigāre

sarculum -ī n

arborēs amputāre

falcula -ae f

stabulum purgāre

vaccās mulgēre

secūris -is f

rutrum -ī n

pāla -ae f

pābulum vaccīs dare

rastellus -ī m

__ ACTIVITĀTĒS _____

A. In each of the following activities, the farmer uses an implement. Underline the correct implement in parentheses:

1. Agricola terram (arātrō/falce) arat.

2. Agricola plantās (situlā aquāriā/sarculō) irrigat.

3. Agricola arborēs (falculā/pālā) amputat.

4. Agricola stabulum (furcā/arātrō) purgat.

5. Agricola segetēs (rutrō/falce) metit.

6. Agricola agrum herbīs malīs (*weeds*) (sarculō/furcā) purgat.

7. Agricola terram (palā/rastellō) vertit (*turns under*).

8. Agricola arborem (secūrī/sarculō) dēcīdit (*cuts down*).

9. Agricola hortum (rastellō/rutrō) ērādit (*rakes*).

10. Agricola faenum (*hay*) (rastellō/falce) secat.

B. Can you identify these implements by sight? Match the following names with the pictures:

arātrum	furca	rutrum
falcula	pāla	sarculum
falx	rastellus	secūris

1. _____   2. _____   3. _____

4. _____   5. _____   6. _____

7. _____   8. _____   9. _____

3 Read the following account of life on the farm:

Agricola est semper occupātus, etiam hieme. Hieme instrūmentum reparat et arborēs amputat. Māne prīmā luce vaccās mulget et eīs pābulum dat. Nōn sōlum stabulum sed etiam cohortem cōtīdiē purgat.

occupātus *-a -um busy*
instrūmentum *-ī n equipment*
  reparō *-āre to repair*
cohors *-tis f barnyard*

Prīmō vēre agrōs arat. Duo bovēs arātrum trahunt. Bovēs sunt lentī sed validī. Agricola, postquam agrōs arāvit, sēmen in terrā serit. In aliō agrō trīticum serit, aliō in agrō hordeum serit, aliō in agrō ocīnum serit. Sī tempestās sicca est, plantās frequenter irrigat.

prīmō vēre *in early spring*

sēmen *-inis n seed*
  trīticum *-ī n wheat*
hordeum *-ī n barley*
  ocīnum *-ī n clover*
siccus *-a -um dry*

Per vēr et aestātem, trīticum et hordeum et ocīnum crescunt. Sed etiam herbae malae in agrīs crescunt. Itaque agricola sarculō herbās malās sarit.

crescō *-ĕre crēvī crētum to grow*
  herba mala *-ae f weed*

Autumnō agricola trīticum et hordeum et ocīnum metit. Trīticum et hordeum plaustrō impōnit. Duo bovēs plaustrum ad āream prope villam trahunt, ubi frūmentum dēteritur. Postquam frūmentum dētrītum est, agricola trīticum et hordeum in horreō condit. Deinde agricola ad agrōs redit et ocīnum metit. Multōs diēs ocīnum in agrō jacet dōnec siccum est. Simul atque ocīnum siccum est, agricola id colligit et in aliā parte horreī condit.

metō *-ĕre messuī messus to harvest, reap*
  impōnō *-ĕre imposuī impositus to put on*
ārea *-ae f threshing floor*
dēterō *-ĕre dētrīvī dētrītus to thresh*
horreum *-ī n barn*
condō *-ĕre condidī conditus to store*
dōnec *until*
colligō *-ĕre collēgī collectus to gather*

— ACTIVITĀS —

C. Respondē Latīnē:

1. Quid facit agricola hieme?

   _____

2. Quō tempore annī agricola agrōs arat?

   _____

3. Quās segetēs agricola in agrīs serit?

   _____

4. Quid facit agricola postquam vaccās mulsit?

   _____

5. Quō tempore annī trīticum et hordeum et ocīnum crescunt?

   _____

6. Quid crescit inter plantās?

   _____

7. Sī caelum siccum est, quid facit agricola?

   _____

8. Quō tempore annī agricola segetēs metit?

   _____

9. Ubi frūmentum dēteritur?

   _____

10. Ubi agricola frūmentum condit?

    _____

 Do you recognize this nursery rhyme?

Puelle caeruleë, age,
flā tuō cornū;
ovēs in prātō,
vaccae in segete;
hōc modō custōdīs ovēs tuās,
sub faenī metā
artē dormiens?

puellus -ī *m little boy*
  age *come*
cornū -ūs *n horn*
seges -etis *m corn* (= *grain field*)
faenum -ī *n hay;* **faenī meta -ae** *f haystack*
artē *fast*

5 The passive forms of **facĕre** are irregular in the present, imperfect, and future tenses:

PRESENT		IMPERFECT		FUTURE	
fīō	fīmus	fīēbam	fīēbāmus	fīam	fīēmus
fīs	fītis	fīēbās	fīēbātis	fīēs	fīētis
fit	fīunt	fīēbat	fīēbant	fīet	fīent

The perfect and pluperfect tenses are regular: **factus sum,** etc.; **factus eram,** etc. The passive infinitive is **fierī.** The passive forms have two basic meanings: *to be made* and *to become, get, turn:*

Inaurēs ex aurō *fiunt*.   *The earrings are made of gold.*
Māla *fiunt* rubra autumnō.   *Apples turn red in the fall.*

___ ACTIVITĀTĒS _____

D. Supply the correct forms of **fierī** in the present tense:

1. Agricola _____ tristis sī imber diū nōn cadit.

2. Ego ipse facile fatīgātus _____ sī celeriter currō.

3. Ego et frāter laetī _____ simul atque ad fundum avī pervenimus.

4. Cūr tam īrātus _____ quandō ego tēcum nōn lūdō?

5. Autumnō diēs _____ frīgidī.

E. Convert the following verbs from the imperfect to the perfect tense:

1. Horreum ex lignō (*wood*) fīēbat. _____

2. Pōmerīdiē nubēs ātrae fīēbant. _____

3. Haec arbor ēnormis fīēbat. _____

4. Ego propter cibum malum aeger fīēbam. _____

5. Nōs mox impatientēs tēcum fīēbāmus. _____

F. Convert the following verbs from the perfect to the pluperfect tense:

1. Labor paulātim (*little by little*) facilior factus est. _____

2. Post tempestātem caelum iterum clārum factum est. _____

3. Propter glaciem, viae perīculōsae factae sunt.   _____

4. Post multōs mensēs sine imbre, agrī siccī factī sunt.   _____

5. Pānis bonus ex hāc farīnā factus est.   _____

6 Now read the story of Cincinnatus, which took place in the early days of Rome. In later centuries, the Romans admired him for preferring a simple life on the farm to high political office in the city:

Lūcius Quinctius Cincinnātus erat honestus patricius Rōmānus. Quamquam consul factus erat, tamen vītam simplicem rūsticam amāvit. Fundus ejus trans Tiberim erat parvus sed prōsperus quia in agrīs dīligentissimē labōrābat. Vītam rusticam vītae urbānae praeferēbat.

honestus -a -um *respectable*
patricius -ī *m patrician*
tamen *still, nevertheless*

Ubi autem hostēs exercitum Rōmānum circumclū-serant, magnus timor senātum populumque Rōmānum occupāvit. "Sōlus Cincinnātus," omnēs aiēbant, "nōs tantā calamitāte conservāre potest." Senātus enim populusque Rōmānus Cincinnātō omnīnō confīdēbant.

circumclūdō -clūděre -clūsī -clūsus *to surround*
timor -ōris *m fear*
occupō -āre *to grip*
aiēbant *(they) said*
tantus -a -um *such a great*
conservō -āre *to save*
enim *for*

Statim lēgātī missī sunt ad Cincinnātum, quī tum agrum arābat. "Hostēs," aiēbant, "exercitum nos-trum circumclūsērunt. Rōma ipsa magnō in perīculō est. Senātus populusque Rōmānus cupiunt tē exer-cituī praeficěre."

lēgātus -ī *m envoy*

praeficiō -ficěre -fēcī -fectus *to put in command of*

Haec verba audiens, Cincinnātus arātrum statim re-līquit, sūdōrem dētersit, togam induit, et ad cūriam festīnāvit, ubi dictātor factus est. Brevī tempore exercitum ex urbe ēduxit et mediā nocte ad castra hostium pervēnit. Postrīdiē prīmā lūce exercitum Rōmānum contrā hostēs duxit et magnā victōriā hostēs superāvit. Cincinnātus Rōmam exercitum et multōs captīvōs reduxit.

relinquō -ěre relīquī relictus *to leave*
sūdor -ōris *m sweat*
dētergeō -ēre dētersī dētersus *to wipe off*
castra -ōrum *npl camp*
postrīdiē *next day*
superō -āre *to defeat*

Senātus populusque Cincinnātum dictātōrem diūtius esse cupīvērunt. Cincinnātus autem hunc honōrem recūsāvit. Post victōriam ad fundum trans Tiberim cupidē sē recēpit et vītam prīvātī ēgit.

diūtius *for a longer time*
recūsō -āre *to turn down*
cupidē *eagerly*
sē recipěre *to retire*
vītam agěre *to lead a life*

___ ACTIVITĀS _____

G. **Vērum aut falsum?** If the statement is true, write **Vērum.** If it is false, write **Falsum** and correct the statement:

1. Cincinnātus erat homo superbus et arrogans.

   _____

2. Cincinnātus vītam urbānam nōn amāvit.

   _____

3. Fundus ejus trans Tiberim erat situs.

   _____

4. Hostēs fundum ejus circumclūserant.

   _____

5. Senātus populusque Rōmānus Cincinnātum omnīnō timēbant.

   _____

6. Ubi lēgātī ad Cincinnātī fundum pervēnērunt, Cincinnātus ocīnum metēbat.

   _____

7. Prīmō Cincinnātus Rōmam īre recūsāvit.

   _____

8. Ubi ad cūriam pervēnit, Cincinnātus consul factus est.

   _____

9. Cincinnātus hostēs celeriter superāvit.

   _____

10. Post victōriam Cincinnātus Rōmae diū habitāvit.

    _____

---

7 As you learned earlier, the fourth principal part of active verbs is the past passive participle. You saw that this participle, plus the present forms of **sum,** can be combined to form the perfect passive tense; and this participle, combined with the imperfect forms of **sum,** forms the pluperfect passive tense:

    Segetēs *messae sunt.*   *The crops were harvested.*   (Perfect tense)
    Segetēs *messae erant.*   *The crops had been harvested.* (Pluperfect tense)

The fourth principal part also functions simply as a participle modifying a noun:

Segetēs *messae* in horreō conditae sunt.	*The harvested crops were stored in the barn.*
Segetēs, ab agricolā *messae,* in horreō conditae sunt.	*The crops harvested by the farmer were stored in the barn.*
Segetēs, ab agricolā exeunte Septembrī *messae*, in horreō Octōbrī conditae sunt.	*The crops, harvested by the farmer at the end of September, were stored in the barn in October.*

Note the position of the participle in each sentence. The participle in Latin does NOT, as in English, come right after the noun it modifies. It comes at the end of the participial phrase. Its modifiers are sandwiched between the noun (**segetēs**) and the participle (**messae**). In the first example, in which there were no modifiers, the participle had to come right after the noun. If you note this principle of Latin word order, you will more easily recognize word groups, that is, words that belong together.

The participle, like any adjective, agrees with the noun it modifies in number, gender, and case. In the sentence above, what is the number of **segetēs?**

_____ What is the gender? _____. What is

the case? _____.

___ ACTIVITĀS _____

H. Read over the following sentences carefully, noting the noun that the missing participle modifies. From the principal parts of the verb given before each sentence, supply the correct form of the participle. Then reread the sentence aloud, making the proper pauses between word groupings:

1. (metō -*ĕre* messuī messus) Trīticum, abhinc duōs diēs _____, ad āream portātum est.

2. (dēterō -*ĕre* dētrīvī dētrītus) Farīna facta est ex frūmentō, in āreā anteā

   _____.

3. (irrigō -*āre* irrigāvī irrigātus) Plantae, ā servīs nostrīs cōtīdiē _____, nunc vigent (*are thriving*).

4. (relinquō -*ĕre* relīquī relictus) Vaccae, in cohorte _____, nullam aquam habent.

5. (arō arāre arāvī arātus) Agrī fertilēs, ā Cincinnātō _____, trans Tiberim sitī erant.

6. (amputō -āre amputāvī amputātus) Arborēs, prīmō vēre _____, multum fructum autumnō ferunt.

7. (serō -ĕre sēvī satus) Sēmen, prīmō vēre in agrīs _____, duodecim diēbus germinat.

8. (frangō -ĕre frēgī fractus) Rāmus arboris, ventō validō _____, trans viam cecidit.

9. (circumclūdō -clūdĕre -clūsī -clūsus) Exercitus Rōmānus, ab hostibus

   _____, ā Cincinnātō līberātus est.

10. (capiō -ĕre cēpī captus) Cincinnātus Rōmam reduxit multōs hostēs, bellō

    recente _____.

From the fourth principal part, as you learned in the last chapter, are derived the doer of the action of the verb and a noun describing that action; for example: **respirātus** (from **respirāre** *to breathe*) gives us **respirātor -ōris** m (*breather, respirator*) and **respirātiō -ōnis** f (*the act of breathing, breath*). Most nouns of the fourth declension come also from the fourth principal part of verbs; for example: **exerceō -ēre** means *to exercise* or *to train*. The fourth principal part is **exercitus,** which means *trained, exercised*. From it we get the noun **exercitus -ūs** m (*trained unit, army*). Here are a few other examples:

vīsus (from **videō**):	**vīsus -us** m *sight, sense of sight*
audītus (from **audiō**):	**audītus -ūs** m *hearing; sense of hearing; audit*
cursus (from **currō**):	**cursus -ūs** m *a run; course*
status (from **stō**):	**status -ūs** m *standing; status*

Do you get the idea? Here's a chance to prove it.

___ ACTIVITĀTĒS _____

I. Write out the nominative of the fourth-declension noun, the genitive ending, the gender, and an English word derived from that Latin noun:

EXAMPLE: **actus** (from   **actus -ūs** m   *doing, action*   *act*
          agō *to do*)

PARTICIPLE	NOUN	MEANING	DERIVATIVE
1. exitus (from **exeō** *to go out*)	_____	*going out*	_____
2. aspectus (from **aspiciō** *to view*)	_____	*a look, view*	_____
3. dēfectus (from **dēficiō** *to fail*)	_____	*a failing*	_____
4. ēventus (from **ēveniō** *to occur*)	_____	*occurrence*	_____
5. intellectus (from **intellegō** *to understand*)	_____	*understanding*	_____

J. Now let's review the entire fourth declension by declining the noun **exercitus:**

	SINGULAR	PLURAL
NOM.	_____	_____
GEN.	_____	_____
ACC.	_____	_____
DAT.	_____	_____
ABL.	_____	_____

QUAESTIŌNĒS PERSŌNĀLĒS

1. Pecūniamne umquam ab amīcīs mūtuātus(-a) es?

_____

2. Sī quid mūtuātus(-a) es, statim id reddistī?

_____

3. Vestēsne an ornāmenta ā frātre aut sorōre mūtuātus(-a) es?

_____

4. Esne tu avidus(-a) amīcōs adjuvāre?

_____

5. Vīsne in fundō habitāre an fundum vīsitāre?

_____

DIALOGUS

Vocābula

modo *just, just now*
immigrō -āre (**in** + *acc*) *to move into*
prōdest *it is good (to)*
quid *anything*
dēsīderō -āre *to need*
licetne mihi *may I*
mūtuor -ārī ātus *to borrow*
avidus -a -um *willing, eager*

vigeō -ēre -uī *to thrive*
quidnī? *why not?*
admodum *very*
obiter *by the way*
dēsiste! *hold it!*
satis *enough*
nebulō -ōnis m *airhead*

COLLOQUIUM

Complete the dialog between the farmer and his new neighbor, Turnus, on the model of the previous conversation:

Salvē, vicīne! Ego sum Turnus, tuus vicīnus novus.
_____
_____
Quid nōmen est tibi?

Salvē, Turne! Ego sum Glaucus
_____
Sī quid dēsīderās, ego....

Optimē, Glauce. Licetne mihi mūtuārī palam et rastellum tuum?

Certē. Vicīnōs meōs
_____

Grātiās. Et licetne mūtuārī sarculum tuum? Agrōs meōs sārīre volō.
_____
_____

Quidnī? Ego quattuor sarcula in horreō habeō.
_____

Splendidē! Tū es homo admodum līberālis.
_____
... et duōs bōvēs et fortasse....,

_____
_____
Fortasse ego sum homo līberālis, sed nebulō nōn sum!

COMPOSITIŌ

You are a famous artist. The President of the United States has commissioned you to paint a large picture of a country scene. Before you begin your painting, you need to draw up your plan of what will be in the painting. In drawing up your list, the following expressions may be helpful. When you are done with the list, you might want to write your descriptions in the panel below:

in abscedentibus	*in the background*
in priōre parte	*in the foreground*
in mediā parte	*in the middle*
ā dextrā	*on the right*
ā sinistrā	*on the left*

THE LATIN CONNECTION

A. The Latin verb **ferō** means *to bear; to produce*. Give the two corresponding English adjectives to define the basic meaning of **fertilis:** _____;

_____. The Romans might speak of **solum fertile** (*fertile soil*); **arborēs fertilēs** (*productive trees*); **montēs aurō fertilēs** (*mountains productive of gold*).

B. The function of the god **Sāturnus** is suggested by the verb **serō serĕre sēvī satus.**

With what activity was he associated? _____ To be able to identify gods and goddesses in art, the ancient artists always represented each deity with a symbol. Do you remember Saturn's symbol? _____ What

day of our week is Saturn's day? _____. The **Sāturnālia** was a major holiday among the Romans, coming at the end of the year and lasting five days. There was an exchange of gifts and merrymaking.

C. Our English word *status* comes from the verb **stō stāre stetī status.** As we saw earlier, **status,** as a fourth-declension noun, means *standing, position*. Explain

what a *status symbol* is and give an example: _____

_____.

What is a status report? _____

_____.

What is a status seeker? _____

The Latin phrase **status quō** has become a regular English noun. It means "the position, or condition, in which (we find ourselves)." Who prefers the **status quō,** the person who is content or the person who wants change?

_____.

D. Can you give the Latin source for the following English derivatives?

1. arable _____	4. detergent _____	7. timorous _____
2. fork _____	5. purge _____	8. hostile _____
3. vaccine _____	6. relinquish _____	9. seminary _____

XIV _Lūsūs_

Defective Verbs; Infinitives

1 Modicum cultūrae

Since Roman boys and girls did not have huge toy stores at which they could choose from an endless variety of toys, they had to get by with simpler toys and rely on their imagination to entertain themselves. One Roman writer, Horace, recalls the first games (**lūsus -ūs** _m_) of his childhood "building toy houses, harnessing mice to a little cart, playing 'odd and even,' and riding a long stick as a hobbyhorse." Children played leapfrog, jumped rope, spun tops, played jacks, rode on swings, played catch, played with dolls, and rolled hoops. The best hoops were decorated with little bells so that they jingled as they rolled.

Boys played a game similar to field hockey with a stick curved at one end like our hockey sticks. They played various games of ball, but none of the games, as far as we know, involved the use of a bat or racket. A very popular ballgame was trigon, played by three players standing to form a triangle. Each player had a leather-covered ball stuffed with hair. The balls were thrown to one another in quick succession. The worst situation was to have two balls coming at you while you still had your own ball in your hand. The winner was the one who dropped the ball least often. A referee judged whether a ball was catchable or not and also counted the number of times each player dropped a ball.

Many of the games that children played were in imitation of adults. They played school, they played soldiers and gladiators using toy wooden swords, and they played chariot racing. A cart or little chariot, just big enough to hold a little girl or boy, would be pulled by a goat, a sheep, or a dog.

We also know of games of skill in which pieces were moved on a game board according to rules similar to those of chess or checkers.

2 Vocābula

calamus -ī m

linea -ae f

hāmus -ī m

piscārī

natāre

rēmus -ī m

rēmigāre

eculeus -ī m

equitāre

pūpā lūděre

pilā lūděre

oscillum -ī n

ad fūnem salīre

oscillāre

arcus -ūs m

sagitta -ae f

culter -trī m vēnāticus

vēnābulum -ī n

canis -is m vēnāticus

vēnārī

— ACTIVITĀS

A. Match the sentences with the pictures they describe:

Piscātor in flūmine piscātur.
Trēs puerī pilā lūdunt.
Puella ad fūnem salit.
Puer oscillat.

Vēnātor cum cane vēnāticō vēnātur.
Puer eculeō equitat.
Puellae pūpīs lūdunt.
Puer duōs rēmōs habet.

1. _____   2. _____

3. _____   4. _____

5. _____   6. _____

7. _____   8. _____

B. Change the subject and verb from the singular to the plural:

1. Piscātor multōs piscēs captat.

   _____

2. Puella in oscillō sedēbat.

   _____

3. Puer pilā lūsit.

   _____

4. Vēnātor vēnābulum ad vulpem conjēcit.

   _____

5. Puer parvulus eculeō equitābat.

   _____

6. Frāter meus arcū et sagittā vēnātur.

   _____

C. Sometimes you need the right equipment to enjoy an activity. Can you identify the following items?

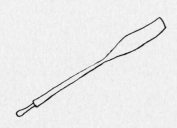

1. _____   2. _____   3. _____

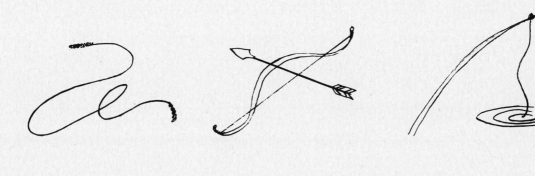

4. _____ **5.** _____ **6.** _____

D. Explain that you use the following items in the activities suggested. Remember that the verb **ūtor ūtī ūsus sum** takes the ablative case:

    Example: (vēnābulum/vēnārī) Ego vēnābulō ūtor cum vēnor. *I use a hunting spear when I hunt.*

1. (calamus et līnea/piscārī)

_____

2. (rēmus/rēmigāre)

_____

3. (oscillum/oscillāre)

_____

4. (fūnis/ad fūnem salīre)

_____

5. (eculeus/equitāre)

_____

6. (arcus et sagitta/vēnārī)

_____

_____

3   Some Latin verbs lack certain forms. They are called DEFECTIVE VERBS. The following verbs have a perfect tense with a present meaning and a pluperfect tense with an imperfect meaning:

meminī	*I remember*	**memineram**	*I remembered*
nōvī	*I know*	**nōveram**	*I knew*
ōdī	*I hate*	**ōderam**	*I hated*

The perfect infinitive, which is formed in all verbs with the perfect stem plus -isse, has a present meaning in these defective verbs:

memin*isse*	*to remember*
nō*visse*	*to know, be familiar with*
ōd*isse*	*to hate*

In all other verbs, the perfect infinitive (perfect stem plus -isse), has a past meaning:

portā*visse*	*to have carried*
mō*visse*	*to have moved*
audī*visse*	*to have heard*

NOTE: **sciō** means *I know a fact*; **nōvī** means *I am familiar with* a person or place.

___ ACTIVITĀTĒS _____

E. Complete the sentences with the correct forms of **meminisse** in the perfect tense:

EXAMPLE: Vēnātor mē meminit. *The hunter remembers me.*

1. Vēnātōrēs hunc locum nōn _____.

2. Vōsne illum piscātōrem _____?

3. Ego et Claudius hunc lūsum bene _____.

4. Ego ipse illum vēnātōrem _____.

5. Piscātor illud flūmen adhūc _____.

F. Complete with the correct forms of **nōvisse** in the pluperfect tense:

EXAMPLE: Ego puellam cum pūpā nōveram. *I knew the girl with the doll.*

1. Vēnātōrēs hanc silvam bene _____.

2. Num tū illum piscātōrem _____.

3. Nōs illōs piscātōrēs adhūc _____.

4. Canis vēnāticus dominum suum statim _____.

5. Ego puellam oscillantem _____.

G. Complete with the correct forms of **ōdisse** in the perfect tense:

1. Ego hunc labōrem neque amō neque _____.

2. Nōs naturāliter hostēs patriae _____.

3. Servī dominum crūdēlem _____.

4. Cūr tū istum mangōnem _____.

5. Frāter meus piscārī _____.

 Now read the following account of a boy's first hunting and fishing trip:

Herī prīmum ego cum patre meō vēnātus sum. Canis vēnāticus noster, Dorceus, nōbīscum vēnit. Dorceus est canis vēnāticus perītus. Sēmitās per campōs optimē nōvit, quia cum patre frequenter vēnātus est.

Pater vēnābulum et cultrum vēnāticum sēcum ferēbat. Ego autem arcum et sagittam mēcum ferēbam. Dorceus avidē praecucurrit, nam sēmitās omnēs nōverat. Repentē cunīculus ex frutectō exsiluit. Ego ipse cunīculum nōn statim conspexī, sed Dorceus cunīculum statim vīderat et eum persecūtus est. Pater vēnābulum conjēcit sed frustrā. Ego arcum intendī sed frustrā. Cunīculus nōn sōlum celer sed etiam astūtus erat. Numquam rectā cucurrit per densum frutectum, sed trānsversē cucurrit. Dorceus quam celerimē cucurrit sed cunīculus etiam celerius cucurrit. Hōc modō cunīculus in densō frutectō facilē effūgit.

Postrīdiē ego et pater piscātī sumus. Tiberis flūmen nōn procul ā domō nostrā abest. Pater meus est piscātor excellens. Ego calamum longum mēcum ferēbam sed pater calamum multō longiōrem sēcum ferēbat. In rīpā flūminis sedēbāmus et escam hāmō impōnēbamus. Simul atque hāmum in aquam injiciēbāmus, piscēs ad escam natāvērunt. Ego excitātus fīēbam et citō hāmum ex aquā extraxī, sed piscem captāvī nullum. "Patientiam, patientiam, mī fīliolē," exclāmāvit pater rīdens. "Nōlī extrahĕre līneam tuam tam citō. Exspectā dōnec piscēs escam sūmunt; tum hāmum ex aquā extrahe."

prīmum *for the first time*
vēnor *-ārī* **vēnātus sum** *to go hunting*
perītus *-a -um experienced*
sēmita *-ae f track, path*
campus *-ī m (untilled) field*
sēcum *with him*
praecurrō *-currĕre -cucurrī -cursum to run out ahead*
repentē *suddenly*
frutectum *-ī n underbrush*
exsiliō *-īre -uī to jump up, jump out*
persequor *-sequī -secūtus est to chase, pursue*
frustrā *in vain*
intendō *-ĕre* **intendī intentus** *to draw*
celer celeris celere *fast*
rectā *in a straight line*
trānsversē *zig-zag*
quam celerrimē *as fast as possible*
effugiō *-ĕre* **effūgī** *to get away, escape*

rīpa *-ae f bank*
esca *-ae f bait*
impōnō *-pōnĕre -posuī -positus (+ dat) to put on*
extrahō *-ĕre* **extraxī extractus** *to pull out*
fīliolus *-ī m dear son*
exspectō *-āre to wait*
dōnec *until*

Ego escam rursus hāmō imposuī et hāmum in aquam injēcī et expectābam. Piscēs rūrsus ad escam natābant. "Patientiam, patientiam!" mēcum cogitābam. Pater mē attentē observāvit sed nihil dixit. Ut piscis escam sumpsit, ego hāmum lentē ex aquā extraxī. Ego meum piscem prīmum captāveram! Hōc modō ego alium piscem ex aliō captāvī.

rursus *again*

mēcum *to myself*
cogitō -āre *to think*

lentē *slowly*

alium ex aliō *one after another*

__ ACTIVITĀTĒS __

H. Respondē ad quaestiōnēs:

1. Quis est Dorceus?

_____

2. Cūr Dorceus sēmitās per campōs optimē nōvit?

_____

3. Quid pater sēcum ferēbat?

_____

4. Quid fīlius sēcum ferēbat?

_____

5. Quid repente ē densō frutectō exsiluit?

_____

6. Quōmodō cunīculus per frutectum densum cucurrit?

_____

7. Quis celerius cucurrit, Dorceus an cunīculus?

_____

8. Ubi pater fīliusque piscātī sunt?

_____

9. Quid pater fīliusque hāmō impōnēbant?

_____

10. Cūr fīlius prīmum piscem nōn captāvit?

_____

I.   We had seen earlier that the perfect active infinitive is formed by adding **-isse** to the perfect stem. Form the perfect active infinitive of the following verbs, which have just occurred in the account of the boy's hunting and fishing trips, and give the English meaning:

> EXAMPLE: **natāre** *to swim*   **natāvisse**   *to have swum*

1.   captāre *to catch*   _____   _____

2.   rēmigāre *to row*   _____   _____

3.   equitāre *to ride*   _____   _____

4.   oscillāre *to swing*   _____   _____

5.   intendĕre *to draw*   _____   _____

6.   conspicĕre *to spot*   _____   _____

7.   effugĕre *to escape*   _____   _____

8.   impōnĕre *to put on*   _____   _____

9.   praecurrĕre *to run ahead*   _____   _____

10.   extrahĕre *to pull out*   _____   _____

5 To form the perfect passive infinitive, add **esse** to the fourth principal part of active verbs (the perfect passive participle):

> EXAMPLES: **portāt*us* (*-a -um*) esse**   *to have been carried*
>   **audīt*us* (*-a -um*) esse**   *to have been heard*

Only transitive verbs (verbs that take a direct object) can form the perfect passive infinitive.

___ ACTIVITĀTĒS _____

J.   Form the present passive infinitive and the perfect passive infinitive of the following verbs from this lesson. Give the English meaning of each:

> EXAMPLE: **lūdō -*ĕre* lūsī lūsus** *to play*:   **lūdī** *to be played*
>   **lūsus esse** *to have been played*

1.   captō captāre captāvī captātus *to catch*

_____   _____   _____   _____

2. conjiciō conjicĕre conjēcī conjectus *to throw*

_____   _____   _____   _____

3. conspiciō conspicĕre conspexī conspectus *to spot*

_____   _____   _____   _____

4. extrahō extrahĕre extraxī extractus *to pull out*

_____   _____   _____   _____

5. impōnō impōnĕre imposuī impositus *to put on*

_____   _____   _____   _____

K. Now give the perfect infinitive of the following deponent verbs. Remember that they are passive in form but active in meaning:

EXAMPLE: **vēnor vēnārī vēnātus sum** *to hunt*:   **vēnātus esse**   *to have hunted*

1. admīror admīrārī admīrātus sum *to admire*: _____   _____

2. conor conārī conātus sum *to try*: _____   _____

3. videor vidērī vīsus sum *to seem*: _____   _____

4. loquor loquī locūtus sum *to speak*: _____   _____

5. nascor nascī nātus sum *to be born*: _____   _____

6. sequor sequī secūtus sum *to follow*: _____   _____

7. ūtor ūtī ūsus sum (+ abl) *to use*: _____   _____

8. morior morī mortuus sum *to die*: _____   _____

9. orior orīrī ortus sum *to rise*: _____   _____

DIALOGUS

Marce, vīsne mēcum lūdĕre? Cum pūpīs lūdĕre aut eculeō equitāre possumus.

Ego, Melissa, nōlō cum pūpīs lūdĕre aut eculeō equitāre. Quid alterī puerī dīcent?

Cupisne trūdĕre mē in oscillō meō aut ad fūnem salīre?

Neque oscillāre neque ad fūnem salīre volō. Ego volō īre vēnātum.

Habēsne arcum et sagittam?

Ita. Etiam vēnābulum et canem vēnāticum habeō. Dorceus nōminātur.

Nonne ferae tē terrent?

Minimē vērō. Leōnēs et tigrēs nōn vēnor. Tantummodo cunīculōs et sciūrōs vēnor.

Vocābula

trūdō -ĕre trūsī trūsus *to push*   **ferae -ārum** *fpl wild animals*

RĒS PERSŌNĀLĒS

Looking over your past life, list the games or activities that you have been involved in either with your sisters and brothers or with your friends. Use the imperfect tense:

1. _____

2. _____

3. _____

4. _____

5. _____

COMPOSITIŌ

You are in charge of arranging a summer program for small boys and girls. Write to their parents, telling them what activities and games the children will engage in at the summer camp:

_____

_____

_____

_____

_____

_____

_____

_____

THE LATIN CONNECTION

A. We had seen at the end of Lesson XII that the last principal part of Latin verbs is often the source of other Latin words. If you drop off the **-us** and add **-iō** to the last principal part, you have the Latin noun that describes the action of the verb:

EXAMPLE: **oscillātus** (*swung*) gives **oscillātiō -ōnis** *f swinging*

Give the action of the following verbs and the meaning; in 5, 6, 8, 9, and 10, give the English noun derived from the verb:

1. equitāre _____ _____

2. piscārī _____ _____

3. vēnārī _____ _____

4. rēmigāre _____ _____

5. extrahĕre _____ _____

6. exspectāre _____ _____

7. cōgitāre _____ _____

8. impōnĕre _____ _____

9. vidēre _____ _____

10. persequī _____ _____

B. The pendulum of a clock is said to *oscillate*. What does it do?

_____

People who cannot make up their minds may *oscillate* between two choices. An *oscillator* is a device for producing alternating current.

C. **Praecurrō** means *I run ahead*. Form the Latin doer of the action from the past participle. _____ What is the English derivative? _____ .

D. **Lūdō** means *I play*. **Collūdō** (from **cum-lūdō**) means *I play with* (someone). As in Exercise A, give the action of this verb in Latin. _____ What is the English derivative? _____ .

E. **Trūdō** means *I push*. What English derivatives come from the principal parts of **intrūdō**? _____ _____ _____ ; of **prōtrūdō**? _____ _____ .

COLLOQUIUM

Take the first part in the dialog with little Marcus. Ask questions that correspond to the answers:

XV Māne et noctū

Indirect Statements

Modicum cultūrae

The Romans in the earliest period of their history allowed their hair, beards, and mustaches to grow freely. Cicero speaks of "the shaggy beard that we see on ancient statues and busts." One reason for this practice was that in those early centuries there were no very sharp razors to make shaving comfortable. Only in the second century B.C. did it become common to cut the hair and shave the beard. According to one author, Varro, who lived in the first century B.C., the first barber came to Italy from Sicily in 300 B.C. But even if there were no public barbershops before 300 B.C., the use of scissors and razors is attested by very early archaeological finds. Scipio Africanus is said to have begun the fashion of daily shaving (around 150 B.C.), which became the common practice after that.

Young men did not shave their first fuzz but allowed it to darken their faces until it was almost a beard; then it was cut and consecrated at a solemn family affair. Growing beards became fashionable again in the second century A.D., when the emperor Hadrian grew a beard to hide his facial blemishes and thereby set a new style. From the time of the emperor Constantine in the fourth century A.D., it became customary for men to be clean-shaven.

Women's hair styles never favored short hair. Every woman chose the style that suited her best. Many of the hair styles in the first centuries A.D. became very elaborate and required the hand of a skillful beautician. False hair, wigs, and dyes were commonly used by women and frequently by men as well. (Men tried all sorts of remedies for baldness and, as a last resort, wore hair pieces to cover their baldness.) Dark hair was typical of Mediterranean people. Some brunettes who wished to be blondes used a dye imported from Northern Europe to bleach their hair or wore blond or red wigs made from the hair of slaves.

Just like modern women, Roman ladies spent time and money on make-up. They wore rouge, lipstick, and eye shadow. They used mascara made of soot from oil lamps to darken their eyelashes and eyebrows. They plucked their eyebrows with tweezers and rubbed off unwanted body hair with pumice. They used face packs and perfumed olive oil to keep their skin soft. And to protect their skin against the rays of the sun, they used parasols. Strangely enough, soap as a cleansing agent was unknown to the Romans until the late fourth century A.D., and even then it was used only to keep wounds clean. But the perfume and cosmetics industry did a booming business to flatter the vanity not only of women but also of some men.

Vocābula

**expergisc*or* -ī
experrectus sum**

**surgō *-ĕre* surrexī
surrectus**

mē lavō *-āre -āvī* lautus

**vestēs induō *-ĕre* ī
indūtus**

**dentēs purgō *-āre -āvī*
*-ātus***

**capillōs crispō *-āre -āvī*
*-ātus***

**capillōs pectō *-ĕre* pexī
pexus**

**barbam rādō *-ĕre* rāsī
rāsus**

**vestēs exuō *-ĕre* -ī
exūtus**

**dormītum eō īre iī/īvī
ītum**

dormiō *-īre -īvī -ītum*

somniō *-āre -āvī -ātum*

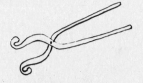

novãcula *-ae* f   **pecten** *-inis* m   **calamistrum** *-ī* n   **speculum** *-ī* n

___ ACTIVITĀS _____

A. Match the descriptions with the pictures:

Melissa capillōs calamistrō crispat.   Claudius sē lavat.
Māter dentēs purgat.   Marcellus vestēs exuit.
Ego dē piscātiōne somniō.   Paula capillōs pectine pectit.
Pater barbam novāculā rādit.   Terentia expergiscitur.

1. _____   2. _____

3. _____   4. _____

5. _____   6. _____

7. _____   8. _____

3 A direct quotation repeats the exact words of a speaker. The Romans did not use quotation marks to set off the direct quotation, but it is customary for us to add the quotation marks:

> **Melissa dīcit: "Pater meus barbam rādit."**
>
> *Melissa says, "My father is shaving."*

An indirect quotation repeats the thoughts but not the exact words of the speaker:

> **Melissa dīcit patrem suum barbam rādĕre.**
>
> *Melissa says that her father is shaving.*

Look at the subject of the indirect quotation. In what case is it? _____

Now look at the verb. What form does it have? _____. In English the indirect statement is often introduced by the conjunction *that*. Sometimes the conjunction *that* is omitted. In Latin no conjunction is ever used to introduce an indirect statement. The Romans simply had a different way of showing that the statement was indirect: by putting the subject into the accusative case and changing the verb to the infinitive.

In Latin, indirect statements are introduced not only by verbs that mean *say* but also by verbs that mean *hear* (**audīre**), *believe* (**crēdĕre**), *know* (**scīre**), *think* (**putāre**), (**consīderāre**), and the like. We have a similar construction in English:

> ***Credō* eum esse reum.**   *I believe him to be guilty.*
> ***Aestimō* eam esse amīcam bonam.**   *I consider her to be a good friend.*

But we don't say: *I say him to be generous.*

When the subject of the indirect statement is the same as the subject of the main verb, the accusative of a reflexive pronoun is used as the subject of the indirect statement:

> DIRECT: **Pater meus dīcit, "Ego dentēs purgō."**
>
> *My father says, "I am cleaning my teeth."*
>
> INDIRECT: **Pater meus dīcit *sē* dentēs purgāre."**
>
> *My father says that he is cleaning his teeth.*

Of course, the predicate adjective in an indirect statement is also in the accusative case and agrees with the subject of the infinitive:

Crēdō hanc *viam* esse *perīculōsam*.   *I believe that this road is dangerous.*

Notice that the present infinitive in the indirect statement represents an act as occurring at the time shown by the tense of the main verb:

Sentiō tempestātem *esse* adversam.   *I realize that the weather is bad.*
Sēnsī tempestātem *esse* adversam.   *I realized that the weather was bad.*

__ ACTIVITĀTĒS __

B. Rewrite each sentence changing the direct quotation to an indirect statement:

1. Pater dīcit: "Ego barbam novāculā rādō."

   _____

2. Melissa dīcit: "Soror mea capillōs pectine pectit."

   _____

3. Claudius dixit: "Ego bene māne (*early in the morning*) surgō."

   _____

4. Marcella dixit: "Frāter meus manūs et faciem lāvat."

   _____

5. Terentia dīcit: "Ego capillōs calamistrō crispō."

   _____

C. Now do just the opposite. Change each indirect statement to a direct statement:

1. Marcella nuntiāvit sē bene māne semper surgĕre.

   _____

2. Paula dīcit frātrem pectinem habēre.

   _____

3. Melissa dīcit sorōrem capillōs numquam crispāre.

   _____

4. Terentia dixit Marcum scholam ōdisse.

   _____

5. Māter putāvit Terentiam vestēs induĕre.

---

4 Now let's look in on a typical situation in a Roman family early in the morning. The mother is in the kitchen, and the children are in their bedrooms:

MĀTER: Melissa et Terentia, surgite! Jam hora diēī tertia est. Melissa, excitā ē somnō frātellum tuum, Claudium.

> excitō -*āre* to wake up
> somnus -*ī* m sleep
> frātellus -*ī* m little brother

MELISSA: Māter, Claudius nōn vult expergiscī. Sub strāgulō jacet et nōn movētur. Dictitat: "Odī expergiscī. Odī oculōs aperīre bene māne."

> strāgulum -*ī* n blanket
> dictitō -*āre* to keep saying

MĀTER: Terentia, experrecta es? Vōcem tuam nōn audiō. Age dum, surgē et ī in Claudī cubiculum et excitā eum ē somnō.

> age dum come on

TERENTIA: Māter, Claudius dīcit sē esse nimis somnolentum et ergō surgĕre nōn posse.

> somnolentus -*a* -*um* sleepy
> ergō therefore

MĀTER: Terentia, extrahe istum pigrum Claudium ē lectulō suō!

> piger pigra pigrum lazy
> lectulus -*ī* m (small) bed

TERENTIA: Māter, frātellus dēnique surrexit, sed lavārī nōn vult. Dīcit aquam esse nimis frīgidam.

> dēnique finally, at last

MĀTER: Claudī, vestēs indue et dentēs purgā. Illud dentifricium faciet dentēs tuōs candidōs et splendidōs.

> dentifricium -*ī* n tooth powder
> candidus -*a* -*um* white
> splendidus -*a* -*um* shiny

CLAUDIUS: Mamma, tunicam meam et calceōs meōs invenīre nōn possum. Et dentifricium invenīre ñon possum. Quis habet dentrificium?

MĀTER: Melissa, ubi est dentifricium? Invenī id prō Claudiō.

TERENTIA: Mater, capillōs meōs pectĕre volō, sed Melissa pectinem meum et speculum meum rursus habet. Melissa rēbus meīs semper ūtitur.

> rursus again

MĀTER: Melissa, ubi est speculum tuum? Redde speculum et pectinem Terentiae. Audīsne mē? Nōlī ūtī rēbus Terentiae.

> reddō -*ĕre* -*idī* -*itus* to give back

MELISSA: Māter, ego ipsa speculum dēsīderō. Capillōs meōs calamistrō crispō. Quōmodō possum capillōs crispāre sine speculō? Māter, Claudius rursus dormītum īvit.

> dēsīderō -*āre* to need

MĀTER: Properāte, līberī! Jentāculum est parātum.

> līberī -*ōrum* mpl children

MELISSA: Veniō, māter.

TERENTIA: Ego quoque veniō.

MĀTER: Claudī, venī statim; aliōquīn ego ipsa veniam et tē ē lectulō tuō extraham! Audīsne me?

> aliōquīn otherwise

CLAUDIUS: Ita, Mamma!

___ ACTIVITĀTĒS _____

D. Respondē ad quaestiōnēs:

1. Quota hōra est cum māter līberōs ē somnō excitat?

_____

2. Quis expergiscī nōn vult?

_____

3. Quamobrem Claudius sē lāvāre nōn vult?

_____

4. Quid Claudius invenīre nōn potest?

_____

5. Quō līberī dentēs purgant?

_____

6. Quamobrem Terentia nōn potest capillōs pectĕre?

_____

7. Quid facit Melissa calamistrō?

_____

8. Quid māter prō līberīs parāvit?

_____

E. **Quid facis bene māne?**

EXAMPLE:

Ego expergiscor.

1. _____   **2.** _____

3. _____

4. _____

5. _____

6. _____

F.   Quid facis noctū?

1. _____

2. _____

3. _____

4. _____

5. _____

6. _____

5 The perfect infinitive in the indirect statement represents an action that occurred earlier than the time shown by the tense of the main verb:

Helena _dīcit_ sē capillōs crispāvisse.	_Helen SAYS that she CURLED her hair._
Helena _dixit_ sē capillōs crispāvisse.	_Helen SAID that she HAD CURLED her hair._

_ ACTIVITĀTĒS _____

G. Rewrite the sentences changing each direct quotation to an indirect statement, making the necessary changes. Remember that you form the perfect active infinitive by adding **-isse** to the perfect active stem:

1. Claudius dixit: "Vēnātor arcum et sagittam habuit."

   _____

2. Publius dīcit: "Piscātōrēs multōs piscēs captāvērunt."

   _____

3. Marcella dixit: "Ego in merīdiem dormīvī."

   _____

4. Tullia dixit: "Ego capillōs pexī."

   _____

5. Claudius dixit: "Ego dē scholā somniāvī."

   _____

H. This time, let's try the opposite. Change each indirect statement to a direct quotation:

1. Marcellus meminit sē dentēs nōn purgāvisse.

   _____

2. Gaius meminit pectinem suum suprā lectum fuisse.

   _____

3. Terentia audīvit Claudium expergiscī nōluisse.

_____

4. Marcus dixit sorōrēs suās capillōs cōtīdiē calamistrō crispāvisse.

_____

5. Pater dīcit sē bene māne barbam rāsisse.

_____

6 You were just reminded that you form the perfect *active* infinitive by adding **-isse** to the perfect active stem: **pexisse** (*to have combed*). Do you remember how to form the perfect *passive* infinitive? What do you add to the fourth

principal part, that is, the perfect passive participle? _____ If you said **esse,** you were correct: **pexus esse** (*to have been combed*). Remember that **pex*us -a -um*** has to agree with the subject:

Capillī illīus puerī videntur   *The hair of that boy seems never*
  numquam pexī esse.   *to have been combed.*

In this example, **pexī** agrees with **capillī.** Furthermore, remember that in what we call "fake passive verbs" the form is passive, but the sense is active:

Sciō Marcum templa Rōmae   *I know that Marcus admired the*
  admīrātum esse.   *temples of Rome.*

In that sentence, **admīrātum esse** is passive in form but active in meaning.

__ ACTIVITĀTĒS _____

I. Rewrite the following sentences, changing each direct quotation to an indirect statement:

  EXAMPLE: Puella dixit: "Capillī meī in tonstrīnā crispātī sunt."
        Puella dixit capillōs suōs in tonstrīnā crispātōs esse.

1. Piscātor dixit: "Trēs piscēs ūnā hōrā captātī sunt."

_____

2. Māter dixit: "Jentāculum parātum est."

_____

3. Marcus dīcit: "Capillī meī pexī sunt."

_____

4. Melissa dixit: "Ego ā mātre vocāta sum."

_____

5. Vēnātor dixit: "Vēnābulum in vulpem conjectum est."

_____

J. Rewrite the following sentences, changing each direct quotation to an indirect statement. But notice that the verb in the direct quotation is a deponent verb, passive in form but active in meaning:

1. Pater dixit: "Omnēs virum fortem admīrātī sunt."

_____

2. Melissa dīcit: "Terentia speculō meō ūsa est."

_____

3. Māter dixit: "Sōl hōrā diēī prīmā ortus est."

_____

4. Marcus dixit: "Avia mea abhinc decem annōs mortua est."

_____

5. Terentia dixit: "Melissa mātrem in culīnam secūta est."

_____

K. We have seen that a verb that is normally transitive (takes a direct object) can be used intransitively by using the passive or the reflexive verb:

EXAMPLE: Cum ego dormiō, mē nōn moveō   *When I sleep, I don't move.*
(nōn moveōr).

Rewrite the following sentences, substituting the reflexive verb for the passive verb. The meaning of the sentence will, of course, remain the same:

1. Marcus cōtīdiē lavātur.   _____

2. Marcus et soror nunc lavantur.   _____

3. Ego mox lavābor.   _____

4. Ego et Paulus māne lavābāmur.   _____

5. Marcus lavārī nōn vult.   _____

DIALOGUS

Vocābula

tonstrīna -ae *f barbershop; beauty salon*
tonstrīx -īcis *f hairdresser*
tondeō -ēre totondī tonsus *to cut*
tingō -ēre tinxī tinctus *to dye, color*
flāvus -a -um *blond*
cōmō -ēre compsī comptus *to do, set (hair)*
ita quidem *yes, indeed*

modus -ī *m style, fashion*
novissimus -a -um *latest*
supercilium -ī *n eyebrow*
ēvellō -ēre ī evulsus *to pluck*
aliquid amplius *anything else*
nempe *well*
palpebra -ae *f eyelash*

RĒS PERSŌNĀLĒS

1. Quotā hōrā expergiscitur māter tua?

2. Expergiscitur pater tuus antequam an postquam māter?

3. Quis excitat tē ē somnō?

4. Surgisne statim an jacēs paulisper sub strāgulō?

5. Quandō dentēs purgās, māne an noctū?

6. Crispāsne capillōs tuōs?

7. Praefersne lavārī aquā frīgidā an tepidā an calidā?

8. Quis in familiā tuā barbam rādit?

9. Dē quō somniās?

10. Habuistīne umquam somnia tumultuōsa (*nightmares*)?

COMPOSITIŌ

List four or five things that you do in the morning before leaving for school:

COLLOQUIUM

Silvia is one of the hairdressers at this beauty salon. Octavia has just come in to have her hair done. Take the role of the hairdresser in this exchange and respond to the customer's questions:

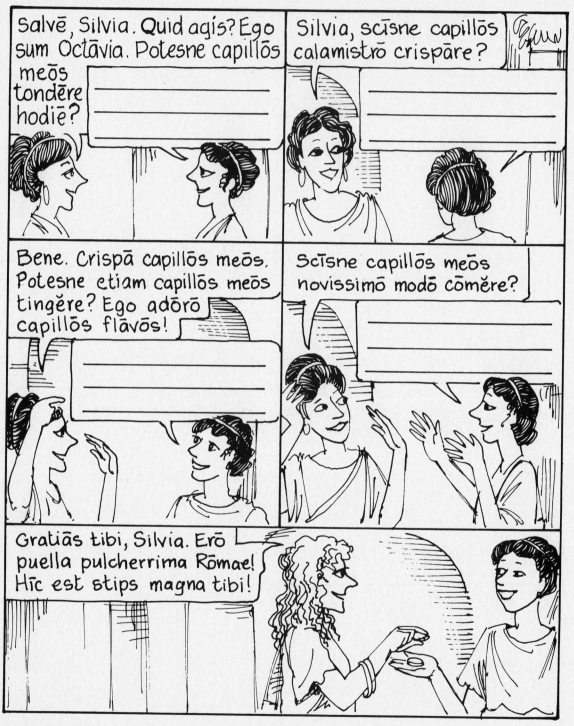

Vocābula

scīsne *do you know how to* **stips** *-is* f *tip*

THE LATIN CONNECTION

A. What is the Latin origin of the following English words? Give a short definition of each English word:

1. dormitory   _____   _____

2. dormant   _____   _____

3. lavatory   _____   _____

4. somnolent   _____   _____

5. somnambulist   _____   _____

6. dentifrice   _____   _____

7. candid   _____   _____

8. candidate   _____   _____

9. mode   _____   _____

10. to tinge   _____   _____

11. to purge   _____   _____

12. purgatory   _____   _____

13. eraser   _____   _____

14. supercilious   _____   _____

B. 1. Roman politicians who ran for office wore a distinctively white toga. The word for flat white is **albus -a -um**. What is the Latin adjective to describe the shiny white toga that candidates wore? _____

2. In which season are trees and plants dormant? _____

3. A capillary is a tiny blood vessel. From its Latin origin, what does such a minute blood vessel resemble? _____ What is the Latin name for it? _____ .

4. When we speak of a lavatory today, we think of a toilet. According to the Latin source, what is a room called a lavatory used for? _____

*Recōgnitiō III
(Lectiōnēs XI–XV)*

Lectiō XI

a. To form the passive voice of the first and third persons, change

-am to **-ar**	**-mus** to **-mur**
-ō to **-or**	**-nt** to **-ntur**
-t to **-tur**	

b. The passive forms of the first and third persons of the **-āre** family of verbs are:

PRESENT:	**vocor**	*I am called*	**vocāmur**	*we are called*
	vocātur	*he/she/it is called*	**vocantur**	*they are called*
IMPERFECT:	**vocābar**	*I was called*	**vocābāmur**	*we were called*
	vocābātur	*he/she/it was called*	**vocābantur**	*they were called*
FUTURE:	**vocābor**	*I will be called*	**vocābimur**	*we will be called*
	vocābitur	*he/she/it will be called*	**vocābuntur**	*they will be called*

c. The passive forms of the first and third persons of the **-ēre** family of verbs are:

PRESENT:	**moveor**	*I am moved*	**movēmur**	*we are moved*
	movētur	*he/she/it is moved*	**moventur**	*they are moved*
IMPERFECT:	**movēbar**	*I was moved*	**movēbāmur**	*we were moved*
	movēbātur	*he/she/it was moved*	**movēbantur**	*they were moved*
FUTURE:	**movēbor**	*I will be moved*	**movēbimur**	*we will be moved*
	movēbitur	*he/she/it will be moved*	**movēbuntur**	*they will be moved*

d. The passive forms of the first and third persons of the **-ĕre** family of verbs are:

PRESENT:	**mittor**	*I am sent*	**mittimur**	*we are sent*
	mittitur	*he/she/it is sent*	**mittuntur**	*they are sent*
IMPERFECT:	**mittēbar**	*I was sent*	**mittēbāmur**	*we were sent*
	mittēbātur	*he/she/it was sent*	**mittēbantur**	*they were sent*
FUTURE:	**mittar**	*I will be sent*	**mittēmur**	*we will be sent*
	mittētur	*he/she/it will be sent*	**mittentur**	*they will be sent*

e. The passive forms of the first and third persons of the **-īre** family of verbs are:

PRESENT:	**audior**	*I am heard*	**audīmur**	*we are heard*
	audītur	*he/she/it is heard*	**audiuntur**	*they are heard*
IMPERFECT:	**audiēbar**	*I was heard*	**audiēbāmur**	*we were heard*
	audiēbātur	*he/she/it was heard*	**audiēbantur**	*they were heard*
FUTURE:	**audiar**	*I will be heard*	**audiēmur**	*we will be heard*
	audiētur	*he/she/it will be heard*	**audientur**	*they will be heard*
INFINITIVE:	**audīrī**			

f. The passive forms of the first and third persons of the **-iō** family of verbs are:

PRESENT:	**accipior**	*I am received*	**accipimur**	*we are received*
	accipitur	*he/she/it is received*	**accipiuntur**	*they are received*
IMPERFECT:	**accipiēbar**	*I was received*	**accipiēbāmur**	*we were received*
	accipiēbātur	*he/she/it was received*	**accipiēbantur**	*they were received*
FUTURE:	**accipiar**	*I will be received*	**accipiēmur**	*we will be received*
	accipiētur	*he/she/it will be received*	**accipientur**	*they will be received*
INFINITIVE:	**accipī**	*to be received*		

Lectiō XII

a. The perfect tense of any verb in the passive voice consists of the perfect passive participle plus the present forms of **sum**:

portātus (*-a -um*) **sum**	*I was carried*	**portātī** (*-ae -a*) **sumus**	*we were carried*
portātus (*-a -um*) **es**	*you were carried*	**portātī** (*-ae -a*) **estis**	*you were carried*
portātus (*-a -um*) **est**	*he/she/it was carried*	**portātī** (*-ae -a*) **sunt**	*they were carried*

PERFECT PASSIVE INFINITIVE: **portātus** (*-a -um*) **esse** *to have been carried*

b. The pluperfect tense of any verb in the passive voice consists of the perfect passive participle plus the imperfect forms of **sum**:

portātus (*-a -um*) **eram**	*I had been carried*	**portātī** (*-ae -a*) **erāmus**	*we had been carried*
portātus (*-a -um*) **erās**	*you had been carried*	**portātī** (*-ae -a*) **erātis**	*you had been carried*
portātus (*-a -um*) **erat**	*he/she/it had been carried*	**portātī** (*-ae -a*) **erant**	*they had been carried*

c. The perfect passive participle has three endings. The subject of the verb will determine which ending is to be used.

d. Certain Latin verbs are called DEPONENT VERBS or "fake passive verbs" because they are passive in form but active in meaning:

admīror -ārī admīrātus sum	*to admire*
loquor loquī locūtus sum	*to speak*
utor utī usus sum (+ *abl*)	*to use*

Lectiō XIII

a. The passive forms of **facĕre** are irregular in the present, imperfect, and future:

PRESENT:		IMPERFECT:		FUTURE:	
fīō	fīmus	fīēbam	fīēbāmus	fīam	fīēmus
fīs	fītis	fīēbās	fīēbātis	fīēs	fīētis
fit	fīunt	fīēbat	fīēbant	fīet	fīent

INFINITIVE: **fīerī**   *to be made; to become, get*

b. The perfect and pluperfect passive forms of **facĕre** are regular: **factus sum,** etc.

c. The perfect participle (the fourth principal part of transitive verbs) combines with the present and imperfect tense of **sum** to form the perfect and pluperfect passive tenses of any verb. But it may also function simply as a participle. In Latin, the participle does not come immediately after the noun it modifies, as in English:

Segetēs, ab agricolā initiō	*The crops harvested by the farmer*
Septembris messae, in horreō mox	*at the beginning of September*
conditae sunt.	*were soon stored in the barn.*

Lectiō XIV

a. Some Latin verbs lack certain forms. They are called DEFECTIVE VERBS. The following verbs have a perfect tense with a present meaning and a pluperfect tense with an imperfect meaning:

meminī	*I remember*	**memineram**	*I remembered*	**meminisse**	*to remember*
nōvī	*I know*	**nōveram**	*I knew*	**nōvisse**	*to know*
ōdī	*I hate*	**ōderam**	*I hated*	**ōdisse**	*to hate*

b. The perfect passive infinitive consists of the perfect passive participle (fourth principal of transitive verbs) plus **esse:**

portā*tus* **(***-a -um***) esse**   *to have been carried*

c. The perfect infinitive of deponent verbs ("fake passive verbs") are passive in form but active in meaning:

conātus esse	*to have tried*
locūtus esse	*to have spoken*

Lectiō XV

a. An indirect statement is expressed in Latin by putting the subject of the direct quotation into the accusative case and changing the verb of the direct quotation to the infinitive. The present infinitive expresses action happening at the same time as that of the main verb; the perfect infinitive expresses action as having occurred before that of the main verb:

Quis dīcit flūmen esse altum?   *Who says that the river is deep?*
Quis dixit flūmen esse altum?   *Who said that the river was deep?*
Quis dixit flūmen fuisse altum?   *Who said that the river had been deep?*

b. If the subject in the indirect statement is the same as the subject of the main verb, the reflexive pronoun is used in the indirect statement:

DIRECT: **Marcus dixit: "Ego sum cīvis**   *Marcus said: "I am a Roman*
          Rōmānus."   *citizen."*
INDIRECT: **Marcus dixit *sē* esse cīvem**   *Marcus said that he was a Roman*
          Rōmānum.   *citizen.*

___ ACTIVITĀTĒS ___

A. Here are twelve people doing things. Complete the description below each picture by using the correct form of a verb chosen from the following list:

crispāre	**expergiscī**	**lūděre**	**purgāre**
dormīre	**induěre**	**oscillāre**	**somniāre**
equitāre	**lavārī**	**piscārī**	**vēnārī**

1. Terentia capillōs calamistrō

_____.

2. Melissa dē amīcō suō

_____.

3. Claudius bene māne

_____.

4. Puerī aquā tepidā

_____.

5. Frātellus eculeō _____ .　　**6.** Pater et fīlius hāmō _____ .

7. Sorōrēs vestēs _____ .　　**8.** Claudia oscillō _____ .

9. Pūblius dentēs dentifriciō

_____ .

10. Marius cum cane vēnāticō

_____ .

11. Jūlia pūpā _____ .　　**12.** Infans artē _____ .

B. Only one of the hunters is fully equipped for the hunt. Pick out the hunter from the description. Place an X in the correct circle:

Vēnātor canem vēnāticum sēcum habet.
Vēnātor arcum habet.
Vēnātor calceōs gestat.

Vēnātor vēnābulum habet.
Vēnātor cultrum vēnāticum habet.
Vēnātor sagittās habet.

C. How many of these words do you remember? Fill in the Latin words, then read down the boxed column to find the mystery word that ties all the other words together:

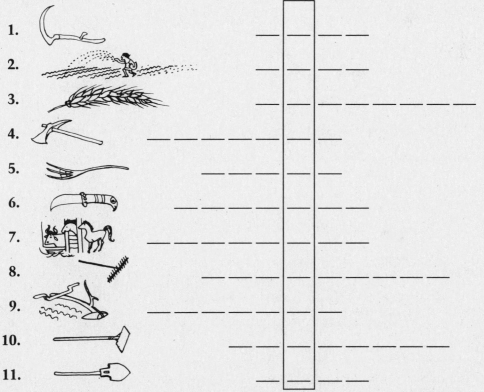

D. Look at this picture of the stars and constellations. Find the six constellations that relate to the myth of Perseus. Make a simple statement in Latin identifying or saying something about each:

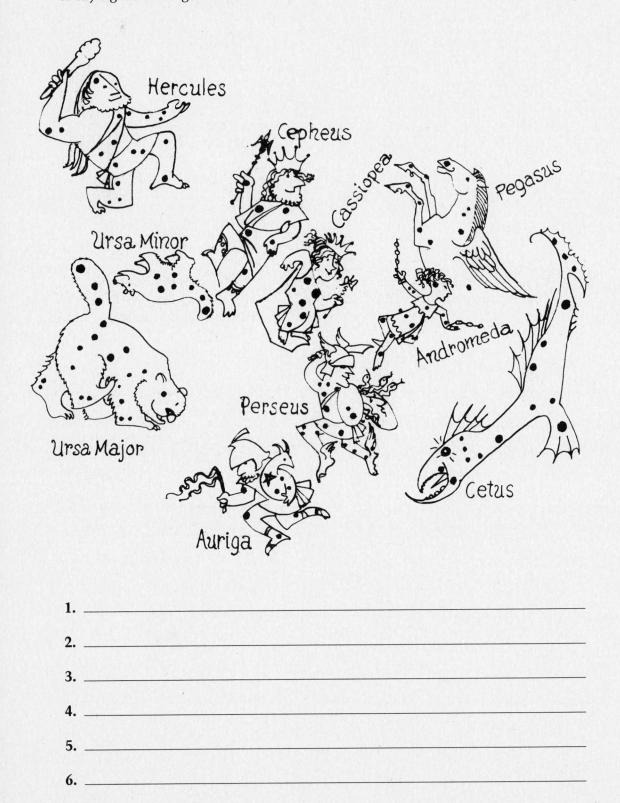

1. _____

2. _____

3. _____

4. _____

5. _____

6. _____

E. Find the hidden objects. Hidden in the barnyard (**cohors**) are eight implements that come in handy on any farm and two animals you will find on any farm. Circle them in the picture and list their Latin names below:

1. _____

2. _____

3. _____

4. _____

5. _____

6. _____

7. _____

8. _____

9. _____

10. _____

F. Cruciverbilūsus:

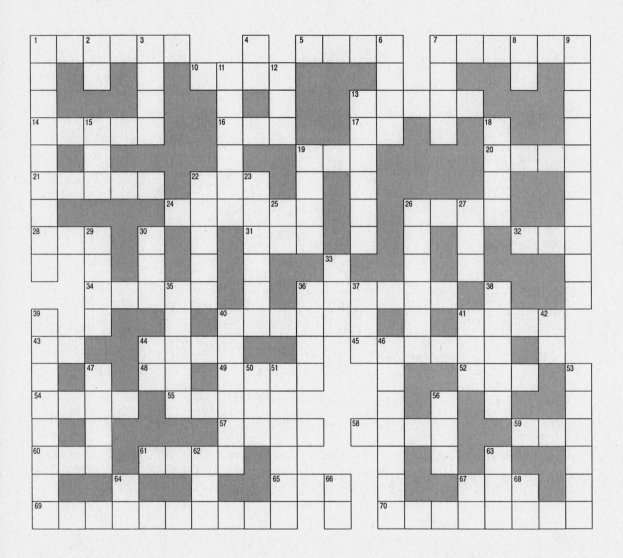

HORIZONTĀLE

1. blond	**26.** quickly	**52.** ox
5. he loves	**28.** where	**54.** trip
7. lightning	**31.** yes	**55.** on top of
10. hope	**32.** go away!	**57.** use
13. chair	**34.** place	**58.** unless
14. whole	**36.** cockroach	**59.** but
16. with	**40.** cages	**60.** to use
17. you are	**41.** his own	**61.** tooth
19. why	**43.** or	**65.** or
20. love	**44.** bait	**67.** to God
21. horn	**45.** again	**69.** most eagerly
22. thing	**48.** you	**70.** pride
24. wind	**49.** in the morning	

PERPENDICULĀRE

1. underbrush	**22.** oar	**41.** under
2. to	**23.** icicle	**42.** if
3. one	**25.** as, when	**46.** last
4. himself	**26.** knife	**47.** sea monsters
6. three	**27.** then	**50.** art, skill
7. scythe	**29.** that	**51.** sailors
8. me	**30.** this	**53.** Gorgon
9. shipwreck	**33.** wing	**56.** I become
11. comb	**35.** bear	**62.** we
12. I am	**36.** well	**63.** through
13. slave	**37.** air	**64.** it
15. three times	**38.** player	**66.** you
18. rarely	**39.** boat	**67.** concerning
19. house	**40.** untilled field	**68.** on account of

G. Unscramble these mythological names. Then unscramble the circled letters to find out what the message is:

A S M D U E   ⬭ ☐ ☐ ☐ ☐ ☐

R S E S U P E   ☐ ☐ ⬭ ☐ ☐ ☐ ⬭

I O S S P E A C A   ☐ ☐ ☐ ☐ ☐ ⬭ ☐ ☐

R A N D O D M A E   ☐ ⬭ ☐ ☐ ☐ ⬭ ☐ ☐ ☐

E C U H E S P   ☐ ☐ ☐ ☐ ☐ ⬭ ☐

S T U E C   ☐ ☐ ⬭ ☐ ☐

Cētus est: ☐ ☐ ☐ ☐ ☐ ☐ ☐ ☐

H. Quid in hāc pictūrā vitiōsum est? What is wrong in this picture? There are ten things wrong with this picture, and it's up to you to find them. Describe them in the spaces provided:

1. _____

2. _____

3. _____

4. _____

5. _____

6. _____

7. _____

8. _____

9. _____

10. _____

I. Picture Story. Can you read this story? Whenever you come to a picture, read it as if it were a Latin word:

Claudius erat   Rōmānus annōrum tredecim.

Claudius cum   rurī habitābat.   sua, quae

Terentia vocāta est, undēcim annōs nāta erat.

suus, quī Gaius vocātus est, octō annōs nātus erat.

Quia aestās erat, Claudius   aut   volēbat. Novum   habēbat. Terentia autem

praeferēbat   aut   lūdĕre aut   .

Frātellus   volēbat. Sed   , quī agricola erat,

in agrīs occupātus erat. Quia diēs clārus erat, pater

faenum   secuit. Deinde pater faenum

collēgit et in   condidit. Deinde pater   ex

prātō in   ēgit (drove) et   eīs dedit.

autem in hortō laborābat. Māter hortum   sāruit et

plantās aquā   . Pōmerīdiē incēpit   et tonāre

(to thunder). Mox   cadĕre incēpit. Tōta familia citō in

villam properāvit.

PARS
QUĀRTA

XVI
Status fēminārum Rōmānārum

-urus Conjugation

1 Modicum cultūrae

Our look at the status of women in Roman times covers a period of over 1000 years. During that long span of time, everything changed, including the status of women. It is easiest to remember Roman history by dividing it into three periods: the period of the kings, or the Monarchy, which lasted 250 years (750 to 500 B.C.); the period of the Republic (500 to 1 B.C.); the period of the Empire (A.D. 1 to 500), when emperors ruled the Roman world. Although the status of women improved during this span of 1000 years, women held a position inferior to that of men. It was truly a man's world.

Women could not vote or hold political office. No woman ever ruled Rome, although women were often very influential behind the scenes. There were no women lawyers or jurors in the courts. A woman had no property rights. As long as she was single (**virgō, -inis** *f*), her father owned everything. As a young girl, she lived under the absolute control of her father; as a married woman (**mātrōna, -ae** *f*), she lived under the absolute control of her husband. He owned her as he owned his house and other property. When he died, she did not inherit anything; everything was passed on to his sons. If he had no sons, the estate went to the nearest male relatives. There was a way around this arrangement. In a marriage called **ūsus,** the wife could retain membership in her father's family; when her father died, she had a right to her inheritance. To gain this right, she simply had to spend a period of three nights a year away from her husband's house. As time went on, this marriage arrangement became more and more common, and the social life of women in general became less and less restrictive.

Even in their names, women were shortchanged. The three-part name for men was not customary for women. A male Roman citizen had three names: **praenōmen, nōmen,** and **cognōmen,** for example, Marcus Tullius Cicero. The **praenōmen** was his first name; the **nōmen,** ending in **-ius,** indicated the clan, or extended family, to which he belonged; the **cognōmen** was the family name. At the same time, one name usually had to do for girls and women. Their names were often the feminine forms of their father's name. Thus Marcus Tullius Cicero named his daughter simply Tullia. There were some names that indicated the order of birth, such as Secunda, Tertia, Maxima (*eldest*). When two names were needed to identify the girl more precisely, the second was likely to be the name of the father or husband in the genitive case.

There is evidence that some girls attended school, but it is not certain that boys and girls attended separate classes. Whether in the city or country, a girl's education under her mother's guidance was directed toward marriage, which occurred as early as the thirteenth or fourteenth year. She learned to spin wool into thread and to weave the thread into garments, to shop and prepare food for the table, and to run the household, including the slaves. When she got married, she brought her husband a dowry in the form of money or landed property. In case of divorce, the husband had to return the dowry to her father. By the time of the Empire, divorce was very common.

In earlier times, dancing, singing, and playing musical instruments were regarded as improper for women. They could not become actresses until the time of the Empire, and even then they were looked down on by most people. Those who really wanted to act on the stage became actresses anyway. They were not allowed to drink wine straight; they watered it down and added honey. You might say that this was the soft drink of antiquity. The ban on drinking straight wine seems to have been very strict in the earliest times. We have the story of a husband who killed his wife because she had drunk his wine.

Still, in comparison to the Greeks and the nations of the Near East, Roman women enjoyed a considerable amount of freedom. Greek women were confined to the women's room in the home so that male visitors would not see them. The married Roman lady, by contrast, carried out her daily occupation in the atrium, the main room and also the most public area of the home. In the dining room, the wife and children sat at the table, while the husband generally reclined. Roman women moved freely in public. They could attend the theater, the amphitheater, the race track, and the public baths at certain hours. A wife went to dinner parties with her husband and attended religious services reserved only for women.

The men in the legislature passed laws to limit the amount of jewelry that women could wear and to crack down on their flashy clothes and their use of carriages, but these laws were generally disregarded.

2 Vocābula

Can you identify these daily activities of Roman women?

domum purgāre

nēre

vestēs texĕre

cibum adpōnĕre

aquam ē cisternā haurīre

3 You have learned the future tense of Latin verbs. In Latin, as in English, the future can be expressed in two ways: "I will clean the house" (**domum purgābō**) and "I am going to clean the house" (**domum purgātūrus(-a) sum**). There is no great difference in meaning between these two forms of the future in English or in Latin. To form this alternate Latin future, take the fourth principal part of the verb, drop the ending, and add **-ūrus, -ūra, -ūrum.** The auxiliary verb (some form of **sum**) can occur before or after the main verb.

Here is a short story of women's activities in a Roman household. Pay attention to the alternate forms of the future in bold type. Notice that the auxiliary verb **sum** can come before or after the verb ending in **-ūrus:**

Pater meus, quī advocātus est, multōs clientēs habet. Hī clientēs sunt etiam ejus amīcī. Clientēs sunt
plēbēī, sed pater est patricius. Quia pater aliquot
amīcōs ad cēnam hodiē **vocātūrus est,** māter et mea
maxima soror omnia **parātūrae sunt.** Prīmum, pater
et clientēs in tablīnum **itūrī sunt,** ubi dē rēbus negō-
tiālibus **locūtūrī sunt.** Deinde ad mensam in trīclīniō
accubitūrī sunt.

plēbēius *-a -um* plebeian,
  common people
  patricius *-a -um* patrician
vocō *-āre* to invite

negōtiālis *-is -e* business
accumbō *-ĕre* accubuī
  accubitum *to recline*

Prīmum māter ad macellum **itūra est,** ubi pānem et holera et vīnum et carnem **obsōnātūra est.** Deinde māter et mea soror maxima, ūnā cum ancillā, tōtam domum **sunt purgātūrae.** Soror cubicula **ordinātūra est.** Māter autem tablīnum et trīclīnium **est purgātūra.** Ancilla aquam **haustūra est** ē cisternā, quae in ātriō sub pavīmentō est. Ancilla pavīmentum in ātriō **est lavātūra.** Quia ego parvulus puer sum, mihi licet tōtum diem lūdĕre, dum aliī tōtum diem labōrant.

eō īre īvī itum *to go*
obsōnō -āre *to shop (for)*
ancilla -ae *f maid*
ordinō -āre *to set in order, arrange*

pavīmentum -ī *n floor*
parvulus -a -um *small, young*
licet mihi *I am allowed*

Māter sororque cēnam in culīnā **coctūrae sunt.** "Simul atque cēnam coxī," ait māter sorōrī," ego cibum convīvīs **sum adpositūra** et tū **es adjūtūra** mē."

convīva -ae *m guest*
adpōnō -ĕre adposuī adpositus *to serve (food)*

Sīc pater **est futūrus** laetus et contentus, et omnēs clientēs **futūrī sunt** grātī.

grātus -a -um *grateful*

___ ACTIVITĀS ___

A. Respondē Latīnē:

1. Quōs pater est vocātūrus ad cēnam?

2. Suntne clientēs plēbēī an patriciī?

3. Estne pater plēbēius an patricius?

4. Quis ad macellum ītūra est?

5. Quid ibī obsōnātūra est?

6. Quis cubicula ordinātūra est?

7. Quis tablīnum et trīclīnium purgātūra est?

8. Quis aquam ē cisternā est haustūra?

_____

9. Ubi est cisterna?

_____

10. Quid ancilla purgātūra est?

_____

In the story you have just read, the verbs ending in **-ūrus** were combined only with the present tense of the verb **sum.** But other tenses of **sum** can be used in the same way as the auxiliary or helping verb:

Māter trīclīnium _purgātūra erat._ Mother was going to clean the dining room.

Pater aliquot clientēs ad cēnam _vocātūrus fuit._ Father was going to invite some clients to dinner.

___ ACTIVITĀTĒS ___

B. Complete the following sentences with the correct imperfect tense of **sum:**

1. Soror mea vestēs lavātūra _____.

2. Ancillae ūtensilia culīnae lavātūrae _____.

3. Pater clientēs ad cēnam nōn vocātūrus _____.

4. Ego et soror domum purgātūrae _____.

5. Claudia, ubi fructūs et holera obsōnātūra _____?

6. Ancillae, quandō cubiculum meum ordinātūrae _____.

C. Complete the following sentences with the correct ending of the verb and the correct form of the auxiliary verb. The principal parts of unfamiliar new verbs and meanings are provided:

1. **suō suĕre suī sūtus** _to sew_

Māter meam tunicam veterem sūt_____ _____.

2. **hauriō -īre hausī haustus** _to draw out_

Terentia, quandō aquam ē cisternā haust_____ _____?

3. neō nēre nēvī nētus *to spin*

Omnēs fīliae meae lānās nēt_____ _____.

4. adpōnō -ĕre adposuī adpositus *to serve*

Servī nostrī vīnum convīvīs adposit_____ _____.

5. obsōnō -āre -āvī -ātus *to shop for*

Māter, sī tū pomerīdiē ad macellum it_____ _____,

obsōnātur_____ _____ holera?

6. texō -ĕre texuī textus *to weave*

Quid ancillae crās text_____ _____, tunicās an stolās?

D. Supply the complete verb in the alternate future form ending with **-ūrus** in place of the regular future tense:

1. Ancillae togās novās texent. _____

2. Quis aquam ē cisternā nunc hauriet? _____

3. Ego ipse aquam ē cisternā numquam hauriam. _____

4. Rōmulus et Remus aquam ē flūmine haurient. _____

5. Avia mea lānās nēbit. _____

6. Ego et amīcae ūtensilia culīnae lavābimus. _____

7. Terentia, num plūs pānis in pistrīnā obsōnābis? _____

8. Duo servulī cibum familiae meae adpōnent. _____

E. Complete the following sentences with the correct form of the **-ūrus** verb and the correct form of **sum** in the perfect tense:

1. Hostēs Rōmae aquam ex aquaeductū publicō haust_____ _____.

2. Quattuor convīvae cum uxōribus ad mensam accubit_____

_____.

3. Puellae lānās nēt_____ _____.

4. Ego et ancillae togās et stolās sūt_____ _____.

5. Māter, ego ipsa stolam meam sūt_____ _____.

6. Servī ūtēnsilia culīnae ē trīclīniō in culīnam portāt_____ _____.

5 A verb with the **-ūrus** ending, but without an auxiliary verb, can be used as a future participle with several meanings:

Senātor ex sellā surrexit,   *The senator rose from his seat,*
   ōrātiōnem habitūrus.   *about to (intending to) give a*
                                     speech.

Used in this way, this form is called the *future participle*.

— ACTIVITĀS

F. Fill in the correct ending of the future participle:

1. Soror mea, comam crispātūr _____, calamistrum ubīque quaesīvit.

2. Convīvae trīclīnium intrāvērunt, prandium sumptūr _____.

3. Ancillae in culīnam ambulāvērunt, ūtensilia lautūr _____.

4. Pater aquam calidam rogāvit, barbam rāsūr _____.

5. Marcella balneum intrāvit, sē lautūr _____.

6. Servī bene māne experrectī sunt, parātūr _____jentāculum.

6 In Chapter XV, you learned how to express an indirect statement with the present and perfect infinitives. Remember that the present infinitive expresses an action occurring at the same time as an action expressed by the tense of the main verb. The perfect infinitive always expresses an action completed BEFORE the time of the main verb. The future infinitive expresses an action occurring AFTER that of the main verb. The future infinitive consists of the future participle plus **esse:**

DIRECT QUOTATION:	**Helena dīcit: "Familia mea domī cēnātūra est."**	*Helen says: "My family is going to eat dinner at home."*
INDIRECT STATEMENT:	**Helena dīcit familiam suam domī cēnātūram esse.**	*Helen says that her family is going to eat dinner at home.*
DIRECT QUOTATION:	**Helena dixit: "Familia mea domī cēnātūra est."**	*Helen said: "My family IS going to eat dinner at home."*
INDIRECT STATEMENT:	**Helena dixit familiam suam domī cēnātūram esse.**	*Helen said that her family WAS going to eat dinner at home.*

___ ACTIVITĀTĒS ___

G. Change each direct quotation to an indirect statement:

1. Cornēlius dīcit: "Ancillae nostrae futūrae sunt fidēlēs."

_____

2. Ancilla dixit: "Dominus noster dōnum mihi datūrus est."

_____

3. Clientēs dixērunt: "Marcus Tullius est futūrus advocātus excellens."

_____

4. Claudia dīcit: "Soror mea capillōs pexūra est."

_____

5. Frātellus dixit: "Māter cēnam excellentem coctūra est."

_____

6. Melissa dixit: "Ancillae crās nōn labōrātūrae sunt."

_____

7. Claudīus dixit: "Ego aliquandō senātor futūrus sum."

_____

8. Servī dixērunt: "Nōs cēnam bonam hodiē adpositūrī sumus."

_____

H. Change the indirect statements to direct quotations:

1. Crēdō mē bene dormītūrum esse.

_____

2. Sciō ancillās futūrās esse industriōsās.

_____

3. Pater dixit mātrem lactūcam et carōtās et cucumerēs in macellō emptūram esse.

_____

4. Vīcīnus meus dixit sē iter per Campāniam factūrum esse.

_____

5. Amīcus ad mē scripsit sē mox in Hispāniam ēmigrātūrum esse.

_____

6. Omnēs dīcunt sē prō patriā moritūrōs esse.

_____

I. Substitute the future infinitive for the present infinitive in the indirect statements. The principal parts of the verb are provided before each sentence:

1. **rādō rādĕre rāsī rāsus**
   Pater dīxit sē barbam novāculō novō rādĕre. _____

2. **surgō *surgĕre* surrexī surrectus**
   Māter dīcit sē bene māne surgĕre. _____

3. **suō suĕre suī sūtus**
   Melissa dīxit ancillam tunicās veterēs nōn suĕre. _____

4. **induō induĕre induī indūtus**
   Pater dīcit convīvās omnēs togam induĕre. _____

5. **purgō -āre -āvi -ātus**
   Māter dīcit frātellum dentēs nōn purgāre. _____

6. **sum esse fuī futūrus**
   Quī in urbe vīvunt dīcunt vītam rūrī multō meliōrem esse. _____

 You have read about the status of Roman women. Now learn something more intimate about a Roman girl by reading a letter that a boy wrote to her and the answer that she sent him:

Cornēlius Clārae salūtem dīcit.*   **salus -ūtis** f *greetings*

Ex quō diē ego tē cum mātre tuā in Forō Rōmānō vīdī et tēcum locūtus sum, tē ubīque quaesīvī. Quotiens ego thermās frequentō, tē quaerō. Quotiens forum aut macellum vīsō, tē quaerō. Crēde mihi, Clāra, erat amor prīmā speciē. Tē vehementer dēsīderō. Sine tē nōn possum vīvĕre. Putō quidem tē esse puellam pulcherrimam tōtīus Ītaliae. Crās ego cum amīcīs ad Circum Maximum itūrus sum, quia gladiātōrēs nōtissimī ibi pugnātūrī sunt. Sperō mē tē ibi rursus cōnspectūrum esse. Ego et amīcī semper in ordine quārtō aut quīntō sedēmus. Quaere nōs ibi! Mūnusculum bellum tibi adferam. Sciō tē nōn Rōmae habitāre sed Arīciae; Arīcia autem nōn procul ab urbe abest. Amor viam semper invenīre potest. Venī, quaesō, sī mē amās. Cūrā ut valeās. Rōmae data.

ex quō diē *ever since the day*
quaerō -ĕre quaesīvī quaesītus *to look for*
quotiens *whenever*
vīsō -ĕre vīsī *to visit*
prīmā speciē *at first sight*
vehementer *terribly*
dēsīderō -āre *to miss*
quidem *really*
nōtus -a -um *well-known, famous*
rursus *again*
ordō -inis m *row*
bellus -a -um *nice*
adferō -ferre -tūlī -lātum *to bring*
quaesō *please*
cūrā ut valeās *take care of yourself*
Rōmae data *mailed in Rome*

Tuus,
Cornēlius

*Typical beginning of a Roman letter.

Clāra Cornēliō salūtem dīcit.

Epistulam tuam magnō cum gaudiō accēpī. Verba tua mē valdē dēlectāvērunt. Ex quō diē ego tē in Forō Rōmānō vīdī et tēcum locūta sum, tē constanter in animō habuī. Ubicumque ego sum, dē tē cōgitō, etiam tum cum domum purgō aut lānās neō aut vestēs texō aut in oppidō obsōnō. Ego quoque tē vehementer dēsīderō. Frequenter cum mātre meā dē tē loquor. Māter putat tē esse juvenem excellentem et hūmānissimum. "Cornēlius," inquit māter, "habitum patricium habet. Oportet tē nūbĕre talī juvenī! Crēde mihi, Clāra, inveniēs nēminem meliōrem." Cum mātre consentiō ex tōtō.

Sciō Arīciam nōn procul ab urbe Rōmā distāre; sciō perinde multōs viātōrēs cōtīdiē ad urbem iter facĕre. Iter ad urbem rārō fēcī, et numquam per mē. Ut scīs, puellae honestae numquam per sē iter faciunt. Praetereā, urbēs magnae mē terrificant. Sī ego Rōmam veniam et tē in Circō Maximō propter turbās magnās nōn conspiciam, venī Arīciam. Domus mea est facilis inventū, quia Arīcia est oppidulum. Venī quam prīmum. Cūrā ut valeās. Arīciae data.

Tua,
Clāra

gaudium **-ī** n joy
dēlectō -āre to delight
constanter constantly
animus **-ī** m mind, heart
  ubicumque wherever
etiam even
  tum cum then when

juvenis **-is** m young man
hūmānus **-a -um** kind
habitus **-ūs** m bearing, looks
  oportet tē you ought
  talis **-is -e** such a
consentiō **-īre consensī**
  consensum to agree
  ex tōtō completely
distō -āre to be distant
perinde furthermore
rārō rarely
  per mē by myself   **ut** as
honestus **-a -um** respectable
praetereā moreover
terrificō -āre to terrify
turba **-ae** f crowd

facilis inventū easy to find
  oppidulum **-ī** n little town
quam prīmum as soon as
  possible

Are you curious to find out what happened? Did Clāra find Cornelius in the Circus Maximus? If you are dying to know the answer, turn your book upside down and find out!

Clāra Rōmam iter fēcit cum mātre. Circum Maximum intrāvit et Cornēlium ubīque quaesīvit sed eum conspicĕre nōn potuit. Oculī ejus erant plēnī lacrimārum. Trīstissima erat. Dēnique Clāra audīvit vōcem dīcentem: "Clāra, Clāra, ego sum hīc! Est tuus Cornēlius!" Clāra cucurrit obvia eī (*to meet him*). Nunc oculī Clārae erant plēnī lacrimārum gaudiī.

DIALOGUS

Vocābula

profundō -ĕre profūdī profūsus *to shed*
amans amantis *m lover, boyfriend*
quondam *once*
accidō -ĕre -ī *to happen*
nebulō -ōnis *m airhead*
argentum -ī *n cash, dough*
jūrō -āre *to swear*

caudex -icis *m blockhead*
jamdūdum *long ago*
repudiō -āre *to jilt*
urbānus -a -um *sophisticated*
crūdus -a -um *crude*
mītis -e *gentle*
marsuppium -ī *n money bag*

QUAESTIŌNĒS PERSŌNĀLĒS

1. Adjuvāsne patrem aut mātrem domī?

   _____

2. Purgāsne et ordinās cubiculum tuum?

   _____

3. Lavāsne ūtensilia culīnae interdum?

   _____

4. Potesne cēnam coquĕre?

   _____

5. Obsōnāsne umquam in macellō cum mātre tuā?

   _____

6. Quis vestēs tuās suit, tū an māter?

   _____

7. Habēsne ancillam domī tuae?

   _____

8. Cōgitāsne fēminās Rōmānās vītam fēlīcem ēgisse _(led)_?

   _____

COMPOSITIŌ

You have learned what the life of women was like in ancient Rome, whether slave or free woman. Can you list three things that Roman girls or women and Americans do that are the same? Can you list three things in which the Roman women were different from American women?

1. _____

2. _____

3. _____

4. _____

5. _____

6. _____

COLLOQUIUM

Complete this dialog between Helena and Agrippina on the basis of the previous conversation:

THE LATIN CONNECTION

A. We have seen the verb **vocāre** used in several senses, but its most common meaning is *to call*. This verb has given us various compounds in English. Give the meaning of the following derivatives of **vocāre** and try to think up a good English sentence for each. Can you supply the noun derived from each derivative?

1. evoke _____   _____

2. convoke _____   _____

3. invoke _____   _____

4. provoke _____   _____

5. revoke _____   _____

6. What is an irrevocable decision? _____

7. What is a vocation? _____ an avocation? _____

B. What is the Latin origin of the following words:

1. utensils _____

2. concoct _____

3. suture _____

4. exhausted _____

5. grateful _____

6. ingrate _____

7. clientele _____

8. Patrick _____

9. ancillary _____

10. repudiate _____

11. consensus _____

12. urbane _____

13. profuse _____

XVII _In officīnā tignāriā_

Present Subjunctive

1 Modicum cultūrae

If you were to travel through the narrow, winding streets of ancient Rome, you would see to the left and right of you master craftsmen (**magister -trī** _m_) in their little workshops (**officīna -ae** _f_), assisted by their young apprentices (**discens -entis** _m_) and other workers. The craftsmen and their families lived in crowded, dingy apartments consisting of a room or two in the upper stories of ramshackle apartment buildings. Fires and collapse of such buildings were very common in Rome. The ground floor was often occupied by workshops, retail stores, and small fast-food restaurants. Craftsmen led a hard life. Work began at sunup and lasted till sundown. The wages earned in these workshops were just enough to keep the people going from day to day.

There were no labor unions in those days to bargain for higher wages or shorter working hours or better working conditions. The owner of a workshop set the wage and that was it. Of course, he had to compete with other shops for the best workers that he could afford to pay. The members of the various trades formed guilds (**collēgium -ī** _n_), which might be called social clubs. There were, for instance, **collēgia** of weavers, shoemakers, blacksmiths, silversmiths, goldsmiths, potters, leather workers, dyers, bakers, barbers, stonemasons, and carpenters. The patroness of many of the **collēgia** was Minerva, the goddess of handicrafts. (Do you remember in which craft she competed with Arachne?) Her temple was located on the Aventine Hill, which was heavily populated with the lower classes (the plebians). Not all guilds chose Minerva as their patroness, however. A wall painting from Pompeii shows that Daedalus, who was regarded as the first carpenter in history, was the patron of the carpenter's guild. It was natural for members of a trade to band together to form **collēgia** because of their common interests. It gave them an opportunity to "talk shop" with one another on holidays and to find out about new developments in their trade. Politicians gradually realized that, if they could win over a **collēgium** with a bribe, they could count on the votes of the members; at the same time, the tradesmen, by selling their votes, had a little more pocket money to make ends meet. The government passed laws to put an end to this cozy arrangement between crooked politicians and poor craftsmen.

In contrast to modern-day factories that hire hundreds and even thousands of workers, the workshops of the Roman tradesmen always remained small. With no electric power to drive machines that could produce in quantity on the assembly line, the tradesmen had to rely on simple tools to do all the work. The Romans were not great inventors. This fact was evident in one area: farming. Cato, who wrote a book on farming around 200 B.C., describes all the tools needed to run a farm. Columella, writing on farming 250 years later, talks of using the same tools. From all evidence, the situation was the same in all the other trades and crafts.

Take the situation of a carpenter (**tignārius -ī** _m_). The tree was chopped down with an axe. The Romans never realized that they could harness the current of the Tiber river to power sawmills. The length of the log was cut by handsaw into boards (**tabula -ae** *f*) and then planed or filed smooth to make them usable for various purposes. This was slow, painstaking work. The Romans were familiar with the lathe (**tornus -ī** *m*), and so they could produce decorative legs for tables, chairs, and the like. Daedalus was believed to have invented the lathe, the saw, the carpenter's level, and other tools. Unfortunately many objects that the carpenters produced decayed in the course of time because of dampness. Nevertheless, the wall paintings from Pompeii and elsewhere in the Roman world show that carpenters could produce very attractive things.

2 Let's look in on a typical carpenter shop in the busy, bustling, noisy **Subūra** section of ancient Rome. Have a good look around so that you will remember the names of the tools:

serra -ae f

malleus -ī m

tignārius -ī m

secūris -is f

scalpellum -ī n

discens -entis m

terebra -ae f

tignum -ī n

tornus -ī m

scōpae -ārum f l p

tabula -ae f

magister -trī m

scobis -is f

runcīna -ae f

clāvus -ī m

3 | You have looked over the carpenter's shop and seen some of his tools. Let's read about an interview between a master carpenter and a new apprentice:

DISCENS: Salvē, magister. Ut intellegō, obligātus sum laborāre in tuā officīnā tignāriā. Nōmen mihi est Marcus Spurius, Marcī fīlius.

MAGISTER: Salvē, Marce. Nōnne cupis fierī tignārius? Immō, quid facĕre potes? Potesne ūtī runcīnā aut scalpellō?

DISCENS: Neque runcīnā neque scalpellō umquam ūsus sum. Usque adhūc scholam frequentābam.

MAGISTER: Potesne serram dūcĕre rectā līneā?

DISCENS: Nōn omnīnō serram dūcĕre possum. Numquam tabulam serrā secuī. Pater meus numquam mē docuit serram dūcĕre.

MAGISTER: Potesne ūtī terebrā?

DISCENS: Terebra? Quid est terebra?

MAGISTER: Hīc est terebra. Terebra est instrūmentum quō tignum aut tabulam perforāmus.

DISCENS: Numquam anteā terebram vīdī, sed volō discĕre terebrā ūtī.

MAGISTER: Potesne ūtī malleō?

DISCENS: Possum. Pater meus malleum domī habet. Ego clāvōs malleō saepe fixī. Ōlim cistam pulchram fabricāvī.

MAGISTER: Potesne tornum tractāre? Potesne pedēs mensae aut sellae tornāre?

DISCENS: Quid est tornus? Numquam dē tornō audīvī. Explicā, quaesō, mihi tornum.

MAGISTER: Tornus est instrūmentum quō rotundāmus lignum, exemplī grātiā, cum pedēs mensae tornāmus. Comprehendisne?

DISCENS: Incertus sum.

MAGISTER: Nōlī timēre. Paulātim docēbō tē ūtī omnibus intrūmentīs in hāc officīnā. Sī dīligenter laborābis et praecepta mea audiēs, fiēs aliquandō tignārius excellens. Hodiē autem officīnam purgābis. Scobis ubīque est. Age, cape scōpās et scobem verre!

obligātus sum *I am supposed*

immō *well*
  runcīna -ae *f plane*
scalpellum -ī *n chisel*

usque adhūc *up till now*
serram dūcĕre rectā līneā *to saw in a straight line*
nōn omnīnō *not at all*
serrā secāre *to saw (cut with a saw)*
terebra -ae *f drill*

instrūmentum -ī *n tool*
perforō -āre *to drill a hole in*

discō -ĕre didicī (+ *inf*) *to learn how to*
figō -ĕre fixī fixus *to drive in*
ōlim *once*
  cista -ae *f box*
fabricō -āre *to make, put together*
tractō -āre *to handle*
  pēs pedis *m leg (of chair, etc.)*
tornō -āre *to turn out (on a lathe)*
explicō -āre -uī -itus *to explain*
rotundō -āre *to make round*
lignum -ī *n wood*
comprehendō -ĕre -ī comprehensus *to understand*
incertus -a -um *uncertain, not sure*
paulātim *little by little*
praeceptum -ī *n instruction*
  audīre *to listen to*
  aliquandō *someday*
scobis -is *f sawdust*
  age *come on*
  scōpae -ārum *fpl broom*
verrō -ĕre -ī versus *to sweep up*

___ ACTIVITĀTĒS _____

A. Imagine that your father has sent you to the hardware store **(taberna ferrāria)** to purchase some tools for work around the house. Write their names below the pictures:

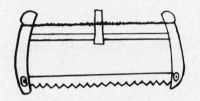

1. _____

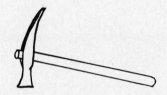

2. _____

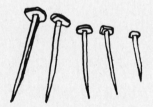

3. _____

4. _____

5. _____

6. _____

B. **Quid faciunt discentēs in officīnā tignāriā?** Match the phrases with the pictures:

Discentēs tignum serrā secant.
Discens scobem scōpīs verrit.
Tignārius pedem mensae in tornō
  tornat.
Discens tignum terebrā perforat.
Discentēs tigna in officīnam portant.

Parvulus cum scobe lūdit.
Tignārius clāvum in tabulam
  malleō fīgit.
Discens tignum runcīnat.
Discentēs cum magistrō loquuntur.
Discens urnam clāvōrum tollit.

1. _____

2. _____

3. _____

4. _____

5. _____

6. _____

7. _____

8. _____

9. _____

10. _____

4 All the verbs that you have used so far have been in the indicative mood. "Mood" does not, of course, refer here to the way a person feels but to the "mode" or way in which the speaker indicates something other than fact. The "indicative mood" of the verb makes a statement of fact. But at times you may want to express a wish or a possibility or deliberation. To express this secondary idea, you change the form of the verb:

WISH:	God *be* with you.
POSSIBILITY:	You *may* always *be* happy.
DELIBERATION:	What am I to do? (or, What *should* I do?)

In the first sentence, the form of the verb was changed to express a wish. In the second sentence, the auxiliary or helping verb *may* is used to show possibility. In the third sentence, *should* is used to show uncertainty. Modern English rarely uses the subjunctive mood. Instead, it normally uses auxiliary verbs (*may*, *should*, *would*, etc.) where subjunctive forms were once used to express shades of meaning other than fact. But just look at a page by a Roman writer, and you will find subjunctive forms all over the place.

The simplest way to explain how to form the present subjunctive is to say that Latin changes the *typical* vowel of the indicative. Look at these two columns:

INDICATIVE	SUBJUNCTIVE
port*ō*	port*em*
port*ās*	port*ēs*
port*at*	port*et*
port*āmus*	port*ēmus*
port*ātis*	port*ētis*
port*ant*	port*ent*

What is the typical vowel of the indicative endings? _____ Which vowel was

substituted for it to make it *sound* different from the indicative? _____ When the Romans heard **portet** instead of **portat,** they immediately realized that **portet** did not simply mean *he carries*, but *he may carry* or *he should carry* or *let him carry.*

Now let's see how the subjunctive is used in Latin. The Romans used the subjunctive with various conjunctions, for instance, to express purpose. In English we express purpose in several ways:

The carpenter works *to support* his family.
in order to support his family.
so that he may support his family.

These three versions all mean exactly the same thing. The most common way to express purpose in English is with the infinitive, as "to support" in the first version. Latin never uses an infinitive to express purpose. The Latin construction is similar to the third version, using the conjunction **ut** *(so that)* and the verb after it in the *subjunctive mood* to express "may support." Latin does not need an auxiliary verb, as English does, but simply changes the vowel in the verb to express purpose. For example, the Latin verb **sustento -āre** means *to support.* Now look at these two sentences:

Tignārius familiam suam *sustentat*. — *The carpenter supports his family.*
Tignārius labōrat ut familiam suam *sustentet*. — *The carpenter works to support his family.*

Because the first sentence simply *indicates* a fact, the verb in both English and Latin is in the *indicative* mood. The second sentence states why the carpenter works (the purpose of his working). To express this purpose, Latin introduces the purpose clause with the conjunction **ut** and puts the verb into the *subjunctive* mood. Did you notice that the final vowel of **sustentat** changed to **sustentet** in the purpose clause of the second sentence?

It is important also to notice that the Latin purpose clause begins with the conjunction (**ut** in this sentence) and ends with the verb (**sustentet**). Seeing word groupings helps you understand the Latin sentence. The negative purpose clause is introduced by the conjunction **nē.** Look at these two sentences:

Fīlius patrem suum non *suscitāt*.
Fīlius tacitē ambulat ne patrem
  suum *suscitet*.

The son does not wake up his father.
The son walks quietly in order not
  to wake up his father.

Again, the first sentence simply *indicates* a fact, and so the verb is in the *indicative* mood. The second sentence contains a clause beginning with the conjunction **nē** and ending with the verb **sustentet** in the *subjunctive* mood.

PITFALL: Don't confuse **ut** (with the indicative, meaning *as* or *when*) with **ut** (with the subjunctive, meaning *in order that* or *so that*).

__ ACTIVITĀS __

C. Rewrite the following sentences, changing the second sentence to a purpose clause:

EXAMPLE: Tignārius labōrat. Familiam sustentat.
     Tignārius labōrat **ut familiam sustentet.**

1. Discentēs veniunt. Officīnam tignāriam purgant.

_____

2. Tignārius serram capit. Tabulam longam serrā secat.

_____

3. Discentēs runcīnā ūtuntur. Tignum grave runcīnant.

_____

4. Ego et discens terebrā ūtimur. Tabulās perforāmus.

_____

5. Tignārius officīnam bene māne intrat. Multās horās ibi labōrat.

_____

6. Discentēs extrā officīnam circumstant. Tornum novum nōn tractant.

_____

7. Discens ē cubiculō suō venit. Amīcum suum nōn ē somnō excitat.

_____

8. Collēgium tignāriōrum in primō ordine sedet. Gladiātōrēs optimōs spectat.

5 To form the subjunctive of the **-āre** family of verbs, you changed the typical vowel **a** to **e.** Now notice what happens in the other families of verbs:

INDICATIVE	SUBJUNCTIVE	INDICATIVE	SUBJUNCTIVE
move*ō*	move*am*	dūc*ō*	dūc*am*
move*s*	move*ās*	dūc*is*	dūc*ās*
move*t*	move*at*	dūc*it*	dūc*at*
move*mus*	move*āmus*	dūc*imus*	dūc*āmus*
move*tis*	move*ātis*	dūc*itis*	dūc*ātis*
move*nt*	move*ant*	dūc*unt*	dūc*ant*

INDICATIVE	SUBJUNCTIVE	INDICATIVE	SUBJUNCTIVE
cap*iō*	cap*iam*	aud*iō*	aud*iam*
cap*is*	cap*iās*	aud*īs*	aud*iās*
cap*it*	cap*iat*	aud*it*	aud*iat*
cap*imus*	cap*iāmus*	aud*īmus*	aud*iāmus*
cap*itis*	cap*iātis*	aud*ītis*	aud*iātis*
cap*iunt*	cap*iant*	aud*iunt*	aud*iant*

Note that the first person singular of the present subjunctive ends in **-m** for all verbs. What is the typical vowel of the subjunctive endings of all families of

verbs except the first? _____Why couldn't this typical vowel be used in the

subjunctive endings of the first family of verbs? _____

_____

__ ACTIVITĀS _____

D. Complete with the correct form of the subjunctive of the verbs in parentheses:

1. (vidēre)   Discens officīnam intrat ut tornum novum _____.

2. (placēre)   Puellae comam calamistrō crispant ut amantibus suīs _____.

3. (facĕre)   Discentēs dīligenter labōrant ut plūs pecūniae _____.

4. (invenīre)   Ego et discentēs interdum latēmus nē magister nōs _____.

5. (emĕre)   Multī officīnam nostram intrant ut sellās et mensās _____.

6. (lavāre)   Ancilla aquam ē cisternā haurit ut ātrium _____.

7. (obsōnāre)   Māter et soror, ītisne nunc in forum ut holera _____?

8. (coquĕre)   Ancillae in culīnam eunt ut cēnam prō convīvīs _____.

9. (audīre)   Discentēs in officīnā conveniunt ut praecepta magistrī _____.

10. (nēre)   Māter in ātriō consīdit ut lānās _____.

6 The subjunctive of the verbs **esse** and **posse** are irregular, that is, they don't fall into the pattern that we just saw for other verbs:

sim	possim
sīs	possīs
sit	possit
sīmus	possīmus
sītis	possītis
sint	possint

— ACTIVITĀS

E. Complete with the correct form of the present subjunctive of the verb in parentheses:

1. (esse)   Parentēs meī Rōmam iter faciunt ut cum avō et aviā _____.

2. (posse)   Ego in prīmō ordine theātrī semper sedeō ut melius vidēre _____.

3. (posse)   Frāter meus prope illam puellam sedet ut cum eā loquī _____.

4. (esse)   Ego et Fabius nunc ex urbe exīmus nē noctū in mediā urbe _____.

5. (posse)   Frātellus aquam ē cisternā haurit ut sē lavāre _____.

6. (esse)   Melissa, manēsne domī ut cum parentibus tuīs _____.

7 The Romans used the subjunctive mood in indirect questions. In English, we change the word order to indicate an indirect question:

DIRECT: **Ubi est pecten meus?**   *Where is my comb?*
INDIRECT: **Caecilia quaerit *ubi pecten suus sit.***   *Caecilia asks where her comb is.*

There are many verbs that can introduce an indirect question. Here are some:

rogāre, interrogāre, quaerĕre, inquīrĕre (*to ask*)
scīre (*to know*) and **nescīre** (*not to know*)
expōnĕre, explicāre (*to explain*)
intellegĕre, vidēre (*to understand*)
ambigĕre (*to be unsure, to wonder*)

There is one peculiarity about the Latin word order in indirect questions. The Romans often put the indirect question first in the sentence. Note the word order of this sentence:

***Ubi discentēs sint* nesciō.**   *I don't know where the apprentices are.*

The Romans said, in effect: "Where the apprentices are I do not know."

__ ACTIVITĀS _____

F. Underline the indirect questions. Then convert the indirect to a direct question:

EXAMPLE: <u>Ubi sim</u> nesciō.   Ubi sum?

1. Magister vult scīre quid nōs faciāmus.

   _____

2. Scīsne quid faciās?

   _____

3. Quid senātor dīcat nōn intellegō.

   _____

4. Cūr tignārius illum malleum habeat nesciō.

   _____

5. Magister quaerit quid discens facĕre possit.

   _____

6. Nōn possum expōnĕre cūr Rōmam sīc amem.

   _____

7. Cūr tignārius īrātus sit nunc videō.

   _____

8. Ambigō num (*whether*) ille Rōmae habitet.

   _____

9. Magister quaerit quandō discentēs labōrātūrī sint.

   _____

10. Qualis persōna tū sīs nesciō.

   _____

⟨8⟩ Daedalus was thought to have been the world's first carpenter and the inventor of some important tools of the trade. That is not his main claim to fame, however. He and his son Icarus were the counterpart of the Wright brothers in antiquity, since they were reputed to have been the first persons to fly. Now read how that came about:

Daedalus cum fīliō Īcarō in insulā Crētā vixit. Tignārius perītissimus erat. Dīcitur invēnisse serram et tornum et multa alia instrūmenta tignāria. Itaque Mīnōs, rex Crētae, Daedalum ad aulam suam vocāvit et dixit: "Monstrum ferōcissimum in aulā habēmus. Hōc monstrum puerōs puellāsque dēvōrat. Vocātur Mīnōtaurus, id est, 'Mīnōis taurus.' Est sēmihomō et sēmitaurus. Jubeō tē labyrinthum aedificāre ut istud monstrum ibi inclūdāmus."

Postquam Daedulus labyrinthum aedificāvit, Mīnōs Daedalum ipsum ūnā cum fīliō Īcarō, in labyrinthō inclūsit quia rex nōluit Daedalum sēcrētum labyrinthī revēlāre cuiquam. Sed Daedalus jānuam sēcrētam labyrinthī facile aperuit et cum fīlio ad montem altum fūgit.

Quōdam diē pater fīliō dixit: "Exulēs in hāc insulā sumus. Neque terra neque mare viam salūtis dat. Sed via per caelum nōbīs patet. Ālās ex avium pennīs faciam ut hōc modō ad salūtem volāre possīmus." Pater fīliusque pennās aquilārum colligunt ut ex hīs pennīs magnās ālās faciant. Dum pater dīligenter labōrat, fīlius cum pennīs lūdit. Pater pennās in ordine pōnit et eās līnō et cērā ligāvit. Dēnique alae erant parātae. Daedalus ālās umerīs fīliī adaptāvit, deinde ipse ālās induit. Mandāta stricta fīliō dedit: "Īcare, mī fīliole, nōlī celsius volāre, nē radiī sōlis cēram ālārum tuārum liquefaciant. Nōlī dēmissius volāre, nē ālae tuae flūctus maris tangant." Ut fīliō mandāta dedit, genae patris maduērunt, et manūs tremuērunt. Ōscula fīliō dat, et ante volat. Fīlius sequitur.

Prīmō Īcarus mandāta patris in memoriā tenēbat. Mox celsius et celsius volāre temptāvit puer et incēpit gaudēre audācī volātū. Radiī sōlis autem cēram ālārum liquefaciēbant. "Pater!" Īcarus clāmāvit, "pater, adjuvā mē, servā mē!" ut in mare cecidit. "Īcare!" clāmāvit anxius pater, "ubi es?" "Īcare" rursus dixit et pennās in flūctibus conspexit. Etiamnunc mare, in quō Īcarus periit, Mare Īcarium vocātur. Postquam pater maestus corpus fīliī sepelīvit, in Ītaliam volāvit.

---

vīvō *-ĕre* vixī *to live*
perītus *-a -um skillful*
Mīnōs *-ōis* m *king of Crete*
sēmihomō *-inis* m *half-man*
sēmitaurus *-ī* m *half-bull*
jubeō *-ēre* jussī jussus *to order*
labyrinthus *-ī* m *labyrinth, maze*
aedificō *-āre -āvī -ātus to build*
inclūdō *-ĕre* inclūsī inclūsus *to lock up*
sēcrētum *-ī* n *secret*
revēlō *-āre to reveal*
cuiquam *to anyone*
exul *-is* m *exiled person*
via salūtis *road to safety*
pateō *-ēre -uī to lie open*
āla *-ae* f *wing*
penna *-ae* f *feather*
colligō *-ĕre* collēgī collectus *to gather*
līnum *-ī* n *twine*
cēra *-ae* f *wax*
ligō *-āre to tie*
adaptō *-āre to adapt*
mandātum *-ī* n *instruction*
celsius *too high*
radius *-ī* m *ray*
liquefaciō *-ĕre -fēcī -factus to melt*
dēmissius *too low*
tangō *-ĕre* tetigī tactus *touch*
gena *-ae* f *cheek*
madeō *-ēre -uī to be wet with tears*
tremō *-ĕre -uī to tremble*
ante *out ahead*
celsius *higher*
gaudeō *-ēre* (+ abl) *to enjoy*
volātus *-us* m *flight*
anxius *-a -um anxious, worried*
rursus *again*
etiamnunc *even now, still today*
pereō *-īre -iī to perish*
maestus *-a -um grieving*
sepeliō *-īre -īvī* sepultus *to bury*

___ ACTIVITĀS _____

G. Respondē Latīnē:

1. Ubi Daedalus habitāvit?

   _____

2. Quis erat fīlius Daedalī?

   _____

3. Quis erat rex insulae?

   _____

4. Quale monstrum rex in aulā habēbat?

   _____

5. Quid rex jussit Daedalum aedificāre?

   _____

6. Quod nōmen erat monstrō?

   _____

7. Cūr Daedalus ex labyrinthō effūgĕre potuit?

   _____

8. Ex quō Daedalus ālās fēcit?

   _____

9. Quid cēram ālārum Īcarī liquefēcit?

   _____

10. Quō volāvit pater post mortem fīliī?

    _____

DIALOGUS

Vocābula

intentē *intently*
Inaugurāsne? *Are you taking the auspices?*
captō -āre *to catch*
sustineō -ēre -uī sustentus *to hold up*

plaudō -ēre plausī plausus *to flap*
tamquam *like*
cauda -ae *f tail*
mementō *remember!*
repente *all of a sudden*

QUAESTIŌNĒS PERSŌNĀLĒS

1. Scīsne ūtī malleō?

2. Potesne serram rectā līneā dūcĕre?

3. Potesne clāvōs fīgĕre?

4. Fabricāvistīne aliquid instrūmentīs tignāriīs?

5. Vidistīne umquam tignārium, tornum tractantem?

6. Purgāsne cubiculum tuum scōpīs?

7. Habetne pater tuus multa instrūmenta tignāria?

8. Ūtitur frequenter pater instrumentīs tignāriīs?

COMPOSITIŌ

Every household has a number of tools that are needed for making repairs around the house. Imagine that your little brother or sister is looking into the tool chest and is asking you what the various tools are used for. Explain how the following tools are used. For example, say, in Latin, of course, "A file is a tool with which . . ."

serra   malleus   secūris   runcīna   terebra

1.

2.

3.

4.

5.

COLLOQUIUM

In this dialog between Tullia and her little brother, Claudius gets stuck for words once in a while. Help him out by supplying the needed words on the model of the previous conversation:

THE LATIN CONNECTION

A. What is the Latin origin of serrated? _____

What is a *serrated* blade? _____

B. What are the Latin origins of the following words and what do they mean?

1. radius _____ _____
2. ligature _____ _____
3. humerus _____ _____
4. aviary _____ _____
5. caudal _____ _____
6. sustain _____ _____
7. precept _____ _____
8. crucifixion _____ _____
9. scalpel _____ _____
10. college _____ _____
11. to turn _____ _____
12. mandate _____ _____
13. liquefy _____ _____
14. tremulous _____ _____
15. tangible _____ _____

C. When we say that a modern factory *manufactures* products, we think immediately of machines as producing various items. But what, according to its Latin

roots, does *manufacture* mean? _____

D. **Secō secāre secuī sectus** means *to cut*. What do the following derivatives mean?

1. vivisection _____

2. intersection _____

3. to dissect _____

4. to bisect _____

5. a sect _____

6. section _____

7. cross-section _____

8. sectional furniture _____

9. secant _____

10. insect _____

XVIII Mons Vesuvius

Imperfect Subjunctive

1 Modicum cultūrae

Of all the natural catastrophes that occurred within Roman memory, by far the most famous was the eruption of the volcano on Mount Vesuvius, which is located about seven miles inland from the Bay of Naples. The eruption occurred on August 24, A.D. 79, at the height of the vacation season, when hordes of vacationers from Rome and elsewhere crowded the resort towns and beaches of the Bay of Naples. A severe earthquake in A.D. 63 had caused heavy damage in the towns of Campania, the district in which Mount Vesuvius lies. Public buildings toppled. Many people were left homeless. A flock of 600 sheep disappeared in a huge crack in the earth's surface. Just before the eruption of Mount Vesuvius in A.D. 79, there were earth tremors, but no one paid much attention to them because they were frequent throughout the district of Campania.

The great eruption lasted three days. When it was over, the towns of Pompeii and Herculaneum were totally destroyed. A teenager, Gaius Plinius Secundus, whom we call Pliny and who lived at Misenum on the northern shore of the Bay of Naples, has left us a short but vivid eyewitness account of what happened during those dreadful hours between August 24 and 26.

A tremendous mushroom cloud was spotted across the Bay of Naples rising high into the sky above Vesuvius. At times the cloud was white, at times it was murky with dust (**pulvis -eris** m) and ashes (**cinis -eris** m). The volcano spewed spectacular sheets of flame at night. Soon thick ash and hot little stones (**lapillī -ōrum** mpl) began to fall over a wide area and cover everything like snow. The thick odor of sulfur was everywhere and made breathing difficult. The next day, the sun was blocked out by the cloud of dust and ashes. Houses shook and were in danger of collapsing. Those who were inside houses ran outside, and those who were outside ran into the houses and public buildings. Children yelled for parents as day turned to night, parents yelled for their children, and husbands yelled for their wives. As people tried to leave the town of Misenum, many lost their way in the pitch darkness. Besides, the earth tremors tossed the vehicles from one side of the road to the other. Many thought that it was the end of the world. Pliny himself believed that he and those around him would die. Tugging his mother by the hand, he forced her to escape with him. When the sun reappeared, the people found that the entire landscape had changed. Everything at Misenum was covered with a deep layer of ash and pumice. And remember that Misenum was located about 15 miles to the northwest of the crater.

At Pompeii, just a couple of miles south of Vesuvius, the situation was far worse. The eruption occurred as the townspeople were sitting in their theater watching a performance. Luckily, the greater part of the population of about 22,000 had time to gather whatever valuables they could carry with them and left town early on the morning of August 24. Some two thousand people died of suffocation. Pompeii was covered to a depth of 20 to 25 feet with ash and pumice. The city was not completely buried; the tops of the walls of many public and private buildings projected from the surface, and so it was possible for the survivors to dig out what valuables they had left behind. Later eruptions and the work of nature and man eventually erased all traces of the city until it was excavated in modern times. Excavations have gone on for well over 100 years; at the present time about 85% of Pompeii has been excavated.

The other town that was destroyed, Herculaneum, lay right on the shore of the Bay of Naples. It was buried in some places to a depth of some 50 feet by a river of volcanic mud, which burst from the crater of Mount Vesuvius and destroyed all the buildings in its wake. A small section of Herculaneum has been excavated because the modern town was built over the old town.

② Vocābula

3 | Read this eyewitness account of the eruption of Vesuvius:

Ego sum Gāius Plīnius, duodēvīgintī annōs nātus. Apud avunculum habitō, cūjus vīlla est suprā collem nōn procul ab orā maritimā. Oppidum Mīsēnum vocātur. Vīlla sita est in septentriōnālī parte sinūs Neāpolītānī. Quōdam diē mensis Augustī ego in āreā domūs legēbam et studēbam. Hōrā ferē septimā, māter mea indicāvit nūbem inūsitātam appārēre trans sinum. Māter clāmāvit: "Spectā nūbem mīram, ex Monte Vesuviō orientem. Quid significat haec nūbēs mīra?"

> **apud** (+ *acc*) *at the house of, with*
> **septentriōnālis** -*is* -*e* *northern*
> **sinus** -*ūs* m *bay*
> **Neāpolītānus** -*a* -*um* of *Naples*
> **āre**a -*ae* f **domus** *yard*
> **ferē** *about, around*
> **inūsitātus** -*a* -*um* *unusual*
> **appāreō** -*ēre* -*uī* *to appear*
> **mīrus** -*a* -*um* *strange*
> **significō** -*āre* *to mean*

Tremor terrae per multōs diēs praecesserat. Ille tremor terrae erat minus formīdābilis quia tremōrēs terrae in Campāniā erant solitī. Ego ipse volēbam continuāre legĕre et studēre, sed māter mea hōc perīculō novō territa erat. Ego librum meum dēposuī et cum tōtā familiā ascendī locum, ex quō illud mīrāculum maximē conspicī poterat. Nūbēs, ex crātēre oriēns, erat candida interdum, interdum erat obscūra et maculōsa. Iam Mons Vesuvius cinerem et fūmum et vapōrem et pūmicem ējiciēbat. Talem ēruptiōnem numquam anteā vīdimus.

> **formīdābil**is -*is* -*e* *frightening*
> **solitus** -*a* -*um* *usual, customary*
> **dēpōnō** -*ēre* **dēposuī** **dēpositus** *to put down*
> **mīrāculum** -*ī* n *strange sight*
> **maximē** *best*
> **crātēr** -*ēris* m *crater*
> **obscūrus** -*a* -*um* *murky*
> **maculōsus** -*a* -*um* *spotty*

Mox dē caelō cadēbat cinis, quī paulātim calidior et densior fīēbat. Iam familia et omnēs oppidānī erant trepidissimī. Aliī intrā tecta manēre cupiēbant, aliī in apertō deambulāre praeferēbant, nam frequentibus vastisque tremōribus tecta nūtāre incipiēbant.

> **oppidānī** -*ōrum* mpl *townspeople*
> **trepidus** -*a* -*um* *alarmed*
> **in apertō** *in the open*
> **deambulō** -*āre* *to walk around*
> **vastus** -*a* -*um* *enormous*
> **nūtō** -*āre* *to totter*
> **cervīcal** -*ālis* n *pillow*
> **moveō** -*ēre* **mōvī** **mōtus** *to cause*
> **tussis** -*is* f *cough, coughing*
> **ululātus** -*ūs* m *wail*
> **vagītus** -*ūs* m *cry*
> **requīrō** -*ēre* **requisīvī** **requisītus** *to look for*
> **vōcibus requīrĕre** *to yell for*
> **conjunx conjugis** mf *spouse*
> **novissimus** -*a* -*um* *last*

In apertō autem ob lapillōs cadentēs, multī cervīcālia capitibus imposuērunt. Praetereā, gravis odor sulfuris erat ubīque et movēbat lacrimās et tussim. Diēs fīēbat nox. Audīvimus ululātūs fēminārum, vagītūs infantium, clāmōrēs virōrum. Aliī requīrēbant vōcibus parentēs; aliī requīrēbant līberōs; aliī requīrēbant conjugēs; aliī requīrēbant amīcōs. Omnēs crēdidērunt illam futūram esse noctem novissimam in mundō.

Dēnique tertiō diē lux rediit et sōl refulsit, sed aër

> **lux lūcis** f *daylight*
> **refulgeō** -*ēre* **refulsī** *to shine again*

erat lūridus. Omnia erant mūtāta. Omnia altō cinere erat obducta tamquam altā nive.

lūridus *-a -um* smoky
altus *-a -um* deep
obductus *-a -um* covered
tamquam *as if*

Postrīdiē nuntius pervēnit, quī dīxit Vesuvium duo oppida dēlēvisse, Pompēiōs et Herculāneum. Ego ipse ēruptiōnem Vesuviī semper in memoriā retinēbō.

postrīdiē *on the following day*

___ ACTIVITĀS _____

A. Respondē Latīnē:

1. Apud quem habitāvit Gāius Plīnius?

2. Ubi erat ejus vīlla?

3. Quis indicāvit Plīniō nūbem inūsitātam?

4. Quid tum Plīnius faciēbat?

5. Ex quō monte nūbēs mīra orta est?

6. Quid per multōs diēs ēruptiōnem praecesserat?

7. Quid Mons Vesuvius ējiciēbat?

8. Quid omnēs oppidānī capitī imposuērunt?

9. Quid omnēs crēdidērunt?

10. Quae oppida Vesuviō dēlēta sunt?

You have learned how to form indirect questions in the present tense. If the verb that introduces the indirect question is in the past tense, the verb in the indirect question is also in the past tense:

Ubi *essem* nescīvī.   *I didn't know where I was.*
Discens exposuit cūr tam sērō   *The apprentice explained why he*
    labōrāret.   *was working so late.*

In both examples, the verb of the indirect question is in the *imperfect* subjunctive. Forming the imperfect subjunctive is simple. Add the personal endings **-m, -s, -t, -mus, -tis, -nt** to the present infinitive of any verb, including **esse** and **posse:**

portāre + m = portāre*m*   portāre + mus = portārē*mus*
portāre + s = portārē*s*   portāre + tis = portārē*tis*
portāre + t = portāre*t*   portāre + nt = portāre*nt*

ACTIVITĀS

B. Underline the indirect question. Then convert the indirect to a direct question:

EXAMPLE: Amita quaesīvit <u>ubi incendium esset</u>.   **"Ubi incendium est?"**

1. Avunculus quaesīvit cūr in āreā domūs sedērem.

2. Cūr tam mīra nūbēs suprā Vesuvium esset nesciēbam.

3. Cūr lapillī dē caelō caderent diū nōn intellexī.

4. Ego ambigēbam quōmodo mē servātūrus essem.

5. Vīcīnus meus ā mē quaesīvit cūr omnēs fūgerent.

6. Oppidānī ā mē rogāvērunt in quā tabernā cervīcālia emĕre possint.

7. Quid in apertō facerētis nesciēbātis.

8. Quid senātor dē causīs ēruptiōnis Montis Vesuviī dīceret nōn intellegēbam.

9. Amita ā mē quaesīvit num familia salva in apertō esset.

10. Ego ab avunculō quaesīvī quid ēruptiōnem Montis Vesuviī movēret (*caused*).

5 The purpose clause, both positive (with **ut**) and negative (with **nē**), requires the imperfect subjunctive if the main verb is in the past tense:

**Multī ex oppidō Mīsēnō fūgērunt
ut mortem certam ēvītārent.**

*Many fled from the town of Misenum
to avoid (or, in order that they
might avoid) certain death.*

Here the main verb (**fūgērunt**) is in the past tense, and so the verb in the purpose clause (**ēvītārent**) is in the imperfect subjunctive.

___ ACTIVITĀTĒS _____

C. Combine the two sentences by making the second sentence a purpose clause:

1. Avunculus meus ad Montem Vesuvium īvit. Nūbem inūsitātam observābat.

2. Multī cervīcālia in capite gestābant. Caput contrā lapillōs prōtegēbant.

3. Līberī ad sinum Neāpolītānum īvērunt. In sinū natābant.

4. Famila mea in apertō dormīvit. Ruīnam (*collapse*) vīllae ēvītābat.

5. Oppidānī Mīsēnum relīquērunt. In aliō oppidō salūtem inveniēbant.

6. Ego et Fabius in āreā domūs sedēbāmus. Librōs cōmicōs ibi legēbāmus.

D. Convert the following sentences from the past to the present tense:

1. Ego et amīcus trans sinum Neāpolītānum nāvigāvimus ut Pompēiōs vīsitārēmus.

2. Ascendistisne Montem Vesuvium ut crātērem vidērētis?

_____

3. Ante ēruptiōnem amita in forum īvit ut obsōnāret.

_____

4. Avus et avia post ēruptiōnem Mīsēnum vēnērunt ut mē vīsitārent.

_____

5. Haec nōn dixī ut tē terrērem.

_____

6. Parentēs per Mīsēnum cucurrērunt ut līberōs requīrerent.

_____

6 Contrary to what you might expect, if there is a verb of fearing (**timeō**, for example) in the main clause, the conjunction **nē** is used to introduce a _positive_ idea, and **ut** is used to introduce a _negative_ idea:

Timeō _ut_ pater veniat.   _I am afraid that my father is NOT coming_
Timeō _nē_ pater veniat.   _I am afraid that my father IS coming._

___ ACTIVITĀS ___

E. Read over the following sentences carefully, remembering that **ut** means _that . . . not_ and **ne** means _that_. The most common verbs of fearing are: **timeō -ēre -uī** and **metuō -ĕre -ī**. Of these, **metuō** expresses a stronger fear. Convert the following sentences from the present to the past by changing the tenses of both verbs:

1. Timeō nē tremor terrae Mīsēnum dēleat.

_____

2. Timēmus ut vīllam nostram servēmus.

_____

3. Metuisne nē pater tē cum amante videat?

_____

4. Omnēs timent nē haec nox sit novissima in mundō.

_____

5. Metuimus ut amīcōs nostrōs ob pulverem et fūmum inveniāmus.

_____

6. Ille metuit nē pūmex et lapillī arborēs ac plantās ac flōrēs dēleant.

_____

7 CONDITIONAL clauses in Latin, as you know, are introduced by the conjunction **sī** (*if*) or **nisi** (*unless, if . . . not*). Look at these two *simple* conditions:

Sī hōc *crēdis*, errās.	*If you believe this, you are wrong.*
Sī Rōmae *manēbis*, Caesarem vidēbis.	*If you stay in Rome, you will see Caesar.*
Nisi dīligenter labōrābis, pecūniam nōn habēbis.	*If you don't work hard, you won't have (any) money.*

In the first sentence, the **sī** clause does not imply that you believe or do not believe. It simply states: *if you believe this*. We therefore call this a *simple* condition. The second **sī** clause is also a simple condition. Notice that the verb of the **sī** clause is in the future tense, while in English we use the present tense (*if you stay*), even though it has a future sense (*if you will stay in Rome*). Don't you agree that the Latin is more precise by using the future tense in the **sī** clause (**manēbis**)? Now look at this sentence:

Sī pecūniam *habērem*, fēlix essem.	*If I had money, I would be happy.*

This **sī** clause implies that I do not have money; therefore, we call it a contrary-to-fact condition. In this situation, Latin puts the verb into the imperfect subjunctive. In English, we use what looks like the past tense of the verb (if I *had*) to express a *present* contrary-to-fact condition, because we mean to say "if I had money right now." The Romans did the same; they used the imperfect tense of the subjunctive.

___ ACTIVITĀTĒS ___

F. Complete the following contrary-to-fact conditions referring to the present time with the correct forms of the imperfect subjective of **habēre** in the **sī clause** and of **esse** in the conclusion:

1. Sī pater pecūniam _____, ille fēlix _____.

2. Sī amīcī meī pecūniam _____, illī fēlīcēs _____.

3. Sī ego et pater pecūniam _____, nōs fēlīcēs _____.

4. Sī tū pecūniam _____, tū fēlix _____.

5. Sī omnēs pecūniam _____, omnēs fēlīcēs _____.

6. Sī tū et frāter pecūniam _____, vōs fēlīcēs _____.

G. Complete the following contrary-to-fact conditions with the correct forms of the verbs in parentheses. The first verb is meant for the **sī** clause:

1. (sedēre/posse)   Sī Plīnius in āreā domūs _____, sinum

vidēre _____.

2. (stāre/cadĕre)   Sī ego in apertō _____, lapillī in caput

meum _____.

3. (habēre/manēre)   Sī oppidānī cervīcālia _____, illī in

apertō _____.

4. (habēre/fugĕre)   Sī familia cisium _____, ex oppidō ad

collēs _____.

5. (habēre/volāre)   Sī ego ālās _____, per aërem

_____.

6. (metuĕre/manēre)   Sī ego ēruptiōnem _____, ego domī

_____.

7. (amāre/relinquĕre)   Sī tū mē vērō _____, tū mē nōn nunc

_____.

8. (habēre/dare)   Sī ego anulum aureum _____, ego eum

tibi _____.

9. (habēre/nēre)   Sī ancillae plūs temporis _____, eae

lānās _____.

10. (esurīre/esse)   Sī tū vērō _____, tū cibum simplicem

_____.

11. (habēre/rādĕre)   Sī ego novāculam _____, ego barbam jam

_____.

12. (pluĕre/manēre)   Sī _____, ego et amīcus in vīllā

_____.

DIALOGUS

Vocābula

adhūc *still*
rēs reī *f situation*
nūper *recently*
omittō -ĕre omīsī omissus *to lose*
dēspērō -āre *to despair*
Quid est? *What's the trouble?*
jam pluit *it has been raining*

urceātim pluĕre *to rain buckets*
jocus -ī *m joke;* **jocum facis!** *you're kidding!*
metō -ĕre messuī messus *to harvest*
abhinc *from here*
salvus -a -um *safe*

RĒS PERSŌNĀLĒS

Imagine that you were in the theater in Pompeii, enjoying the show when you and the audience heard a loud roar as Mount Vesuvius erupted and you saw the mushroom cloud rise high into the air. (One can easily see the top of Vesuvius from the theater of Pompeii.) Look over the list of things that you could possibly do in that emergency. But be careful! Number the items from 1 to 12, writing 1 in the block of the item that you would take care of first, 2 in the block of the item that you would take care of next, and so on to the end of the list:

☐ Ex urbe statim fugerem.

☐ Cibum et potiōnem prō fugā colligerem.

☐ Parentēs meōs requīrerem.

☐ Domum dīrēctō īrem.

☐ Pecūniam meam caperem.

☐ Ex theātrō currerem.

☐ Amīcōs meōs adjuvārem.

☐ Canem (aut fēlem) meum servārem.

☐ Cīvēs veterēs adjuvārem.

☐ Raedam aut cisium requīrerem.

☐ Magistrum meum servārem.

☐ Amīcīs valē dīcerem.

COMPOSITIŌ

Imagine that your are the mayor of Pompeii. Mount Vesuvius has just erupted. People are in a panic. You stand on a platform in the forum as crowds of people wonder what they should do. Should they stay in their houses, should they walk slowly out of the city, should they run out of the city, should they look for their children, should they get a carriage and ride out, should the slaves help their masters, should the children look for their parents? Should they take food and money with them? Should they cover their heads against the falling ash? They look to you for advice. Use the imperative form, positive or negative, in telling people what to do. Address your orders to men, women, children, or slaves.

_____

_____

_____

_____

_____

_____

COLLOQUIUM

How good is your memory? How many of the missing words can you supply in this dialog between a farmer and his sympathetic friend?

THE LATIN CONNECTION

Given the Latin source for the following words:

1. eruption _____

2. miracle _____

3. intrepid _____

4. desperate _____

5. sulfur _____

6. joke _____

7. appear _____

8. formidable _____

9. inevitable _____

10. incinerate _____

11. pulverize _____

12. perfume _____

13. vapor _____

14. significant _____

15. deposit _____

16. vast _____

17. conjugal _____

18. mundane _____

19. lurid _____

20. crater _____

21. pumice _____

22. sinuses _____

23. apparent _____

24. indication _____

XIX *Jūstitia crīminālis*

Pluperfect Subjunctive

1 Modicum cultūrae

No profession was considered more honorable or more useful among the Romans than the practice of law. It provided the surest road to political success. Some Romans made it to the top by being great generals in the Roman army, but the vast majority of politicians traveled the legal road to power and wealth. A father who wanted his sons to succeed took them to the Roman Forum to learn public speaking and to study law. Later, the father would put his sons under the care of a famous statesman or teacher. That is how Cicero's father introduced his son to famous legal experts in Rome, and Cicero went on to become the most famous lawyer in the Roman world.

There are, of course, some important differences between a Roman advocate and a modern lawyer. It is quite normal nowadays for lawyers to make their living exclusively from the practice of law. In Rome, however, the practice of law was only one of the many activities of a politician. The financial side of law was of minor importance. The politician practiced law only for the authority and political prestige that it would bring him. In fact, a law was passed in 204 B.C. that forbade anyone to accept money or a gift for pleading a case in court. Demanding a fee in advance, as many lawyers do today, was considered particularly dishonorable. There was even a difference in name between the advocate (**advocātus -ī** m), who gave legal help to clients to advance his political career, and the lawyer of the lower classes (**causidicus -ī** m), who regularly accepted fees to defend people in court. The **advocātus** looked down on the **causidicus.** In the course of time, it became not unusual for a client at the end of a trial to pay the advocate who had successfully defended him. But payment was never compulsory.

If a person wanted to bring a civil (as opposed to a criminal) suit against someone, he had to go out and arrest that man himself and haul him into court. To make sure that the defendant could not complain that he had not been summoned, the accuser took several witnesses with him to issue the summons. The accuser and the defendant then went before the chief justice (**praetor -ōris** m) for a hearing (**praejūdicium -ī** n). The **praetor** decided whether there were grounds for a lawsuit and set the fine or other punishment if the defendant were to be found guilty in a trial.

Another difference is that in a Roman civil case the lawyer (**advocātus**) merely helped out his client: he stood near him, made suggestions, and spoke on his behalf, as a character witness would today. The client had to speak for himself. Today, by contrast, the lawyer in a civil case handles the whole case, and the

325

client is there to remind the lawyer of some last-minute detail that he thinks will help his case.

In a criminal case, the accused had to act as his own lawyer. There was no public prosecutor or district attorney to prosecute the criminal; it was left for one private citizen to prosecute another. The defendant had the right to a public trial and to cross-examine his accuser. Much publicized criminal trials and famous criminal lawyers attracted huge crowds in the Roman Forum. The accuser and the accused surrounded themselves in court with influential friends, whose very presence might influence the jurors. Lawsuits were heard before a panel of up to 50 or 60 jurors (**jūdex -icis** m) chosen from a list of about 4,000 men of the upper classes, presided over by a **praetor.**

Roman trials were short, lasting generally one day or less. Complicated and important cases could last several days, but, unlike some modern cases, they did not drag on for weeks, months, and years. In a case of capital punishment, the convicted criminal could appeal only once: to the assembly of citizens. But there were no endless appeals as in our courts today.

If a person was found guilty, he could be fined or deprived of some of his civil rights, such as the right to vote or to run for office. In more serious cases, he could be sent into exile or executed. If he was a Roman citizen, he could not be crucified or scourged, but there were many ways in which he could be punished. A Roman citizen could be thrown down the Tarpeian Cliff of the Capitoline Hill or strangled in prison or starved to death there. He could be sentenced to work in the mines, from which he would never again see the light of day. He could be sentenced to fight wild beasts in the arena or fight to death as a gladiator. Sometimes a murderer would be sewn up in a sack with a rooster, an ape, and a snake and be thrown into the Tiber to drown. Beheading was common. Death by fire was sometimes the punishment for committing arson.

There were no long prison sentences because there were no huge penitentiaries such as we have today. There was only one small prison in all of Rome, at the foot of the Capitoline Hill. It was actually an ancient cave that was converted into a prison, which can still be visited today, although it has been converted into a Christian chapel. A prisoner was kept there before trial if he could not put up bail and would be taken there at times after conviction to be executed. The great lawyer Cicero was sent into exile because he had some political prisoners put to death there without benefit of trial.

In the early days of Rome, the death penalty was often inflicted for what we would call minor offenses, but in later centuries the convicted person was permitted to go into voluntary exile even before the trial was over.

It may seem strange that Rome got along for 700 years without a police force to maintain order. Magistrates, like the **aediles** (**aedīlis -is** m), had certain police powers and must have had a group of men to maintain order in the streets and to make arrests. But it was the Emperor Augustus who, near the end of his reign in A.D. 14, created a new force, organized in a semimilitary fashion. There were seven cohorts, each consisting of one thousand men called **vigilēs** (**vigil** *-is* m). They served both as firemen and policemen. They were recruited from former slaves. Their chief, who could be called the fire and police chief, had the title of prefect. He was a member of the middle class. Such was the arrangement for the city of Rome. Other cities and towns generally copied the Roman model in creating their fire brigade and police force.

2 Vocābula

jūdicium -ī n

praetor -ōris m

tribūnal -ālis n

jūdex -icis m

jūdex -icis m

subsellium -ī n

advocātus -ī m

advocātus -ī m

accūsātor -ōris m

reus -ī m

testis -is m

testēs -ium mpl

ACTIVITĀS

A. Look over the courtroom (**jūdicium**) in the courthouse (**basilica -ae** *f*) and then try to answer these questions in Latin:

1. Quis in tribunālī sedet? _____

2. Quī in subselliīs sedent? _____

3. Quot jūdicēs in hōc jūdiciō sunt? _____

4. Quis accūsat reum? _____

5. Quis dēfendit reum? _____

6. Statne an sedet reus? _____

7. Quis adjuvat accūsātōrem? _____

8. Quem indicat accūsātor? _____

3 Listen in on the conversation between two robbers in their little room in an apartment building after pulling off a robbery. Pay special attention to the verbs in bold type. They are in the pluperfect subjunctive to indicate past contrary-to-fact conditions:

LONGĪNUS: Dēnique salvī sumus in hōc stabulō. Ego autem exanimātus sum.

SABĪNUS: Dīc mihi, quantum argentum in saccō est? Sumusne nunc dīvitēs?

LONGĪNUS: Quantum argentum in saccō sit nesciō. Possumus argentum ēnumerāre sērius. Prīmum animam recipiāmus! Numquam anteā tam rapidē cucurrī.

SABĪNUS: Cōgitāsne argentārium in tabernā argentāriā nōs recognōvisse?

LONGĪNUS: Nesciō. Vīdistīne ejus vultum? Ego vīdī nōnnullōs testēs, extrā argentāriam tabernam stantēs. Cōgitāsne aliquem ex testibus nōs recognōvisse? Vīdistīne vigilem in angulō stantem? In quem partem vigil spectābat? Meā opīniōne, sī iste nōs **vīdisset,** nōs certē **apprehendisset.**

SABĪNUS: Etiamsī vigil nōs **vīdisset,** numquam nōs **captāvisset.** Cucurrimus tamquam cervī. Praetereā, iste est nimis crassus ut nōs captet.

LONGĪNUS: Sī argentārius aut ūnus ex testibus nōs **captāvisset,** nōs in jūdicium **rapuisset.** Sī vigil ipse nōs **apprehendisset,** in carcere nunc sederēmus.

SABĪNUS: Nōlī mentiōnem facĕre dē jūdiciō aut dē carcere. Mentiō dē carcere praecipuē mē trepidissimum semper facit.

LONGĪNUS: Immō, aperiāmus saccum et videāmus quid intus sit. Nunc tempus est praedam dividĕre. Ēnumerābō dēnāriōs: ūnus, duo, trēs, quattuor, quīnque . . .

Tunc maximē vigil jānuam pulsāvit et in eōrum cellam inruit. "Vōs latrōnēs, nōlīte movērī! Vīdistisne meam clāvam? Mēherculē, ego eā ūtar sī necesse est. Tradite mihi illum saccum pecūniae. Venīte mēcum!" Vigil deinde manicās eīs induit.

LONGĪNUS: Domine, quōmodo scīvistī ubi cella mea sit?

VIGIL: Est simplex. Ecce, est forāmen in īmō saccō. Ut vōs latrōnēs cucurristis, nummī per hōc forāmen in crepīdinem dēcidēbant. Illī nummī mē dīrectō ad cellam vestram duxērunt. Ego vōs accūsō latrōciniī.

---

stabulum -ī *n hole-in-the-wall*
exanimātus -*a* -*um* *out of breath*
argentum -ī *n cash, dough*
saccus -ī *m bag*
ēnumerō -*āre* *to count up*
sērius *later*
animam recipĕre *to catch (one's) breath*
argentārius -ī *m banker*
taberna argentāria *f bank*
recognoscō -*ĕre* **recognōvī recognitus** *to recognize*
vultus -*ūs* *m expression*
nōnnullī -*ae* -*a* *some*
testis -*is* *mf witness*
aliquis *someone*
angulus -ī *m corner*
pars partis *f direction*
apprehendō -*ĕre* -ī **apprehensus** *to arrest*
etiamsī *even if*
tamquam *like*
cervus -ī *m deer*
nimis crassus ut *too fat to*
in jūdicium *to court*
rapiō -*ĕre* -*uī* -*tus* *to haul off*
carcer -*eris* *m jail*
praecipuē *in particular*
trepidus -*a* -*um* *nervous*
immō *well*
intus *inside*
praeda -*ae* *f loot*

tunc maximē *just then*
pulsō -*āre* *to knock at*
inruō -*ĕre* -ī *to rush in*
latrō -*ōnis* *m robber*
clāva -*ae* *f billyclub*
mēherculē! *so help me!*

Domine *Sir*
cella -*ae* *f (little) room*
forāmen -*inis* *n hole*
in īmō saccō *in the bottom of the bag*
nummus -ī *m coin*
crepīdō -*inis* *f sidewalk*
dēcidō -*ĕre* -ī *to fall (down)*
latrōcinium -ī *n robbery*

__ ACTIVITĀTĒS _____

B. Respondē Latīnē:

1. Quis latrōcinium committēbant?

_____

2. Quis erat illō tempore in tabernā argentāriā?

_____

3. Quid latrōnēs ex tabernā cēpērunt?

_____

4. Quō latrōnēs post latrōcinium fūgērunt?

_____

5. Ut fugēbant, nōnne latrōnēs conspexērunt vigilem?

_____

6. Cūr vigil nōn posset captāre latrōnēs, etiamsī vigil latrōnēs vīdīsset?

_____

7. Cūr latrōnēs pecūniam nōn statim numerāvērunt?

_____

8. Habitābantne latrōnēs in domō aut in insulā?

_____

9. Quis jānuam latrōnum pulsāvit?

_____

10. Quid vigil manibus latrōnum induit?

_____

C. How much of a **vigil** are you? Try to answer these questions without looking again on the scene of the robbery. Give yourself one demerit every time you have to turn back to look at the robbery scene to answer the questions:

1. Quota hōra erat quandō latrōnēs ex tabernā exībant?

_____

2. Quot virī in crepīdine erant?

_____

3. Quot fēminae in crepīdine stābant?

_____

4. Quot testēs vīdērunt latrōnēs ex tabernā currentēs?

_____

5. Quot persōnae in raedā sedēbant?

_____

6. Ante quam tabernam stetit vigil?

_____

7. Quid vigil manū dextrā tenēbat?

_____

8. Gerēbantne latrōnēs barbam?

_____

9. Quae tabernae erant proximae tabernae argentāriae?

_____

10. Ubi erat canis?

_____

 To form a contrary-to-fact condition referring to the past, the PLUPERFECT SUBJUNCTIVE is used:

Sī tē _vīdissem,_ tē _salūtāvissem._   _If I had seen you, I would have greeted you._

Here the speaker implies that he had not, in fact, seen you. The pluperfect subjunctive, like the imperfect subjunctive, is easy to form. Just as the endings **-m, -s, -t, -mus, -tis, -nt** were added to the _present_ infinitive to form the imperfect subjunctive, so these same endings are added to the _perfect_ infinitive to form the _pluperfect subjunctive._ Do you remember how to form the perfect infinitive? Add **-isse** to the perfect stem, which is found in the third principal part of the verb minus the personal ending:

portāv + isse + m = portāvissem	portāv + isse + mus = portāvissēmus
portāv + isse + s = portāvissēs	portāv + isse + tis = portāvissētis
portāv + isse + t = portāvisset	portāv + isse + nt = portāvissent

__ ACTIVITĀTĒS _____

D. Change the following sentences from present to past contrary-to-fact conditions:

> EXAMPLE: **Sī pecūniam *habērem*, fēlix *essem*.**
> **Sī pecūniam *habuissem*, fēlix *fuissem*.**

1. Sī ego cervīcal capitī impōnerem, salvus essem.

   _____

2. Sī ego et dominus cervīcālia capitī impōnerēmus, salvī essēmus.

   _____

3. Nisi collem ascenderem, ēruptiōnem Vesuviī vidēre nōn possem.

   _____

4. Sī in āreā domūs manērem, māter mē nōn invenīret.

   _____

5. Sī nōs prope Montem Vesuvium vīverēmus, magnō in perīculō essēmus.

   _____

6. Amīcī, sī cervīcālia capitī impōnerētis, salvī essētis.

   _____

E. Change the following past contrary-to-fact to present contrary-to-fact conditions:

1. Sī tū in crepīdine stetissēs, latrōcinium vīdissēs?

   _____

2. Sī multam pecūniam habuissēs, eam in tabernā argentāriā dēposuissēs?

   _____

3. Sī latrōnēs raedam habuissent, eī salvī effūgissent.

   _____

4. Sī vigil nōn tam crassus fuisset, latrōnēs facilē apprehendisset.

   _____

5. Sī ego vigilem in angulō stantem vīdissem, eum salūtāvissem.

   _____

6. Sī plūs temporis habuissēmus, prius (*sooner*) ad tē litterās scripsissēmus.

   _____

5 | Longinus and Sabinus were hauled into court. To get the trial scene fixed in your mind, look at this picture. Then read the record of their trial in the Basilica Jūlia in the Roman Forum, just across from the **cūria.**

Jūdicium Longīnī atque Sabīnī in Basilicā Jūliā

PRAETOR: Petītor, quis es tū et quem accūsās?

ACCUSĀTOR: Vir illūstris, ego sum argentārius. Nōmen mihi est Lūcius Laelius Lepidus, Lepidī fīlius.* Tabernam argentāriam in Subūrā exerceō. Taberna mea est optima taberna argentāria tōtīus Romae et . . . .

PRAETOR: Satis, satis! Quid reī fēcērunt? Quid est crīmen?

ACCUSĀTOR: Ego sum victima latrōciniī. Hunc crīminālem et ejus socium accūsō latrōciniī. Ego jūs-

petītor -ōris m *plaintiff*

vir illūstris *Your Honor*

exerceō -ēre -uī -itus *to manage, run*

satis *enough*

jūstitia -ae f *justice*

*Very formal, proud response.

titiam crīminālem flāgitō. Herī post merīdiēm grassātor iste cum sociō suō argentāriam tabernam meam intrāvit et saccum pecūniae clepsit. Nisi magnā cum vōce exclāmāvissem, hīc grassātor tōtam pecūniam meam clepsisset. Ubi sunt jūs et ordō in hāc urbe? Istī grassātōrēs poenam dare debent. Rogō ut tū hōs reōs sevērē pūniās.

PRAETOR: Reë, estne hōc vērum? Intrāvistīne tabernam argentāriam et pecūniam clepsistī? Quod nōmen est tibi?

LONGĪNUS: Sum Longīnus. Numquam anteā pecūniam umquam clepsī. Vir illūstris, ego sum innocens; nōn sum latrō; nēmō in totā urbe est honestior quam ego. Jūdicēs, vidētis quam pauper ego sim. Ecce meam tunicam sordidam! Ecce calceōs meōs! Sunt plēnī forāminum. Sī ego et socius pecūniam clepsissēmus, nunc vestēs novās gestārēmus. Negō mē latrōcinium commīsisse.

ADVOCĀTUS: Cliens meus, jūdicēs, est homō honestus. Familiam suam amat, uxōrem amat, līberōs suōs amat; ille etiam canēs vīcīnitātis amāt. Spectāte lacrimās ejus! Nē condemnētis hunc miserum hominem. Absolvite eum.

PRAETOR: Vigil, habēsne testimōnium in hunc reum?

VIGIL: Vir illūstris, nisi ego ipse Longīnum ex tabernā argentiā currentem vīdissem, eum nōn accūsārem. Habēbat saccum pecūniae in manū. Socius ejus etiam intererat. Ambō in culpā sunt. Longīnum et Sabīnum usque ad eōrum cellam secūtus sum. Quandō cellam intrāvī, ego invēnī hōs duōs grassātōrēs, rīdentēs et praedam ēnumerāntēs. Sint jūs et ordō in viīs urbis nostrae! Flāgitō jūstitiam crīminālem.

PRAETOR: Jūdicēs, absolvētisne reōs an condemnābitis? Prōnuntiāte sententiam vestram.

JŪDICĒS: Vir illūstris, hōs latrōnēs condemnāmus. Eōs nōn ad bestiās damus neque ad mūnus glādiātōrium condemnāmus. Neque dē Rūpe Tarpeiā eōs praecipitābimus. Purgantō viās urbis per trēs annōs.

PRAETOR: Sīc fīat.

---

flāgitō *-āre* to demand
grassātor *-ōris* m hoodlum
   socius *-ī* m accomplice
clepō *-ĕre* clepsī cleptus
   to steal
jūs jūris n law
ordō *-inis* m order
   poena *-ae* f penalty;
   poenam dare to pay the
   penalty
pūniō *-īre -īvī -ītus* to punish

quam *than*
quam *how*

negō *-āre* to deny
   committō *-ĕre* commīsī
   commissus to commit

vīcinitās *-ātis* f
   neighborhood
condemnō *-āre* to condemn
absolvō *-ĕre -ī* absolūtus
   to acquit
testimōnium *-ī* n evidence
   in (+ acc) against

intersum *-esse -fuī* to be
   involved
   ambō *-ae -ō* both
   in culpā esse to be guilty

prōnuntiō *-āre* to pronounce
   sententia *-ae* f verdict

ad bestiās dare to make
   (them) fight wild beasts
   mūnus *-eris* n show,
   contest; ad mūnus
   gladiātōrium to fight as
   gladiators
Rūpēs *-is* f Cliff
praecipitō *-āre* to throw
   down
   purgantō they shall clean
sīc fīat so be it

___ ACTIVITĀS _____

F. Respondē Latīnē:

1. In quā parte urbis erat taberna argentāria?

_____

2. Quis erat accūsātor?

_____

3. Quī erant reī?

_____

4. Quis dīxit sē esse victimam latrōciniī?

_____

5. Quis jūstitiam crīminālem flāgitāvit?

_____

6. Quis grassātor saccum argentī manū tenēbat?

_____

7. Quis dīxit sē numquam anteā pecūniam clepsisse?

_____

8. Num vērum est Longīnum fuisse honestissimum hominem in urbe Rōmā?

_____

9. Quis testimōnium dedit Longīnum uxōrem et līberōs et canēs vīcīnitātis amāre?

_____

10. Quam poenam grassātōrēs dabunt?

_____

DIALOGUS

Vocābula

festīnō -āre *to rush*
celeber -bris -bre *famous*
fīō fierī factus sum *to take place; to become*
dēfensor -ōris m *defense lawyer*
spērō -āre *to hope*

aliquandō *someday*
potestās -ātis f *power*
auctōritās -ātis f *authority, prestige*
prōsum prōdesse prōfuī (+ dat) *to be good for*

QUAESTIŌNĒS PERSŌNĀLĒS

1. Nōvistīne (*do you know*) advocātum clārum?

   _____

2. Estne advocātus in familiā tuā?

   _____

3. Cupisne esse advocātus/advocāta aliquandō?

   _____

4. Estne vigil in familiā tuā?

   _____

5. Praefersne esse advocātus/advocāta an vigil an medicus/medica?

   _____

6. Quis est ūtilior (*more useful*), advocātus an vigil?

   _____

7. Sī nullam pecūniam habērēs, cibumne cleperēs?

   _____

8. Sī latrōnem ex tabernā currentem vidērēs, apprehenderēsne eum aut vocārēs vigilem?

   _____

9. Sī amīcus aut amīca in carcere esset, eum aut eam vīsitārēs?

   _____

10. Praefersne potestātem auctōritātemque an jūstitiam lībertātemque?

   _____

COLLOQUIUM

Complete the dialog on the model of the previous conversation:

COMPOSITIŌ

You are a police officer in your hometown. Someone has just attempted to hold up the bank. As you come around the corner on your beat, a suspicious-looking character comes running from the scene of the crime. Since it is a small town, you know everyone in town. But this fellow is an outsider. You nab him. List the questions that you will ask him to determine whether he is the culprit.

1. _____
2. _____
3. _____
4. _____
5. _____

THE LATIN CONNECTION

What are the Latin origins of the following derivatives?

1. accusation _____
2. judicial _____
3. sack _____
4. testimony _____
5. angle _____
6. incarcerate _____
7. intrepid _____
8. victim _____
9. kleptomaniac _____
10. penal _____
11. justice _____
12. jury _____
13. order _____
14. culpable _____
15. subpoena _____
16. prejudice _____
17. comprehend _____
18. mention _____
19. cell _____
20. innocent _____
21. negate _____
22. absolve _____
23. ambidextrous _____
24. criminal _____
25. commit _____
26. tribunal _____
27. pronounce _____
28. sentence _____

XX *Rēs pūblica*

Ablative Absolute

1 Modicum cultūrae

Who ruled Rome? What kind of government did Rome have? During the first 250 years of its existence, seven kings ruled Rome, one after the other, beginning with Romulus. The king consulted the senate, which in Romulus's time is said to have consisted of 100 elder citizens, who met in the senate building (cūria *-ae f*) in the Roman Forum. Eventually the senate numbered 300 senators, who were former officials. A senator could easily be recognized. He wore a white toga with a broad crimson border and a special gold ring. He also wore special shoes, tied with red laces around his ankles and just below the knee.

When the last Roman king, Tarquin the Proud, was overthrown, the Romans decided to elect two men called consuls (consul *-is m*) to head the government, which the Romans called **rēs pūblica,** the Republic. Each consul had the right to veto the acts of the other. If war broke out, the consuls were also the commanders on the battlefield. The consuls held office for only one year and gave their names to that year. The Romans could not, of course, use the familiar abbreviations B.C. and A.D. to date their years. They would say "when so-and-so and so-and-so were consuls." (They also counted the years from the founding of Rome in 753 B.C.) Each consul had a bodyguard of twelve men, called lictors (lictor *-ōris m*), each of whom carried a bundle (fascēs *-ium mpl*) of rods (virga *-ae f*) and an axe (secūris *-is f*) as a symbol of the consul's power to inflict corporal punishment and even capital punishment on those guilty of serious crimes. Lictors had the daily task of walking before the consuls to clear the way for them through the crowds. For centuries, only men of the Roman nobility, the patricians, could be elected consul. Consuls had the power to call a meeting of the senate and preside over it. They had the right to have the auspices taken. At the end of their terms, they spent another year governing one of the Roman provinces. Can you imagine our country headed by two presidents, each of whom could veto the action of the other? Worse yet, can you imagine presidential elections every year? Strangely enough, the Romans made this system work for almost 500 years.

The consuls couldn't do everything by themselves, and so two men called praetors were eventually elected by the Assembly of the People to serve as judges. The praetors were more like the members of our Supreme Court. As Rome grew bigger and more complicated, the number of praetors increased. For a long time, only patricians could be elected praetor. As the representative of the consul, the praetor had the right to preside over the Assembly of the People and conduct military affairs under the direction of the consul. Although the praetor had great power, he was inferior to the consuls; this inferior position was clearly indicated to the public by the fact that a praetor was escorted by only six lictors, whereas a consul had twelve. During his year in office in Rome, the praetor was in charge of the judicial system; in the following year he, like the consuls, went out to govern one of the provinces.

As the city grew, another two men, called aediles (**aedīlis -is** m), were elected by the Assembly of the People to supervise the construction of public buildings. They also had charge of the temples, baths, marketplaces, and streets. It was their duty to see to it that law and order were kept in public places, and so they had certain police powers. They were also in charge of public events, such as gladiatorial shows, chariot and horse races, and performances in the theater.

Ranking below the praetors were the quaestors (**quaestor -ōris** m), who were in charge of the public treasury. They collected all the money that was due the state and made such payments from the treasury as the law or the proper magistrate required. They were also in charge of all public records. A large number of clerks worked under their direction. Quaestors, like the consuls, praetors, and aediles, held office for one year. After their year in office in Rome, they served as second in command to some provincial governor. A man had to hold at least the office of quaestor in order to become a life member of the senate.

Usually, a man of ambition moved up the political ladder from quaestor to consul. This sequence was called the **cursus honōrum,** or career of public offices. The Latin word **honor -ōris** m was used to refer to a political office because that's what it was: simply an honor. The magistrates received no salary. Under these conditions, only the rich could afford to run for office. The struggle of the lower classes for the right to hold high office went on for centuries. They finally succeeded.

In times of national emergency, a dictator was appointed, and all the other officers stepped down temporarily. The dictator was escorted by twenty-four lictors, indicating that his power was equal to the combined powers of the two consuls. He could hold office for the emergency or for six months, whichever ended first. His powers were so great that everyone feared that, if he were left in office more than six months, he might be tempted to become dictator for life. Julius Caesar was named dictator for life, and that is why many Roman senators feared him and put him to death on the Ides of March (March 15), 44 B.C.

Rome never had a democracy. After the early kings ceased to rule, certain families of the upper class, the patricians, held the high offices of government, while the people of the lower classes, the plebeians, fought for civil rights. Just as the plebeians were finally enjoying their full civil rights, the Republic came to an end and was replaced by the Empire. The first emperor was Augustus. Emperors ruled the Roman world in one form or another for the next 500 years.

2 Vocābula

fascēs -ium mpl
virga -ae f secūris -is f
sceptrum -ī n
consul -is m
toga -ae (f) praetexta
corrigia -ae f
lictor -ōris m
calceus -i (m) consulāris

praetor -ōris m
sella -ae (f) curūlis

quaestor -ōris m

aedīlis -is m

__ ACTIVITĀS _____

A. Match the descriptions with the appropriate pictures:

> **Consul togam praetextam induit.**
> **Lictor fascēs suprā umerum sinistrum portat.**
> **Consul calceum corrigiā rubrā ligat.**
> **Sex lictōrēs praetōrem prōsequuntur** (*escort*).
> **Quaestor pecūniam numerat.**
> **Aedīlis cōnstructiōnem templī cūrat** (*supervises*).
> **Duodecim lictōrēs cōnsulem prōsequuntur.**
> **Cōnsul sceptrum manū dextrā tenet.**

1. _____

2. _____

3. _____

4. _____

5. _____

6. _____

7. _____ 8. _____

```
3
```
What would it have been like to be the son of a famous politician and lawyer in ancient Rome? This is how Cicero's son saw it:

Nōmen mihi est Marcus Tullius Cicerō. Pater meus idem nōmen habet. Pater est ambitiōsissimus senātor. Vult esse cīvis prīmus Rōmae. Abhinc quattuor annōs, pater meus erat candidātus, nam volēbat fīerī consul. Erant multī competītōrēs. Nōn omnēs competītōrēs erant amīcī patris. Exemplī grātiā, Clōdius et Catilīna erant inimīcī. Petītiō duōs mensēs dūrāvit.

> competītor -ōris m opponent
> petītiō -ōnis f campaign
> dūrō -āre to last

Ego puer quattuordecim annōrum eram, sed ego omnia bene in memōriā teneō. Cōtīdiē clientēs, officiī grātiā, ad domum nostram vēnērunt. In ātriō congregātī sunt. Bene māne pervēnērunt. Interdum collēgium tignāriōrum, interdum collēgium pistōrum aut tonsōrum patrem meum vīsitāvit. Ātrium nostrum paene semper plēnum clientium erat. Nullum locum habēbam ubi ego lūderem.

> officiī grātiā to pay their
>   respects
> congregor -ārī -ātus sum to
>   congregate
> perveniō -īre pervēnī to
>   arrive
> paene almost
> sportula -ae f lunch basket

Māter cum sorōre meā, Tulliā, et cum ancillīs, sportulam clientibus parābat, nam sīc mōs erat. Clientēs semper sportulās exspectābant. Deinde pater jūs et rem pūblicam cum clientibus disputāvit, quia pater meus advocātus perītissimus est. Posteā clientēs patrem ad forum prōsecutī sunt. In forō pater ōrātiōnēs longās habēbat, et populō multa prōmīsit. Deinde pater per omnēs vīcōs urbis in togā candidā ambiit, nam sīc mōs est. Postrēmō, diēs suffrāgiī aderat.

> mōs mōris m custom
> rēs pūblica f politics
> disputō -āre to discuss
> prōsequor -ī prōsecūtus sum
>   to escort
> ōrātiōnem habēre to give a
>   speech
> vīcus -ī m ward
> ambiō -īre -iī -ītum to
>   campaign
> suffrāgium -ī n vote; diēs
>   suffrāgiī election day
> adsum adesse adfuī to be
>   at hand

Cīvēs Rōmānī omnēs in Campum Martium īvērunt ut suffrāgium ferrent et duōs consulēs ex tam multīs competītōribus ēligerent. Pater meus et socius ejus, Gāius Antōnius, consulēs ēlectī sunt. Mīlia cīvium patrī "tibi fēlīciter!" acclāmāvērunt.

Quandō pater ē Campō Martiō discessit, ut in forō apud populum appārēret, duodecim lictōrēs, fascēs in umerō sinistrō portantēs, eum prōsecūtī sunt. Post eum multī senātōrēs et clientēs et amīcī et familia secūtī sunt. In curiā pater togam candidam exuit et togam praetextam cum lātō clāvō induit. Porrō, calceōs consulārēs cum corrigiīs rubrīs induit. Mox pater ē cūriā exiit et rostra ante cūriam ascendit. Ut pater in sellā curūlī sedēbat, omnēs in forō "tibi fēlīciter!" acclāmāvērunt. Pater deinde ōrātiōnem habuit ut omnibus suffrāgātōribus gratiās ageret.

Quam superbus patre meō eram! Exemplum mīrābile mihi praebuit.

suffrāgium ferre *to cast a ballot*
ēligō -ere ēlēgī ēlectus *to elect, choose*
tibi fēlīciter! *congratulations!, bravo!*
acclāmō -āre *to shout*
apud (+ acc) *before*
appāreō -ēre -uī *to appear*
praetexta *crimson-bordered*
lātus -a -um *broad*
clāvus -ī m (crimson) *stripe*
porrō *besides, furthermore*
corrigia -ae f *shoelace*
rostra -ōrum npl *rostrum, (speaker's) platform*
sella curūlis *official chair*
suffrāgātor -ōris m *voter*
superbus -a -um (+ abl) *proud of*
exemplum praebēre *to set an example*
mīrābilis -is -e *wonderful*

ACTIVITĀS

B. Respondē Latīnē:

1. Quot annōs abhinc erat Marcus Tullius candidātus?

2. Quot mensēs dūrāvit petītiō?

3. Quī erant competītōrēs inimīcī?

4. Quae collēgia domum Cicerōnis vīsitābant?

5. Quid pater in ātriō disputāvit?

6. Quō cīvēs Rōmānī īvērunt ut suffrāgia ferrent?

7. Quot lictōrēs Marcum Tullium in forum prōsecūtī sunt?

8. Quid lictōrēs suprā umerum sinistrum portābant?

___

9. Ubī pater in sellā curūlī sedēbat et ōrātiōnem habēbat.

___

10. Quamobrem Marcus Tullius hanc ōrātiōnem habuit.

___

 The Latin verb systems did not have past active participles except in "fake passive" (deponent) verbs. The Romans could not say "having seen," "having heard," and the like. They could say **secūtus** *having followed* and **locūtus** *having spoken* because **sequor sequī secūtus sum** and **loquor loquī locūtus sum** are "fake passives":

> **Haec *locūtus*, rostra ascendit.**   *Having said this, he went up to the rostrum.*

But if they wanted to use the verb **dīcō**, they could NOT say: **Haec *dictus*, rostra ascendit.**

Why not? Because **dictus** means *having been said*. What did the Romans do? They put the noun or pronoun—in this instance a pronoun—and the past passive participle into the ABLATIVE CASE:

> **Hīs *dictīs*, consul rostra per gradūs ascendit.**   *Having said this (literally, these things having been said), the consul climbed the steps to the rostrum.*

If you wanted to translate this sentence literally, you would say: *These things having been said, the consul climbed the rostrum by the steps.* Of course, that's pretty clumsy English. A better translation would be: *Having said this, . . .* or *After he had said this, . . .* or *When he had said this, . . .*, or *As soon as he had said this, ...* When translating this kind of construction, you can use any conjunction that fits the situation.

This construction is called ABLATIVE ABSOLUTE because the noun (or pronoun) and the participle are in the ABLATIVE CASE and because it is grammatically independent of the main clause, that is, there is no conjunction to connect this clause with the rest of the sentence. "Absolute" comes from the verb **absolvō absolvēre absolvī absolūtus.** This verb has several meanings: *to release; to acquit; to free; to complete.* An ABLATIVE ABSOLUTE, therefore, is a phrase that is "complete in itself" and "freed" from the main clause without a conjunction. The noun or pronoun may stand in the ablative absolute only when it refers to a person or thing different from the main clause.

__ ACTIVITĀTĒS __

C. Convert the subordinate clause to an ablative absolute:

EXAMPLE: **Cicerō, postquam ōrātiōnem *habuit*, domum rediit.**
Ōrātiōne habitā, Cicerō domum rediit. } *After giving his speech, Cicero returned home.*

NOTE: Because the word **Cicerō** comes at the beginning of the sentence and before **postquam** of the dependent clause, you can expect **Cicerō** to be the subject of both the dependent clause and the main clause.

EXAMPLE: **Postquam Cicerō ōrātiōnem *habuit*, turba "tibi fēlīciter" acclāmāvit.**
Ōrātiōne ā Cicerōne habitā, turba "tibi fēlīciter" acclāmāvit. } *After Cicero had given his speech, the crowd cried "Bravo!"*

NOTE: Because in this second example the word **Cicerō** comes after the conjunction **postquam,** we know that **Cicerō** is the subject only of the dependent clause and that there will be a different subject (**turba**) in the main clause.

1. Praetor, postquam jūs disputāvit, basilicam intrāvit.

_____

2. Marcus, ubi competītōrēs conspexit, nihil dixit.

_____

3. Aedīlis, simul atque forum intrāvit, rostra per gradūs ascendit.

_____

4. Clientēs, postquam sportulam accēpērunt, abīvērunt.

_____

5. Consul, postquam sceptrum accēpit, in sellā curūlī consēdit.

_____

6. Postquam cīvēs suffrāgia tulērunt, Cicerō in forō appāruit.

_____

D. Change each ablative absolute to a dependent clause, using the conjunction that best suits the sentence: **ubi** (*when*), **cum prīmum, simul atque** (*as soon as*), **postquam** (*after*):

1. Consulibus novīs ēlectīs, populus deīs grātiās ēgit.

_____

2. Cērā pennārum liquefactā, Īcarus dē caelō in mare cecidit.

_____

3. Rēgibus expūlsīs, populus Rōmānus duōs consulēs ēlēgit.

_____

4. Latrōnibus comprehēnsīs, testēs nōn jam erant territī.

_____

5. Saccō argentī cleptō, grassātōrēs ex tabernā argentāriā ruērunt.

_____

6. Latrōciniō commissō, grassātōrēs poenam dedērunt.

_____

E. Underline the dependent clause and then change it to an ablative absolute:

1. Cum prīmum advocātus reum accūsāvit, praetor in tribūnālī consēdit.

_____

2. Ubī populus Cicerōnem ēlēgērunt, Catilīna ex urbe fūgit.

_____

3. Postquam Marcus Tullius ōrātiōnem habuit, populus applausit.

_____

4. Cum prīmum tignārius officīnam aperuit, turba introībat.

_____

5. Postquam ancillae cēnam parāvērunt, convīvae trīclīnium intrāvērunt.

_____

6. Simul atque ego vigilem vocāvī, grassātōrēs tabernam meam relīquērunt.

_____

5 | Although Latin has no past active participle, it does have a present active participle, which can be used in the ablative absolute:

Populō _audiente_, praetor   _As the people were listening, the_
ōrātiōnem habuit.   _praetor gave a speech._

___ ACTIVITĀTĒS _____

F. Convert the ablative absolute to a dependent clause, using the conjunction **ubi** (*when*), **ut** (*as*), or **dum** (*while*). Always use the present tense (called historical present) with the conjunction **dum:**

1. Daedalō dīligenter labōrante, Īcarus cum pennīs lūdēbat.

   _____

2. Omnibus clientibus tacentibus, advocātus loquī incēpit.

   _____

3. Familiā dormiente, latrō vīllam intrāvit.

   _____

4. Consule in sellā curūlī sedente, praetor suprā rostra stābat.

   _____

5. Competītōribus domī manentibus, Marcus Tullius per urbem ambiit.

   _____

6. Candidātō togam candidam gestante, consul togam praetextam gestābat.

   _____

G. Change the dependent clause to an ablative absolute:

1. Dum populus consulem exspectat, competītōrēs suprā rostra appāruērunt.

   _____

2. Ut praetor per Sūbūram ambulābat, sex lictōrēs prope forum stābant.

   _____

3. Ut populus suffrāgia ferēbat, turba in Campō Martiō dē lībertāte clāmābat.

   _____

4. Dum māter in macellō obsōnat, infans constanter vagiēbat.

   _____

5. Dum clientēs in ātriō stant, ego et pater sportulās suprā mensam pōnēbāmus.

   _____

6. Dum pater dīcit, omnēs in ātriō silēbant.

   _____

The verb **sum** has no present participle. It would be **ens entis,** which is used with a few verbs, such as **absum** (*I am absent*); the participle is **absens** (abs + ens -entis). But since the participle of **sum** does not exist, an ablative absolute that would normally contain it consists usually of two nouns in the ablative:

**Marcellō dūce, exercitus
Rōmānus Germānōs vīcit.**

Under the leadership of Marcellus (literally, Marcellus [being] the leader), the Roman army defeated the Germans.

A common use of this type of ablative absolute is in the dating of Roman years:

**Marcō Tulliō Gāiō Antōniō
consulibus, rēs pūblica erat
salva.**

In the consulship of Marcus Tullius and Gaius Antonius (literally, Marcus Tullius [and] Gaius Antonius [being] consuls), the government was safe.

ACTIVITĀTĒS

H. Convert each ablative absolute to a dependent clause introduced by **ubi:**

1. Rōmulō rēge, vīta erat simplex.

2. Antōniō praetōrē, jūdicia erant jūsta.

3. Tarquiniō Superbō rēge, populus Rōmānus rebellāvit (*rebelled*).

4. Appiō Claudiō consule, mīlitēs Rōmānī prīmam viam longam mūnīvērunt (*built*).

5. Serviō Tulliō rēge, mūrus prīmus Rōmae aedificātus est.

6. Lūciō Domitiō aedīle, templum novum in Aventinō colle aedificātum est.

I. In the following sentences, the noun or pronoun and the participle are provided in the nominative case. Change them to the ablative case to form an ablative absolute:

1. _____, omnēs cīvēs deīs grātiās ēgērunt.
   consul ēlectus

2. _____, reus sē dēfendet.
   praetor praesens

3. _____, iter per Campāniam fēcimus.
   urbs relicta

4. _____, consul dē rostrīs dēscendit.
   haec verba dicta

5. _____, consul irātus fīēbat.
   ōrātiō audīta

6. _____, servī laetissimī erant.
   dominus absēns

7. _____, oppidānī Mīsēnī erant trepidī.
   mīra nūbēs vīsa

8. _____, argentārius in tabernam suam rediit.
   latrōnēs comprehēnsī

J. At the beginning of each of the following sentences, you will see a noun in the nominative case and an infinitive. Construct an ablative absolute by changing the noun to the ablative case and the infinitive to a present participle in the ablative case. Note that the "fake passive" verbs have *active* forms and *active* meanings in the present participles (**loquens -entis** *speaking*, **admīrans -antis** *admiring*, **moriens -entis** *dying*, **oriens -entis** *rising*):

> EXAMPLE: (mīlitēs audīre) _____ dux ōrātiōnem habuit.
> **Mīlitibus audīentibus,** dux ōrātiōnem habuit.
> *As the soldiers listened, the general made a speech.*

1. (consul jubēre) _____, lictōrēs fascēs virgārum et secūrim portant.

2. (consulēs jubēre) _____, lictor secūrim ē fascibus remōvit.

3. (consulēs praeesse) _____ populus "vōbīs fēlīciter" acclāmāvit.

4. (populus admīrārī) _____, consul rostra ascendit.

5. (advocātus dēfenděre) _____, reus ā jūdicibus absolūtus est.

6. (consul loquī) _____, omnēs senātōrēs in cūriā sīlēbant.

7. (sōl orīrī) _____, populus in Campum Mārtium inīvērunt.

8. (sōl caděre) _____, populus domum rediit.

9. (consul morī) _____, lictōrēs fascēs dēmittēbant (*lowered*).

10. (consul praesiděre) _____, senātus legem novam tulit (*passed*).

QUAESTIŌNĒS PERSŌNĀLĒS

1. Praefersne rēgem et rēgīnam praesidentī in patriā nostrā?

2. Vīdistīne umquam candidātum?

3. Praefersne vītam pūblicam an prīvātam quandō adultus (-a) eris?

4. Spērāsne aliquandō collēgium frequentāre?

5. Praefersne collēgium prope domum tuam an collēgium procul ā domō?

6. Paterne tuus collēgium frequentāvit?

7. Māterne tua collēgium frequentāvit?

8. Habēsne sorōrem an frātrem quī nunc collēgium frequentat?

DIALOGUS

Unde venīs, Claudī?

Salvē, Marcelle. Ā Campō Martiō veniō.

Cūr tam laetus es? Numquam tē tam laetum vīdī.

Comitia hodiē in Campō Martiō erant. Multī ex omnī parte urbis ibi erant.

Tū suffrāgium ferre nōndum potes. Tū nimis parvus es. Quī candidātī vīcērunt?

Quī victōrēs sint an quī victī sint nesciō. Candidātī mihi nōn cūrae sunt.

Cūr tandem in Campum Martium īvistī, sī candidātī tibi nōn cūrae sunt.

Immō, amāns mea, in margine Campī Martiī habitat. Eam, nōn candidātōs, vīsitābam. Quotiēns ego eam vīsitō, laetissimus sum.

Vocābula

comitia -ōrum npl elections
victus -ī m loser
mihi nōn cūrae sunt (they) are of no concern to me
cūr tandem just why

immō well, . . .
amāns -antis f girlfriend
margō -inis m edge, fringe
quotiēns whenever

COLLOQUIUM

In this dialog Marcellus wants to know why his friend went to the Campus Martius. Complete this conversation, taking the role of the friend and giving your own reasons for going to the Campus Martius:

THE LATIN CONNECTION

A. **1.** From which Latin verb does our word *status* come? Give all the principal

parts. _____

2. The following words come from the same Latin verb. Explain their meanings
in relation to their Latin origin:

a. stable _____

b. stability _____

c. instability _____

d. constant _____

e. stature _____

B. The **fascēs** symbolized a Roman magistrate's power of life and death over the

people. What is a fascist? _____

_____

C. What is the Latin origin of the following words:

1. rostrum _____   6. to rebel _____

2. mores _____   7. apprehend _____

3. acclaim _____   8. honest _____

4. absent _____   9. congregation _____

5. scepter _____   10. office _____

D. Roman political campaigns involved language that has given us several familiar English words. What are the Latin sources for the following words? Can you explain the English words with respect to their roots?

1. elect   _____   6. suffrage   _____

2. election   _____   7. ambition   _____

3. eligible   _____   8. competitor   _____

4. electoral college   _____   9. petition   _____

5. candidate   _____   10. honor   _____

_____ COMPOSITIŌ _____

If you were walking in the crowded Roman Forum and a consul were to come through it, you would undoubtedly be able to pick him out from the crowd. Explain why you would be able to do so.

_____

_____

_____

_____

_____

Recōgnitiō IV
(Lectiōnēs XVI–XX)

Lectiō XVI

a. To form the ALTERNATE FUTURE, add the ending **-ūrus (-a -um)** to the stem of the perfect participle (the fourth principal part) of a verb. Then combine this form with the forms of **sum:**

vocātūrus (-a) sum	*I'm going to call*	**vocātūrī (-ae) sumus**	*we're going to call*
vocātūrus (-a) es	*you're going to call*	**vocātūrī (-ae) estis**	*you're going to call*
vocātūrus (-a) est	*he/she is going to call*	**vocātūrī (-ae) sunt**	*they're going to call.*

This alternate future may also mean *I am about to call* or *I intend to call.*

b. In the same way, a past tense of **sum** (**eram** or **fuī**) can be added:

vocātūrus (-a) eram/fuī   *I was going to call, I was about to call, I intended to call*

c. The verb with the **-ūrus** ending, but without a form of **sum,** may be used as a future participle, with several meanings:

Senātor ex sellā surrexit, ōrātiōnem **habitūrus.**	*The senator rose from his seat, about to give a speech/intending to give a speech.*

d. The future infinitive consists of the future participle plus **esse.** In an indirect statement, the future infinitive represents an action occurring after the action of the main verb:

Helena dixit sē domī *cēnātūram* esse.	*Helen said that she would dine at home/was going to dine at home.*

Lectiō XVII

a. A verb in the SUBJUNCTIVE MOOD expresses something other than simple fact. The present subjunctive expresses a wish, possibility, doubt, or polite command. The present subjunctive is formed by changing the *typical* vowel in the ending of a verb:

vocem	moveam	dūcam	capiam	audiam
vocēs	moveās	dūcās	capiās	audiās
vocet	moveat	dūcat	capiat	audiat
vocēmus	moveāmus	dūcāmus	capiāmus	audiāmus
vocētis	moveātis	dūcātis	capiātis	audiātis
vocent	moveant	dūcant	capiant	audiant

Note that the first person subjunctive of all families of verbs ends in **-m.**

b. The subjunctive forms of **esse** and **posse** are irregular:

sim	possim
sīs	possīs
sit	possit
sīmus	possīmus
sītis	possītis
sint	possint

c. Certain Latin conjunctions require the subjunctive. The conjunction **ut** with the verb in the subjunctive gives us a purpose clause:

Labōrāmus ut edāmus.   *We work in order to eat.*

The conjunction **nē** with the verb in the subjunctive gives us a negative purpose clause:

Labōrāmus nē famem habeāmus.   *We work in order not to go hungry.*

Lectiō XVIII

a. The imperfect subjunctive is formed by adding the endings **-m, -s, -t, -mus, -tis, -nt** to the present infinitive of any verb:

vocāre + m = vocārem   vocāre + mus = vocārēmus
vocāre + s = vocārēs   vocāre + tis = vocārētis
vocāre + t = vocāret   vocāre + nt = vocārent

b. If the verb that introduces an indirect question is in the past tense, the verb in the indirect question is in the imperfect subjunctive:

Ubi *essem* nescīvī.   *I didn't know where I was.*

c. A purpose clause, whether positive (with **ut**) or negative (with **nē**), requires a verb in the imperfect subjunctive if the main verb of the sentence is in the past tense:

Multī Mīsēnō fūgērunt ut mortem certam ēvītārent.   *Many fled from Misenum to avoid certain death.*

d. After a verb of fearing (such as **timeō, metuō**), the conjunction **nē** is used to introduce a *positive* idea and **ut** is used to introduce a *negative* idea:

> **Timeō *nē* pater veniat.**   *I am afraid that my father is coming.*
> **Timeō *ut* pater veniat.**   *I am afraid that my father is not coming.*

If the verb in the main clause is in the past tense, the verb in the subordinate clause is also in the past tense:

> **Metuī nē amita sērius *pervenīret*.**   *I was afraid that my aunt would*
> **Metuī ut amita mea hodiē**   *arrive late.*
> **pervenīret.**   *I was afraid that my aunt would*
>   *not arrive today.*

e. In simple conditions, the verb of the **sī** clause as well as the verb of the conclusion is in the indicative mood. Contrary-to-fact conditions, however, referring to the present tense require a verb in the **sī** clause in the imperfect subjunctive:

> **Sī amīcōs *habērem*, fēlix *essem*.**   *If I had friends, I'd be happy.*

Lectiō XIX

a. To form the pluperfect subjunctive, add the endings **-m, -s, -t, -mus, -tis, -nt** to the perfect active infinitive of any verb:

> **vocāv + isse + m = vocāvisse*m***   **vocāv + isse + mus = vocāvissē*mus***
> **vocāv + isse + s = vocāvissē*s***   **vocāv + isse + tis = vocāvissē*tis***
> **vocāv + isse + t = vocāvisse*t***   **vocāv + isse + nt = vocāvisse*nt***

b. To form a contrary-to-fact condition referring to the past, use the pluperfect subjunctive:

> **Sī tē *vīdissem*, tē *salūtāvissem*.**   *If I had seen you, I would have greeted you.*

c. It is possible to have the verb of the **sī** clause in the pluperfect subjunctive, and the verb of the conclusion in the imperfect subjunctive:

> **Sī dīligentius *labōrāvissem*, dīves**   *If I had worked harder, I'd be rich*
> **nunc *essem*.**   *now.*

Lectiō XX

a. An ABLATIVE ABSOLUTE usually consists of a noun and a participle in the ablative case. The noun cannot be related to any word in the main clause:

> **Hīs *dictīs*, senātor rostra ascendit.**   *Having said this (literally, these*
>   *words having been said), the*
>   *senator climbed the rostrum.*

b. The ablative absolute may consist of a noun and a present active participle in the ablative case. The present participle of deponent verbs is active in form and meaning:

> **Deīs adjuvantibus, ego consul fīam.**
>
> *With the help of the gods, I shall become consul.*
>
> **Senātōre loquente, consul abiit.**
>
> *While the senator was talking, the consul left.*

c. The verb **sum** has no present participle. An ablative absolute that would normally contain that participle, consists usually of two nouns in the ablative case:

> **Marcellō dūce, vincēmus.**
>
> *Under the leadership of Marcellus (literally, Marcellus being the leader), we shall win.*

d. The ablative absolute is equivalent to various adverbial clauses using the conjunctions (*when, while, because, although, if*) depending on the context:

> **Discipulīs loquentibus, magistra erat īrāta.**
>
> *Because the students were talking, the teacher was angry.*

— ACTIVITĀTĒS

A. Following the clues given, complete the descriptions under the pictures, using the following phrases:

lānās net	reum indicat	manicās induit
saccum pecūniae clepit	suffrāgium fert	cibum convīvīs adpōnit
capitī impōnit	pūmicem et fūmum ējicit	latrōnēs persequitur
holera obsōnat	serrā secat	per gradūs ascendit

1. Cīvis Rōmānus _____

_____ .

2. Tignārius tabulam _____

_____ .

3. Vigil latrōnī _____

_____ .

4. Plīnius cervīcal _____

_____ .

5. Ancilla _____

_____ .

6. Amita _____

_____ .

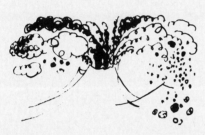

7. Mons _____

_____ .

8. Senātor rostra _____

_____ .

9. Vigil duōs _____

_____ .

10. Accūsātor _____

_____ .

11. Latrō _____

_____ .

12. Servus _____

_____ .

B. Word search. There are 15 words related to Roman law hidden in this puzzle. Circle them from left to right, right to left, up or down, or diagonally and then write them in the spaces below:

L	A	M	U	I	C	I	D	U	J
A	D	V	X	L	S	X	R	U	U
N	V	M	I	U	A	E	S	S	D
U	O	A	J	G	C	T	U	Z	I
B	C	N	Q	R	I	E	R	Q	C
I	A	I	A	T	R	L	X	O	E
R	T	C	I	S	O	C	I	U	S
T	U	A	P	R	A	E	T	O	R
A	S	A	C	I	L	I	S	A	B
A	C	C	U	S	A	T	O	R	Q

1. _____   9. _____

2. _____   10. _____

3. _____   11. _____

4. _____   12. _____

5. _____   13. _____

6. _____   14. _____

7. _____   15. _____

8. _____

C. Here are 10 pictures showing what activities various Romans were engaged in. Complete the description below each picture by using the correct perfect tense form of the appropriate verb from the following list:

gerĕre	texĕre	haurīre	volāre	clepĕre
loquī	verrĕre	habēre	ūtī	accumbĕre

1. Ancilla aquam ē cisternā _____ .

2. Māter atque fīlia tunicās _____ .

3. Senātor ōrātiōnem _____ .

4. Daedalus per aërem _____ .

5. Convīvae ad mensam _____ .

6. Serva cubiculum scōpīs _____ .

7. Advocātus cum reō _____ .

8. Latrō ānulum aureum _____ .

9. Tignārius terebrā 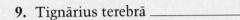.

10. Senātōrēs togās praetextās _____.

D. Cruciverbilūsus:

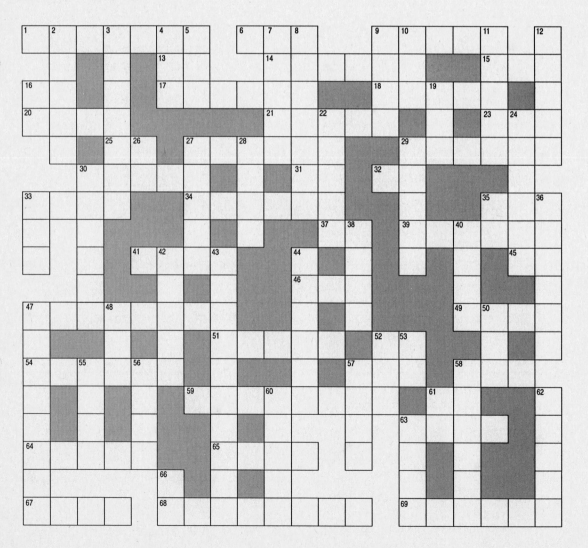

HORIZONTĀLE

1. to avoid
6. so
9. such a
13. you are
14. to harvest
15. or
16. he/she/it goes
17. immediately
18. they were
20. take (imperative)
21. whole
23. so
25. again, back (*prefix*)
28. to tie

29. cause (*acc*)
30. previously, before
31. on
32. if
33. urn
34. so great (*fpl*)
35. at that time, then
37. on account of
39. apartment building
41. to be
45. or
46. not
47. cistern
49. then

51. well known, noted
52. it
54. rostrum
57. I will go
58. heart
59. you loved (*sing.*)
61. she
63. rose
64. I wear
65. Roman male dress
67. royal (court)
68. courthouse
69. speech

PERPENDICULĀRE

2. old
3. shop, inn
4. thing
5. it is
7. aunt
8. memory
9. three
10. air
11. enough
12. also
19. wing
22. I hold
23. he
24. board

26. and
27. broad
28. cheek
29. citizen
30. mind
33. to use
35. you
36. handcuff
38. well
40. they are
42. saw
43. out of breath
44. corners

47. shoelace
48. so many
50. one (*masc. abl.*)
52. there
53. I give
55. his own
56. I shave
57. trip
58. camp
60. policeman
61. I go
62. robber
63. rarely
66. from

E. Here's a puzzle that will test your command of Latin vocabulary. Transform one word into another, by changing one letter at a time:

EXEMPLUM:
$$
\begin{array}{cccc}
C & O & M & A \\
\underline{R} & \underline{O} & \underline{M} & \underline{A} \\
\underline{R} & \underline{O} & \underline{S} & \underline{A} \\
\underline{R} & O & T & \underline{A}
\end{array}
$$

U N U S   R U R S U S   N O V U S   F E R O

_ _ _ _   _ _ _ _ _ _   _ _ _ _ _   _ _ _ _

_ _ _ _   _ _ _ _ _ _   _ _ _ _ _   _ _ _ _

A V I S   C U R V U S   M O D U S   T E R O

F. The consul in the **cūria** has asked you to go outside to fetch one of his lictors. You find five of them standing right outside the senate building. Pick out the right lictor from the consul's description to you:

Capillōs densōs habet.
Calceōs gestat.
Barbam curtam gerit.
Semper subrīdet.

Fascēs ejus secūrim nōn habent.
Fascēs suprā umerum sinistrum portat.
Tenet sagulum *(his cape)* manū dextrā.
Tunicam suprā genū gerit.

G. Unscramble the words. Then unscramble the circled letters to find out where these things come from:

P O R A V   ⬕ ☐ ☐ ⬕ ☐

U M F U S   ☐ ⬕ ☐ ☐ ☐

L U S U F R   ☐ ☐ ⬕ ☐ ☐ ☐

L A M M F A   ☐ ☐ ⬕ ☐ ☐ ☐

E X M U P   ☐ ☐ ⬕ ⬕ ☐

N I C I S   ⬕ ☐ ⬕ ☐ ☐

Haec omnia ējiciuntur ___ ___ ___ ___ ___ ___ ___ ___ .

H. Each group of words below belongs to the same grammatical category (part of speech); for example, all verbs, all adjectives, all adverbs, except for ONE word in each group. Find the grammatical misfit in each group and cross it out. Write the grammatical category of each group (adjectives, adverbs, ablative nouns, conjunctions, or other) in the spaces:

1. posteā ut postquam simul atque dum   _____

2. macellum tablīnum forum pavīmentum iterum _____

3. quaerĕre fugĕre induĕre suĕre mare   _____

4. ibi mox suprā etiam deinde   _____

5. humānus rūrsus honestus sōlus novus   _____

6. argentō malleō clāvō populō plaudō   _____

7. inter tandem per ob propter   _____

8. dum id ista eadem ille   _____

I. How many of these words do you remember? Fill in the Latin words, then read down the boxed column to find out to whom these objects belong:

1. _ _ _ _ _ _ _ _

2. _ _ _ _ _

3. _ _ _ _ _ _

4. _ _ _ _ _ _

5. _ _ _ _ _ _

6. _ _ _ _

7. _ _ _ _ _ _

8. _ _ _ _ _ _

9. _ _ _ _ _ _ _

J. The words of each numbered group in the left column belong to the same category or topic. Look over the words in the right column to see to which group they belong. Write the matching letter in the space provided:

1. pūmex, cinis, vapor, fūmus _____

2. malleus, clāvus, serra, secūris _____

3. praetor, jūdex, jūdicium, basilica _____

4. suffrāgium, competītor, candidātus, suffrāgātor _____

5. aedīlis, consul, dictātor, praetor _____

6. Mīsēnum, Rōma, Pompēiī, Herculāneum _____

7. obsōnāre, coquĕre, nēre, suĕre _____

8. trīclīnium, cubiculum, ātrium, peristȳlium _____

a. quaestor
b. Arīcia
c. tablīnum
d. tornus
e. crātēr
f. texĕre
g. petītiō
h. reus

K. The Latin Connection. In the space provided, write the Latin word from which the English word is derived:

1. matron _____
2. virgin _____
3. patrician _____
4. apposition _____
5. context _____
6. oration _____
7. resurrection _____
8. noted _____
9. humane _____
10. distant _____
11. profuse _____
12. repudiate _____
13. mitigate _____
14. tabulate _____
15. turn _____
16. perforate _____
17. evident _____
18. insular _____
19. deposition _____
20. judicious _____
21. durable _____
22. prosecute _____
23. margin _____
24. servile _____
25. amicable _____

Proficiency Test

I. Speaking

a. Your teacher will award up to 10 points for your oral performance in the classroom.

b. Oral Communication Tasks (20 points)

Your teacher will administer a series of communication tasks in four categories. Each task prescribes a simulated conversation in which you play yourself and the teacher assumes the role indicated in the task. Each task requires at least four utterances on your part, for which you can earn up to five points of credit. An utterance is any spoken statement that leads to accomplishing the stated task. Assume that in each situation you are speaking with a person who speaks Latin. You receive no credit for Yes-No answers or simple repetitions.

II. Listening Comprehension

a. Multiple Choice (English) (20 points)

Part IIa consists of ten questions. For each question, you will hear some background information in English. Then you will hear a passage in Latin *twice*, followed by a question in English. After you have heard the question, look at the question and the four suggested answers in your book. Choose the best suggested answer and write its number in the space provided.

1 What was Marcellus' problem? _____

    1. He didn't do his homework.   3. He left his homework at home.
    2. He was late for school.   4. He wants to leave school early.

2 What items on the menu did Claudius not order? _____

    1. Asparagus and cucumbers.   3. Lettuce and carrots.
    2. Milk and wine.   4. Bread and roast.

3 Which season of the year is it? _____

    1. Summer.   3. Winter.
    2. Fall.   4. Spring.

4 What mode of transportation does Linus prefer? _____

    1. A wagon, because he likes oxen.
    2. A cisium, because it travels fast.
    3. A carriage, because it goes neither too fast nor too slow.
    4. A carpentum, because he likes the company of women.

5 What is the good news? _____

   1. He is going to have a birthday party.
   2. He will be allowed to stay home tomorrow.
   3. He is going to have friends over for the weekend.
   4. He and the family are going on a fun trip.

6 Why shouldn't you go into the barnyard? _____

   1. There's a wild bull there that will attack you.
   2. You might let out the cows.
   3. You might scare the horses.
   4. The watchdogs in there might bite you.

7 What did your sister buy your mother for her birthday? _____

   1. A new dress.   3. A pair of golden earrings.
   2. A golden necklace.   4. A beautiful gold ring.

8 In which Olympic event does Lucius expect to compete and win? _____

   1. Swimming.   3. Wrestling.
   2. Boxing.   4. Running.

9 Which of the tasks did Gaius not like? _____

   1. Carrying bags of flour.   3. Tending the oven.
   2. Turning the mill.   4. Making the dough.

10 What does Gloria not like about her new boyfriend? _____

   1. He brags too much.   3. He's too quiet.
   2. He's stuck-up.   4. He talks too much.

b. Multiple Choice (Latin) (10 points)

Part IIb consists of five questions. For each question, you will hear some background information in English. Then you will hear a passage in Latin *twice*, followed by a question in Latin. After you have heard the question, look at the question and the four suggested answers in your book. Choose the best suggested answer and write its number in the space provided.

11 Cūr tū laetissimus(-a) eris? _____

   1. Multam pecūniam habēbis.   3. Multōs amīcōs habēbis.
   2. Dōnum mīrābile accipiēs.   4. Bonam fortūnam habēbis.

12 Cūr Titus vult fierī medicus: _____

   1. Medicī aegrōs sānāre possunt.   3. Medicī numquam aegrī fiunt.
   2. Medicī fiunt dīvitēs.   4. Omnēs admīrantur medicōs.

13 Quem Marcus nōn amat?   _____

    1. Puellās in officīnā tignāriā.   3. Magistrum sevērum et arrogantem.
    2. Alterōs discentēs.   4. Canem ferōcem in officīnā tignāriā.

14 Ubi Marīa animālia ferōcia vīdit?   _____

    1. In vīvāriō.   3. In āreā domūs.
    2. In silvā.   4. In campō.

15 Quid Jūlīa herī frequentāvit?   _____

    1. Convīvium.   3. Nuptiās.
    2. Scholam.   4. Macellum.

c. Multiple Choice (Visual) (10 points)

Part IIc consists of five questions. For each question, you will hear some background information in English. Then you will hear a passage in Latin *twice*, followed by a question in English. After you have heard the questions, look at the question and four pictures in your book. Choose the picture that best answers the question and circle its number.

16 Which picture best describes Melissa's task at home?

    1   2   3   4

17 For which sport is your friend training?

    1   2   3   4

18 For what did your friend Julia shop?

     1   2   3   4

19 What did the police officer do?

     1   2   3   4

20 Which scene best describes what the little brother is doing?

     1   2   3   4

III. Reading

a. Multiple Choice (English) (12 points)

Part IIIa consists of six questions or completions in English, each based on a reading selection in Latin. For each, choose the expression that best answers the question or completes the statement. Base your choice on the content of the reading selection. Write the number of your answer in the space provided.

21

> Balneum nostrum in mediā urbe sītum est. Balneum habet nōn sōlum frīgidārium sed etiam caldārium et lacōnicum. Praetereā, vōs potestis natāre ab sōlis ortū ad sōlis occāsum. In āreā nostrā, potestis vōs exercēre aut pilā lūdĕre aut ad fūnem salīre. In hortīs nostrīs dēambulāre potestis.

The owner of this public bath wishes to advertise that _____

1. the entrance fee is cheap.
2. there are facilities for many kinds of activities.
3. it's a good place to meet friends.
4. the food is excellent.

22

> ### VIR QUAESĪTUS OB LATRŌCINIUM!
>
> Latrō, circā vīgintī annōs nātus, cum capillīs rubrīs et barbā longā et tunicā sordidā. Vir habet sīcam, et est periculōsissimus. Recentissimē vīsus est in mediā Subūrā. Magnum praemium ob captūram hujus latrōnis.

This notice, posted in the forum, is for _____

1. a job opening in center city.
2. a warrant for someone's arrest.
3. a recruiting call for the army.
4. a call for community improvement.

23

Ego ex Germāniā veniō. Duodēvīgintī annōs nātus sum. In bellō Germānicō, ego ab Rōmānō exercitū captus eram. In Germāniā, parentēs meī erant agricolae sed ego scholam frequentāvī. Lūdī magister meus erat Rōmānus. Possum Latīnē legĕre et scrībĕre. Ego etiam Latīnē bene loquor.

This slave on the auction block could best be employed as   _____

1. a farm hand.
2. a shepherd.
3. a scribe or secretary.
4. a carpenter.

24

> ### Dāte huic excellentī hominī suffrāgia vestra!!
>
> *Aulus Gabinius, vir patricius, amīcus populī, petit consulātum. Erat aedīlis honestissimus, deinde praetor jūstissimus. Nunc vult fierī consul. Hīc honestus homō dēsīderat vestra suffrāgia. Ille dēsīderat auxilium vestrum. Cīvēs omnēs, adjuvāte hunc honestum magistrātum.*

This poster in the Campus Martius is   _____

1. a decree honoring a national hero.
2. the publication of a list of officials.
3. a plea for better working conditions.
4. a political campaign notice.

25

> Valerius parentibus suīs salūtem dīcit. Quattuor mensēs abhinc in urbem Rōmam pervēnī. Rōma est urbs multō major quam Lānuvium. Ego bene māne surgō et per viās citō ambulō ad domum medicī, ubi ego medicīnae studeō. Medicus est magister sevērus sed intellegentissimus. Pōmerīdiē ego cum medicō cōtīdiē aegrōs vīsitō. Ego dīligenter observō quid medicus faciat. Hōc modō ego multum dē medicīnā discō.

What is Valerius writing about? _____

1. He is sick and needs a doctor.
2. The city is a dangerous place.
3. The doctors can't cure him.
4. His routine as a medical student.

26

> ### Taberna Vestīaria
> #### Via Campagna
> #### Rōmae
>
> Adfer tēcum hanc chartam, ubi tabernam nostram vīsitās. Nam per hanc chartam tū vestēs aut calceōs emĕre potes parvō pretiō. Necesse est, autem, scrībĕre nōmen tuum in īmā chartā.
>
> ....
> nōmen tuum

This form is used _____

1. to buy clothes at a low price.
2. to apply for a job as sales clerk.
3. to win a free pair of shoes.
4. to rent this clothing store.

b. Multiple Choice (Latin) (8 points)

Part IIIb consists of four questions or completions in Latin, each based on a reading selection in Latin. For each choose the expression that best answers the question or completes the statement. Write the number of your answer in the space provided.

27

QUIS EST HĪC? ILLE EST FĪLIUS DANAĒS. PARMAM SPECULĀREM SINISTRĀ MANŪ TENET; GLADIUM CURVUM DEXTRĀ MANŪ TENET. SOLEĀS ALĀTĀS IN PEDIBUS GERIT. PER ĀĒREM VOLĀRE POTEST.

Ille est _____

1. Juppiter.
2. Herculēs.
3. Apollō.
4. Perseus.

28

VENĪTE ET EMITE PARVŌ PRETIŌ!

IN NOSTRĀ TABERNĀ VENDITĀMUS SCŪTA, GALEĀS, OCREĀS, GLADIŌS, PARMĀS, RĒTIA, TRIDENTĒS.

EMITE HAEC IN TABERNĀ NOSTRĀ ET ERITIS VICTŌRĒS IN ARĒNĀ.

Quis emit tālēs rēs in hāc tabernā? _____

1. Lictōrēs.
2. Āthlētae.
3. Gladiātōrēs.
4. Vigilēs.

29

Virgō (24 Augustī - 23 Septembris)

Quia signum tuum zōdiacī Virgō est, tū es persōna astūta et cauta. Itaque per proximum mensem, antequam aliquid faciēs, dīligenter cōnsīderā valetūdinem tuam, quoniam valetūdō tua erit incerta. Sī febrem habēs, sī pallidus(-a) es, sī frons tua calida est, sī dolōrem capitis habēs, vīsitā statim medicum tuum.

Quid indicat hōroscopium tuum per proximum mensem? _____

1. Amīcus tuus fiet aeger.
2. Valetūdō tua in perīculō erit.
3. Omnēs discipulī fient aegrī.
4. Tū prō medicō labōrābis.

30

Ecce, omnēs agricolae!!

Sī tū agricola es, multīs instrūmentīs ūsūrus es.

—Tū terram *arātrō* arās.
—Tū segetēs *falce* metis.
—Tū agrum herbīs malīs *sarculō* purgās.
—Tū arborēs *falculā* amputās.
—Tū stabulum *furcā* purgās.

Tū potes emĕre omnia haec instrūmenta minimō pretiō in tabernā nostrā.

Potes emĕre haec instrūmenta in _____

1. tabernā ferrāriā.
2. tabernā chartāriā.
3. tabernā tignāriā.
4. tabernā argentāriā.

IV. Writing

a. Notes (6 points)

Write two notes in Latin as directed below. Each note must consist of at least 12 words.

1. You went on a tour to Rome. Write a note in Latin, telling your friend back home what you visited and what you did or saw there.

   _____

   _____

   _____

   _____

2. You have been invited to a birthday party, but you can't go because you don't feel well. Write a note in Latin, telling your friend what's wrong with you and that you can't go the party.

   _____

   _____

   _____

   _____

b. List (4 points)

Write two lists in Latin as directed below. Each list must contain four items.

1. Your friend is going to visit the zoo. In Latin, list the four most interesting animals in the zoo that you wouldn't want your friend to miss seeing.

   _____   _____

   _____   _____

2. You have invited your friend to your home for the weekend. In Latin, list four things that you two could do to enjoy yourselves. Use the infinitive form.

   _____   _____

   _____   _____

Vocābula
Latīna-Anglica

The masculine, feminine, and neuter forms are given for adjectives: **clārus -a -um; facilis -is -e.** Adjectives of the third declension with one ending are followed by a semicolon and the genitive singular: **vetus; veteris.** Endings are italicized to distinguish them clearly from the stems of words. The following abbreviations occur:

abl	= ablative		*interj*	= interjection
acc	= accusative		*m*	= masculine
adj	= adjective		*n*	= neuter
adv	= adverb		*pl*	= plural
conj	= conjunction		*pref*	= prefix
dat	= dative		*prep*	= preposition
f	= feminine		*pron*	= pronoun
indecl	= indeclinable		*rel*	= relative

ā, ab *prep* (+ *abl*) from; by; after; **nōmināre ā sē** to name after oneself

ā, ab- *pref* from, away

abeō -īre -iī or **-īvī -itum** to go away, leave

abhinc *adv* from here; ago; **abī abhinc!** go!, leave!

absolvō -ĕre -ī absolūtus to acquit

absum abesse āfuī to be distant

accendō -ĕre accendī accensus to light

accidō -ĕre -ī to happen

accipiō -ĕre accēpī acceptus to accept, receive

acclāmō -āre -āvī -ātus to shout (*in approval*)

accumbō -ĕre accubuī accubitum to recline (*at the table*)

accūsātor -ōris *m* plaintiff, prosecutor

accūsō -āre -āvī -ātus to accuse, charge

ācer ācris ācre sharp, keen

aciēs -ēī *f* battle line

activitās -ātis *f* activity

actor -ōris *m* actor

actrix -īcis *f* actress

acūleus -ī *m* sting

acūtus -a -um sharp

ad *prep* (+ *acc*) to; for (the purpose of)

ad- *pref* to, toward; intensely

adamō -āre -āvī -ātus to love deeply

adaptō -āre -āvī -ātus to adapt, fit

addūcō -ĕre adduxī adductus to take to

adeō adīre adiī aditum to go to, approach

adferō -ferre -tulī -lātus to bring to; to bring along

adhibeō -ēre -uī -itus to show

adhūc *adv* till now, still

adjacens -entis adjacent

adjaceō -ēre -uī to lie next to

adjuvō adjuvāre adjūvī adjūtus to help

admīrābilis -is -e wonderful

admīror -ārī -ātus sum to admire

admodum *adv* very

adōrō -āre -āvī -ātus to adore, worship

adpōnō -ĕre adposuī adpositus to serve (*food*)

adsum adesse adfuī to be present; to be at hand

adversārius -ī *m* opponent

adversus -a -um bad

advocātus -ī *m* advocate, lawyer

aedēs -is *f* shrine; **aedēs -ium** *fpl* home

aedificō -āre -āvī -ātus to build

aedīlis -is *m* aedile (*an official*)

aër aëris *m* air

aestās -ātis *f* summer

aestimō -āre -āvī -ātus to consider, think

aestus -ūs *m* tide

aetās -ātis *f* age

Aethiopia -ae *f* Ethiopia

afficiō afficĕre affēcī affectus to influence

Āfrica -ae *f* Africa

ager agrī *m* field; **agrī -ōrum** *mpl* countryside

agitō -āre to drive

agō agĕre ēgī actus to drive; to lead (*a life*); **age!** *interj* come!, come on!

agricola -ae *m* farmer

aiēbant they said

Ajax -ācis *m* Ajax

āla -ae f wing; **ālās plaudĕre** to flap the wings
ālātus -a -um winged
Alba Longa -ae f town in Latium, 15 miles southeast of Rome
alea -ae f die; **aleā lūdĕre** to play dice; to gamble
aliēnus -ī m stranger, foreigner
aliōquīn adv otherwise
aliquandō adv someday
aliquid amplius anything else
aliquis alicūjus pron someone
aliquot indecl adj some
alius -a -ud other, another; **alius ex aliō** one after another
alter altera alterum the other
altus -a -um high, tall; deep
amābilis -is -e lovable
amans -antis mf lover; m boyfriend; f girlfriend
amārus -a -um bitter
ambigō -ĕre to wonder, be uncertain
ambiō -īre -iī -ītum to campaign
ambitiōsus -a -um ambitious
ambō -ae -ō both
amīca -ae f (girl)friend
amīcus -a -um friendly
amīcus -ī m (boy)friend
amita -ae f aunt
āmittō -ĕre āmīsī āmissus to lose
amō amāre amāvī amātus to love
amor -ōris m love
amphitheātrum -ī n amphitheater
amphora -ae f amphora (large storage jar)
amputō -āre -āvī -ātus to prune
Amūlius -ī m brother of King Numitor and uncle of Rhea Silvia
an conj or
ancilla -ae f maid
Andromeda -ae f daughter of King Cepheus and Queen Cassiopea
angulus -ī m corner
angustus -a -um narrow
anicula -ae f little old lady
anima -ae f breath; **animam recipĕre** to catch one's breath
animal -ālis n animal
animus -ī m mind, heart

annus -ī m year
ante prep (+ acc) in front of, before; adv out ahead; previously
anteā adv previously, before
antecēdo -cēdĕre -cessī to go before, precede
antequam conj before
ānulus -ī m ring
anus -ūs f old lady
anxius -a -um anxious, worried
aperiō -īre aperuī apertus to open
apertus -a -um open; **in apertō** in the open
apis -is f bee
apodytērium -ī n dressing room
appareō -ēre -uī -itum to make one's appearance, show up, appear
applaudō -ĕre applausī applausus to applaud
apprehendō -ĕre -ī to arrest
appropinquō -āre -āvī -ātus (+ dat) to approach
Aprīlis -is m: **mensis Aprīlis** April
apud prep (+ acc) among; at the house of, with; before, in the presence of
aqua -ae f water
Aquārius -ī constellation Aquarius (water carrier)
aquila -ae f eagle
ara -ae f altar
Arachnē -ēs f Arachne (Lydian girl, changed into a spider)
arānea -ae f spider
arātrum -ī n plough
arbor -oris f tree
arca -ae f chest
arcus -ūs m bow
Ardea -ae f town in Latium
ardeō -ēre arsī arsum to burn, glow
ārea -ae f open space; threshing floor; **ārea domūs** yard
arēna -ae f sand; arena
argentārius -a -um banker's, of a bank; m banker; **taberna argentāria** bank
argentum -ī n cash, dough
Arīcia -ae f town in Latium, about 18 miles south of Rome
armārium -ī n cupboard, closet, cabinet

arō -āre -āvī -ātus to plough
arrogans; arrogantis arrogant
Ariēs -etis m Constellation Aries (ram)
ars artis f skill
artē adv fast, sound (asleep)
articulus -ī m joint; **dolor articulōrum** arthritis
artifex; artificis artistic, skillful
arx arcis f citadel
ascendō -ĕre -ī ascensum to climb; to rise
Asia -ae f Asia
aspectus -ūs m look, view
aspiciō -ĕre aspexī aspectus to watch, look at
assum -ī n roast
assūmō -ĕre -psī -ptus to assume
astrologia -ae f astrology
astrologus -ī m astrologer
astrum -ī n star
astūtus -a -um clever, astute
asȳlum -ī n asylum, refuge
āter ātra ātrum dark, black
āthlēta -ae m athlete
āthlēticus -a -um athletic
atque conj and
ātrium -ī n entrance room
attentē adv carefully, attentively, closely
auctōritās -ātis f authority, prestige
audax; audācis bold
audiō -īre -īvī -ītum to hear; to listen to
audītōrium -ī n lecture hall
audītus -ūs m hearing
augur -uris m augur
augurāculum -ī n place of augury
Augustus -ī m Augustus (first Roman emperor); **mensis Augustus** August
aula -ae f palace
aurātus -a -um gold-plated
aureus -a -um gold(en)
aurīga -ae m charioteer
auris -is f ear
autem adv now, however
autumnus -ī m autumn
avārus -a -um greedy
avē interj hello!
Aventīnus -a -um Aventine (Hill)
avia -ae f grandmother
avidē adv eagerly

avidus -a -um eager, willing
avis -is f bird
avus -ī m grandfather

balneolum -ī n little bath
balneum -ī n bath; **balnea
-ōrum** npl public bath
barba -ae f beard; **barbam rādĕre**
to shave off the beard
basilica -ae f courthouse
bellum -ī n war
bellus -a -um nice
bene adv well, fine; **bene māne**
early in the morning
beneficium -ī n kindness, good
deed
benignē adv warmly, kindly
benignus -a -um kind
bestia -ae f beast; **ad bestiās
dare** to condemn to fight
wild beasts
bestiārius -ī m wild-animal
fighter
bibliothēca -ae f library
bibō -ĕre bibī bibitus to drink
bis adv twice
blandus -a -um endearing
blatta -ae f cockroach
bonus -a -um good
bōs bovis m ox
Bovillae -ārum fpl town in
Latium about 10 miles south
of Rome
bracchium -ī n arm; claw
brevis -is -e short, brief
Britannia -ae f Britain, England

cadō -ĕre cecidī cāsum to fall
caedēs -is f murder; kill
caelum -ī n sky; heaven
Caesar -aris m Caesar
caestus -ūs m boxing glove
calamistrum -ī n curling iron
calamitās -ātis f calamity
calamus -ī m fishing pole
calceus -ī m shoe
caldārium -ī n hot room, hot
bath
calidus -a -um hot
calx calcis f heel
Campānia -ae f district in
central Italy, south of
Latium
campus -ī m (untilled) field;
Campus Mārtius Field of
Mars

Cancer -crī m constellation
Cancer (crab)
candēlābrum -ī n candlestick,
candelabrum
candidātus -a -um whitened; m
candidate
candidus -a -um white
canis -is m dog; **Canis Major** m
constellation Canis Major
(bigger dog); **Canis Minor**
constellation Canis Minor
(smaller dog); **canis vēnāticus**
hunting dog
caper caprī m goat
capillī -ōrum mpl hair; **capillōs
crispāre** to curl the hair;
capillōs pectĕre to comb the
hair
capiō capĕre cēpī captus to
take; to capture
Capitōlīnus -a -um Capitoline;
m Capitoline (Hill)
Capricornus -ī m constellation
Capricorn
captīvus -ī m captive, prisoner
captō -āre -āvī -ātus to catch
Capuā -ae f city in Campania,
south of Rome
caput -itis n head; **Caput
Medūsae** constellation Caput
Medusa (head of Medusa)
carcer -eris m jail
carmen -inis n song
carōta -ae f carrot
carpentum -ī n two-wheeled buggy
carpō -ĕre -sī -tus to find fault
with, carp at
carrūca -ae f traveling carriage;
currūca dormītōria sleeping
carriage
carrus -ī m two-wheeled cart
cārus -a -um dear; expensive
casa -ae f house, hut
Cassiopēa -ae f wife of
Cepheus, king of Ethiopia
castor -oris m beaver
castra -ōrum npl camp
cāsus -ūs m case; **eō casū** in
that case
catasta -ae f slave block
catulus -ī m cub
cauda -ae f tail
caudex -icis m blockhead
caupō -ōnis m innkeeper
caupōna -ae f inn
causa -ae f cause; **causā** (+ gen)
for the sake of

causidicus -ī m lawyer
cautus -a -um cautious
cavea -ae f cage
caverna -ae f hole
celeber -bris -bre famous
celebrō -āre -āvī -ātus to
celebrate
celer celeris celere fast
cella -ae f (little) room; storeroom
celsus -a -um high; **celsius** too
high
cēna -ae f dinner, supper
cēnō -āre -āvī -ātus to eat
supper, dine
Cēpheus -ī m king of Ethiopia
cēra -ae f wax
cerebrōsus -a -um hot-headed
certāmen -inis n contest
certē adv certainly, surely;
without fail
certō -āre -āvī -ātus to compete
certus -a -um certain, sure
cervīcal -ālis n pillow
cervix -īcis f neck
cervus -ī m deer
ceterī -ae -a remaining, rest of;
et cetera and so forth
cētus -ī m sea monster
cibus -ī m food; meal
cicōnia -ae f stork
cinis -eris m ashes
circumambulō -āre -āvī to walk
around
**circumclūdō -clūdĕre -clūsī
-clūsus** to surround
circumstō -stāre -stetī to stand
around
circus -ī m racetrack
cisium -ī n two-wheeled carriage
cista -ae f box
cisterna -ae f cistern
cito adv quickly
cīvis -is mf citizen
cīvitās -ātis f state
clāmō -āre -āvī -ātus to shout
clārus -a -um clear; bright;
famous
claudō -ĕre clausī clausus to
close
clāva -ae f billyclub
clāvus -ī m (crimson) border;
nail
clepō -ĕre -sī -tus to steal
cliens -entis m client
cōgitō -āre -āvī -ātus to think;
cōgitāre sēcum to think to
oneself

cōgō *-ĕre* coēgī coactus to force

cohors *-tis* f barnyard

collēgium *-ī* n guild, college

colligō *-ĕre* collēgī collectus to gather

collis *-is* m hill

color *-ōris* m color

Columba *-ae* f constellation Columba (dove)

columna *-ae* f column

coma *-ae* f hair

cōmicus *-a -um* comic, funny

comitia *-ōrum* npl elections

comittō *-ĕre* commīsī commissus to commit

commūnis *-is -e* common

cōmō *-ĕre* compsī comptus to do, set (*hair*)

compeditī *-ōrum* mpl members of a chain gang

competītor *-ōris* m opponent

comprehendō *-ĕre -ī* comprehensus to arrest; to understand

condemnō *-āre -āvī -ātus* to condemn

condiscipulus *-ī* m classmate

condō *-dĕre -didī -ditus* to store; to found (*a city*)

confīdō *-ĕre* confīdī confīsus sum (+ *dat*) to trust

congregō *-āre -āvī -ātus* to congregate

conjiciō *-ĕre* conjēcī conjectus to hurl; to guess

conjungō *-ĕre* conjunxī conjunctus to join

conjunx *-jugis* mf spouse

cōnor *-ārī -ātus* sum to try

conscendō *-ĕre -ī* to climb aboard

consentiō *-īre* consensī consensus to agree

conservō *-āre -āvī -ātus* to save

consīderō *-āre -āvī -ātus* to consider

consīdō *-sīdĕre -sēdī -sessum* to sit down

consilium *-ī* n idea; plan; advice; consilium inīre to form a plan

consistō *-ĕre* constitī to stop; to take up position

cōnsobrīnus *-ī* m cousin

conspiciō *-ĕre* conspexī conspectus to spot

constanter adv constantly

constellātiō *-ōnis* f constellation

constituō *-ĕre -ī -tus* to decide

constō *-āre -stetī* (+ *abl* of cost) to cost

constructiō *-ōnis* f construction

consul *-is* m consul

consulāris *-is -e* consular, of a consul

consultō *-āre -āvī -ātus* to consult

consūmō *-sūmĕre -sumpsī -sumptus* to consume, eat

contendō *-ĕre ī* contentum to fight, contend

contineō *-ĕre -uī* to hold together; to contain

contingit *-ĕre -tingī -tactum* to happen; contingit it happens; sīc contingit (*dat*) that's what happens to

continuō adv continuously; continuō inspicĕre to keep on looking

continuō *-āre -āvī -ātus* to continue

continuus *-a -um* continuous

contrā adv on the other hand; prep (+ *acc*) against

contrōversia *-ae* f controversy, argument

conveniō *-īre* convēnī conventum to come together, gather; to agree

convertō *-ĕre -ī* conversus to turn; oculōs convertĕre in (+ *acc*) to turn to look at

convīva *-ae* mf (dinner) guest

convocō *-āre -āvī -ātus* to call together

coquō *-ĕre* coxī coctus to cook; to bake

cor cordis n heart

coram prep (+ *abl*) in the presence of

corbis *-is* f basket

corōna *-ae* f crown

cornū *-ūs* n horn

corpus *-oris* n body

corrigia *-ae* f shoelace

coruscō *-āre -āvī* to flash

cōtīdiē adv daily

crās adv tomorrow; crās manē tomorrow morning

crassus *-a -um* fat

crātēr *-ēris* m crater

credō *-dĕre -didī -ditum* (+ *dat*) to believe

crepīdō *-inis* f sidewalk

creō *-āre -āvī -ātus* to create

crescō *-ĕre* crēvī crētum to grow

crīmen *-inis* n charge; crime

crīminālis *-is -e* criminal; crīminālis *-is* m criminal

crispō *-āre* to curl

crocodīlus *-ī* m crocodile

crūdēlis *-is -e* cruel

crūdus *-a -um* crude

cruentus *-a -um* bloody

crūs crūris n leg

cubiculum *-ī* n bedroom

cubitum *-ī* n elbow

cucumis *-eris* m cucumber

cūjus whose

culpa *-ae* f fault, guilt; in culpā esse to be guilty

culter *-trī* m knife; culter vēnāticus hunting knife

cultūra *-ae* f culture

cum prep (+ *abl*) with; against (*an opponent*)

cum conj when; cum subitō when suddenly

cum prīmum adv as soon as possible

cuniculus *-ī* rabbit

cupidē adv eagerly

cupiō *-ĕre -īvī* or *-iī -ītus* to wish, want

cūr adv why; cūr tandem just why

cūra *-ae* f care, worry, concern; cūrae esse to be of concern

cūria *-ae* f senate building

cūrō *-āre -āvī -ātus* to take care, see to it; to supervise

curriculum *-ī* n chariot; racetrack

currō *-ĕre* cucurrī cursum to run

currus *-ūs* m chariot

cursor *-ōris* m runner

cursus *-ūs* m course; cursus honōrum career of public offices

curtus *-a -um* short

curvus *-a -um* curved

Danaē *-ēs* f (acc: Danaen) mother of Perseus

datus *-a -um* mailed; Rōmae data (epistula) mailed in Rome

dē prep about, concerning

dē- *pref* down; thoroughly

deambulō *-āre -āvī* to stroll, walk around

dēbeō *-ēre -uī -itum* to owe

decem *indecl* ten

December *-bris m*: mensis December December

dēcernō *-cernĕre -crēvī -crētus* to decide

dēcidō dēcidĕre dēcidī to fall down

dēcīdō dēcīdĕre dēcīdī dēcīsus to cut down

decōrō *-āre -āvī -ātus* to decorate

dēdicō *-āre* to dedicate

dēductiō *-ōnis f* bridal procession

defectus *-ūs m* defect, failing

dēfendō *-dĕre -dī -sus* to defend

dēfensor *-ōris m* defense lawyer

dēficiō *-ficĕre -fēcī -fectum* to run low

deinde *adv* then

dēlectāmentum *-ī n* entertainment

dēlectō *-āre -āvī -ātus* to delight

dēleō *-ēre -ēvī -ētus* to destroy

dēmissus *-a -um* low; demissior too low

dēmittō *-ĕre dēmīsī dēmissus* to drop; to get rid of

dēnārius *-ī m* "dollar"

dēnique *adv* finally, at last

dēnotō *-āre -āvī -ātus* to mark down

dens dentis *m* tooth

densus *-a -um* dense, thick

dentifricium *-ī m* tooth powder

dēpendeō *-ēre -ī* to hang down

dēpōnō *-ĕre dēposuī dēpositus* to put down

dēserta *-ōrum npl* desert

dēsīderō *-āre -āvī -ātus* to need; to miss; to desire

dēsistō *-ĕre dēstitī* to stop; dēsiste! hold it!

dēspērātus *-a -um* desperate

dēspērō *-āre -āvī -ātus* to despair

dētergeō *-ēre dētersī dētersus* to wipe off

dēterō *-ĕre dētrīvī dētrītus* to thresh

dēterreō *-ēre -uī -itus* to frighten away; to prevent, deter

dētrahō *-ĕre dētraxī dētractus* to pull off

dētruncō *-āre -āvī -ātus* to cut off; to behead

dēveniō *-īre dēvēnī dēventum* to come down

dēvorō *-āre -āvī -ātus* to devour

dexter *-tra -trum* right

dialogus *-ī m* conversation, dialog

dictātor *-ōris m* dictator

dīcō dīcĕre dixī dictus to say

dictitō *-āre -āvī -ātus* to keep saying

diēs *-ēī m* day

difficilis *-is -e* difficult

diffīdō *-ĕre -ī* (+ *dat*) to distrust

digitus *-ī m* finger

dignus *-a -um* (+ *dat*) deserving of

dīligenter *adv* carefully; diligently, hard

dīmittō *-ĕre dīmīsi dīmissus* to get rid of

dīrectē *adv* directly

dīrectō *adv* directly

discēdō *-ĕre discessī discessum* to depart, leave

discens *-entis m* apprentice

discipulus *-ī m* pupil, student

discō *-ĕre didicī* to learn

disputō *-āre -āvī -ātus* to discuss

distō *-āre* to be distant

discobolus *-ī m* discus thrower

discus *-ī m* discus

diū *adv* long, for a long time; diū et ācriter long and hard; diūtius for a longer time

dīves; dīvitis rich; dīvitēs *mpl* the rich

dō dare dedī datus to give

doceō *-ēre -uī -tus* to teach; to tell, explain

dolor *-ōris m* pain; dolor capitis headache

domesticus *-a -um* domestic

domina *-ae f* lady of the house, mistress; domina! madam!

dominus *-ī m* master, owner; domine! sir!

domus *-ūs f* home; domī at home; domō from home; domum (to) home

dōnec *conj* until

dōnum *-ī n* gift

dormiō *-īre -īvī -ītum* to sleep; dormītum īre to go to sleep

dūcō *-ĕre duxī ductus* to lead; in mātrimōnium dūcĕre to marry

dum *conj* while

duo duae duo two

duodēvīgintī *indecl* eighteen

duplex; duplicis double

dūrō *-āre -āvī* to last

dūrus *-a -um* rough, hard, tough

ē- *pref* out; thoroughly, up

ē (ex) *prep* (+ *abl*) out of

ecce! look!

eculeus *-ī m* hobbyhorse

edō esse ēdī ēsum to eat

ēdō ēdĕre ēdidī ēditus to provide

ēducō *-āre -āvī -ātus* to raise

efficiō *-ĕre effēcī effectus* to bring about, cause

effugiō *-ĕre -ī* to escape, run away, get away

ego *pron* I

ējiciō *-ĕre ējēcī ējectus* to throw out, eject

ejus *pron* his, her, its

elephantus *-ī m* elephant

ēlegans; ēlegantis elegant

elementum *-ī n* element

ēligō *-ĕre ēlēgī ēlectus* to elect, choose

ēmigrō *-āre -āvī -ātum* to move, emigrate

emō emĕre ēmī emptus to buy

enim *conj* for

ēnormis *-is -e* enormous

ēnumerō *-āre -āvī -ātus* to count up

eō īre īvī/iī itum to go; eāmus let's go!

epistula *-ae f* letter

equitō *-āre -āvī* to ride (a horse)

equus *-ī m* horse

ērādō *-ĕre ērāsī ērāsus* to rake

ergā *prep* (+ *acc*) toward

ergastulum *-ī n* prison farm

ergō *adv* therefore

errō *-āre -āvī -ātum* to be wrong, err; to wander

ēruptiō *-ōnis f* eruption

esca *-ae f* bait

essedum *-ī n* (light two-wheeled) carriage

ēsuriō *-īre* to be hungry, go hungry

etiam *adv* even; also

etiamnunc *adv* even now, still today

etiamsī *conj* even if
Eurōpa -ae *f* Europe
ēvellō -ĕre -ī ēvulsus to pluck
ēveniō -īre ēvēnī ēventum to occur
ēventus -ūs *m* occurrence, event
ēvītō -āre -āvī -ātus to avoid
ex- *pref* out; thoroughly, up
ex *prep* (+ *abl*) out of, from, of; **ex hōc** from now on
exanimātus -a -um out of breath
exardescō -ĕre exarsī to flare up
excellens; excellentis excellent
excipiō -ĕre excēpī exceptus to welcome; to catch
excitātus -a -um excited
excitō -āre -āvī -ātus to awaken
exemplum -ī *n* example; **exemplī grātiā** for example; **exemplum praebēre** to set an example
exeō exīre exīvī *or* **exiī exitum** to go out
exerceō -ēre -uī -itus to train; to run (*a shop, company*); **sē exercēre** to train, practice, exercise
exercitātiō -ōnis *f* exercise
exercitus -ūs *m* army
exhauriō -īre exhausī exhaustus to draw out, drain
exhibeō -ēre -uī -itus to show
exinde *adv* thereafter
exitus -ūs *m* exit, going out
expellō -ĕre expulī expulsus to expel, drive out
expergiscor -ī experrectus sum to wake up
explicō -āre -uī -itus to explain
expōnō -ĕre exposuī expositus to explain
exprimō -ĕre expressī expressus to express
exsiliō -īre -uī to jump up, jump out
exspectō -āre -āvī -ātus to wait (for)
extrā *prep* (+ *acc*) outside of
extrahō -ĕre extraxī extractus to pull out
exul -is *m* exiled person, exile
exultō -āre -āvī to exult
exuō exuĕre exuī exūtus to take off

fabricō -āre -āvī -ātus to make, put together
facile *adv* easily
facilis -is -e easy; **facilis inventū** easy to find
faciō -ĕre fēcī factus to do, make; to cause
faenum -ī *n* hay
falcula -ae *f* pruning knife
falx -cis *f* scythe
famēs -is *f* hunger
familia -ae *f* family; household; **familia rūstica** slaves on a country estate; **familia urbāna** slaves belonging to a city household
farīna -ae *f* flour
fascēs -ium *mpl* fasces (*rods and ax carried by the lictors*)
fascia -ae *f* bandage
fastīdiōsus -a -um picky
fatigātus -a -um exhausted
Februārius -ī *m*: **mensis Februārius** February
fēlīciter! congratulations (**tibi** to you)!, bravo!
fēlix; fēlīcis happy; lucky
fēmina -ae *f* woman
femur -oris *n* thigh
fenestra -ae *f* window
ferae -ārum *fpl* wild animals
ferē *adv* about, around, approximately
ferō ferre tulī lātus to bring, carry; to take
Fērōnia -ae *f town south of Rome*
ferox; ferōcis *adj* ferocious
ferula -ae *f* whip
fessus -a -um tired
festīnō -āre -āvī to rush; to hurry up
fēstus -a -um festive; **fēstus diēs** holiday, feast day
fidēlis -is -e faithful
fīgō -ĕre fixī fixus to drive in
fīliolus -ī *m* baby boy; dear son
fīō fierī factus sum to be made; to become, get, turn; to take place; **fīat sīc** so be it
flāgitō -āre -āvī -ātus to demand
flamma -ae *f* flame
flammeus -a -um orange, flame-colored
flāvus -a -um blond

fleō flēre flēvī flētum to cry
flō flāre flāvī flātum to blow
flōridus -a -um of flowers, flowery
flōs flōris *m* flower
flūctus -ūs *m* wave
fluitō -āre -āvī to float
flūmen -inis *n* river
fluō fluĕre fluxī fluxum to flow
flūvius -ī *m* stream
focus -ī *m* fireplace, hearth
fons fontis *m* fountain, spring
forāmen -inis *n* hole
forīs *adv* outside, out of doors
forma -ae *f* shape
Formiae -ārum *fpl town in Latium, south of Rome*
formīca -ae *f* ant
formīdābilis -is -e frightening
forsitan *adv* perhaps, maybe
fortassē *adv* perhaps, maybe
forte *adv* by chance; **sī forte tē vidēbō** if I happen to see you
fortis -is -e brave
fortiter *adv* bravely
fortūna -ae *f* fortune
fortūnātus -a -um fortunate
forum -ī *n* marketplace; **forum boārium** cattle market
Forum Appiī *n town in Latium, 43 miles southeast of Rome*
fractus -a -um broken
frangō -ĕre frēgī fractus to break
frātellus -ī *m* little brother
frāter -tris *m* brother
frāterculus -ī *m* little brother
frātricīdium -ī *n* fratricide
fremō -ĕre -uī -itum to roar
frequens; frequentis frequent
frequenter *adv* frequently
frequentō -āre -āvī -ātus to attend
frīgidārium -ī *n* cold bath, cold room
frīgidus -a -um cool
frons frontis *f* forehead
frūctus -ūs *m* fruit
frūmentum -ī *n* grain; wheat
frūstrā *adv* in vain, to no purpose
frūtectum -ī *n* underbrush
fuga -ae *f* escape
fugiō -ĕre fūgī fūgitūrus to flee, run away

fugitīvus *-ī* m fugitive
fulm*en* *-inis* n lightning
fulmin*at* *-āre* *-āvit* to lighten
fūmus *-ī* m smoke
Fundī *-ōrum* mpl *town in Latium, southeast of Rome*
fundō *-ĕre* **fūdī fūsus** to pour
fund*us* *-ī* m farm
fūn*is* *-is* m rope; **ad fūnem salīre** to jump rope
furc*a* *-ae* f fork
furnus *-ī* m oven; furnace
furtim *adv* stealthily; **furtim rēpĕre** to sneak
futūr*a* *-ōrum* npl future

gale*a* *-ae* f helmet
Galli*a* *-ae* f Gaul
gallīn*a* *-ae* f chicken
gaude*ō* *-ēre* (+ *abl*) to enjoy
gaudium *-ī* n joy
gelid*us* *-a* *-um* cold
Geminī *-ōrum* mpl *constellation Gemini (twins)*
gen*a* *-ae* f cheek
gen*er* *-erī* m son-in-law
genocīdium *-ī* n genocide
genū *-ūs* n knee
genus *-eris* n kind, type
Germānia *-ae* f Germany
Germānī *-ōrum* mpl Germans
germicīdium *-ī* n germicide
germin*ō* *-āre* *-āvī* *-ātum* to germinate, sprout
ger*ō* **gerĕre gessī gestus** to wear; to carry; **bellum gerĕre** to fight a war
gest*ō* *-āre* *-āvī* *-ātus* to wear; to carry
gladiāt*or* *-ōris* m gladiator
gladiātōri*us* *-a* *-um* gladiatorial
gladi*us* *-ī* m sword
glori*a* *-ae* f glory
Gorgō *-ōnis* f Gorgon (*female monster*)
grabāt*us* *-ī* m cot
grad*us* *-ūs* m step; **per gradūs ascendĕre** to go up the steps
Graeci*a* *-ae* f Greece
Graec*us* *-a* *-um* Greek
grandin*at* *-āre* *-āvit* to hail
grand*is* *-is* *-e* big, huge
grand*ō* *-inis* m hail
grassāt*or* *-ōris* m hoodlum
grātiā *prep* (+ *gen*) for the sake of; **exemplī grātiā** for example

grāt*us* *-a* *-um* grateful
gravāt*us* *-a* *-um* heavy
grav*is* *-is* *-e* heavy; serious
gust*ō* *-āre* *-āvī* *-ātus* to taste, eat
gymnasium *-ī* n gymnasium

habe*ō* *-ēre* *-uī* *-itus* to have
habit*ō* *-āre* *-āvī* *-ātum* to live, dwell
habit*us* *-ūs* m bearing, looks; condition
hām*us* *-ī* m hook
harēn*a* *-ae* f sand
harūsp*ex* *-icis* m diviner, soothsayer
hast*a* *-ae* f spear
hauri*ō* *-īre* **hausī haustus** to draw
herb*a* *-ae* f grass; herb; **herba mala** weed
herbicīdium *-ī* n herbicide
Herculāneum *-ī* n *town on the Bay of Naples*
herī *adv* yesterday
hīc *adv* here
hīc haec hōc *pron* this
hinc *adv* from here; **hinc . . . hinc** on one side . . . on the other side
hippodromos *-ī* m racetrack, hippodrome
hodiē *adv* today
holus *-eris* n vegetable
homicīdium *-ī* n homicide
hom*ō* *-inis* m person; **hominēs** people
honest*us* *-a* *-um* honest; respectable
hon*or* *-ōris* m political office
hōr*a* *-ae* f hour
hordeum *-ī* n barley
hōroscopium *-ī* n horoscope
horreum *-ī* n barn
horribil*is* *-is* *-e* horrible
hort*us* *-ī* m garden; **hortī publicī** park
hospitālit*ās* *-ātis* f hospitality
host*is* *-is* m enemy
hūc *adv* here, to this place
hūmid*us* *-a* *-um* humid

ibi *adv* there
ic*ō* **icĕre īcī ictus** to hit; to sting
ict*us* *-ūs* m bite, sting

īdem eadem idem *pron, adj* the same
ign*is* *-is* m fire
ille illa illud *pron* that
imbecill*us* *-a* *-um* weak
imb*er* *-bris* m rain
immigr*ō* *-āre* *-āvī* (in + *acc*) to move into
immō *adv* well
impōn*ō* *-ĕre* **imposuī impositus** (+ *dat*) to put on
īm*us* *-a* *-um* lowest; **in īmō saccō** at the bottom of the bag
in *prep* (+ *acc*) against; into; to; (with *abl*) in; on
inaugur*ō* *-āre* *-āvī* *-ātum* to look for an omen, take the auspices
inaur*is* *-is* f earring
incendium *-ī* n fire
incend*ō* *-ĕre* *-ī* **incensus** to light
incert*us* *-a* *-um* unsure, uncertain
incipi*ō* *-ĕre* **incēpī inceptus** to begin
incit*ō* *-āre* *-āvī* *-ātus* to urge on
inclūd*ō* *-ĕre* **inclūsī inclūsus** to lock up; to enclose
indic*ō* *-āre* *-āvī* *-ātus* to point out
indīc*ō* *-ĕre* **indīxī indictus** to declare
indu*ō* *-ĕre* *-ī* **indūtus** to put on
industri*us* *-a* *-um* industrious
ine*ō* **inīre iniī** or **inīvī initum** (in + *acc*) to go into
inf*ans* *-antis* mf baby
infanticīdium *-ī* n infanticide
inf*ēlix* *-ēlīcis* unhappy; unlucky
inferī *-ōrum* mpl the dead; underworld
infest*us* *-a* *-um* hostile
inflammāt*us* *-a* *-um* inflamed
infund*ō* *-ĕre* **infūdī infūsus** to pour into
inhabit*ō* *-āre* *-āvī* *-ātus* to inhabit
inimīc*us* *-a* *-um* unfriendly
inimīc*us* *-ī* m (personal) enemy
injici*ō* *-ĕre* **injēcī injectus** to throw into
innoc*ens* *-entis* innocent
inop*s* *-is* helpless
inquiēt*us* *-a* *-um* restless

inquirō -*ere* inquisīvī inquisītus to ask, enquire
inruō -*ere* -ī to rush in
inscrībō -*ere* inscripsī inscriptus to write on
insecticīdium -ī *n* insecticide
insectum -ī *n* insect
inserō -*ere* -uī -tus to insert, put into
inspiciō -*ere* inspexī inspectus to look into
instrūmentum -ī *n* tool; equipment
insula -ae *f* apartment building; island
intellectus -ūs *m* understanding, intellect
intellegens; intellegentis intelligent
intellegō -*ere* intellexī intellectus to understand
intendō -*ere* -ī intentus to draw
intentē *adv* intently
inter *prep* (+ *acc*) between; during; **inter sē** with each other
interdum *adv* at times, sometimes
interrogātum -ī *n* question
interrogō -āre -āvī -ātus to ask
intersum -esse -fuī to be involved, participate; (with *dat* or *in* + *abl*) to be present at, participate in
intrō -āre -āvī to enter
intus *adv* inside
inūsitātus -a -um unusual
inveniō -īre invēnī inventus to find, come upon, to invent
invideō -*ere* invīdī (+ *dat*) to envy
invīsibilis -is -e invisible
ipse ipsa ipsum *pron* -self; himself; herself; itself
īra -ae *f* anger
īracundus -a -um quick-tempered
īrātus -a -um angry
īre see **eō**
irrigō -āre -āvī -ātus to water
irrītābilis -is -e irritable
iste ista istud *pron* that
ita *adv* so, thus; yes; **ita est** that's right; **ita quidem** yes indeed; **itane?** is that so?
Ītalia -ae *f* Italy
itaque *conj* and so

iter -ineris *n* trip; **iter facere** to take a trip, travel
iterum *adv* again
Itrī -ōrum *mpl* town south of Rome in Latium

jaceō -*ere* -uī to lie (down)
jactō -āre -āvī -ātus to toss; **sē jactāre dē** (+ *abl*) to boast about
jaculātor -ōris *m* hurler
jaculum -ī *n* javelin
jam *adv* already; by now, now; **jam trēs hōrās labōrō** I have been working for three hours
jamdudum *adv* long ago
jamprīdem *adv* long ago
janua -ae *f* door
Jānuārius -ī *m*: **mensis Jānuārius** January
jentāculum -ī *n* breakfast
jocus -ī *m* joke; **jocum facis!** you're kidding!
juba -ae *f* mane
jubeō -*ere* jussī jussus to order
jūdex -icis *m* judge; juror
jūdicium -ī *n* trial; court; courtroom; verdict
Jūlius -ī *m*: **mensis Jūlius** July
jungō -*ere* junxī junctus to join
Jūnius -ī *m*: **mensis Jūnius** June
jūrō -āre -āvī -ātus to swear
jūs jūris *n* law
jūstitia -ae *f* justice
jūstus -a -um just, fair
jūvenis -is *m* young man
juvō -āre jūvī jutus to help

labor -ōris *m* work; **labōrēs** troubles
labōrō -āre -āvī -ātus to work
labyrinthus -ī *m* labyrinth, maze
lac lactis *n* milk
lacōnicum -ī *n* sauna
lacrima -ae *f* tear
lacrimō -āre -āvī to cry
lactūca -ae *f* lettuce
laetus -a -um happy
lāna -ae *f* wool; **lānās nēre** to spin wool
laniō -āre -āvī -ātus to tear up
lanista -ae *m* trainer
Lānuvium -ī *n* town in Latium, south of Rome
lapillus -ī *m* little stone
Larēs -ium *mpl* household gods

lateō -*ere* -uī to hide
Latīnē *adv* (in) Latin; **Latīnē docēre** to teach Latin; **Latīnē loquī** to speak Latin
Latium -ī *n* district in central Italy just south of the Tiber river
latrīna -ae *f* toilet
latrō -ōnis *m* robber
lātus -a -um broad
laudō -āre -āvī -ātus to praise
laureus -a -um of laurel
lavō -āre lāvī lautus to wash; **sē lavāre** to wash (oneself)
lectīca -ae *f* litter
lectulus -ī *m* (small) bed
legātus -ī *m* envoy, delegate
legiō -ōnis *f* legion
legō -*ere* lēgī lectus to read
lentē slowly
lentus -a -um slow
Leō -ōnis *m constellation Leo (lion)*
leopardus -ī *m* leopard
levō -āre -āvī -ātus to lift
libenter *adv* gladly
liber -brī *m* book
liberālis -is -e generous
liberī -ōrum *mpl* children
līberō -āre -āvī -ātus to free, liberate
lībertās -ātis *f* liberty
Libra -ae *f constellation Libra (scales)*
lībum -ī *n* cake
licet -*ere* -uit it is allowed; **licet mihi** I am allowed, I may; **licet** *interj* well!
lictor -ōris *m* lictor, bodyguard
lignum -ī *n* wood
ligō -āre -āvī -ātus to tie
lilium -ī *n* lily
līmen -inis *n* threshold, doorstep
līnea -ae *f* line; string
līnum -ī *n* twine
liquefaciō -facere -fēcī -factus to melt
litterae -ārum *fpl* letter
lituus -ī *m* augur's staff
locus -ī *m* place; **in locō** (+ *gen*) in place of; **locus dēstinātus** destination
longē *adv* far
longinquus -a -um distant, far, far away
longus -a -um *adj* long

loquor loquī locūtus sum to speak

lūceō -ēre luxī to shine

luctātor -ōris m wrestler

lūdō -ĕre lūsī lūsus to play

lūdus -ī m game; school; **lūdī** public games

lūna -ae f moon

lupa -ae f (female) wolf

lupus -ī m (male) wolf

lūridus -a -um smoky, yellowish

lūsor -ōris m player

lustrō -āre -āvī -ātus to look over

lūsus -ūs m game

lūx lūcis f light; daylight; **prīmā lūce** at dawn

Lydia -ae f country in Asia Minor

macellum -ī n produce market, grocery store

macula -ae f spot

maculōsus -a -um spotty

madeō -ēre -uī to be wet (with tears)

maestus -a -um grieving

magis adv more; **magis et magis** more and more

magister -trī m teacher; master craftsman

magistra -ae f teacher

magnificē adv magnificently

magnificus -a -um magnificent

magnopere adv greatly

magnus -a -um big; important; great; loud

Maius -ī m: **mensis Maius** May

major major majus bigger; older

maleficium -ī n evil deed

malleus -ī m hammer

mālum -ī n apple

malus -a -um bad

mamma -ae f mom, mommy

mandātum -ī n instruction

māne adv in the morning

maneō -ēre mansī mansūrus to stay

mangō -ōnis m slave dealer

manīcae -ārum fpl handcuffs

mannus -ī m pony

manus -ūs f hand

mare -is n sea

margō -inis m edge, fringe, border

marīnus -a -um sea-, of the sea

maritimus -a -um sea-, of the sea

marītus -ī m husband

marsuppium -ī n moneybag

Martius -ī m: **mensis Martius** March

matella -ae f chamberpot

māter -tris f mother

mathēmaticus -ī m astrologer; mathematician

mātricīdium -ī n matricide

mātrimōnium -ī n marriage; **in mātrimōnium dūcĕre** to marry

mātrōna -ae f married woman

maximē adv best

maximus -a -um biggest; oldest

mē pron me; **mēcum** with me, to myself

medeor -ērī (+ dat) to heal

medica -ae f (female) doctor

medicus -ī m doctor

Medūsa -ae f one of the three Gorgons

mehercule interj by heaven!, so help me!

mel mellis n honey

melior melior melius better

melius adv better

meminī -isse to remember; **mementō!** remember!

memoria -ae f memory; **in memoriā tenēre** to remember, keep in mind

mens -tis f mind

mensa -ae f table; **Mensa** constellation Mensa

mensis -is m month

mentiō -ōnis f mention

mereō -ēre -uī -itus to earn

merīdiēs -ēī m noon

meta -ae f stack; **faenī meta** haystack

metō -ĕre messuī messus to reap, harvest

metuō -ĕre ī to fear

meus -a -um my

migrō -āre -āvī to move

mīles -itis m soldier

Minerva -ae f goddess of handicrafts

minimē adv no; **minimē vērō** no; not at all

minimus -a -um smallest; youngest

Mīnōs -ōis m king of Crete

minor minor minus smaller; younger

Mīnōtaurus -ī m Minotaur

Minturnae -ārum fpl town in Latium, south of Rome

mīrābilis -is -e wonderful

mīrāculum -ī n miracle; strange sight

mīrus -a -um strange

Mīsēnum -ī n town on the northern tip of the Bay of Naples

miser -era -erum poor, miserable

mītis -is -e gentle; tame, mild

modicum -ī n a bit, modicum

modo adv just, just now; **modo . . . modo** sometimes . . . sometimes

modus -ī m way, method; style, fashion

mola -ae f mill, flour mill

momentum -ī n importance; **momentum temporis** moment

moneō -ēre -uī -itus to warn

mons montis m mount

monstrō -āre -āvī -ātus to show

mora -ae f delay

morior morī mortuus sum to die

mortālitās -ātis f mortality

mōrus -ī f mulberry tree

mōs mōris m custom

mōtiō -ōnis f movement

moveō -ēre mōvī mōtus to move; to cause

mox adv soon; then

mulgeō -ēre mulsī mulsus to milk

multī -ae -a many

multitūdō -inis f crowd

multō adv much, by much; **multō nimis lentus** much too slow; **multō plūra** many more

multum adv a lot

multus -a -um much

mūlus -ī m mule

mundus -ī m world; **in mundō** on earth

mūniō -īre -īvī or **-iī -ītus** to fortify; to build (a road)

mūnus -eris n show, contest; **ad mūnus gladiātōrium condemnāre** to condemn to fight as a gladiator

mūnusculum -*ī n* (little) present

mūrus -*ī m* wall; **mūrum dūcĕre** to build a wall

mūsculus -*ī m* muscle

mūtābilis -*is* -*e* fickle, changeable

mūtō -*āre* -*āvī* -*ātus* to change

mūtuor -*ārī* -*ātus* **sum** to borrow

mūtuus -*a* -*um* mutual

nam *conj* for, because

nascor nascī nātus sum to be born

nātālis -*is* -*e*: **diēs nātālis** birthday

natātiō -*ōnis f* swim

natō -*āre* -*āvī* to swim

nātus -*a* -*um* born; (*with number of years*) old

naufrāgium -*ī n* shipwreck

nāvicula -*ae f* boat

nāvis -*is f* ship; **nāvis magister** captain

nē *conj* (*with purpose clauses*) that not; (*after verbs of fearing*) that

nē *adv* not; **nē . . . quidem** not even

-**ne** *adv interrogative particle expecting a yes or no answer*

Neāpolītānus -*a* -*um adj* Neapolitan

nebula -*ae f* fog, mist

nebulō -*ōnis m* airhead

necō -*āre* -*āvī* -*ātus* to kill

nectō -*ĕre* **nexī nexus** to tie

negō -*āre* -*āvī* -*ātus* to deny

negōtiālis -*is* -*e* business

negōtiātor -*ōris m* businessman

nēmō -*inis m* no one

nempe *adv* well, as you know

neō nēre nēvī nētus to spin

neque . . . neque *conj* neither . . . nor

nesciō -*īre* -*īvī or* -*iī* -*ītum* not to know

niger -*gra* -*grum* black

nihil *indecl* nothing

nīmīrum *adv* of course

nimis *adv* too

nimium *adv* too

ningit -*ĕre* **ninxit** to snow

nisi *conj* unless; except

**nix nivis f* snow

nōbilitās -*ātis f* nobility

nōbilis -*is* -*e* noble

noceō -*ēre* -*uī* (+ *dat*) to harm

noctū *adv* at night

nōlō nōlle nōluī to not want, to be unwilling; **nōlī (nōlīte)** (+ *inf*) do not . . .!

nōmen -*inis n* name; clan name

nōminō -*āre* -*āvī* -*ātus* to name

nōn *adv* no; not; **nōn jam** no longer; **nōn modo . . . sed etiam** not only . . . but also; **nōn procul abhinc** not far from here

nōndum *adv* not yet

nōnne *adv introduces a question expecting a yes answer*

nōnnullī -*ae* -*a* some

nōs *pron* we; us

noster -*tra* -*trum* our

notō -*āre* -*āvī* -*ātus* to notice

nōtus -*a* -*um* well known, noted

novācula -*ae f* razor

nōvī nōvisse to know, to be acquainted with

novissimus -*a* -*um* latest, last

novus -*a* -*um* new

**nox noctis f* night

nūbēs -*is f* cloud

nūbilus -*a* -*um* cloudy, overcast

nūbō -*ĕre* **nupsī nupta** (+ *dat*) to marry

nūgae -*ārum fpl* nonsense; **nūgās!** nonsense!

nullus -*a* -*um* no

num *adv introduces a question expecting a negative answer*

num *conj* whether

numerō -*āre* -*āvī* -*ātus* to count

Numitor -*ōris m king of Alba Longa, grandfather of Romulus and Remus*

nummus -*ī m* coin

numquam *adv* never

nunc *adv* now

nuntiō -*āre* -*āvī* -*ātus* to announce

nūper *adv* recently

nupta -*ae f* bride

nuptiae -*ārum fpl* wedding

nuptiālis -*is* -*e* wedding, nuptial

nūtō -*āre* -*āvī* to totter

nūtriō -*īre* -*īvī or* -*iī* -*ītus* to nourish; to nurse

**nux nucis f* nut

ob *prep* (+ *acc*) on account of, because of

obductus -*a* -*um* covered

obēdiens; obēdientis obedient

obēdiō -*īre* -*īvī or* -*iī* (+ *dat*) to obey

obiter *adv* by the way

oblectāmentum -*ī n* delight

obligō -*āre* -*āvī* -*ātus* to bind, oblige; **obligātus sum** (+ *inf*) I am supposed to

oblongus -*a* -*um* oblong

obscūrus -*a* -*um* murky

observō -*āre* -*āvī* -*ātus* to observe

obsōnō -*āre* -*āvī* to shop (*for groceries*); to go shopping

obstinātus -*a* -*um* obstinate, stubborn

obvius -*a* -*um*: **īre obvius** (+ *dat*) to go to meet

occidens -*entis* setting

occīdō -*ĕre* -*ī* **occīsus** to kill

occultō -*āre* -*āvī* -*ātus* to hide

occupātus -*a* -*um* busy

occupō -*āre* -*āvī* -*ātus* to seize, grip

occurrō -*ĕre* -*ī* **occursum** (+ *dat*) to run into, meet

ōceanus -*ī m* ocean

ocīnum -*ī n* clover

ocrea -*ae f* shinguard

Octōber -*bris m*: **mensis Octōber** October

oculus -*ī m* eye

ōdī ōdisse to hate

odor -*ōris m* odor

offendō -*ĕre* -*ī* **offensus** to offend

officīna -*ae f* workshop

officium -*ī n* duty; **officiī grātiā** to pay one's respects

ōlim *adv* once

olīvētum -*ī n* olive grove

Olympia -*ae f site of ancient Olympic games in Greece*

Olympicus -*a* -*um* Olympic

ōmen -*inis n* omen

omittō -*ĕre* **omīsī omissus** to skip, forget about; to lose

omnīnō *adv* entirely, completely; **nōn omnīnō** not at all

omnis -*is* -*e* every, each; **omnēs (omnia)** all

onerō -*āre* -*āvī* -*ātus* to load

onus -*eris n* burden, weight

opiniō -ōnis f opinion

oportet -ēre -uit it befits;
 oportet tē you ought

oppidānī -ōrum mpl
 townspeople

oppidulum -ī n little town

oppidum -ī n town

oppugnō -āre -āvī -ātus to
 charge, attack

optimus -a -um best

opus -eris n work

ōra -ae f shore; ōra maritima
 seashore

ōrātiō -ōnis f speech; ōrātiōnem
 habēre to give a speech

orbis -is m globe; orbis
 terrārum the world

ordinō -āre -āvī -ātus to
 arrange, set in order

ordō -inis m row; order; jūs et
 ordō law and order

oriens -entis rising

orior orīrī ortus sum to rise

ōrō -āre -āvī -ātus to beg

oscillō -āre -āvī to swing

oscillum -ī n swing

osculum -ī n kiss

ovīle -is n sheep fold

ovis -is f sheep

pābulum -ī n fodder, feed

paenē adv almost

paenitet -ēre -uit to cause
 regret; mē paenitet I am
 sorry, I regret

pala -ae f spade

palaestra -ae f palaestra,
 wrestling place; exercise yard

palaestricus -ī m coach

pallidus -a -um pale

palma -ae f palm

palpebra -ae f eyelash

pānis -is m bread; pānēs loaves
 of bread

panthēra -ae f panther

pāpiliō -ōnis m butterfly

parens -entis mf parent

pariēs -etis m (inner) wall

parma -ae f (small, round)
 shield

pars partis f part; direction

parvulus -a -um small, young

parvulus -ī m little boy, young
 boy

parvus -a -um small, young

passus -ūs m pace; mīlle passūs
 a mile

pastor -ōris m shepherd

pateō -ēre -uī to lie open

pater -tris m father

patiens patientis patient

patientia -ae f patience

patria -ae f country, native
 land, native city

patricīdium -ī n patricide

patricius -a -um patrician

paulātim adv little by little

paulisper adv for a little while

paulō adv a little; paulō post a
 little later

pauper pauperis paupere poor

pavīmentum -ī n pavement, floor

pāvō -ōnis m peacock; Pāvō
 constellation Pāvō

pax pācis f peace

pecten -inis m comb

pectō -ěre pexī pexus to comb

pectus -oris n breast, chest

pecūlium -ī n personal savings

pecūnia -ae f money

pējor pējor pējus worse

pellis -is f hide, skin, pelt

penna -ae f feather

pensitō -āre -āvī -ātus to pay

per prep (+ acc) through; per
 mē by myself

per- pref thoroughly, up
 (perficiō I finish up)

perdō -děre -didī -ditus to
 destroy

pereō -īre -iī to die, perish

perfodiō -īre perfōdī perfossus
 to stab

perforō -āre -āvī -ātus to drill a
 hole in; to pierce, perforate

perīculōsus -a -um dangerous

perīculum -ī n danger

perinde adv furthermore;
 perinde ac just as

peristȳlium -ī n (colonnaded)
 garden, courtyard

perītus -a -um experienced,
 skilled

perpaucī -ae -a very few

perpetuus -a -um constant; in
 perpetuum forever; in
 perpetuum exinde ever after

persequor -sequī -secūtus sum
 to chase, pursue

persōna -ae f person

persōnālis -is -e personal

perterritus -a -um scared stiff

pertineō -ēre -uī to belong to; to
 pertain to

perveniō -venīre -vēnī -ventum
 to arrive (ad or in + acc at);
 to reach

pēs pedis m foot; leg; īre
 pedibus to go on foot

pessimus -a -um worst

pesticīdium -ī n pesticide

petītiō -ōnis f campaign

petītor -ōris m plaintiff

petō -ěre -īvī -ītus to chase
 (after)

pexus -a -um (past participle of
 pectō) combed

philosophus -ī m philosopher

Pictor -ōris m constellation
 Pictor (the Painter)

pictūra -ae f painting, picture

piger pigra pigrum lazy

pila -ae f ball; pilā lūděre to
 play ball; pila nivea snowball

pīlentum -ī n women's carriage

pingō -ěre pinxī pictus to
 embroider; to paint

pinguis -is -e fat

pinna -ae f fin

pīrāta -ae m pirate

piscātiō -ōnis f fishing

piscīna -ae f swimming pool;
 fish pond

piscis -is m fish; Piscēs
 constellation Pisces

piscor -ārī -ātus sum to go
 fishing

pistor -ōris m baker

pistrīna -ae f bakery

placeō -ēre -uī -itum (+ dat) to
 please; urbs mihi placet I like
 the city

plānē adv clearly, plainly

planēta -ae f planet

planta -ae f plant; sole

plaudō -ěre plausī plausum to
 flap

plaustrum -ī n wagon

plēbēius -a -um plebian

plēnus -a -um (+ gen) full of

plerīque pleraeque pleraque
 most

pluit -ěre pluit to rain

plūs adv more; plūs temporis
 more time

Plūtō -ōnis m king of the
 underworld

pluvia -ae f rain

pluvius -a -um rain-, of rain;
 rainy; pluvius arcus rainbow

polītus -a -um polite, refined

pollex -icis m thumb
Polydectēs -ae m (acc: **Polydectēn**) king of the island of Seriphos
pōmerīdiē adv in the afternoon
pompa -ae f procession
Pompēiī -ōrum mpl city in Campania, a few miles south of Mount Vesuvius
pōnō -ĕre posuī positus to put; to ask
popīna -ae f snack shop, restaurant
populāris -is -e popular
populus -ī m people
porcus -ī m pig
porrō adv besides, furthermore
porta -ae f gate; **Porta Capēna** gate in the ancient Roman wall marking the beginning of the Via Appia
possideō -ēre possēdī possessus to own
possum posse potuī to be able
post prep (+ acc) behind; after
post- pref behind, after
post adv afterwards, later; **paulō post** a little later
posteā adv afterwards, later on
posterus -a -um following
postis -is m doorpost
postmerīdiē adv in the afternoon
postquam conj after
postrīdiē adv on the following day
postulō -āre -āvī -ātum to demand
potestās -ātis f power
potiō -ōnis f drink
pōtō -āre -āvī pōtus to drink
praecēdō -ĕre praecessī praecessum to go before, precede
praeceptum -ī n instruction
praecipitō -āre -āvī -ātus to throw down (headfirst)
praecipuē adv especially
praecurrō -currĕre -cucurrī -cursum to run out ahead
praeda -ae f loot
praedīcō -ĕre -dīxī -dictus to predict
praeferō -ferre -tulī -lātus to prefer
praeficiō -ficĕre -fēcī -fectus to put (someone) in command of

praeiūdicium -ī n pretrial hearing
praemium -ī n award
praenōmen -inis n first name
praesideō -sidēre -sēdī to sit before; to preside
praesum -esse -fuī to be in charge; to preside
praetereā adv besides, moreover
praetereō -īre -īvī or **-iī -itum** to pass
praeternāvigō -āre -āvī -ātum to sail by
praetextus -a -um having a border; **toga praetexta** toga with a broad crimson border
praetor -ōris m praetor
prandium -ī n lunch
prātum -ī n meadow
prīmō adv first; at first
prīmum adv first (of all); for the first time
prīmus -a -um first; **prīmō vēre** in early spring
prius adv first; sooner
prīvātus -a -um private; m private citizen
prō- prep (+ abl) on behalf of, for; instead of
prō pref forward, forth
probātiō -ōnis f test
prōcēdō -cēdĕre -cessī to proceed, go on
procul adv at a distance, far; **procul ab** (+ abl) far from
prōdeō -īre -iī -itum to step forward
prodest see **prosum**
prōfundō -fundĕre -fūdī -fūsus to shed
prōhibeō -ēre -uī -itus to prohibit; to prevent
prōiciō -ĕre prōiēcī prōiectus to throw forward, project
prōmittō -mittĕre -mīsī -missus to promise; **multa prōmittĕre** to make many promises
prōnuba -ae f bridesmaid, matron of honor
prōnuntiō -āre -āvī -ātum to pronounce
prope prep (+ acc) near
properō -āre -āvī to rush, hurry
propter prep (+ acc) on account of
prōrsum adv absolutely
prosperus -a -um favorable

prōsequor prōsequī prōsecūtus sum to escort
prōsum prōdesse prōfuī (+ dat) to be good for
prōtegō -tegĕre -tēgī -tectus to protect
prōvocō -āre -āvī -ātus to challenge
proximus -a -um (+ dat) next (to)
prūdens; prūdentis prudent
pūblicus -a -um public
puella -ae f girl
puellus -ī m little boy
puer -ī m boy
pugil -is m boxer
pugnō -āre -āvī -ātus to fight
pulcher -chra -chrum handsome; beautiful
pulchritūdō -inis f beauty
pulsō -āre -āvī -ātus to batter, pound; to knock at
pulvis -eris m dust
pūniō -īre -īvī or **-iī -ītus** to punish
pūpa -ae f doll
purgō -āre -āvī -ātus to clean
purpureus -a -um crimson

quaerō -ĕre quaesīvī quaesītus to look for
quaesō please
quaestiō -ōnis f question
quaestor -ōris m quaestor (financial officer)
quālis -is -e what kind of
quam adv how; **quam superbus** how proud
quam conj as; than; **quam celerrimē** as fast as possible; **quam prīmum** as soon as possible
quamdiū adv how long
quamobrem adv why; that's why
quamquam conj although
quandō adv when
quattuor indecl four
quārtus -a -um fourth
quī quae quod rel pron who, which, that
quī quae quod interrogative adj which, what
quia conj because
quīcumque quaecumque quodcumque pron whoever, whatever

quid *pron* what; (*after* **sī**) anything; **quid est?** what's the trouble?; **quid est tibi?** what's wrong with you?

quīdam quaedam quoddam *pron* a certain; **quōdam diē** one day

quidem *adv* really; in fact

quidnam? *pron* just what?

quidnī *adv* why not

quīnque *indecl* five

quis *pron* who?

quō *adv* where(to)

quō *adv*: **quō magis . . . eō magis** the more . . . the more

quōmodo *adv* how

quondam *adv* once

quoque *adv* too

quot *indecl* how many

quotiens *adv* how often; *conj* whenever

quōusque *adv* how long

radius *-ī m* ray; spoke

raeda *-ae f* four-wheeled carriage; **raeda meritōria** rental carriage

raedārius *-ī m* driver, coachman

rapidē *adv* rapidly, fast

rapiō *-ĕre -uī -tus* to seize, kidnap; **in jūdicium rapĕre** to haul off to court

rārō *adv* rarely

rastellus *-ī m* rake

ratiō *-ōnis f* reason

re- *pref* back; backward; again

rebellis *-is -e* rebellious

rebellō *-āre -āvī -ātum* to rebel

recens; recentis recent

recipiō *-ĕre recēpī receptus* to take back; **sē recipĕre** to retire

recognoscō *-ĕre recognōvī recognitus* to recognize

rectus *-a -um* straight; **rectā lineā** in a straight line

recūsō *-āre -āvī -ātus* to refuse

reddō *-ĕre redidī reditus* to return, give back

redeō *-īre -iī itum* to return, go back

redūcō *-dūcĕre -duxī -ductus* to lead back

refugiō *-ĕre -ī* to fall back

refulgeō *-ēre refulsī* to shine again

regiō *-ōnis f* region

regnō *-āre -āvī -ātum* (+ *dat*) to rule over

regnum *-ī n* kingdom

relinquō *-ĕre relīquī relictus* to leave

remigō *-āre -āvī* to row

rēmus *-ī m* oar

reparō *-āre -āvī -ātus* to repair

repente *adv* all of a sudden, suddenly

repentīnus *-a -um* sudden

rēpō *-ĕre -sī -tum* to crawl

reportō *-āre -āvī -ātus* to bring back

repudiō *-āre -āvī -ātus* to jilt

repugnō *-āre -āvī* to fight back

requīrō *-ĕre requisīvī requisītus* to look for; **vōcibus requīrĕre** to yell for

rēs reī f thing; situation; matter; **rēs pūblica** government; politics

respirātiō *-ōnis f* breathing; breath

respirātor *-ōris m* respirator

respirō *-āre -āvī -ātum* to breathe

respondeō *-ēre -ī responsum* to answer

restō *-āre restitī* to remain, be left over

rētē *-is n* net

retiārius *-ī m* netman

retineō *-ēre -uī retentus* to hold back, retain

reus *-ī m* defendant; guilty one

revēlō *-āre -āvī -ātus* to reveal

rex rēgis *m* king

rīma *-ae f* crack

rīpa *-ae f* bank

rōbustus *-a -um* strong, robust

rogō *-āre -āvī -ātus* to ask

Rōmānus *-a -um* Roman

Rōmulus *-ī m first king of Rome*

rostra *-ōrum npl* rostrum, speaker's platform

rota *-ae f* wheel

rotundō *-āre -āvī -ātus* to make round

ruber rubra rubrum red

rūgiō *-īre -iī* to roar

ruīna *-ae f* collapse

runcīna *-ae f* (carpenter's) plane

runcīnō *-āre -āvī -ātum* to plane

ruō *-ĕre -ī -itūrus* to rush

rūpēs *-is f* cliff

rursus *adv* again

rūs rūris *n* country; **rūre** from the country; **rūrī** in the country; **rūs** (*acc*) to the country

rutrum *-ī n* shovel

Sabīnus *-a -um* Sabine; **Sabīnī** Sabines (*ancient neighbors of Rome*)

saccus *-ī m* bag

saepe *adv* often

sagitta *-ae f* arrow

Sagittārius *-ī m constellation Sagittarius*

saliō *-īre -iī* to jump; **ad fūnem salīre** to jump rope

salūs *-ūtis f* greeting; safety; **salūtem dare** *or* **dīcĕre** to send greetings

salvē! (salvēte!) hello!

salvus *-a -um* safe

sandalium *-ī n* sandal

sānē *adv* yes

sānitās *-ātis f* health; sanity

sānō *-āre -āvī -ātus* to heal

sānus *-a -um* sound, healthy

sarculum *-ī n* hoe

sariō *-īre -uī* to hoe

satis *adv* enough

Sāturnalia *-ium npl feast in honor of Saturn*

saxum *-ī n* rock

scaena *-ae f* scene

scalpellum *-ī n* chisel

scēptrum *-ī n* scepter

schola *-ae f* school

scientia *-ae f* science; knowledge

sciō scīre scīvī scītus to know

sciūrus *-ī m* squirrel

scobis *-is f* sawdust

scopae *-ārum fpl* broom

scopulus *-ī m* (projecting) cliff

Scorpiō *-ōnis m constellation Scorpio*

scrībō *-ĕre scripsī scriptum* to write

Sculptor *-ōris m constellation Sculptor*

scūtum *-ī n* (oblong) shield

secō *-āre -uī -tus* to cut

secrētum *-ī n* secret

secrētus *-a -um* secret

secūris *-is f* (*acc:* **securim**) axe

sēcūritās *-ātis f* security

sed *conj* but

sedeō -ēre sēdī sessum to sit
seges -etis f crop; corn
sēgregō -āre -āvī -ātus to keep apart
sēligō -ĕre sēlēgī sēlectus to choose
sella -ae f chair; **sella curūlis** official chair; **sella gestātōria** sedan chair
semel adv once
sēmen -inis n seed
sēmihomō -inis m half-man
sēmita -ae f track, path
sēmitaurus -ī m half-bull
semper adv always
senātor -ōris m senator
sensus -ūs m sense
sententia -ae f verdict
sentiō -īre sēnsī sēnsus to realize
sepeliō -īre -īvī sepultus to bury
septem indecl seven
September -bris m: **mensis September** September
septentriōnālis -is -e northern; **ex septentriōnibus flantēs** blowing from the north
sequor -ī secūtus sum to follow
serēnus -a -um calm, clear
sērius adv later; (too) late
sērius -a -um serious
Serīphus -ī f Greek island
serō -ĕre sēvī sātus to sow
serō adv late
serpens -entis m serpent
serpō -ĕre -sī to crawl
serra -ae f saw; **serram dūcĕre** to saw; **serrā secāre** to saw
serta -ae f garland
sērus -a -um late
serva -ae f (female) slave
serviō -īre -iī (+ dat) to serve, be a slave to
servō -āre -āvī -ātus to save
servulus -ī m young slave
servus -ī m slave
sī conj if
sibi reflexive pron to himself/ herself/itself/themselves
sīc adv in this way, thus; so
sīca -ae f dagger
siccus -a -um dry
Sicilia -ae f Sicily
sīcut conj just as, like
significō -āre -āvī -ātus to mean
signum -ī n sign
silentium -ī n silence

sileō -ēre -uī to be silent
silva -ae f forest, woods
similis -is -e similar, alike
simplex; simplicis simple
simul atque conj as soon as
sincērus -a -um sincere
sine prep (+ abl) without
singula -ōrum npl details
sinister -tra -trum left
sinus -ūs m bay
situla -ae f bucket
situs -a -um located
socius -ī m accomplice
sōl -is m sun
solea -ae f sandal
solitus -a -um usual, customary
sōlus -a -um alone, only
somniō -āre -āvī -ātum to dream
somnium -ī n dream; **somnium tumultuōsum** nightmare
somnolentus -a -um sleepy
somnus -ī m sleep
sordidus -a -um dirty
soror -ōris f sister
Spartacus ī m gladiator who led a revolt
speciēs -ēī f sight, appearance; **prīmā speciē** at first sight
spectāculum -ī n show
spectator -ōris m spectator
spectō -āre -āvī -ātus to watch, look at
speculāris -is -e adj mirrorlike, shiny
speculum -ī n mirror
spēlunca -ae f cave
spērō -āre -āvī -ātus to hope (for)
spēs spēī f hope
spīna -ae f spine
splendidus -a -um splendid; shiny
sportula -ae f food basket, lunch basket
stabulum -ī n stable; dingy room, hole-in-the-wall
stadium -ī n stadium
stagnum -ī n pond
statim adv immediately
statua -ae f statue
status -ūs m standing, status
stella -ae f star
stīria -ae f icicle
stō stāre stetī statum to stand
stragulum -ī n blanket
strictus -a -um strict

studeō -ēre -uī to study
studiōsus -a -um studious
sub prep (+ abl) under; at the foot of; **sub nocte** before nightfall
subeō -īre -īvī or **-iī -itum** to go up, climb
subigō -igĕre -ēgī -actus to knead
subitō adv suddenly
subrīdeō -rīdēre -rīsī -rīsum to smile
subsellium -ī n bench; juror's bench
Subūra -ae f noisy commercial center in Rome
successus -ūs m success
sūdō -āre -āvī -ātum to sweat
sūdor -ōris m sweat
sufflāmen -inis n brake
sufflāminō -āre -āvī -ātum to brake; **rotam sufflāmināre** to put on the brake
suffrāgātor -ōris m voter
suffrāgium -ī n vote; **diēs suffrāgiī** election day; **suffrāgium ferre** to cast a vote
suīcīdium -ī n suicide
sulfur -uris n sulfur
sum esse fuī futūrus to be
summus -a -um highest
suō suĕre suī sūtus to sew
superbia -ae f pride
superbus -a -um (+ abl) proud of
supercilium -ī n eyebrow
superō -āre -āvī -ātus to overcome, defeat
superior -ior -ius higher
superstitiō -ōnis f superstition
superstitiōsus -a -um superstitious
suprā (+ acc) on; on top of
suprēmus -a -um highest
surgō -ĕre surrexī surrectum to rise, get up
sustentō -āre -āvī -ātum to support, sustain
sustineō -ēre -uī to hold up
suus -a -um his/her/its/their own

taberna -ae f shop, store; booth; tavern; **taberna ferrāria** hardware store; **taberna vīnāria** wine shop

tablīnum -ī *n* study, den
tabula -ae *f* board
taeda -ae *f* torch
Talassiō! *interj* traditional wedding cry
tālis -is -e such a
tam *adv* (before adjectives and adverbs) so; **tam ... quam** as ... as
tamen *adv* still, nevertheless
tamquam *conj* like; as if
tandem *adv* finally; **cūr tandem** just why
tangō -ĕre tetigī tactus to touch
tantum *adv* only
tantummodo *adv* only
tantus -a -um so much; such a great
tardus -a -um slow
Taurus -ī *m* constellation Taurus (bull)
tectum -ī *n* roof; house
tēla -ae *f* cobweb
tempestās -ātis *f* weather; storm
templum -ī *n* temple; section of the sky marked for augury
temptō -āre -āvī -ātus to try
tempus -oris *n* time; **tempus annī** season
tempus -oris *n* temple
teneō -ēre -uī -tum to hold; to occupy, live in
tener -eris -ere tender, soft
tepidārium -ī *n* warm room, warm bath
tepidus -a -um lukewarm
ter *adv* three times
terebra -ae *f* drill
tergum -ī *n* back
terra -ae *f* earth
terreō -ēre -uī -itus to frighten
terrificō -āre -āvī -ātus to terrify
territus -a -um frightened, scared
tertius -a -um third
testimōnium -ī *n* evidence, testimony
testis -is *m* witness
texō -ĕre -uī -tum to weave
theātrum -ī *n* theater
thermae -ārum *fpl* public baths
thēsaurus -ī *m* treasure
Thrācia ae *f* Thrace (country north of Greece)
tibi *pron* to you

tībia -ae *f* flute; **tībiā cantāre** to play the flute
tībīcen -inis *mf* flute player
tignārius -a -um of a carpenter; **tignārius** *m* carpenter
tignum -ī *n* beam
tigris -is *f* tiger
timeō -ēre -uī to fear, be afraid (of)
timidus -a -um timid
timor -ōris *m* fear
tingō -ĕre tinxī tinctus to dye, color
titulus -ī *m* sign, label
toga -ae *f* toga
tollō -ĕre sustulī sublātus to raise
tomāclum -ī *n* sausage
tondeō -ēre totondī tonsus to cut
tonitrus -ūs *m* thunder
tonō -āre -uī to thunder
tonsor -ōris *m* barber
tonstrīna -ae *f* beauty salon; barbershop
tonstrīx -īcis *f* hairdresser
tornō -āre -āvī -ātus to turn out (on a lathe)
tornus -ī *m* lathe
tot *indecl* so many
tōtus -a -um whole, entire; **ex tōtō** completely
tractō -āre -āvī -ātus to handle
trahō -ĕre traxī tractus to pull, draw
trans *prep* (+ acc) across
transeō -īre -iī -itum to move
transversē *adv* zigzag
tremō -ĕre -uī to tremble
tremor -ōris *m* tremor
trepidus -a -um alarmed; nervous
trēs trēs tria three
tribūnal -ālis *n* judge's bench
trīclīnium -ī *n* dining room
tridens -entis *m* trident
tristis -is -e sad
trīticum -ī *n* wheat
trochus -ī *m* hoop
tū *pron* you
tum *adv* then, at that time; **tum cum** then when
tumeō -ēre -uī to swell
tumens -entis swollen
tumor -ōris *m* swelling, lump
tunc *adv* then; **tunc maximē** just then

tunica -ae *f* tunic
turba -ae *f* crowd, mob
tussis -is *m* (acc: **tussim**) cough, coughing
tuus -a -um your
tympanum -ī *n* (solid) wheel; drum
tyrannicīdium -ī *n* tyrannicide

ubi *adv* where; *conj* when
ubīcumque *adv* wherever
ubīque *adv* everywhere
ullus -a -um any
ultimus -a -um last, final
ultrā *adv* more; *prep* (+ acc) beyond
ululātus -ūs *m* wail, cry
umerus -ī *m* shoulder
umquam *adv* ever
ūnā *adv* together; **ūnā cum** together with
unctiō -ōnis *f* massage, rubdown
unctōrium -ī *n* massage room
unde *adv* where (from)
unguis -is *m* fingernail
undique *adv* everywhere
ūnitās -ātis *f* unity
ūnus -a -um one
urbānus -a -um sophisticated
urbs urbis *f* city
urceātim *adv* by the bucket; **urceātim pluĕre** to rain buckets
urna -ae *f* urn
ursa -ae *f* bear; **Ursa major** constellation Ursa Major (Big Dipper); **Ursa Minor** constellation Ursa Minor (Little Dipper)
ursus -ī *m* bear
usque *adv* right up to; **usque adhūc** up till now
ut *conj* (with indicative mood) as, when; (with subjunctive mood) to, in order to
ūtensilia -ium *npl* utensils; **ūtēnsilia culīnae** dishes
utique *adv* at least
ūtor ūtī ūsus sum (+ abl) to use
utrimque *adv* from both sides
uxor -ōris *f* wife; **uxōrem dūcĕre** to get married

vacca -ae *f* cow
vāgiō -īre -iī or **-īvī** to cry
vāgītus -ūs *m* cry (of a baby)
valdē *adv* a lot, hard

valeō *-ēre -uī* to be fine; to be well; **Vale!** Good-bye!

valētūdō *-inis* f health

validus *-a -um* strong

vallēs *-is* f valley

valvae *-ārum* fpl folding doors

vastus *-a -um* enormous, vast

vehementer *adv* hard; terribly

vehiculum *-ī* n vehicle

vēlāmen *-inis* n wrap, shawl

vēlox; vēlōcis fast

vēlum *-ī* n curtain; **vēla dare** to set sail

vēnābulum *-ī* n hunting spear

vēnātiō *-ōnis* f wild-animal hunt

vēnātor *-ōris* m hunter

venēnātus *-a -um* poisonous

venditor *-ōris* m vendor

veniō *-īre* vēnī ventum to come

vēnor *-ārī -ātus* sum to hunt, go hunting

ventus *-ī* m wind

vēr vēris n spring

verberō *-āre -āvī -ātus* to beat

vērō *adv* in fact

verrō *-ere -ī* versus to sweep up

versō *-āre -āvī -ātus* to turn

vertebra *-ae* f vertebra

vertō *-ere -ī* versus to turn

vērus *-a -um* true

vester *-tra -trum* your

vestīgium *-ī* n footprint

vestis *-is* f clothing; **vestēs exuěre** to undress; **vestēs induěre** to get dressed

Vesuvius *-ī* m *volcanic mountain southeast of Naples*

veterānus *-ī* m veteran

vetus; veteris old

vexillum *-ī* n flag

via *-ae* f road; **via strāta** paved road, highway; **via salūtis** road to safety

Via Appia *-ae* f Appian Way (*first Roman highway*)

Via Lactea *-ae* f Milky Way

viātor *-ōris* m traveler

vīcēsimus *-a -um* twentieth

vīcīnitās *-ātis* f neighborhood

vīcīnus *-a -um* neighboring

victima *-ae* f victim

victor *-ōris* m victor, winner

victōria *-ae* f victory

victus *-ī* m loser

vīcus *-ī* m ward; block

videō *-ere* vīdī vīsus to see

videor vidērī vīsus sum to seem

vigeō *-ēre -uī* to thrive

vigil *-is* m policeman, fireman

vīlla *-ae* f farm house, country house

vīnārius *-a -um* (of) wine

vincō *-ere* vīcī victus to win, conquer

vīnum *-ī* n wine

viola *-ae* f violet

violentus *-a -um* violent

vir *-ī* m man; **vir illustris!** your honor!

virga *-ae* f rod, stick

virgō *-inis* (single) girl; **Virgō** *constellation Virgo*; **Virgō Vestālis** Vestal Virgin

vīsitō *-āre -āvī -ātus* to visit

vīsne *see* volō

vīsō *-ere -ī* to look at; to visit

vīsus *-ūs* m sight

vīta *-ae* f life; **vītam agěre** to lead a life

vitiōsus *-a -um* faulty, wrong, defective

vivārium *-ī* n zoo

vīvō *-ere* vixī victum to live

vīvus *-a -um* alive

vocābulum *-ī* n word

vocō *-āre -āvī -ātus* to call; to invite

volātus *-ūs* m flight

volō *-āre -āvī -ātum* to fly

volō velle voluī to want, wish; **vīsne?** do you want, wish?

volvō *-ere -ī* volūtum to roll

vōs *pron* you

vōx vōcis f voice; cry; **magnā cum vōce** in a loud voice

vulnerātus *-a -um* wounded

vulnerō *-āre -āvī -ātus* to wound

vulnus *-eris* n wound

vultur *-is* m vulture

vultūs *-ūs* m looks, expression

zōdiacus *-ī* m zodiac; **zōdiacus circulus** zodiac

zōdiacus *-a -um* zodiacal

Vocābula Anglica-Latīna

able; be able possum posse potuī

about (*concerning*) dē (+ *abl*); (*approximately*) circā

absolutely prōrsum

accept accipiō -ĕre accēpī acceptus

accomplice socius -ī *m*

account: on account of ob (+ *acc*), propter (+ *acc*)

ache dolor -ōris *m*

acquit absolvō -ĕre -ī absolūtus

across trans (+ *acc*)

activity activitās -ātis *f*

actor actor -ōris *m*

actress actrix -īcis *f*

adapt adaptō -āre -āvī -ātus

adjacent adjacens -entis

admire admīror -ārī -ātus sum

adore adōrō -āre -āvī -ātus

advocate advocātus -ī *m*

aedile aedīlis -is *m*

afraid: be afraid of timeō -ēre -uī

after *conj* postquam; *prep* post (+ *acc*)

afternoon: in the afternoon pōmerīdiē

afterwards posteā

again iterum, rursus

against in (+ *acc*); (*an opponent*) cum (+ *abl*), contrā (+ *acc*)

age aetās -ātis *f*

ago abhinc

agree conveniō -venīre -vēnī -ventum

air aër aëris *m*

alarmed trepidus -a -um

alike similis -is -e

alive vīvus -a -um

all omnēs -ēs -ia; **not at all** nōn omnīnō

almost paene

already jam

also etiam

altar ara -ae *f*

although quamquam

always semper

ambitious ambitiōsus -a -um

among apud (+ *acc*)

amphitheater amphitheātrum -ī *n*

amphora amphora -ae *f*

and atque, et

anger īra -ae *f*

angry īrātus -a -um

animal animal -ālis *n*

announce nuntiō -āre -āvī -ātus

another alius -a -um

answer respondeō -ēre -ī responsum

ant formīca -ae *f*

anxious anxius -a -um

any ullus -a -um

anything else aliquid amplius

apartment building insula -ae *f*

appear appareō -ēre -uī -itum

applaud applaudō -ĕre applausī, applausum

apple mālum -ī *n*

apprentice discens -entis *m*

approach appropinquō -āre -āvī -ātus (+ *dat*)

arena arēna -ae *f*

argument contrōversia -ae *f*

arm bracchium -ī *n*

army exercitus -ūs *m*

around (*approximately*) ferē, circā

arrange ordinō -āre -āvī -ātus

arrest comprehendō -ĕre -i comprehensus

arrogant arrogans; arrogantis

arrow sagitta -ae *f*

arthritis dolor -ōris *m* articulōrum

artistic artifex; artificis

as ut (*with indicative*); **as . . . as** tam . . . quam; **as if** tamquam; **as soon as possible** cum prīmum

ashes cinis -eris *m*

ask inquirō -ĕre inquisīvī inquisītus; rogō -āre -āvī -ātus; (*questions*) pōnō -ĕre posuī positus

assume assūmō -ĕre -psī -ptus

astrologer astrologus -ī *m*

astrology astrologia -ae *f*

athlete āthlēta -ae *m*

athletic āthlēticus -a -um

attack oppugnō -āre -āvī -ātus

attend frequentō -āre -āvī -ātus

attentively attentē

augur augur -uris *m*

augur's staff lituus -ī *m*

augury augurium -ī *n*; **place of augury** augurāculum -ī *n*

aunt amita -ae *f*

auspices: take the auspices inaugurō -āre -āvī -ātum

authority auctōritās -ātis *f*

autumn autumnus -ī *m*

avoid ēvitō -āre -āvī -ātus

awaken excitō -āre -āvī -ātus

award praemium -ī *n*

away ā, ab prep (+ *abl*)

axe secūris -is *f* (*acc* secūrim)

baby infans -antis *mf*

back tergum -ī *n*

bad malus -a -um; (*unfavorable*) adversus -a -um

bag saccus -ī *m*

bait esca -ae *f*

bake coquō -ĕre coxī coctus

baker pistor -ōris *m*

bakery pistrīna -ae *f*

ball pila -ae *f*; **play ball** pilā lūdĕre

bandage fascia -ae *f*

bank taberna (-ae *f*) argentāria; (*of river*) rīpa -ae *f*

banker argentārius -ī *m*

barber tonsor -ōris *m*

barbershop tonstrīna -ae *f*

barley hordeum -ī *n*

barnyard cohors -tis *f*

basket corb*is -is mf*
bath balneum *-ī n; (cold bath)*
  frīgidārium *-ī n; (hot bath)*
  caldārium *-ī n; (warm bath)*
  tepidārium *-ī n; (large public*
  baths) therm*ae -ārum fpl;*
  (small bath) balneolum *-ī n*
batter pulsō *-āre -āvī -ātus*
battle line aci*ēs -ēī f*
bay sinus *-ūs m*
be sum esse fuī futūrus
beam tignum *-ī n*
bear *(male)* ursus *ī m; (female)*
  urs*a -ae f*
beard barb*a -ae f*
bearing habitus *-ūs m*
beast bestia *-ae f*
beat verberō *-āre -āvī -ātus*
beautiful pul*cher -chra -chrum*
beauty pulchritūdō *-inis f*
beauty salon tonstrīn*a -ae f*
beaver cast*or -oris m*
because quod, quia, quoniam;
  because of ob *(+ acc)*, propter
  (+ acc)
become fīō fierī factus sum
bed lect*us -ī m; (small)* lectulus
  -ī m
bedroom cubiculum *-ī n*
bee ap*is -is f*
before *prep* ante *(+ acc); (in the*
  presence of) apud *(+ acc);*
  conj antequam
beg orō orāre orāvī orātus
begin incipiō *-ĕre* incēpī
  inceptus
behalf: on behalf of prō *(+ abl)*
behead dētruncō *-āre -āvī -ātus*
behind post *(+ acc)*
believe crēdō *-dĕre -didī -ditum*
  (+ dat)
belong (to) pertineō *-ēre -uī*
bench subsellium *-ī n*
besides praētereā
besides porrō
best *adj* optimus *-a -um; adv*
  maximē
better *adj* melior melior
  melius; *adv* melius
between inter *(+ acc)*
beyond ultrā *(+ acc)*
big magnus *-a -um*
bigger major major majus
biggest maximus *-a -um*
billyclub clāv*a -ae f*
bind obligō *-āre -āvī -ātus*
bird av*is -is f*
birth *adj* nātāl*is -is -e*

birthday diēs *(-ēī m)* nātālis
bit modic*um -ī n*
bite ictus *-ūs m*
bitter amārus *-a -um*
black āter ātra ātrum, nig*er -ra*
  -um
blanket strāgulum *-ī n*
block vicus *-ī m*
blockhead caud*ex -icis m*
blond flāvus *-a -um*
bloody cruentus *-a -um*
board tabul*a -ae f*
boast (about) sē jactāre (dē + ₁bl)
boat nāvicul*a -ae f*
body corpus *-oris n*
bold audax; audācis
book li*ber -brī m*
booth tabern*a -ae f*
border margō *-inis m; (crimson)*
  clāvus *ī m*
born nātus *-a -um;* **be born**
  nascor nascī nātus sum
borrow mūtuor *-ārī -ātus* sum
both ambō *-ae -ō*
bottom īmus *-a -um;* **at the**
  bottom of the bag in īmō
  saccō
bow arcus *-ūs m*
box cist*a -ae f*
boxer pugil *-is m*
boxing glove caestus *-ūs m*
boy puer *-ī m*
boyfriend am*ans -antis m*
brake sufflāminō *-āre -āvī -ātus*
brake *n* sufflām*en -inis n;* **put**
  on the brake rotam
  sufflāmināre
brave fort*is -is -e*
bravely fortiter
bravo! fēlīciter!
bread pān*is -is m;* **loaves of**
  bread pān*ēs mpl*
break frangō *-ĕre* frēgī fractus
breakfast jentāculum *-ī n*
breath anim*a -ae f;* **catch one's**
  breath animam recipĕre; **out**
  of breath exanimātus *-a -um*
breathe respirō *-āre -āvī -ātum*
bride nupt*a -ae f*
bridal procession dēductiō *-ōnis*
  f
brief brev*is -is -e*
bright clārus *-a -um*
bring ferō ferre tulī lātus; **bring**
  about efficiō *-ĕre* effēcī
  effectus; **bring along** adferre;
  bring back reportō *-āre -āvī*
  -ātus

Britain Britanni*a -ae f*
broad lātus *-a -um*
broken fractus *-a -um*
broom scōp*ae -ārum fpl*
brother frā*ter -tris m;* **little**
  brother frātellus *-ī m*
buck dēnārius *-ī m*
bucket situl*a -ae f;* **to rain**
  buckets urceātim pluĕre
buggy *(two-wheeled)*
  carpentum *-ī n*
build aedificō *-āre -āvī -ātus;*
  (road) mūniō *-īre -īvī -ītum*
bull taurus *-ī m*
burden onus *-eris n*
burn ardeō *-ēre* arsī arsum
bury sepeliō *-īre -īvī* sepultus
business negōtium *-ī n; adj*
  negōtiāl*is -is -e*
businessman negōtiāt*or -ōris m*
busy occupātus *-a -um*
but sed
butterfly pāpiliō *-ōnis m*
buy emō emĕre ēmī emptus

cabinet armārium *-ī n*
cage cave*a -ae f*
cake lībum *-ī n*
calamity calamit*ās -ātis f*
call vocō *-āre -āvī -ātus;* **call**
  together convocō *-āre -āvī*
  -ātus
calm serēnus *-a -um*
camp castra *-ōrum npl*
campaign petītiō *-ōnis f*
candelabrum candēlābrum *-ī n*
candidate candidātus *-ī m*
candlestick candēlābrum *-ī n*
captain nāvis magis*ter -trī m*
captive captīvus *-ī m*
capture capiō capĕre cēpī
  captus
care cūr*a -ae f*
career *(political)* cursus *(-ūs m)*
  honōrum
carefully dīligenter
carp at carpō *-ĕre -sī -tus*
carpenter tignārius *-ī m*
carriage *(traveling)* carrūc*a -ae*
  f; (two-wheeled) cisium *-ī n;*
  (light two-wheeled) essedum
  -ī n; (four-wheeled) raed*a -ae*
  f; (women's) carpentum *-ī n,*
  pilentum *-ī n*
carrot carōt*a -ae f*
carry gerō gerĕre gessī gestus;
  ferō ferre tulī lātus
cart *(two-wheeled)* carrus *-ī m*

case casus -ūs m; **in that case**
eō casū
cash argentum -ī n
catch captō -āre -āvī -ātus
cattle market forum boārium -ī
n
cause n causa -ae f
cause efficiō -ĕre effēcī effectus
cautious cautus -a -um
cave spelunca -ae f
celebrate celebrō -āre -āvī -ātus
certain quīdam quaedam
quoddam; (sure) certus -a -um
certainly certē
chain gang compeditī -ōrum
mpl
chair sella -ae f
challenge prōvocō -āre -āvī
-ātus
chamberpot matella -ae f
chance: by chance forte
change mūtō -āre -āvī -ātus
changeable mūtābilis -is -e
charge oppugnō -āre -āvī -ātus;
crīmen -inis n
chariot curriculum -ī n
charioteer aurīga -ae m
chase persequor -sequī -secūtus
sum
cheek gena -ae f
chest arca -ae f
chicken gallīna -ae f
children līberī -ōrum mpl
chisel scapellum -ī n
choose ēligō -ĕre ēlēgī ēlectus
cistern cisterna -ae f
citadel arx arcis f
citizen cīvis -is mf
city urbs urbis f
classmate condiscipulus -ī m
claw bracchium -ī n
clean purgō -āre -āvī -ātum
clear clārus -a -um
clearly plānē
clever astūtus -a -um
client cliens -entis m
cliff scopulus -ī m
climb ascendō -ĕre -ī ascensum;
climb aboard conscendō -ĕre
-ī
close claudō -ĕre clausī clausus
closely attentē
closet armārium -ī n
clothing vestis -is f
cloud nūbēs -is f
cloudy nūbilus -a -um
clover ocinum -ī n
coach palaestricus -ī m

coachman raedārius -ī m
cobweb tēla -ae f
cockroach blatta -ae f
coin nummus -ī m
cold gelidus -a -um; frīgidus -a
-um
collapse ruīna -ae f
college collēgium -ī n
color n color -ōris m
color tingō -ĕre tinxī tinctus
column columna -ae f
comb pectō -ĕre pexī pexus;
pecten -inis m
come veniō -īre -ī ventum;
come on! age!; **come together**
conveniō -venīre -vēnī
-ventum; **come upon** inveniō
-īre invēnī inventus
comic cōmicus -a -um
commit committō -ĕre
commīsī commissus
common commūnis -is -e
compete certō -āre -āvī -ātus
completely omnīnō
concern cūra -ae f; **be of**
concern to cūrae esse (+ dat)
concerning dē (+ abl)
condemn condemnō -āre -āvī
-ātus
condition habitus -ūs m
congratulations! fēlīciter!
congregate congregō -āre -āvī
-ātus
consider cōnsīderō -āre -āvī
-ātus
constant perpetuus -a -um
constantly constanter
constellation constellātiō -ōnis
f
construction constructiō -ōnis f
consul consul -is m
consular consulāris -is -e
consult consultō -āre -āvī -ātus
consume consumō -sūmĕre
-sumpsī -sumptus
contain contineō -ēre -uī
contentus
contend contendō -ĕre -ī -tum
contest certāmen -inis n
continue continuō -āre -āvī
-ātus
continuous continuus -a -um
continuously continuō
controversy contrōversia -ae f
cook coquō -ĕre coxī coctus
cool frīgidus -a -um
corn seges -itis f
corner angulus -ī m

cost constō -stāre -stetī (+ abl)
cot grabātus -ī m
cough tussis -is m (acc: tussim)
count numerō -āre -āvī -ātus;
count up ēnumerō -āre -āvī
-ātus
country (native land) patria -ae
f; (opposite of city) rūs rūris
n; **from the country** rūre; **in**
the country rūrī; **to the**
country rūs
course cursus -ūs m; **of course**
nīmīrum
court jūdicium -ī n
courthouse basilica -ae f
courtroom jūdicium -ī n
courtyard peristȳlium -ī n
cousin consōbrīnus -ī m
countryside agrī -ōrum mpl
covered obductus -a -um
cow vacca -ae f
crab cancer -crī m
crack rīma -ae f
crater crātēr -ēris m
crawl rēpō -ĕre -sī -tum
create creō -āre -āvī -ātus
crime crīmen -inis n
criminal crīminālis -is -e;
crīminālis -is m
crimson purpureus -a -um
crocodile crocodīlus -ī m
crop seges -etis f
crowd multitūdō -inis f
crown corōna -ae f
crude crūdus -a -um
cruel crūdēlis -is -e
cry intr fleō flēre flēvī flētum;
(of a baby) vāgiō -īre -iī or -īvī
ītum; vagītus -ūs m
cub catulus -ī m
cucumber cucumis -eris m
culture cultūra -ae f
cupboard armārium -ī n
curl crispō -āre -āvī -ātus
curling iron calamistrum -ī n
curtain vēlum -ī n
curved curvus -a -um
custom mōs mōris m
cut secō -āre -uī -tus; (hair)
tondeō -ēre totondī tonsus;
cut down dēcīdō -cīdĕre -cīdī
-cīsus
customary solitus -a -um

dagger sīca -ae f
daily cōtīdiē
danger perīculum -ī n
dangerous perīculōsus -a -um

dark āter ātra ātrum
day diēs -ēī *m;* **one day** quōdam
  diē; **on the following day**
  postrīdiē
daylight lux lūcis *f*
dear cārus -a -um
decide dēcernō -cernĕre -crēvī
  -crētus
declare indīcō -ĕre indixī indictus
decorate decorō -āre -āvī -ātus
deep altus -a -um
deer cervus -ī *m*
defeat superō -āre -āvī -ātus
defect defectus -ūs *m*
defend dēfendō -dĕre -dī -sus
defendant reus -ī *m*
defense lawyer dēfensor -ōris *m*
delay mora -ae *f*
delegate legātus -ī *m*
delight dēlectō -āre -āvī -ātus;
  oblectāmentum -ī *n*
demand postulō -āre -āvī -ātus
den tablīnum -ī *n*
dense densus -a -um
deny negō -āre -āvī -ātus
depart discēdō -ĕre discessī
  discessum
desert dēserta -ōrum *npl*
desire dēsīderō -āre -āvī -ātus
despair dēspērō -āre -āvī -ātus
desperate dēspērātus -a -um
destination locus (-ī *m*)
  dēstinātus
destroy deleō -ēre -ēvī -ētus
details singula -ōrum *npl*
deter dēterreō -ēre -uī -itus
devour dēvorō -āre -āvī -ātus
dictator dictātor -ōris *m*
die alea -ae *f;* **play dice** aleā
  lūdĕre
die morior morī mortuus sum
difficult difficilis -is -e
diligent dīligens, diligentis
dine cēnō -āre -āvī -ātus
dining room trīclīnium -ī *n*
dinner cēna -ae *f;* **eat dinner**
  cēnō -āre -āvī -ātus
direction pars partis *f*
directly dīrectō
dirty sordidus -a -um
discus discus -ī *m*
discus thrower discobolus -ī *m*
dishes ūtensilia (-ium *npl*)
  culīnae
dispute disputō -āre -āvī -ātus
distance: at a distance procul
distant longinquus -a -um; **be
  distant** absum abesse āfuī

distrust diffīdō -ĕre -ī (+ *dat*)
do faciō -ĕre fēcī factus; (*hair*)
  cōmō -ĕre -compsī comptus
doctor medicus -ī *m;* medica
  -ae *f*
dog canis -is *m*
doll pūpa -ae *f*
dollar dēnārius -ī *m*
door: folding doors valvae
  -ārum *fpl*
doorpost postis -is *m*
doorstep līmen -inis *n*
double duplex; duplicis
dough (*money*) argentum -ī *n*
dove columba -ae *f*
drain exhauriō -īre exhausī
  exhaustus
draw trahō -ĕre traxī tractus;
  (*water, etc.*) hauriō -īre hausī
  haustus; (*bow*) intendō -ĕre -ī
  intentus
dream somniō -āre -āvī -ātus;
  somnium -ī *n*
dress: get dressed vestēs induō
  -ĕre -ī
dressing room apodȳtērium -ī *n*
drill perforō -āre -āvī -ātus;
  terebra -ae *f*
drink potō -āre -āvī potus; potiō
  -ōnis *f*
drive agitō -āre -āvī -ātus; agō
  agĕre ēgī actus; **drive in** (*nail*)
  fīgō -ĕre fixī fixus
driver raedārius -ī *m*
drop dēmittō -ĕre dēmīsī
  dēmissus
drum tympanum -ī *n*
dry siccus -a -um
during inter (+ *acc*)
dust pulvis -eris *m*
duty officium -ī *n*
dwell habitō -āre -āvī -ātum
dye tingō -ĕre tinxī tinctus

each omnis -is e
eager avidus -a -um
eagerly avidē; cupidē
eagle aquila -ae *f*
ear auris -is *f*
early in the morning bene
  māne
earn mereō -ēre -uī -itus
earring inauris -is *f*
earth terra -ae *f*; (*world*)
  mundus -i *m*; **on earth** in
  mundō
easy facilis -is -e
eat ēdō esse ēdī ēsum

edge margō -inis *m*
elbow cubitum -ī *n*
elect ēligō -ĕre ēlegī ēlectus
election day diēs (-ēī *m*)
  suffrāgiī
elections comitia -ōrum *npl*
elegant ēlegans; ēlegantis
element elementum -ī *n*
embroider pingō -ĕre pinxī
  pictus
emigrate ēmigrō -āre -āvī -ātus
enclose inclūdō -ĕre inclūsī
  inclūsus
endearing blandus -a -um
enemy (*public*) hostis -is *m*;
  (*personal*) inimīcus -ī *m*
England Britannia -ae *f*
enjoy gaudeō -ēre (+ *abl*)
enormous ēnormis -is -e
enough satis
enter intrō -āre -āvī
entertainment dēlectāmentum
  -ī *n*
entire tōtus -a -um
entirely omnīnō, ex tōtō
envoy legātus -ī *m*
envy invideō -ēre invīdī (+ *dat*)
equipment instrūmentum -ī *n*
err errō -āre -āvī -ātum
eruption ēruptiō -ōnis *f*
escape *intr* effugiō -ĕre -ī
escape *n* fūga -ae *f*
escort prōsequor prōsequī
  prōsecūtus sum
especially praecipuē
even etiam; **even if** etiamsī;
  even now etiamnunc
event eventus -ūs *m*
ever umquam; **ever after** in
  perpetuum exinde
every omnis -is -e
everywhere ubīque; **from
  everywhere** undique
evidence testimōnium -ī *n*
example exemplum -ī *n;* **for
  example** exemplī grātiā
excellent excellens; excellentis
except nisi
excited excitātus -a -um
exercise exerceō -ēre -uī -itum;
  reflex sē exercēre
exercise yard palaestra -ae *f*
exhausted fatigātus -a -um
exile exilium -ī *n;* (*person in
  exile*) exul -is *m*
exit exitus -ūs *m*
expel expellō -ĕre expulī
  expulsus

expensive cārus -a -um
experienced perītus -a -um
explain explicō -āre -uī -itus
express exprimō -ĕre expressī
   expressus
expression (on face) vultus -ūs m
exult exultō -āre -āvī
eye oculus -ī m
eyebrow supercilium -ī n
eyelash palpebra -ae f

fact: in fact quidem, vērō
failing dēfectus -ūs m
fair jūstus -a -um
faithful fidēlis -is -e
fall cadō -ĕre cecidī casum; fall
   down dēcidō -cidĕre -cidī
family familia -ae f
famous clārus -a -um
far adj longinquus -a -um; adv
   longē; by far longē; far away
   longinquus -a -um; far from
   procul ab (+ abl)
farm fundus -i m
farmhouse vīlla -ae f
farmer agricola -ae m
fasces fascēs -ium mpl
fashion modus -ī m
fast celer celeris celere; adv
   rapidē; (asleep) artē; as fast as
   possible quam celerrimē
fat crassus -a -um
fault culpa -ae f; find fault with
   carpō -ĕre carpsī carptus
faulty vitiōsus -a -um
favorable prōsperus -a -um
fear timeō -ēre -uī; timor -ōris m
feather penna -ae f
feed pabulum -ī n
ferocious ferox; ferōcis
festive festus -a -um
few paucī -ae -a; very few
   perpaucī -ae -a
fickle mūtābilis -is -e
field (untilled) campus -ī m;
   (tilled) ager agrī m
fight pugnō -āre -āvī -ātum
fin pinna -ae f
final ultimus -a -um
finally dēnique
find inveniō -īre invēnī
   inventum
fine adv bene; be fine valeō -ēre
   -uī
finger digitus -ī m
fingernail unguis -is m
fire ignis -is m; incendium -ī n
fireman vigil -is m

fireplace focus -ī m
first prīmus -a -um; first name
   praenōmen -inis n; for the
   first time prīmum; adv
   prīmō; at first prīmō; first of
   all prīmum
fish piscor -ārī -ātus sum; piscis
   -is m
fishing pole calamus -ī m
fish pond piscīna -ae f
fit adaptō -āre -āvī -ātus
flag vexillum -ī n
flame flamma -ae f; flame-
   colored flammeus -a -um
flap plaudō -ĕre plausī plausum
flare up exardescō -ĕre exarsī
flash coruscō -āre -āvī
flee fugiō -ĕre fūgī fūgitum
flight volātus -ūs m
float fluitō -āre -āvī -ātum
floor pavīmentum -ī n
flour farīna -ae f
flour mill mola -ae f
flow fluō fluĕre fluxī fluxum
flowery floridus -a -um
flute tībia -ae f; play the flute
   tībiā cantāre
flute player tībīcen -inis m
fly volō -āre -āvī -ātum
fodder pabulum -ī n
fog nebula -ae f
follow sequor -ī secūtus sum
food cibus -ī m
foot pēs pedis m; go on foot īre
   pedibus; at the foot of sub (+
   abl)
footprint vestīgium -ī n
for prep (for the purpose of) ad
   (+ acc); (on behalf of) prō (+
   abl); conj enim, nam
force cogō -ĕre coēgī coāctus
forehead frons frontis f
foreigner aliēnus -ī m
forest silva -ae f
forever in perpetuum
forget about omittō -ĕre omīsī
   omissus
fork furca -ae f
fortify muniō -īre -īvī or -iī -ītum
fortunate fortunātus -a -um
fortune fortuna -ae f
found condō -dĕre -didī -ditus
fountain fons fontis m
fourth quārtus -a -um
fratricide frātricīdium -ī n
free līberō -āre -āvī -ātus
frequent frequens; frequentis
friendly amīcus -a -um

frighten terreō -ēre -uī -itus;
   frighten away dēterreō -ēre
   -uī -itus; frightened territus
   -a -um
frightening formīdābilis -is -e
fringe margō -inis m
from ā, ab (+ abl); from now on
   ex hōc
fruit fructus -ūs m
fugitive fugitīvus -a -um
full plēnus -a um; full of plēnus
   (+ gen)
funny cōmicus -a -um
furnace furnus -ī m
furthermore porrō
future futūra -ōrum npl

gamble aleā lūdĕre
game lūdus -ī m; public games
   lūdī -ōrum mpl
garden hortus -ī m
garland serta -ae f
gate porta -ae f
gather colligō -ĕre collectus;
   conveniō -venīre -vēnī
   -ventum
Gaul Gallia -ae f
generous līberālis -is -e
genocide genocīdium -ī n
gentle mitis -is -e
Germans Germānī -ōrum mpl
Germany Germānia -ae f
germicide germicīdium -ī n
germinate germinō -āre -āvī
   -ātum
get (become) fiō fierī factus
   sum; get away effugiō -ĕre;
   get up surgō -ĕre surrexī
   surrectum
gift donum -ī n
girl puella -ae f
girlfriend amans -antis f
give dō dare dedī datus
gladiator gladiātor -ōris m
gladiatorial gladiātōrius -a -um
gladly lībenter
globe orbis -is m
glory gloria -ae f
glow ardeō -ēre arsī arsum
go eō īre īvī or iī itum; go away
   abeō -īre -iī or -īvī, -itum; go
   away! abī abhinc!; go into
   ineō inīre iniī or inīvī initum
   (in + acc); go on prōcēdō
   -cēdĕre -cessī -cessum; go out
   exeō exīre exīvī or exiī
   exitum; go to adeō adīre adiī
   aditum

goat cape*r* caprī *m*
gold-plated aurāt*us -a -um*
golden aure*us -a -um*
good bon*us -a -um;* **good deed**
  beneficium ī *n;* **be good for**
  prōsum prōdesse prōfuī (+
  dat)
government rēs (reī *f*) pūblica
grandfather av*us -ī m*
grandmother avi*a -ae f*
grass herb*a -ae f*
grateful grāt*us -a -um*
great magn*us -a -um*
Greece Graeci*a -ae f*
greedy avār*us -a -um*
Greek Graec*us -a -um*
greeting salus *-ūtis f;* **send**
  greetings salūtem dīcĕre
grieving maest*us -a -um*
grip occupō *-āre -āvī -ātus*
grocery store macell*um -ī n*
grow crescō *-ĕre* crēvī crētum
guess conjici*ō -ĕre* conjēcī
  conjectus
guest convīv*a -ae mf*
guild collēgi*um -ī n*
guilt culp*a -ae f*
gymnasium gymnasi*um -ī n*

hail grandin*at -āre -avit;* grando
  -inis m
hair com*a -ae f,* capillī *-ōrum*
  mpl
half-bull sēmitaur*us -i m*
half-man sēmihom*ō -inis m*
hammer malle*us ī m*
hand man*us -ūs f;* **on the other**
  hand contrā; **be at hand**
  adesse
handcuff manic*a -ae f*
handle tractō *-āre -āvī -ātus*
handsome pul*cher -chra*
  -chrum
hang down dēpende*ō -ēre -ī*
happen accidō *-ĕre -ī;* **if I**
  happen to see you sī forte tē
  vidēbō
happy laet*us -a -um*
hard dūr*us -a -um; adv*
  (*strenuously*) vehementer;
  (*diligently*) dīligenter
hardware store tabern*a (-ae f*)
  ferrāria
harm noce*ō -ēre -uī* (+ *dat*)
harvest metō *-ĕre* messuī
  messus
hate odī odisse
have habe*ō -ēre -uī -itus*

hay faen*um -ī n*
haystack met*a -ae f*
head cap*ut -itis n*
headache dolor (*-ōris m*) capitis
heal sānō *-āre -āvī -ātus*
health sānit*ās -ātis f*
healthy sān*us -a -um*
hear audi*ō -īre -īvī -ītus*
hearing audīt*us -ūs m*
heart cor cordis *n*
heaven cael*um -ī n;* **by heaven!**
  mehercule!
heavy grav*is -is -e*
heel calx calcis *f*
hello! salvē! (*pl:* salvēte!)
helmet gale*a -ae f*
help juvō *āre -ī* jutus; **so help**
  me! mehercule!
helpless inops; inopis
her ejus
herbicide herbicīdi*um ī n*
here hīc; (*to this place*) hūc;
  from here hinc
hide occultō *-āre -āvī -ātus;*
  late*ō -ēre -uī*
hide pell*is -is f*
high alt*us -a -um,* cels*us -a -um*
higher superi*or -ior -ius*
highest summ*us -a -um*
highway vi*a* (*-ae f*) strata
hill coll*is -is m*
his ejus
hit icō icĕre īcī ictus
hobbyhorse ecule*us -ī m*
hoe sari*ō -īre -uī;* sarcul*um ī n*
hold tene*ō -ēre -uī* tentus; **hold**
  it! dēsiste!; **hold back** retineō
  -ēre -uī retentus; **hold**
  together contine*ō -ēre -uī*
  contentus
hole forām*en -inis n;* (*of a*
  mouse, ant) cavern*a -ae f*
holiday fest*us* di*ēs (-ēī) m*
home dom*us -ūs f*
homicide homicīdi*um -ī n*
honest honest*us -a -um*
honey mel mellis *n*
honor: **your honor!** vir illūstris!
hoodlum grassāt*or -ōris m*
hook ham*us -ī m*
hoop troch*us -ī m*
hope (for) spērō *-āre -āvī -ātus;*
  spēs speī *f*
horn corn*u -ūs n*
horoscope horoscopi*um -ī n*
horrible horribil*is -is -e*
horse equ*us -ī m*
hospitality hospitālit*ās -ātis f*

hostile infest*us -a -um*
hot-headed cerebrōs*us -a -um*
hot room caldāri*um -ī n*
hour hōr*a -ae f*
house tect*um -ī n*
household famili*a -ae f;*
  household gods Lar*ēs -um*
  mpl
how quōmodō; **how long**
  quōusque; **how many** quot;
  how often quotiens; **how**
  proud quam superbus
however autem
huge grand*is -is -e*
humid hūmid*us -a -um*
hunger fam*ēs -is f*
hungry: **be hungry** ēsuri*ō -īre*
hunt vēnor *-ārī -ātus* sum;
  vēnāti*ō -ōnis f*
hunter vēnāt*or -ōris m*
hunting dog can*is (-is m*)
  vēnāticus
hunting spear vēnābul*um -ī n*
hurl conjici*ō -ĕre* conjēcī
  conjectus
hurler jaculāt*or -ōris m*
hurry properō *-āre -āvī -ātum*
husband marīt*us -ī m*
hut cas*a -ae f*

icicle stiri*a -ae f*
idea consili*um -ī n*
if sī
immediately statim
importance moment*um -ī n*
important magn*us -a -um*
in in (+ *abl*); **in front of** ante (+
  acc)
industrious industri*us -a -um*
infanticide infanticīdi*um -ī n*
inflamed inflammāt*us -a -um*
influence afficiō afficĕre affēcī
  affectus
inhabit inhabitō *-āre -āvī -ātus*
inn caupōn*a -ae f*
innkeeper caup*ō -ōnis m*
innocent innocens; innocentis
insect insect*um -ī n*
insecticide insecticīdi*um -ī n*
insert inserō *-ĕre -uī -tus*
inside intus
instead of prō (+ *abl*)
instruction mandāt*um -ī n*
intellect intellect*us -ūs m*
intelligent intellegens;
  intellegentis
intently intentē
into in (+ *acc*)

invent invenīō -īre invēnī inventus
invisible invīsibilis -is -e
invite vocō -āre -āvī -ātus
irritable irrītābilis -is -e
island insula -ae f
Italy Ītalia -ae f
its ejus

jail carcer -ĕris m
javelin jaculum -ī n
jilt repudiō -āre -āvī -ātus
join jungō -ĕre junxī junctus
joint articulus -ī m
joke jocus -ī m
joy gaudium -ī n
judge jūdex -icis m; **judge's bench** tribūnal -ālis n
jump saliō -īre -iī; **jump rope** ad fūnem salīre; **jump up** exsiliō -īre -iī
juror jūdex -icis m
just jūstus -a -um; *adv* modō; **just as** sīcut, perinde ac; **just now** modō; **just what?** quidnam?

keep retineō -ēre -uī -tentus; **keep in mind** in memoriā tenēre
kidnap rapiō -ĕre -uī -tus
kill necō -āre -āvī -ātus; caedēs -is f
kind benignus -a -um
kindness beneficium -ī n
king rex rēgis m
kingdom rēgnum -ī n
kiss osculum -ī n
knead subigō -igĕre -ēgī -actus
knee genu -ūs n
knife culter -trī m
knock at pulsō -āre -āvī -ātus
know sciō scīre scīvī scītum; (*a person, place*) cognoscō -ĕre cognōvī cognitus; **not know** nesciō -īre -īvī or -iī -ītus; **well known** nōtus -a -um
knowledge scientia -ae f

label titulus -ī m
labyrinth labyrinthus -ī m
lady of the house domina -ae f
last dūrō -āre -āvī
last novissimus -a -um
late sērus -a -um; *adv* sērō
later post(eā); **a little later** paulō post; **later on** posteā
latest novissimus -a -um

lathe tornus -ī m
Latin Latīnus -a -um; **learn Latin** Latīnē discĕre; **teach Latin** Latīnē docēre; **speak Latin** Latīnē loquī
law jūs jūris n; **law and order** jūs et ordō
lawyer advocātus -ī m
lazy piger pigra pigrum
lead dūcō -ĕre duxī ductus; (*a life*) agĕre, dūcĕre; **lead back** redūcō -dūcĕre -duxī -ductus
learn discō -ĕre didicī
least: at least utique
leave relinquō -ĕre relīquī relictus; abeō -īre -iī or -īvī -itum
lecture hall auditōrium -ī n
left sinister -tra -trum
leg crūs crūris n; (*of chair, table*) pēs pedis m
legion legiō -ōnis f
leopard leopardus -ī m
letter epistula -ae f
lettuce lactūca -ae f
liberate līberō -āre -āvī -ātus
liberty lībertās -ātis f
library bibliothēca -ae f
lictor lictor -ōris m
lie (down) jaceō -ēre -uī; **lie next to** adjacēre
life vīta -ae f; **lead a life** vītam agĕre, vītam dūcĕre
lift levō -āre -āvī -ātus
light incendō -ĕre -ī; lūx lūcis f
lighten fulminat -āre -āvit
lightning fulmen -inis n
like placet -ēre -uit; **I like the city** urbs mihi placet; *prep* sīcut, tamquam
lily līlium -ī n
line līnea -ae f
listen to audiō -īre -īvī -ītus
litter lectīca -ae f
little: a little paulō; **a little later** paulō post; **little by little** paulātim
live vīvō -ĕre vīxī victum; (*dwell*) habitō -āre -āvī -ātum
load onerō -āre -āvī -ātus
located situs -a -um
lock up inclūdō -ĕre inclūsī inclūsus
long longus -a -um; *adv* (*for a long time*) diū; **for a longer time** diūtius; **long ago** jamdūdum, jam prīdem; **long and hard** diū et acriter

look m aspectus -ūs m; (*on the face*) vultus -ūs m; **looks** habitus -ūs m
look spectō -āre -āvī -ātus; **look!** ecce; **look at** aspiciō -ĕre aspexī aspectus; **look for** quaerō -ĕre quaesīvī quaesītus; **look over** lustrō -āre -āvī -ātus
loot praeda -ae f
lose amittō -ĕre amīsī amissus
loser victus -ī m
lot: a lot multum
loud magnus -a -um
lovable amābilis -is -e
love amō -āre -āvī -ātus; amor -ōris m
lover amans -antis mf
low dēmissus -a -um
lowest īmus -a -um
lucky felīx; fēlīcis
lunch basket sportula -ae f
lurid lūridus -a -um

madam domina -ae f
magnificent magnificus -a -um
maid ancilla -ae f
mailed datus -a -um
make faciō -ĕre fēcī factus; fabricō -āre -āvī -ātus; **make one's appearance** appareō -ēre -uī
man vir virī m
mane juba -ae f
many multī -ae -a; **many more** multō plūrēs
mark down dēnotō -āre -āvī -ātum
marketplace forum -ī n
marriage matrimōnium -ī n
married woman mātrōna -ae f
marry nūbō -ĕre nupsī nupta (+ dat)
massage unctiō -ōnis f
massage room unctōrium -ī n
master dominus -ī m; **master craftsman** magister -trī m
mathematician mathēmaticus -ī m
matricide mātricīdium -ī n
matron of honor prōnuba -ae f
matter rēs reī f
maybe forsitan, fortasse
maze labyrinthus -ī m
meadow prātum -ī n
meal cibus -ī m
mean sigificō -āre -āvī -atus

meet occurrō *-ĕre -ī* occursum
 (+ *dat*); **go to meet** obvius (*-a
 -um*) īre (+ *dat*)
melt lique*faciō -facĕre -fēcī
 -factus*
memory memoriā *-ae f*
mention mentiō *-ōnis f*
method modus *-ī m*
mild mītis *-is -e*
mile mille passūs *-uum mpl*
milk mulgeō *-ēre* mulsī
 mulsus; lac lactis *n*
Milky Way Via (*-ae f*) Lactea
mind animus *-ī m*
Minotaur Mīnōtaurus *-ī m*
miracle mīrāculum *-ī n*
mirror speculum *-ī n*;
 mirrorlike speculāris *-is -e*
miss dēsīderō *-āre -āvī -ātus*
mist nebula *-ae f*
mistress domina *-ae f*
mob turba *-ae f*
moment momentum (*-ī n*)
 temporis
mommy mamma *-ae f*
money pecūnia *-ae f*
month mensis *-is m*
moon lūna *-ae f*
more *adv* magis, plūs; **more
 and more** magis et magis;
 more time plūs temporis; **the
 more . . . the more** quō magis
 . . .eō magis
moreover praetereā
morning: in the morning māne;
 early in the morning bene māne
mortality mortālitās *-ātis f*
most plerīque pleraeque pleraque
mother māter *-tris f*
mount mons montis *m*
move moveō *-ēre* mōvī mōtus;
 (*change residence*) migrō *-āre
 -āvī -ātum*; **move into**
 immigrō *-āre -āvī -ātum*
movement motiō *-ōnis f*
much multus *-a -um*; *adv*
 multō; **much too slow** multō
 nimis lentus
mulberry tree mōrus *-ī f*
murder caedēs *-is f*
murky obscurus *-a -um*
muscle mūsculus *-ī m*
mutual mūtuus *-a -um*
my meus *-a -um*

nail clāvus *-ī m*
name nōminō *-āre -āvī -ātus*;
 nōmen *-inis n*

narrow angustus *-a -um*
native city patria *-ae f*
native land patria *-ae f*
near *prep* prope (+ *acc*)
neck cervix *-īcis f*
need dēsīderō *-āre -āvī -ātus*
neighbor vīcīnus *-ī m*
neighborhood vīcīnitās *-ātis f*
neighboring vīcīnus *-a -um*
neither neque; **neither . . . nor**
 neque . . . neque
nervous trepidus *-a -um*
net rēte *-is n*
netman rētiārius *-ī m*
never numquam
nevertheless tamen
new novus *-a -um*
next (to) proximus *-a -um* (+
 dat)
nice bellus *-a -um*
night nox noctis *f*; **at night**
 noctū
nightmare somnium (*ī n*)
 tumultuōsum
no minimē, minimē vērō, nōn;
 no longer nōn jam; *adj* nullus
 -a -um; **no one** nēmō *-inis m*
nobility nōbilitās *-ātis f*
nonsense nūgae *-ārum fpl*;
 nonsense! nūgās!
noon merīdiēs *-ēī m*
northern septentriōnālis *-is -e*
not nōn; **not only . . . but also**
 nōn modō. . . sed etiam; **not
 yet** nōndum
noted nōtus *-a -um*
nothing nihil
notice notō *-āre -āvī -ātus*
nourish nūtriō *-īre -īvī* or *iī
 -ītus*
now nunc; autem; **by now** jam
nurse nūtriō *-īre -īvī* or *iī -ītus*
nuptial nuptiālis *-is -e*

oar rēmus *-ī m*
obedient obēdiens; obēdientis
obey obēdiō *-īre -īvī* or *-iī* (+
 dat)
oblige obligō *-āre -āvī -ātus*
oblong oblongus *-a -um*
observe observō *-āre -āvī -ātus*
occupy occupō *-āre -āvī -ātus*;
 (*live in*) teneō *-ēre -uī -tum*
occur ēveniō *-īre* ēvēnī
 ēventum
occurrence ēventus *-ūs m*
ocean oceanus *-ī m*
odor odor *-ōris m*

offend offendō *-ĕre -ī* offensus
office honor *-ōris m*
often saepe
old lady anus *-ūs f*
older major major majus (nātū)
oldest maximus *-a -um* (nātū)
Olympic Olympicus *-a -um*
omen ōmen *-inis n*
on in (+ *abl*), suprā (+ *acc*)
one ūnus *-a -um*
once ōlim, quondam; (one
 time) semel
only tantummodo
open apertus *-a -um*; **in the
 open** in apertō
opinion opiniō *-ōnis f*
opponent adversārius *-ī m*,
 competītor *-ōris m*
or an
orangey flammeus *-a -um*
order jubeō *-ēre* jussī jussus; **in
 order to** ut (*with
 subjunctive*)
other alius *-a -um*; **one after the
 other** alius ex aliō; **the other**
 alter altera alterum
otherwise aliōquīn
ought oportet *-ēre -uit*; **I ought
 to** oportet mē (+ *inf*)
our noster *-tra -trum*
out ahead ante
out of ē (ex) (+ *abl*)
outdoors forīs
outside forīs; **outside of** extrā
 (+ *acc*)
oven furnus *-ī m*
overcast nūbilus *-a -um*
overcome superō *-āre -āvī -ātus*
owe debeō *-ēre -uī -itum*
own: his/her/its/their own suus
 -a -um
owner dominus *-ī m*
ox bōs bovis *m*

pace passus *-ūs m*
pain dolor *-ōris m*
paint pingō *-ĕre* pinxī pictus
painting pictūra *-ae f*
palace aula *-ae f*
pale pallidus *-a -um*
palestra palaestra *-ae f*
palm palma *-ae f*
panther panthēra *-ae f*
parent parens *-entis mf*
part pars partis *f*
participate (in) intersum *-esse
 -fuī* (*dat* or in + *abl*)
path sēmita *-ae f*

patience patientia -ae f
patient patiens; patientis
patrician patricius -a -um
patricide patricīdium -ī n
pavement pavīmentum -ī n
pay pensitō -āre -āvī -ātus
peace pax pācis f
peacock pāvō -ōnis f
people hominēs -um mpl; populus -ī m
perhaps forsitan, fortasse
perish periō -īre -iī
person persōna -ae f, homō -inis m
personal persōnālis -is -e
pertain (to) pertineō -ēre -uī
pesticide pesticīdium -ī n
philosopher philosophus -ī m
picky fastidiōsus -a -um
picture pictūra -ae f
pierce perforō -āre -āvī -ātus
pig porcus -ī m
pillow cervīcal -ālis n
pirate pirāta -ae m
place locus -ī m
plainly plānē
plaintiff accusātor -ōris m
plan consilium -ī n
plane runcīnō -āre -āvī -ātus; runcīna -ae f
planet planēta -ae f
plant planta -ae f
play lūdō -ĕre lūsī lūsus
player lūsor -ōris m
please placeō -ēre -uī -ītum (+dat); **please!** quaesō
plebeian plebeius -a -um
plough arō -āre -āvī -ātus; arātrum -ī n
pluck ēvellō -ĕre -ī evulsus
point out indicō -āre -āvī -ātus
poisonous venēnātus -a -um
policeman vigil -is m
polite polītus -a -um
politics rēs (reī f) publica
pond stagnum -ī n
pony mannus -ī m
poor (unfortunate) miser -era -erum; (moneyless) pauper pauperis paupere
popular populāris -is -e
pound pulsō -āre -āvī -ātus
pour fundō -ĕre fūdī fūsus; **to pour into** infundĕre
power potestās -ātis f
practice exerceō -ēre -uī -itus; sē exercēre
praetor praetor -ōris m

praise laudō -āre -āvī -ātus
pretrial hearing praejūdicium -ī n
precede praecēdō -ĕre praecessī praecessum
predict praedīcō -ĕre -dixī dictus
prefer praeferō -ferre -tulī -lātus
presence: in the presence of coram (+ abl)
present mūnusculum -ī n
present: be present adsum -esse -fuī; **be present at** intersum -esse -fuī (dat or in + abl)
preside praesideō -sidēre -sēdī
prestige auctoritās -ātis f
prevent dēterreō -ēre -uī -itus
previously ante(ā)
pride superbia -ae f
prisoner (of war) captīvus -ī m
prison farm ergastulum -ī n
private privātus -a -um; **private citizen** privātus -ī m
proceed precēdō -cēdĕre -cessī -cessum
procession pompa -ae f
produce market macellum -ī n
prohibit prōhibeō -ēre -uī -itus
promise prōmittō -mittĕre -mīsī -missus
pronounce prōnuntiō -āre -āvī -ātus
prosecutor accusātor -ōris m
protect prōtegō -tegĕre -tēgī -tectus
proud (of) superbus -a -um (+ abl)
prudent prūdens; prūdentis
prune amputō -āre -āvī -ātus
pruning knife falcula -ae f
public pūblicus -a -um
public baths thermae -ārum fpl
pull trahō -ĕre traxī tractus; **pull off** dētrahō -ĕre dētraxī dētractus; **pull out** extrahō -ĕre extraxī extractus
punish pūniō -īre -īvī or -iī -ītus
pupil discipulus -ī m
pursue persequor -sequī -secūtus sum
put pōnō -ĕre posuī positus; **put down** dēpōnō -ĕre dēposuī dēpositus; **put on** (impose) impōnō -ĕre imposuī impositus (+ dat); (clothes) induō -ĕre -ī indūtus

quaestor quaestor -ōris m
question quaestiō -ōnis f

quick-tempered īrācundus -a -um
quickly cito

racetrack circus -ī m
rain pluit -ĕre pluit; pluvia -ae f
rainbow pluvius arcus -ūs m
raise (children) ēducō -āre -āvī -ātus
rake ērādo -ĕre ērāsī ērāsum; rastellus -ī m
rapid rapidus -a -um
rarely rārō
ray radius -ī m
razor novācula -ae f
reach perveniō -īre -ī -tum ad or in (+ acc)
read legō -ĕre lēgī lectus
realize sentiō -īre sensī sensus
really quidem
reap metō -ĕre messuī messus
reason ratiō -ōnis f
rebellious rebellis -is -e
receive accipiō -ĕre accēpī acceptus
recent recens; recentis; **recently** nūper
recline accumbō -ĕre accubuī accubitum
recognize recognoscō -ĕre recognōvī recognitus
red ruber rubra rubrum
refined polītus -a -um
refuge asȳlum -ī n
refuse recūsō -āre -āvī -ātus
region regiō -ōnis f
regret paenitet -ēre -uit; **I regret** mē paenitet
remain maneō -ēre -uī; (be left over) restō -āre restitī
remaining ceterī -ae -a
remember in memoriā tenēre
repair reparō -āre -āvī -ātus
republic rēs (reī f) pūblica
respectable honestus -a -um
rest of ceterī -ae -a
restaurant popīna -ae f
restless inquiētus -a -um
retain retineō -ēre -uī retentus
retire sē recipĕre
return (go back) redeō -īre -iī -itum
reveal revēlō -āre -āvī -ātus
rich dīves; dīvitis; **the rich** dīvitēs mpl
rid: get rid of dēmittō -ĕre dēmīsī dēmissus
ride equitō -āre -āvī

right dexter -tra -trum; **right up to** usque ad (+ acc)

ring ānulus -ī m

rise surgō -ĕre surrexī surrectum; ascendō -ĕre -ī ascensum

rising oriens; orientis

river flūmen -inis n

road via -ae f

roar fremō -ĕre -uī -itum

roast assum -ī n

robber latrō -ōnis m

robust rōbustus -a -um

rock saxum -ī n

rod virga -ae f

roll volvō -ĕre -ī volūtus

Roman Rōmānus -a -um

roof tectum -ī n

room cella -ae f

rope fūnis -is m; **jump rope** ad fūnem salīre

rostrum rostra -ōrum npl

rough dūrus -a -um

row remigō -āre -āvī; ordō -inis m

rule (over) regnō -āre -āvī -ātum (+ dat)

run (a shop, company) exerceō -ēre -uī -itus; currō -ĕre cucurrī cursum; **run away** effugiō -ĕre -ī; **run into** occurrō -ĕre -ī occursum (+ dat); **run low** deficiō -ĕre -fēcī -fectum

runner cursor -ōris m

rush festīnō -āre -āvī -ātum

sad tristis -is -e

safe salvus -a -um

safety salus -ūtis f

sail nāvigō -āre -āvī -ātum; **sail by** praeternāvigō; **set sail** vēla dare

sake: for the sake of causā (+ gen)

same īdem eadem idem

sand arēna -ae f

sandal sandalium -ī n

sanity sānitās -ātis f

sauna laconicum -ī n

sausage tomāclum -ī n

save conservō -āre -āvī -ātus

saw serrā secō -āre -uī -tus; serram dūcĕre; serra -ae f

sawdust scobis -is f

say dīcō dīcĕre dixī dīctus

scared territus -a -um; **scared stiff** perterritus -a -um

scene scaena -ae f

scepter sceptrum -ī n

school schola -ae f; lūdus -ī m

science scientia -ae f

scorpion scorpiō -ōnis m

sculptor sculptor -ōris m

scythe falx -cis f

sea mare -is n; adj. marīnus -a -um, maritimus -a -um; **sea monster** cētus -ī m

seashore ora (-ae f) marītima

season tempus (-oris n) annī

secret sēcrētus -a -um; sēcrētum -ī n

security sēcuritās -ātis f

sedan chair sella (-ae f) gestatōria

see videō -ēre vīdī vīsus; **see to it that** cūrāre ut

seed sēmen -inis n

seem videor vidērī vīsus sum

seize rapiō -ĕre -uī -tus; occupō -āre -āvī -ātus

self (himself) ipse; (herself) ipsa; (itself) ipsum

senate building cūria -ae f

senator senātor -ōris m

sense sensus -ūs m

serious gravis -is -e

serpent serpens -entis m

serve (food) adpōnō -ĕre adposuī adpositus

set (hair) cōmō -ĕre compsī comptus; **set in order** ordinō -āre -āvī -atus

setting occidens; occidentis

sew suō suĕre suī sūtus

shape forma -ae f

sharp acūtus -a -um

shawl vēlāmen -inis n

shed prōfundō -fundĕre -fūdī -fūsus

sheep ovis -is f; **sheep fold** ovīle -is n

shepherd pastor -ōris m

shield (round) parma -ae f; (oblong) scutum -ī n

shine luceō -ēre luxī; **shine again** refulgeō -ēre refulsī

shinguard ocrea -ae f

shiny splendidus -a -um

ship nāvis -is f

shipwreck naufrāgium -ī n

shoe calceus -ī m

shoelace corrigia -ae f

shop obsōnō -āre -āvī -ātus

shop taberna -ae f

shore ora -ae f

short brevis -is -e

shoulder umerus -ī m

shout clāmō -āre -āvī -atus; (in approval) acclāmō

shovel rutrum -ī n

show adhibeō -ēre -uī -itus; **show up** appareō -ēre -uī; spectāculum -ī n

shrine aedēs -is f

side latus -eris n; **from both sides** utrimque

sidewalk crepīdō -inis f

sight speciēs -ēī f; **at first sight** prīmā speciē

sign signum -ī n; titulus -ī m

silence silentium -ī n

silent: be silent sileō -ĕre -uī

similar similis -is -e

simple simplex; simplicis

sincere sincērus -a -um

sir! domine!

sister soror -ōris f

sit sedeō -ēre sēdī sessum; **sit down;** consīdō -sīdĕre -sēdī -sessum

situation rēs rēī f

skill ars artis f

skilled perītus -a -um

skillful artifex; artificis

skin pellis -is f

skip omittō -ĕre omīsī omissus

sky caelum -ī n

slave serva -ae f; servus -ī m

slave block catasta -ae f

slave dealer mangō -ōnis m

sleep dormiō -īre -īvī -ītum; **go to sleep** dormītum īre; somnus -ī m

sleepy somnolentus -a -um

slow lentus -a -um

small parvus -a -um; parvulus -a -um; **smaller** minor minor minus; **smallest** minimus -a -um

smile subrīdeō -rīdĕre -rīsī -rīsum

smoke fūmus -ī m

snack shop popīna -ae f

snow ningit -ĕre ninxit; nix nivis f

snowball pila (-ae f) nivea

so ita, sīc; **and so** itaque; **so many** tot; **so much** tantus -a -um

soft tener -eris -ere

soldier mīles -itis m

sole planta -ae f

some aliquot

someday aliquandō
someone aliquis alicūjus
son fīlius -ī m
song carmen -inis n
soon mox; **as soon as possible** cum prīmum
sooner prius
soothsayer haruspex -icis m
sophisticated urbānus -a -um
sorry: I am sorry mē paenitet
sound sānus -a -um; **be sound asleep** dormīre artē
sow serō -ĕre sēvī sātus
spade pala -ae f
speak loquor loquī locūtus sum
spear hasta -ae f
spectator spectātor -ōris m
speech orātiō -ōnis f; **give a speech** orātiōnem habēre
spider arānea -ae f
spin neō nēre nēvī nētus
splendid splendidus -a -um
spoke radius -ī m
spot conspiciō -ĕre conspexī conspectus
spot macula -ae f
spotty maculōsus -a -um
spouse conjunx -jugis mf
spring fons fontis m; (season) vēr vēris n
sprout germinō -āre -āvī -ātum
squirrel sciūrus -ī m
stable stabulum -ī n
stack mēta -ae f
stadium stadium -ī n
stand stō stāre stetī statum; **stand around** circumstō -stāre -stetī
standing statūs -ūs m
star stella -ae f
state cīvitās -ātis f
statue statua -ae f
status status -ūs m
stay maneō -ēre mansī mansūrus
steal clepō -ĕre -sī -tus
step gradus -ūs m; **go up the steps** per gradūs ascendĕre; **step forward** prōdeō -īre -iī -itum
stick virga -ae f
still adhūc; (nevertheless) tamen; **still today** etiamnunc
sting icō icĕre īcī ictus; ictus -ūs m
stone: little stone lapillus -ī m
stop (doing something) dēsistō -ĕre dēstitī; (stand still) consistō -ĕre constitī

store condō -dĕre -didī -ditus; taberna -ae f
storeroom cella -ae f
stork cicōnia -ae f
storm tempestās -ātis f
straight rectus -a -um
strange mīrus -a -um
stranger aliēnus -ī m
stream flūvius -ī m
strict strictus -a -um
string līnea -ae f
stroll dēambulō -āre -āvī
strong validus -a -um
stubborn obstinātus -a -um
student discipulus -ī m
studious studiōsus -a -um
study studeō -ēre -uī; (room) tablīnum -ī n
style modus -ī m
success successus -ūs m
such talis -is -e
sudden repentīnus -a -um; **suddenly** subitō
suicide suicīdium -ī n
sulfur sulfur -uris n
summer aestās -ātis f
sun sōl -is m
superstition superstitiō -ōnis f
superstitious superstitiōsus -a -um
supervise cūrō -āre -āvī -ātus
supper cēna -ae f; **eat supper** cēnō -āre -āvī
support sustentō -āre -āvī -ātum
supposed: I am supposed to obligātus sum (+ inf)
surely certē
surround circumclūdō -clūdĕre -clūsī -clūsus
swear jurō -āre -āvī -ātum
sweat sūdō -āre -āvī -ātus
sweep (up) verrō -ĕre -ī versus
swell tumeō -ēre -uī
swim intr natō -āre -āvī
swim natātiō -ōnis f
swimming pool piscīna -ae f
swing oscillō -āre -āvī -ātum; oscillum -ī n
swollen tumens -entis
sword gadius -ī m

table mēnsa -ae f
tail cauda -ae f
take (seize) capiō capĕre cēpī captus; (bring) ferō ferre tulī lātus; **take back** recipiō -ĕre -cēpī -ceptus; **take care** cūrō -āre -āvī -ātus; **take to** addūcō -ĕre adduxī adductus

tall altus -a -um
tame mītis -is -e
taste gustō -āre -āvī -ātus
tavern taberna -ae f
teach doceō -ēre -uī -tus
teacher magister -trī m, magistra -ae f
tear lacrima -ae f
tear up laniō -āre -āvī -ātus
temple (building) templum -ī n; (head) tempus -oris n
tender tener -eris -ere
terribly vehementer
terrify terrificō -āre -āvī -ātus
test probātiō -ōnis f
testimony testimōnium -ī n
than quam
that ille illa illud; iste ista istud
theater theātrum -ī n
then (next) deinde; (at that time) tum; **just then** tunc maxime; **then when** tum cum
there ibi
thereafter exinde
therefore ergo
thick densus -a -um
thigh femur -oris n
thing rēs rēī f
think cōgitō -āre -āvī -ātus; **think to oneself** cōgitāre sēcum
third tertius -a -um
this hīc haec hōc
three trēs trēs tria; **three times** ter
thresh dēterō -ĕre dētrīvī dētrītus
threshing floor ārea -ae f
threshold līmen -inis n
thrive vigeō -ēre -uī
through per (+ acc)
throw jaciō -ĕre jēcī jactus; **throw down** dējiciō -ĕre dējēcī dējectus; **throw into** injiciō -ĕre injēcī injectus; **throw out** ējiciō -ĕre -ējēcī ējectus
thumb pollex -icis m
thunder tonō -āre -uī; tonitrus -ūs m
thus ita, sīc
tide aestus -ūs m
tie ligō -āre -āvī -ātus
tiger tigris -is f
till now adhūc
time tempus -oris n; **at that time** tum
timid timidus -a -um

to ad (+ *acc*); ut (*with subjunctive*)
today hodiē
toga tog*a -ae f*
together ūnā; **together with** ūnā cum (+ *abl*)
toilet latrīn*a -ae f*
tomorrow crās
too (*excessively*) nimis; (*also*) quoque
tool instrūment*um ī n*
tooth dens dentis *m*
top: at the top of the page in summā pagīnā; **on top of** suprā (+ *acc*)
torch taed*a -ae f*
toss jactō *-āre -āvī -ātus*
totter nūtō *-āre -āvī*
touch tangō *-ĕre* tetigī tactus
tough dūr*us -a -um*
toward erga (+*acc*)
town oppid*um -ī n*
townspeople oppidānī *-ōrum mpl*
track sēmit*a -ae f*
train exerceō *-ēre -uī -itus*; sē exercēre
trainer lanist*a -ae m*
travel iter faciō *-ēre* fēcī factus
traveler viāt*or -ōris m*
treasure thesaur*us -ī m*
tree arb*or -oris f*
tremble tremō *-ĕre -uī*
tremor trem*or -ōris m*
trial jūdici*um -ī n*
trident trid*ens -entis m*
trip iter itineris *n*; **take a trip** iter facĕre
troubles labōr*ēs -um mpl*
true vēr*us -a -um*
trust confīdō *-ĕre* confīdī confīsum (+ *dat*)
try temptō *-āre -āvī -ātus*
tunic tunic*a -ae f*
turn convertō *-ĕre -ī* conversus; **turn out** (*on a lathe*) tornō *-āre -āvī -ātus*; (*become*) fiō fierī factus sum

twentieth vīcēsim*us -a -um*
twice bis
twin gemin*us -ī m*
twine līn*um -ī n*
two duo duae duo
tyrannicide tyrannicīdi*um -ī n*

uncertain incert*us -a -um*
under sub (+ *abl*)
underbrush frūtect*um -ī n*
understand intellegō *-ĕre* intellexī intellectus
understanding intellect*us -ūs m*
underworld inferī *-ōrum mpl*
undress vestēs exuō *-ĕre -ī*
unfriendly inimīc*us -a -um*
unhappy infēlix; infēlīcis
unity ūnit*ās -ātis f*
unless nisi
unsure incert*us -a -um*
until donec
unusual inūsitāt*us -a -um*
unwilling: be unwilling nōlō nōlle nōluī
up till now usque adhūc
urge on incitō *-āre -āvī ātus*
urn urn*a -ae f*
us nōs
use ūtor ūtī ūsus sum (+ *abl*)
usual solit*us -a -um*
utensils ūtensili*a -ium npl*

vain: in vain frustrā
valley vall*ēs -is f*
vast vast*us -a -um*
vegetable hol*us -eris n*
vendor vendit*or -ōris m*
verdict jūdici*um -ī n*
very admodum
veteran veterān*us -ī m*
victim victim*a -ae f*
victory victōri*a -ae f*
view aspect*us -ūs m*
violet viol*a -ae f*
visit vīsitō *-āre -āvī -ātus*

voice vōx vōcis *f*; **in a loud voice** magnā cum vōce
vote suffrāgi*um -ī n*; **cast a vote** suffrāgium ferre
voter suffrāgāt*or -ōris m*
vulture vultur *-is m*

wagon plaustr*um -ī n*
wailing ululāt*us -ūs m*
wait exspectō *-āre -āvī -ātum*; **wait for** exspectāre
wake up expergiscor *-ī* experrectus sum
walk ambulō *-āre -āvī*; **walk around** dēambulāre
wall mūr*us -ī m*; (*between rooms*) pari*ēs -etis m*
wander errō *-āre -āvī -ātum*
want volō velle voluī; **not want** nōlō nōlle nōluī
war bell*um -ī n*
ward vīc*us -ī m*
warm tepid*us -a -um*; **warm bath** tepidāri*um -ī n*
warmly benignē
warn moneō *-ēre -uī -itus*
wash lavō *-āre -ī* lāvī lautus
watch spectō *-āre -āvī -ātus*
water irrigō *-āre -āvī -ātus*; aqu*a -ae f*
wave fluct*us -ūs m*
way mod*us -ī m*; **by the way** obiter; **in this way** sīc
wear gestō *-āre -āvī -ātus*
weather tempest*ās -ātis f*
weave texō *-ĕre -uī -tus*
wedding nupti*ae -ārum fpl*; *adj* nuptiāl*is -is -e*
weed herb*a* (*-ae f*) mala
weight on*us -eris n*
welcome excipiō *-ĕre* excēpī exceptus
well: be well valeō *-ēre -uī*; *adv* bene; (*interj*) nempe
wet madid*us -a -um*
what? quid?